NORTHUMBRIA AD 367–867

Northumbria
AD 367–867
EARTH-HALL, RING-GIFT AND HEAVEN'S FIELD

MAX ADAMS *and*
COLM O'BRIEN

First published in 2025 by
John Donald, an imprint of Birlinn Ltd
West Newington House
10 Newington Road
Edinburgh
EH9 1QS

www.birlinn.co.uk

ISBN: 978 0 85976 742 2

Copyright © Max Adams and Colm O'Brien 2025

The right of Max Adams and Colm O'Brien to be identified as the authors of this work has been asserted by them in accordance with the Copyright, Designs and Patents Act 1988.

All rights reserved. No part of this publication may be reproduced, stored or transmitted in any form without the express written permission of the publisher. This includes the use or reproduction in any manner for the purpose of training artificial intelligence technologies or systems. This work is reserved from text and data mining (Article 4(3) Directive (EU) 2019/790).

British Library Cataloguing-in-Publication Data
A catalogue record for this book is available from the British Library

Typeset by Hewer Text UK Ltd, Edinburgh

Papers used by Birlinn Ltd are from well-managed forests and other responsible sources

Printed and bound in Britain by Clays Ltd, Elcograf S.p.A.

For our friends in the Bernician Studies Group
and in the Lands of Éogain, past and present

CONTENTS

List of illustrations	ix
Preface	xiii
Genealogies	xvii

Part I: 367–642   1
   Chronology I: 367–642   3
 1 Marcher-wards: 367–450   7
 2 Earth-halls: 451–616   39
 3 Edwin: Ring-giver 616–633   64
 4 Oswald: Heaven's field 633–642   91

Part II: 643–737   117
   Chronology II: 643–737   119
 5 Oswiu: God-friend 643–670   127
 6 Ecgfrið: Peace-weavers 671–685   155
 7 Aldfrið: Word-smiths 685–705   182
 8 The Angelcynn: 706–737   212

Part III: 738–867   241
   Chronology III: 738–867   243
 9 Sky-flame: 738–803   251
10 Shield-clash: 804–867   281

Northumbrian regnal list	309
Notes on the written sources	311
Notes	315
Bibliography	341
Image credits	367
Subject index	369
Name index	379

LIST OF ILLUSTRATIONS

Front endpaper: Northumbria in the Early Medieval period 367–867
Rear endpaper: Northumbrian empires 600–800

Plates

1. Bamburgh Castle: ancestral seat of the Bernician kings from the sixth century.
2. Heavenfield, where Oswald raised a cross the night before battle.
3. Reconstruction at Jarrow Hall of the excavated Hall 'A' at Thirlings.
4. Reconstruction at Jarrow Hall of an Early Medieval sunken-floored building.
5. The church at Lastingham, founded by Cedd in about 654 on the edge of moorland.
6. The medieval churches on Lindisfarne, likely on the site of the original foundation of 635.
7. The ramparts of Old Oswestry hill fort, perhaps the site of King Oswald's final battle in 642.
8. Stained-glass window at St John Lee near Hexham, depicting the scene at Heavenfield before the battle of Denisesburn.
9. Yeavering Bell: Iron Age hill fort and, below, the site of the royal township of Ad Gefrin.
10. The great enclosure ditch at Yeavering, re-excavated in 2023.
11. The Norman chancel arch and nave of St Cuthbert's church at Norham.
12. The site of Old Melrose monastery in a bend of the River Tweed.
13. Escomb church, County Durham: a seventh-century foundation close to the Roman fort at Binchester.
14. The carved stone 'Frith' stool at Hexham Abbey – perhaps the episcopal throne of St Wilfrid.
15. Reconstruction drawing imagining Hexham Abbey as originally built in the seventh century.

16 Alcuin: a nearly contemporary portrait of the Northumbrian and Carolingian scholar in his last years.
17 Whitby Abbey: the medieval ruins on the site of the probable royal monastic complex of Streanæshealh founded in the seventh century.
18 The Franks Casket, carved from whalebone, generally regarded as a product of eighth-century Northumbrian craftsmanship.
19 Plan of the church of the Holy Sepulchre, Jerusalem, from De Locis Sanctis, copied in Northumbria.
20 The *Codex Amiatinus*: a complete Bible, produced at Wearmouth–Jarrow in 716.
21 The so-called St Cuthbert Gospel – the oldest surviving intact binding on an English book.

In-text figures

Hadrian's Wall: the definition of Rome's Northern Frontier	9
From Roman military granary to mead hall: the excavations at Birdoswald	19
The claustrophobic intimacy of the seventh-century crypt at Ripon belies the extravagant feast that accompanied its dedication	53
York's minster: founded in the ruins of the Roman fortress by Bishop Paulinus in 627	75
Yeavering's great halls: reconstructed Viking Age hall at Fyrkat, Jutland, Denmark	78
Modern statue of St Aidan on Lindisfarne	99
Iona Abbey: the foundation of Colm Cille in the sixth century and mother house of the Northumbrian church on Lindisfarne	102
Dere Street, the Roman road linking York in Deira with the Tyne at Corbridge and the Antonine Wall at Edinburgh	130
Sculptured frieze at All Saints' church, Hovingham, North Yorkshire	141
Roman *spolia* from the town of *Coria* (Corbridge) in Wilfrid's crypt at Hexham	162
Bede's church at Jarrow on the south bank of the River Tyne	172

List of illustrations

The tall, narrow chancel arch of the seventh-century church of St John, Escomb, County Durham	174
Aberlemno II: battle scene depicted on the reverse of a shaped cross-slab	180
Incised cross grave marker from Cooley graveyard, Moville, County Donegal	190
Seventh- or eighth-century high cross in the graveyard of St Cuthbert's church, Bewcastle, Northumberland	192
Obverse and reverse designs on a *sceat* of King Aldfrið	197
The 'Anglian tower' in York, perhaps part of a seventh-century refurbishment of the city's defences	202
Whithorn Priory, which stands on the site of the monastic church and settlement called *Candida Casa* by Bede	221
Detail of the carved interlace relief and runic inscription on the high cross at Ruthwell Kirk, Dumfriesshire	225
Artist's impression of the monastic complex at Hoddom	227
Silver penny of King Eanred	288
Scandinavian place-names, a familiar feature of East and North Yorkshire	302
Ryton church overlooking the Tyne at its lowest historical fording point	306

Maps and plans

1	Southern Northumbria: topography and settlement	13
2	Northern Northumbria: topography and settlement	15
3	Northern Northumbria: the 'cultural corelands'	26
4	Southern Northumbria: the 'cultural corelands'	27
5	J.R. Mortimer's plan of burials along Sledmere Green Lane	46
6	The kingdom of Elmet reconstructed	70
7	The royal township at Yeavering, first identified from the air and confirmed as Bede's *Ad Gefrin* by Brian Hope-Taylor's excavations	80

8 Sprouston, on the south bank of the River Tweed.
  Ian Smith's plan of the layout — 84
9 The excavated settlement of a *comes* at Thirlings,
  in the Milfield Plain, Northumberland — 87
10 West Heslerton, East Yorkshire: the most thoroughly
   excavated Northumbrian settlement — 90
11 Excavated features at the unique funerary complex at
   Street House, Loftus, in the Cleveland Hills — 106
12 Plan of part of the excavated settlement at Shotton, central
   Northumberland — 108
13 Deiran monasteries and churches — 139
14 The natural and ecclesiastical topography of Ripon — 147
15 Bernician monasteries and churches — 150
16 Hexham: the abbey church dominated a prominent hill
   overlooking the River Tyne — 159
17 Distribution of coins of King Aldfrið — 199
18 The territorial interests of the monastic community on Lindisfarne — 261
19 Distribution of coins of King Eadberht and Archbishop Ecgberht — 269
20 Distribution of *stycas* of Kings Eanred and Æðelred II — 285
21 Excavated structures of the Early Medieval settlement
   at Green Shiel on Holy Island — 294

PREFACE

It is thirty years since Nick Higham (1993) published *The Kingdom of Northumbria AD 350–1100*; and twenty since David Rollason's (2003) *Northumbria 500–1100*: both landmarks in the historiography of Early Medieval North-East England. Between the two, in *Northumbria's Golden Age* (1999), Jane Hawkes and Susan Mills collected a number of 'state of the art' papers together for an equally significant volume. Since then, a second important collection of papers, edited by David Petts and Sam Turner (2011), *Early Medieval Northumbria: Kingdoms and Communities, AD 450–1100*, showed that the pace of development in new source materials – particularly metal-detected finds and excavated settlements – and new thinking, especially in historical geography, is quickening. The outstanding collection of papers published under the title *Finds from the Frontier*, edited by Rob Collins and Lindsay Allason-Jones (2010), has had a profound effect on all future work. The state of the art in Northumbrian Early Medieval studies is excitingly dynamic. A broader perspective, looking at Northumbria from the outside, is now coming into focus, typified by John Blair's (2018) monumental survey *Building Anglo-Saxon England*, which reveals a much more sophisticated and organised idea of royal administration and of economic and social dynamism than we could have dared propose a few decades ago.

In undertaking the daunting task of following in these footsteps and in those of the late Dame Rosemary Cramp (1929–2023), the great Early Medieval archaeologist, we now have sufficient material at our disposal to frame this new volume on Early Medieval Northumbria around the mere half-millennium between the so-called Barbarian Conspiracy of AD 367 and the fall of York to the Danish army in 867 – convenient historical book-ends. Our narrative stops short of exploring what is popularly known as the Viking Age, and beyond – it would have required another whole volume, and the expertise of other scholars.

Addressing those themes that form repeating patterns in the history of what we think of as Middle Britain – identity, the Christian conversion, the dynastic politics of Northumbrian kings, its relations with neighbours, allies and friends abroad – we have been inclined in some cases to reinforce long-held ideas; in others to nuance or update them. We like to think that our own individual and collaborative researches, as field archaeologists and colleagues in the Bernician Studies Group, have given fresh slants to the story. We are both enthusiastic students of Bede and of Northumbria's links with the northern part of the island of Ireland. Colm O'Brien has made a specialism of reconstructing Northumbria's Early Medieval territorial geographies. Max Adams writes broad narratives encompassing themes of landscape and regionality. But we are both, at heart, excavators, and the increase in published archaeological fieldwork over the last three decades has made it possible to draw a fuller, if still far from complete, picture of settlement and ecclesiastical archaeology. Widely available remote sensing – geophysics and LiDAR (Light Detection and Ranging), in particular – have greatly enhanced archaeologists' ability to identify and map previously unknown or enigmatic sites and local landscapes, without recourse to excavation.

Two minor revolutions of the last two decades have particularly influenced our thinking. First, the work of historical geographers, especially that of Professor Brian Roberts, has allowed sense to be made of relations between cultural identity and the evolution of landscapes. Second, a huge increase in the recovery of metalwork, particularly coins, has enabled numismatists to offer a counter-narrative to the historical sources, particularly for the eighth and ninth centuries when annalistic material is so conspicuously lacking.

By and large, our narrative structure is based around the reigns of those Northumbrian kings for whom biographies can be sketched in outline. Within those, we have attempted to make connections both backward and forward in time. In particular, we have focused on the theme of territorial lordship – the ways in which élites exercised power over, and in turn drew their power from, stable, hierarchically organised, known parcels of land: from the *familia* or farm of Bede, through a holistic structure of *vills* and *villae regiae* to the shire and beyond. Both secular and ecclesiastical power were mediated through this hierarchy, reinforcing and reinforced by customary law and so robust that they were able to accommodate radically novel political and social realities from the seventh century onwards when, increasingly, rights to exact tribute and services from land were 'booked' by charter: first for the early monastic foundations; later for most secular land transactions.

For the general reader, as well as for the student of Northumbrian history, comprehension of its complexities is daunting. While we urge readers to try (or go back to) reading Bede, the greatest historian of the Early Middle Ages, we are aware that keeping up with the names of kings, the different narrative sources, the geographies and dates is enough to make one's head spin. To that end, we have provided a series of maps that will allow those geographies to become familiar and, through them, we have plotted the key themes as they develop in the narrative. We have also provided a concise timeline of events in three parts; genealogies of the principal early Northumbrian dynasties; and lists of kings' reigns compiled from the most trustworthy sources. Footnotes give brief explanatory notes; endnotes give reference citations.

The study of Early Medieval Northumbria never stands still. Long-awaited publications and major new research projects will shift perspectives once more – although we are grateful to many colleagues for allowing access to pre-publication material, and to their current thinking on a wide range of themes. Where possible, we have acknowledged them in the text, but we would like to thank the following individually: Brian Roberts and David Petts; Sarah Semple and Roger Miket; Dominic Powlesland, Jane Kershaw, Richard Carlton, Hermann Moisl, Brian Lacey, Sam Turner, Maria Duggan and our friends the members of the Bernician Studies Group. Diana Whaley very generously read the manuscript and has sharpened it on many points, not least by correcting any linguistic solecisms. We would also like to acknowledge the very kind help of the librarians at the University of Newcastle, the Society of Antiquaries of Newcastle upon Tyne and the Lit. and Phil., Newcastle upon Tyne. Our wives, Sarah Annesley and Anne Liddon, are owed more thanks than words can adequately convey.

The authors of long historical narratives must, in the end, confront the impossibility of including 'everything'. We are painfully conscious that neither of us is an artefact specialist or art historian, although there is much excellent scholarship in these areas. We have also chosen not to spend too much time engaging with the invasion/immigration, Briton vs Anglo-Saxon debate. That is partly a matter of taste; partly a reflection of the fact that science is now changing perspectives on ethnic and genetic identity at a pace which means inevitably anything we say now might shortly be used in evidence against us. In any case, we feel that the debate is in some respects immaterial: we know that Early Medieval people and communities were mobile and dynamic. But the regional diversity and strong identities that we detect – sometimes defined by what people were not, as much as what they were – are based solidly in place, topography, soil and in the deep time of prehistory. All else is mutable.

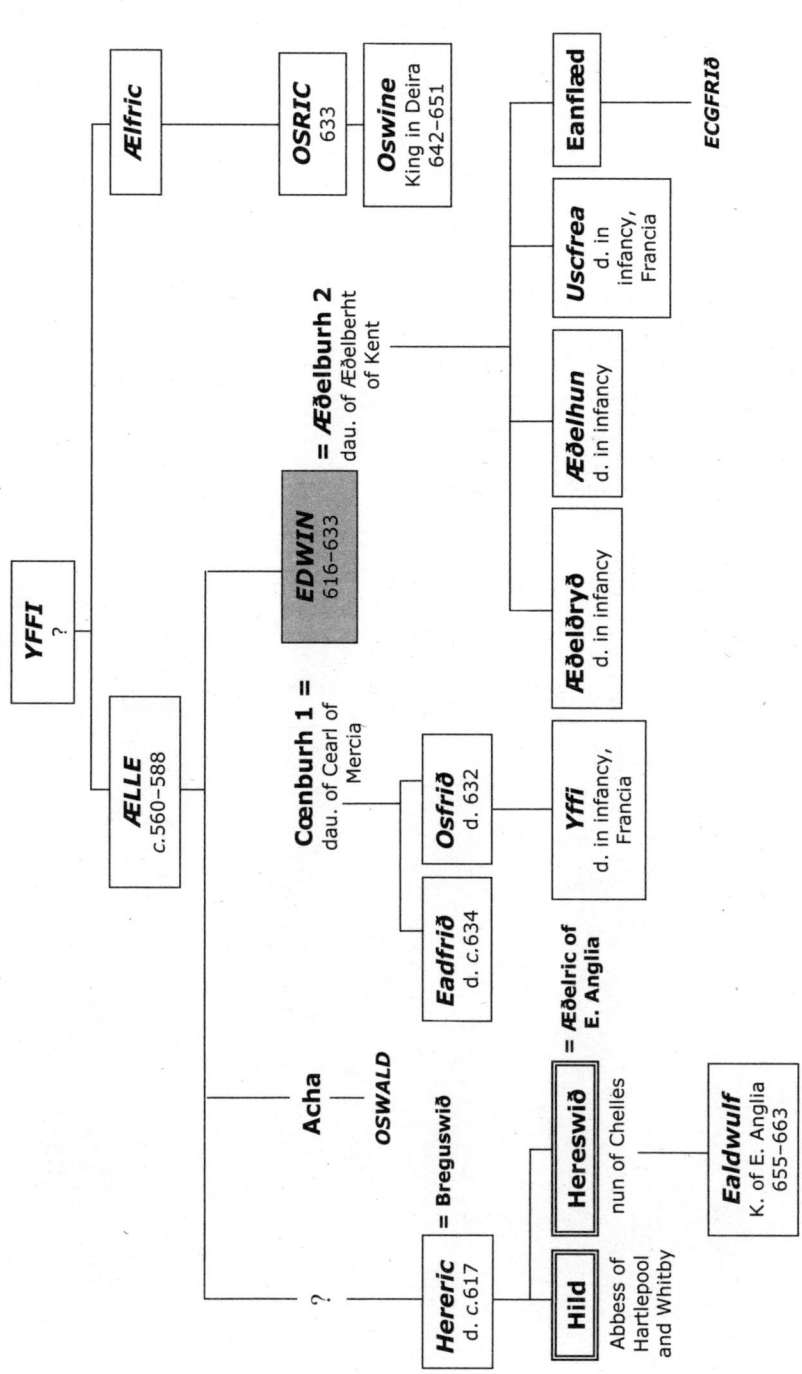

The seventh-century Deiran royal house

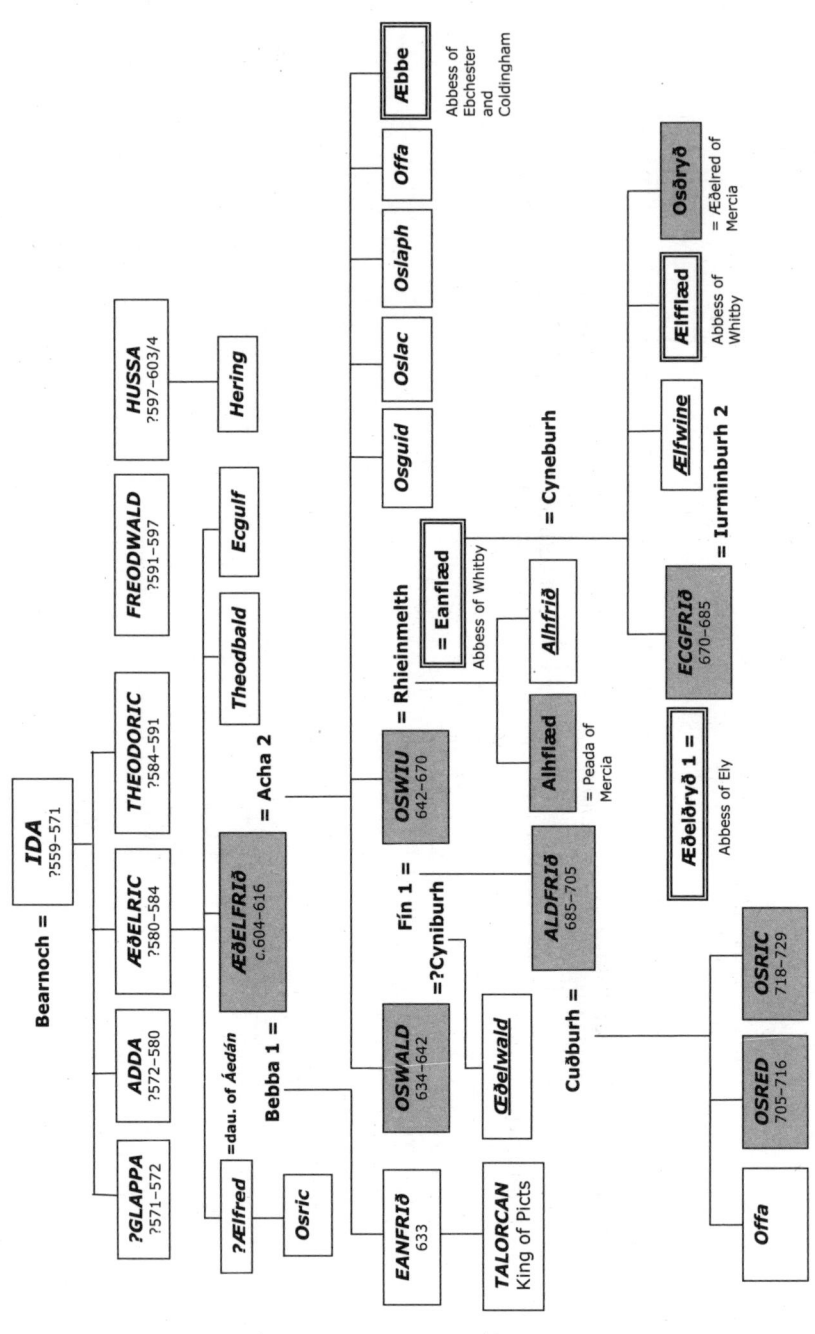

The seventh- and early eighth-century Bernician royal house

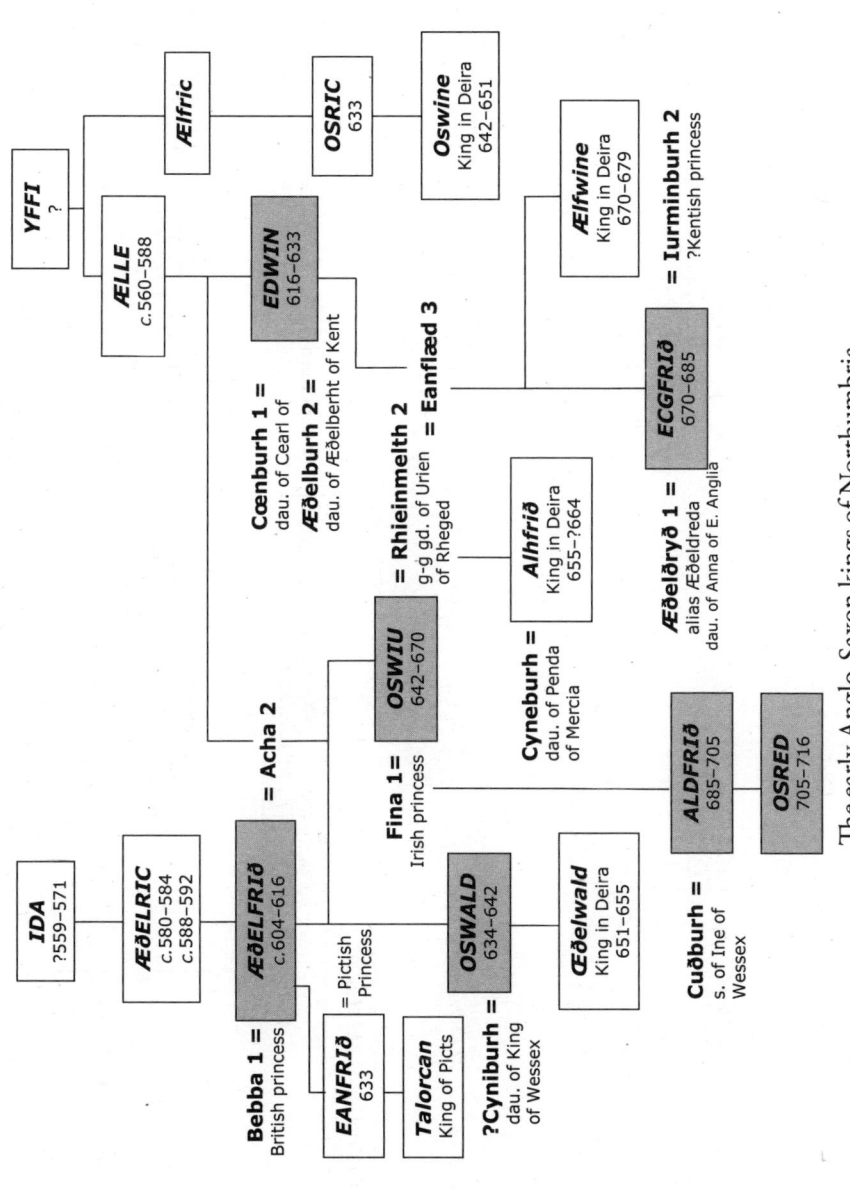

The early Anglo-Saxon kings of Northumbria

PART I: 367–642

CHRONOLOGY I: 367–642

367 – The so-called 'Barbarian Conspiracy', in which tribes north of Hadrian's Wall overrun it with connivance of its garrisons (*Res Gestae* 27.9).*

368 – Count Theodosius is sent to Britain: he recaptures London, restores order and the forts.

369 – Theodosius routs the invaders and begins re-fortifying the frontier. No Roman troops are now stationed north of the Wall. Watch and signal towers on the Yorkshire coast are probably built at this time, between Filey and Huntcliffe.

383 – Magnus Maximus, commander in Britain, usurps the throne from Emperor Gratian (375–83); he crosses to Gaul with elements of the British army.

408–9 – Constantine 'III' is recognised as co-Emperor by Honorius; the army in Britain rebels against him, and the Britons expel the Roman administration (Zosimus VI.v.2).

410 – *Britanniae Saxonum incursionae devastatae (Chronica Gallica).*

415 – A possible approximate date for the birth of St Patrick, based on Charles Thomas's 'single, late Patrick' model.

425 – The so-called Kentish Chronicle, cited by Nennius's *Chronographer*, dates Vortigern's coming to power (*HB* 66).

428 – The English come to Britain (*HB* 66).

429 – Bishop Germanus of Auxerre visits Britain with a delegation to put down heresy (*Vit Germ* 12–18).

---

* See the primary sources section of the bibliography for keys to abbreviations.

437 – The Battle of Wallop, as dated by Nennius's *Chronographer* (*HB* 66): a possible civil war in Britain. A 'quarrel' between Vitalinus and Ambrosius.

449 – 'Traditional' (calculated by Bede and the *ASC*) date of arrival of Hengist and Horsa in Kent and the wars against Vortigern.

480 – The earliest plausible date for Gildas writing the *De Excidio* (more likely closer to 500; possibly as late as 540).

⋮

547 – The traditional date of Ida's arrival at Bamburgh (calculated by Bede) and the foundation of the kingdom of Bernicia.

559 – Beginning of Ida's reign in Bernicia (our amended chronology).

560 – The beginning of Ælle's reign in Deira.

565 – The founding of the monastery on Iona (*ASC*).

572 – The death of Ida; succeeded by Adda (amended chronology).

580 – The death of Adda; succeeded by Æðelric (amended chronology).

584 – The death of Æðelric; succeeded by Theodoric (amended chronology); the probable date of the siege of Lindisfarne by Urien of Rheged (undated in *HB* 63); Urien is betrayed and killed by Morcant.

588 – Ælle of Deira dies (*ASC*) [?]; Æðelric succeeds.

590 – Possible historical context for the Battle of *Catræth* between warriors of the Gododdin and an Anglian warband.

591 – The death of Theodoric; succeeded by Freodwald (amended chronology).

592/3 – [?] The death of Æðelric and succession of Æðelfrið as king in Deira. He takes Bebba as his Bernician wife?

593 – The death of Colm Cille on Iona (traditionally 597 but see Lacey 2013); the death of Freodwald; succeeded by Hussa (amended chronology).

597 – The arrival of St Augustine's Christian mission in Kent (*ASC* F).

604 – The death of Hussa of Bernicia; he is succeeded by King Æðelfrið (amended chronology) who defeats Áedán mac Gabráin, King of the Dál Riata Scots, at the Battle of Degsastan as the culmination of a long-running war. Æðelfrið's brother Theobald is killed. Dál Riata is now tributary to Northumbria.

615/6? – The Battle of Chester: King Æðelfrið defeats British warbands under Solon, son of Conan of Powys and possibly a Mercian warband under Cearl (613 in *AC*). Edwin, son of Ælle, prince of Deira, marries Cœnburh of Mercia, daughter of Cearl (Bede *HE* II.14); then takes refuge with the royal family of East Anglia.

616 – King Æðelfrið is ambushed and killed by King Rædwald of East Anglia at Bawtry in the Battle of the River Idle (Bede *HE* II.12 but undated by Bede). Edwin becomes King of Deira, having fought beside Rædwald.

619 – [?] Edwin expels King Ceretic from the British kingdom of Elmet (*HB* 63).

c.622 – Edwin campaigns against Man and Anglesey and besieges Cadwallon on Priestholm.

625 – King Edwin marries a Christian princess, Æðelburh of Kent. Paulinus is consecrated Bishop of York (Bede *HE* II.9).

626 – An assassination attempt at Easter on King Edwin by an agent of the Wessex King Cwichelm. Edwin recovers from his wounds and wages war on Cwichelm (Bede *HE* II.9).

[?] Birth of Eanflæd, daughter of Edwin and Æðelburh.

627 – King Edwin is baptised in a new wooden church at York by Bishop Paulinus. Mass baptisms follow in the River Swale (beside the *villa regia* of *Catræth*) and at Edwin's refurbished palace at Yeavering (Bede *HE* II.14).

632/3 – Edwin is killed at the Battle of Hatfield/*Meicen* by Penda of Mercia (633 in *ASC*) fighting with Cadwallon of Gwynedd. Edwin's son Osfrið is also killed; the other, Eadfrið, flees to or is taken into Mercia and later killed there (Bede *HE* II.20).

633 – Northumbria collapses into its constituent kingdoms; reverts to paganism under Eanfrið (son of Æðelfrið) and Osric (cousin of Edwin), both killed by Cadwallon. Cadwallon wastes Northumbria (Bede *HE* III.1).

634 – Eanfrið sues for peace with Cadwallon in Bernicia and is murdered with his companions.

Oswald returns from exile to claim the Northumbrian kingdom, with a [?] retinue including Dál Riatan and Ionan warriors. He defeats and kills King Cadwallon at the Battle of *Denisesburn* after raising his cross at Heavenfield (Bede *HE* III.2).

635 – Oswald sends for Aidan, an Irish monk/bishop from the Scottish island of Iona, to convert Northumbria to Irish Christianity. Aidan establishes a monastery on the island of Lindisfarne and becomes its first bishop (Bede *HE* III.3).

Oswald is present at King Cynegils's baptism into the Roman church.

Likely date of the marriage of Oswiu to Rhieinmelth, granddaughter of Urien of Rheged (*HB*).

638 – The siege of Edinburgh – by Oswald/Oswiu? (*AU*).

642 – King Oswald is killed in the Battle of *Maserfelth* (*ASC* A). He is succeeded by his brother Oswiu in Bernicia and by Oswine (son of Osric: a cousin of Edwin) in Deira.

1

MARCHER-WARDS: 367–450

Conspiracy and crisis – North of Humber
– Fort, town, villa – Territorial lordship –
Cultural corelands – Patrick, Gildas, Nennius

Only the thinnest of threads seem to connect the ordered, wealthy, urbane and civilised society of Roman Britain with the warlike tribal kingdoms of the Anglo-Saxons, Picts and Britons portrayed by their historians just a few centuries after Rome's fall around AD 400. Those threads of continuity – geographical, social and institutional – are the more difficult to detect because of a seemingly overwhelming discontinuity in narrative history, in the settlement record, in language and material culture.

The political instability that severed Britain from the Roman Empire in the first decade of the fifth century can be traced at least as far back as the year 350, when *Britannia*'s governors declared their support for a usurper, Magnentius. His defeat by Constantius II the following year, in a battle in the Balkans, was followed by savage reprisals against *Britannia*'s propertied classes and the suicide of its *vicarius*, or prefect.[1] Eight years later the Emperor Julian sent a huge fleet of 600 ships across the Channel to extract the province's grain harvest to feed his Continental armies.[2] That same year, 359, when a score or more of British bishops attended a church council at *Ariminum* (Rimini), three of them had to be subsidised out of public funds.[3] A year later, according to Ammianus Marcellinus,* the last great Classical historian, Britain's northern frontier zone, along the line of Hadrian's Wall, was attacked: 'the wild tribes of the Scots and Picts broke their undertaking to keep peace, laid waste the country near the frontier and caused alarm among the provincials, who were exhausted by the repeated disasters they had suffered'.[4]

---

* Writing in Rome in the 380s. *Res Gestae* 27.8.

The outcome of a campaign to repel the invaders, under a commander named Lupicinus, is unrecorded; but in any case the restoration of military control over the northern frontier lasted less than a decade. Ammianus recalled how, in 367, the Emperor Valentinian was marching with an army from Amiens towards Trier on the Moselle when he received intelligence of a conspiracy of northern barbarians – Picts, Scots and the shadowy Attacotti – which had brought Britain to its knees. Count Nectaridus, the commander of *Britannia*'s East Coast defences,* had been killed. The *dux* of the northern frontier, General Fullofaudes,† had been ambushed and cut off by the enemy.[5]

Despite the distractions of a punitive campaign against the Alamanni of the Upper Rhine, Emperor Valentinian sent a small army to Britain in the following year under a promising commander named Theodosius. He discovered evidence of an army coup and of the betrayal of the frontier intelligence and scouting corps, the *milites areani*: bribed or coerced by northern tribes to look the other way.[6] Theodosius's forces rounded up looters and army deserters, restored property and disbanded the scouting corps. He was also said to have restored cities and garrisons, reinforced guard posts and defences and brought order to the province. Nevertheless, the shocking speed and ferocity of this incursion, the failure of the frontier defences and the exposure of fatal weaknesses in Britain's political leadership and military intelligence, reverberated long afterwards.

Historians have seen in the events of 367–9 a pivotal marker for the eventual end of Britain as a Roman province two generations later. In those decades chroniclers' very sparse notices of events in Britain tell of a succession of usurpers setting themselves up as would-be emperors, using the province and its armies as a platform to launch bids for the imperial throne across the English Channel.‡ The most significant of these was Theodosius's nephew and comrade-in-arms on the 368 expedition: Magnus Maximus, who launched his own imperial bid in Britain in the 380s and whose name, intriguingly, appears in the genealogies of the earliest Welsh kings.

The decisive crisis came in 408–9 when, according to the historian Zosimus, writing a century later but drawing on a lost, more nearly contemporary account by Olympiodorus:

---

* Formally *Comes littoris Saxonici per Britanniam*.
† The *Dux Britanniarum*, with his headquarters at York.
‡ For a fuller summary of these events, see Adams 2021a, 49ff.

Hadrian's Wall: the definition of Rome's Northern Frontier

the barbarians beyond the Rhine made such unbounded incursions over every province, as to reduce not only the Britons, but some of the Celtic nations also, to the necessity of revolting from the empire, and living no longer under the Roman laws but as they themselves pleased. The Britons therefore took up arms, and incurred many dangerous enterprises for their own protection, until they had freed their cities from the barbarians who besieged them.[7]

The *Chronica Gallica** paints an even starker image, which needs no translation: *Britanniae Saxonum incursionae devastatae.*

* * *

There are strong hints of a political crisis in the South in the 420s – of factional and religious tensions, perhaps of civil war: a pro-Roman and anti-Roman party in competition for power; the arrival of proxy armed forces from the near Continent.[8] But a narrative history for the lands north of the Humber is almost non-existent before the end of the sixth century, by which time warlord dynasties bearing native British or Germanic names, speaking a novel language, were vying for control of a politically unrecognisable landscape of petty kingdoms. By then Britain no longer had any functioning urban centres; no civil service or state functionaries; no currency aside from recycled Roman coins; no market economy and barely any relations with Continental Europe. The last stratigraphic phases of buildings, streets and defences in Britain's Roman towns are often found to be covered by a thick layer of what is called, enigmatically but literally, 'dark earth': their apparently deserted streets and buildings became the back-filled graves of an empire.

Archaeologists, hoping to fill in at least some of the gaps, and to flesh out the disaster narratives of Roman historians, are confronted with a raft of challenges: the lack of dateable coinage from British sites after about 400; the absence of new masonry construction; an extreme paucity of diagnostic finds – decorated pottery, metalwork or textiles – and no chronological context, no history, in which to situate the dramatic changes they see in settlement, agriculture, environment and population.

The archaeological record is a generally reliable witness to catastrophe: fires leave layers of charcoal which can be broadly dated using the radiocarbon 14 isotope. Forts, towns and rural settlements, abandoned in extreme hurry, leave tell-tale signs: unburied bodies, whole pots lying on the floors of

---

* Compiled, judging by the latest entry, in 452.

houses and barns – the artefacts of daily routines interrupted. But across more than a century of research, in hundreds of excavations, archaeologists of the frontier zone expecting to uncover tell-tale signs of destruction or massacre in its forts, *vici*, *coloniae* and villas have failed to detect wholesale destruction: a Pompeii full of hastily abandoned houses, skeletons littering the streets, a dramatic hiatus in daily life. The crises of 360, 367 and 408 have left little obvious evidence in the soil.

Archaeologists have, nevertheless, seen discontinuities in negatives: the apparent gradual abandonment of forts and villas after the middle or end of the fourth century and a chronic lack of evidence for a thriving rural or urban population.* From the point of the view of the grand urbanising Roman project – with its civic buildings and sewers, its roads, public baths and an immense web of markets, towns and literate civil servants, its professional armies, grand country houses set in well-ordered estates and its sense of unshakeable cultural purpose – the political and social upheavals of the fourth century look like the end of an epoch: almost the end of civilisation.

The words of very few, if telling, witnesses – a clerical confession; a smattering of barely credible saints' lives; pseudo-historical annal entries and an excoriating sermon – survive to sketch a picture of the aftermath. They portray a litany of invasions, civil wars, famine, fire and plague; of Briton against Saxon, of pagan against Christian. But the dispassionate testimony of archaeological excavation and survey, of historical geography, of place-names and pollen samples, tells a different story. The peoples of the lands north of the Humber endured; they adapted. They still raised cattle, grew cereals and vegetables; forged decorative arts and weapons; spun and wove cloth; buried their dead; explored new means of expression and identity that were nevertheless rooted in the deep, sometimes mythic past. They farmed with pragmatism but with an eye to the caprices of their gods. They glorified warfare and treasure in an imaginative world full of warrior heroes and vengeful smiths, dragons and fantastical creatures. They knew who they were, and who they were not. They venerated their ancestors and generally treated their

---

* A number of coastal signal stations between Huntcliffe in the north and Filey in the south are conventionally dated to the post-360 political landscape. North of Hadrian's Wall, forts like *Bremenium*, at High Rochester, seem to have been abandoned or destroyed some time during the middle of the fourth century (Crow 2004). (Ottaway (2013) has good material on York's signal stations.)

dead with reverence, sometimes with fear. In peace and war they valued reciprocity in gift, service, loyalty, comradeship, reward, punishment and revenge. They feared exclusion, exile and lordlessness above all else. In surviving, they came to experiment with a form of hierarchical lordship in which ceorl, thegn, ealdorman and king, bound by the agricultural wealth of the earth, embedded communities and power structures in their landscapes. Those landscapes – topographies of river valley, fertile plains, coastal margins, wooded hillsides and open upland pastures, of soils and climate – are tangible threads linking the present with the past: age-old constraints and opportunities familiar to farmers, travellers, armies and traders across millennia.

Meteorologically, Britain is divided into four zones: a mild, wet South-west; a cool, wet North-west; a cool, dry North-east; and a mild, dry, more continental South-east. The most fertile lands lie towards the east and south. The easiest, best-drained arable lay on the gravels and alluvial silts of broad river valleys; heavier, more intractable but more fertile soils were to be found on the clay lands of the Midlands and North-east.

The estuary of the River Humber penetrates some 60km (40 miles) inland from the east coast, fed by the broad and powerful River Trent that rises in Staffordshire, and by the many rivers that drain east off the Pennine chain of hills: Swale, Ure, Ouse, Nidd, Wharfe, Aire, Calder and Don. Ferries have crossed and ships navigated the Humber's dangerous waters time out of mind; even so, it is both a formidable barrier to movement and a natural frontier between North and South.

The head of the Humber catchment is low-lying, prone to flooding and periodically inundated by floods so as to make habitation and agriculture marginal or impossible. Some Roman-period settlements here were buried by a metre or so of alluvium during the late fourth century, a time when broadly cooler and wetter conditions prevailed.[9] North of the Humber, framing the east side of the Vale of York – also prone to flooding then, as now – the chalk Wolds are relatively dry, with few permanent watercourses. These uplands had long before been cleared and demarcated by prehistoric herders; they were rich in surviving prehistoric earthworks, burial mounds and standing stones. Beyond, the Vale of Pickering paradoxically carries the River Derwent inland from near the coast at Filey towards the Ouse at Selby, draining the deeply incised southern slopes of the more formidable North Yorkshire Moors.*

---

* Rising to 454m OD (almost 1,500ft) at Urra Moor.

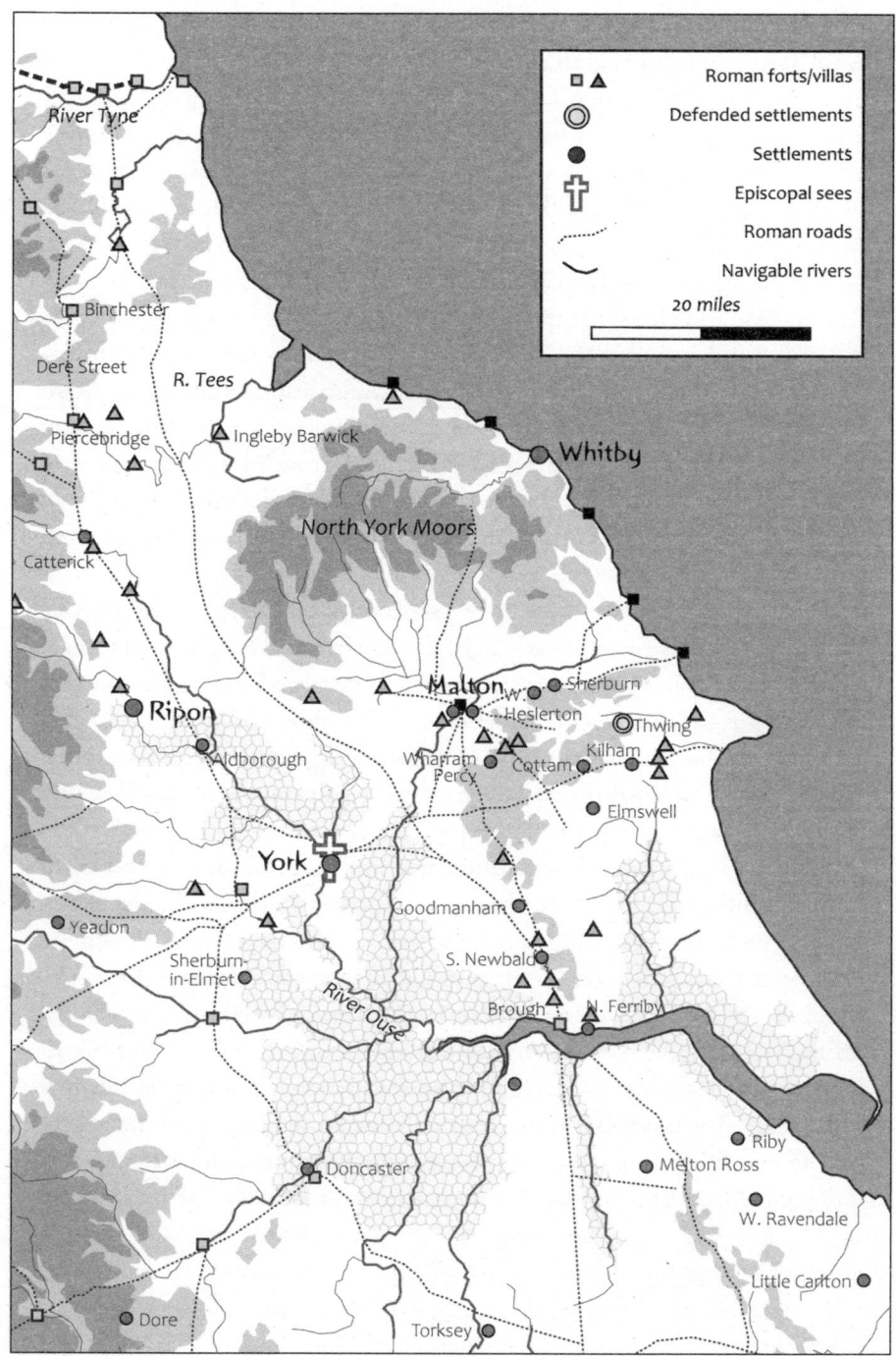

Map 1 Southern Northumbria: topography and settlement

A Roman road, Dere Street, linked Lincoln (*Lindum colonia*) and York (*Eboracum*) to the forts along Hadrian's Wall, skirting the low ground along the west edge of the Vale of York at the foot of the Pennine chain. A more or less parallel road running along the east side of the vale linked a key Humber estuary crossing at Brough (Roman *Petuaria*), and the western fringe of the Wolds and Moors to another key river crossing the River Tyne at Gateshead.*
Here, a bridge, the *Pons Aelius*, met Hadrian's Wall at what is now Newcastle. Both roads crossed the broad, fertile plain of the River Tees: to the west at Piercebridge and to the east at Croft.

West from Newcastle, the Tyne–Solway Gap was not merely a convenient straight line linking east and west coasts with the frontier defences of the Wall: it enjoys the least difficult terrain for passage across the Pennines. In the Roman period the Tyne was navigable perhaps only 20km or so inland† and the River Eden only as far as Carlisle (*Civitas Carvetiorum*). But a road – the Stanegate – joined Dere Street at *Coria* (Corbridge) with Carlisle, servicing the Wall forts, shrinking the distance between east and west ports of trade and providing rapid military access along the whole frontier line. Long sections of the Stanegate may still be driven – or walked: from Fourstones village near Hexham along a minor road almost as far as the much-excavated fort at Vindolanda; thence its line can be traced in fields north of General Wade's Military Road as far as Greenhead; from then on it is largely followed by the course of the modern A69. The deeply incised gorge of the Tipalt Burn is crossed here by a bridge and, rising up the west side onto rough pastures lying at over 200m (650ft) above sea level, the sense of coming into a border land as one passes from Northumberland into Cumbria is palpable; even the weather seems suddenly to change, presaging something much more exposed and remote.

Tynedale also benefits from fertile soils and south-facing slopes: it is abundant in early settlement evidence and is still valued as prime agricultural real estate. North of the Tyne, relatively modest rivers run east off the North Pennines and Cheviot Hills: the Wansbeck, Coquet, Aln and then the more substantial Tweed, whose headwaters lie close to the source of the north-west-draining Clyde. Each of the east-draining rivers is a partial barrier to traffic along the fertile coastal plain of Northumberland. Dere Street crossed

---

* *Ad Caprae Caput*: literally 'the goat's head'.
† The debate over the highest navigable reach is unresolved. At a stretch, Corbridge may have been reachable with flash weirs; more likely Wylam, as now, was the navigable limit.

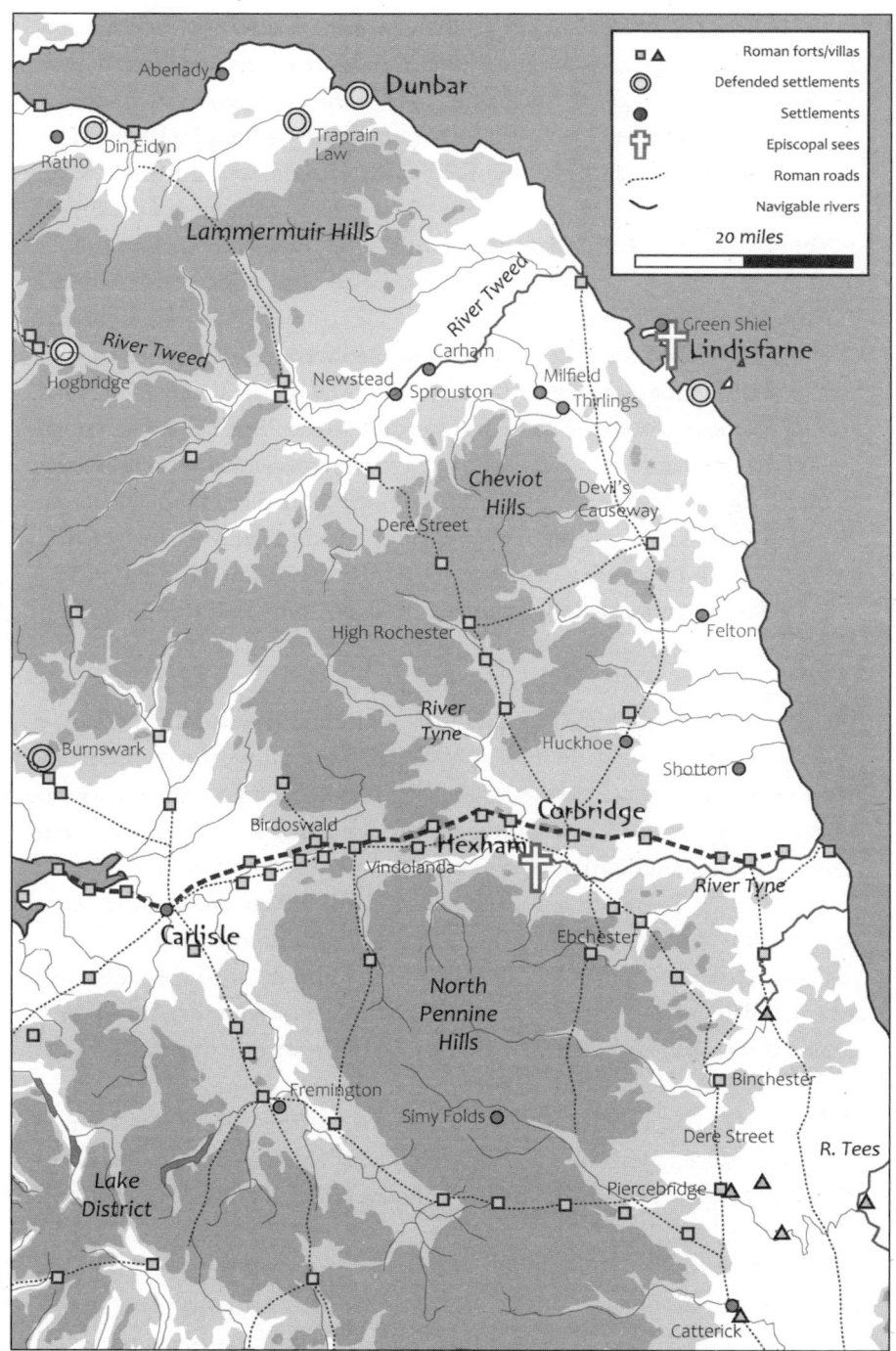

Map 2 Northern Northumbria: topography and settlement

the Tyne at Corbridge (*Coria*), pierced the Wall at what is now Portgate, and drove across the high country towards the River Forth and the second-century Antonine Wall, at Edinburgh (*Din Eidyn*). An offshoot road, the Devil's Causeway, linked Dere Street with the Tweed-mouth port of Berwick; another, putatively, ran north from the Tyne at *Pons Aelius*, perhaps crossing the River Coquet near Felton.

The Tweed Valley is broad and fertile. Well-populated and culturally cohesive in later prehistory, it came periodically under the control of the Roman military with the strategically key fort of Newstead overlooking a river crossing at Melrose. The Lammermuir Hills and Southern Uplands of Scotland are thinly populated: this is cattle and sheep country, of wide upland pastures, wooded valleys and heather moors. But coastal lowlands around Dunbar and the Forth estuary see concentrations of early settlements. These are the East Lothian heartlands of the legendary Gododdin. To the south and west, along the coast of Dumfries and Galloway, fringing the Solway Firth and bounding the Irish Sea, productive farmland and maritime access fostered cultural and economic relations with Ireland and Man: connecting, rather than dividing peoples.

* * *

The origins of Early Medieval kingdoms, as they are expressed in these diverse geographies, are to be found in the political and economic accommodations made by devolved tribal entities in the fragmenting Roman Empire; and in the layers of soil that archaeologists call late Roman horizons. By the fourth century Britain's southern provinces were no longer militarised. Britons were Roman citizens, barred from bearing arms and fully integrated into the imperial system of *civitates* – former tribal areas with regional capitals governed by primarily indigenous élites. But Britain must pay its way, and it became a net exporter of grain, cloth and the mineral wealth of its metal ores: gold, copper, tin, iron, silver and lead. North of the Humber the armies of the frontier were paid for by those taxes – the exploitive price of peace.

Under the late Empire, civil and military administrative powers were progressively separated from one another and devolved to its regions. Taxes formerly levied in coin and bullion came to be extracted in kind as the *iugum*, a render of labour and goods imposed on its citizens by the *civitates*. Instead of being exported to Rome these were consumed directly and, therefore, locally. At the same time, the defences of the northern frontier came to rely not on the field armies or *comitatenses* – élite professional units recruited from across the Empire and sent to serve in distant provinces – but on *limitanei* or frontiersmen, recruited from and embedded within regional and local communities.[10]

On Britain's northern frontier, along Hadrian's Wall and its forts, the *limitanei* were largely drawn from the native British population, often serving under officers posted from far-flung lands, under the overall command of the *Dux Britanniarum* at York. The *limitanei* patrolled and policed the frontier zone and the lands to the north; gathered and passed on intelligence of possibly hostile actions; controlled passage through the line of the frontier and protected the landed economic assets that lay to the south – particularly, perhaps, the state-controlled lead mines of the North Pennines.[11] On retirement they were given land on which to settle, farm and raise the next generation of troops. Son might follow father into military service on the Wall; generations of the same family might depend on the forts, and, in turn, the proper functioning of the frontier relied on these communities. They became interdependent.

The fort of *Banna* (Birdoswald) is perched on the high watershed of the Rivers Tyne and Irthing between what are now Cumbria and Northumberland, not far from the pass at Greenhead. Excavations here in the 1990s, under the direction of Tony Wilmott, revealed local expressions of these broader trends in telling detail. The playing card-shaped fort developed across three centuries, its north wall and entrance incorporated into the line of the Wall, facing the high country beyond the frontier. *Banna* was manned by an auxiliary cohort recruited from *Dacia* (roughly modern Romania). In its shadow a civilian settlement, or *vicus*, grew up during the third century. By the beginning of the fourth century the garrison consisted of *limitanei*, the locally recruited frontier troops. Evidence for its fortunes after this time focuses on the sites of two *horrea*, or granaries, which stood inside the west gate immediately south of the *Via Principalis*. These were huge stone structures, each more than 30m long, with heated flagstone floors and external buttresses, designed to store and secure the garrison's grain and other foodstuffs.

The first signs that the fort was adapting to new realities on the frontier come after about 350, when the flagstone floor in the south granary was lifted, the sub-floor was filled in and then the flags were replaced. All the coins from the sealed deposit below the re-laid flags dated to 348 or before, providing a *terminus post quem*: a date after which the alterations must have been made.[12] A series of stone hearths excavated at the west end of this re-purposed granary shows that whatever was still being stored there, the *horrea* had now also taken on a domestic function – fireplaces being incompatible with grain storage. From the layers that accumulated around these hearths, excavators recovered a gold earring, a black glass ring and a coin from the reign of Emperor Theodosius* (dated to 388–395).

Some time during this period the roof of the north granary collapsed, indicating that it was no longer being maintained for its original function. It seems to have been quarried for stone and other materials and used for the dumping of rubbish. Coins found sealed beneath these layers range in date from the 340s to the reign of Emperor Valentinian I (364–378), including coins of a type known as *Fel Temp Reparatio* (348–364), from a legend borne on the reverse which ironically translates as 'the restoration of happy times'. A distinctive, 'sub-Roman' type of penannular brooch was also recovered from these deposits.[13]

Later, two successive timber structures were erected on the site of the north granary. The first was constructed so that its massive posts sat on top of the truncated stone walls. It was given a new stone floor, sealing the rubbish layers and dated finds beneath. Later again a second timber building was constructed – this time shifted 3m or so north and west so that it only partly overlay the former granary. It now intruded onto the south side of the *Via Principalis* but, significantly, it aligned with a re-modelled west gate, so that on entering the fort from the west, one's view was dominated by its gable end. This structure was supported by paired posts on stone post pads and measured 23m by 8.6m: on the same scale and alignment as its predecessors but shorter by some 6m. What had been a military granary seems now to have morphed into an Early Medieval mead hall.

Tony Wilmott, in considering how long this sequence of buildings can be taken beyond the sealed evidence below its floors, argues that the revival of the north granary site must have taken place at or after the final abandonment of the south granary – dated to the reign of Theodosius – and was its direct replacement. He also argues that two timber structures built on stone foundations would enjoy substantial life spans, and that the whole sequence might run through, and beyond, the fifth century.[14]

The last army pay wagons turned up no later than the late 390s. That *Banna* and its garrison survived and functioned as a military command after that date demonstrates that here, at least, localised military authority, and the economy to support it, successfully evolved. The grandiosity of the architecture shows that the garrison commander and his troops were not merely huddling in the ruins of the former imperial army fortress – they were the

---

* Son of the army commander sent to Britain in 368.

From Roman military granary to mead hall: the excavations at Birdoswald

direct successors of its imperial commanders. In later centuries the commanders of such units might be called *mearc-weardas*, literally 'marcher-wards' or 'border-sentinels' – an Old English kenning for a wolf. The modern-day visitor to Birdoswald, confronted with the formal, excavated remains of the Roman fort and the massive timber posts placed in their sockets by English Heritage to evoke the epochal cultural shift here in the fifth century, is struck with awe at idea that this is where what used to be called the Dark Ages began.

To the east and south, along the Stanegate, the much-excavated fort at Vindolanda shows signs of late occupation and, potentially, of flourishing Christian worship – a possible thread, like territorial lordship, linking the late Roman world with the Early Medieval. The defences seem to have been refurbished in the late fourth century. A building in the courtyard of the remodelled *praetorium*, constructed with a west-facing apse, is interpreted by its excavators as a church.[15] Here also a tombstone dated tentatively to around 500 was inscribed with the Brittonic name BRIGOMAGLOS, meaning 'high lord'; the accompanying words [HI]C IACIT ('here lies') are typical of Christian burial at this time.[16] A rectangular stone slab found in a pit near the south wall of the fort, inscribed with a *chi rho* monogrammed cross, is possibly a portable altar stone, and other buildings late in the site's sequence are speculatively regarded as possible churches.[17] This interpretation depends on the idea that an apse at one end of a rectangular building is diagnostic of a church, but this form of building is not uncommon within southern Scotland and Northumberland, seen for example at Traprain Law hillfort, in the settlement enclosure of Huckhoe and elsewhere.

Around 30 miles to the south-east along Dere Street, the Roman fort at Binchester commanded a key crossing of the River Wear and here a similarly long sequence of occupation extends its life beyond the beginning of the fifth century. During the early to mid fourth century a new and elaborate *praetorium*, or headquarters complex, was constructed. Around 370 – perhaps in the aftermath of the crisis of 367 – a large bath house was added; then enlarged. After a number of refurbishments that would seem to take the bath house complex beyond the year 400, its furnace became choked with rubble. A smithing forge was installed in one room, while another seems to have been used as an abattoir. Material from the collapse of the bath house vault was cut by a grave dating to the sixth century.[18] Elsewhere on the site large quantities of animal bone were recovered from pits and a distinctive penannular brooch was also found.[19]

Close to the mouth of the River Tyne, the Wall supply fort of *Arbeia* at South Shields reveals a contrasting sequence over a period that extends the site's life well into the century after the end of Roman rule. Here, the forecourt of the *principia* seems to have been partially transformed into a building which has been interpreted as a church.[20] A ditch was cut through the metalled surface of a road which contained a coin of 388–402. Afterwards, a new timber gate was installed, with a portal bearing similarities with the gateway remodelling at Birdoswald. An inhumation cemetery was established inside the walls, and, in a courtyard house, two bodies were interred, bearing identical injuries and dating to the early part of the fifth century.[21] Here, the evidence argues for striking discontinuity, albeit spread across decades well into the fifth century. The implication is, perhaps, that coastal forts were more vulnerable to disruptive external forces than those inland.

Rob Collins has studied the material culture of the northern frontier and sees in these structural adaptations a broader trend towards relatively smaller garrisons of *limitanei*, perhaps of 120–150 active soldiers, stationed along the frontier during the fourth century. Their commanders were men of high status, reflecting increased independence and roles that spanned civilian and military governance. They modified their accommodation and the internal structures of their forts as local need arose: to store produce rendered in kind; to act as assembly sites for those communities dependent on them. They were supported by self-sustaining industries and technologies. 'Public' buildings were privatised and headquarter compounds often turned over to butchery, metalworking, accommodation or worship. They increasingly preferred to build in timber even if their new structures were essentially conceived on imperial models.[22]

In later Roman towns, roadside settlements and forts these trends – recognisable from large-scale depositions of animal bone, forging waste, metalwork, ancillary workshop debris and remodelled public space – seem from an urbane, Roman point of view like societal failure, even disaster. In the frontier zone it looks more like the emergence of a new sort of locally invested power: territorial lordship. Where piles of animal bone scattered about former public spaces look from one point of view like anarchy and squatting, from another they look like the concentration of animals rendered as tax in kind, butchered, consumed and perhaps partly redistributed through gifts and feasting from a central facility – the fort, where the commander now lived in a converted granary like a warrior in his mead hall. Thickly accumulating layers of so-called dark earth are not necessarily evidence of abandonment, but of a perquisite: cattle belonging to dependents were wintered inside the forts' walls for protection, adding a valuable layer of manure to the commander's kitchen garden. Scrap metalwork brought in as bullion, part of a render, was now recycled into distinctive brooches with hybrid Roman, native and Continental affinities, given as tokens of loyalty and esteem to reward officers, clients and local allies, or traded further afield. In turn, burials within forts and towns look like reinforcements of identity and belonging.

A late fourth-century military commander cut off from regular supplies and coin for salaries, severed from the political control and direction of commissars and already embedded within a civilian community to which his soldiers belong, must needs make do. Farmers and craftspeople within the hinterland of a fort find their produce requisitioned locally rather than taxed in coin at distant markets; their labour is bent to refurbishing the commander's accommodation; to tending his cattle. In return, they are protected from the predations of rival garrisons and raiders from beyond the horizon. The former granaries of the fort are repurposed as semi-domestic, semi-public spaces where supplies are gathered and kept safe, where complainants and supplicants are heard; justice meted out; feasts held on the quarter days; gifts given in exchange for loyal service, on marriage and, perhaps, to cement local alliances under which the garrison extended its protection and patronage to settlements beyond its immediate hinterland.

The historical geographer Brian Roberts has observed that along the length of Hadrian's Wall the boundaries of historic townships, as recorded on the first Ordnance Survey maps in the middle of the nineteenth century but likely much more ancient, almost never butt up against the Wall, as one might expect of so formidable a barrier.[23] When the smallest units of territorial lordship emerge in documentary sources in the seventh century, they centre on the *vill*, a large farmstead to which services and food renders were brought from a known, more or less bounded area of agricultural production: a theoretically centripetal model. In the case of the *vills* or townships along the Wall, which evolved into the historic townships of the Medieval period, the centres of many of these *vills* were its forts.*

If local territorial lordship developed in some of the Wall forts, similar types of evidence, albeit fragmented, can also be found elsewhere. Carlisle stands at the west end of Hadrian's Wall in the tribal lands of the *Carvetii*.[24] Carlisle was *Caer Ligualid* in Old Welsh, *Lugubaliam civitatem* in Bede's Latin, a first-century fortress controlling both a key crossing of the River Eden at the head of the Solway Firth. It lay at a critical intersection of routes running north into what is now South-west Scotland, east along the Stanegate towards the River Tyne, south towards Chester and south-east towards Catterick and York. It later became the *civitas* capital. Here, the central range of the *principia* was refurbished, with a new hypocaust sub-floor heating system, which seems to have functioned well into the fifth century, judging by a late coin sequence and evidence for butchery.[25] Mike McCarthy, Carlisle's principal archaeologist over many years, sees strong indications of decline from the town's thriving apogee in the third century; but he acknowledges that an emphasis in later decades on livestock management, the presence of dark earth deposits and a number of drinking vessels, may indicate adaptation rather than abandonment. Carlisle was later patronised by the Northumbrian royal house, who gave land here in the seventh century to the Lindisfarne community for the establishment of a nunnery.

---

* Roberts points out forcefully that a simplistic survival from fort to *vill* cannot be asserted; the townships have long, complex, nuanced histories; they are 'residuals'. Roberts 2010, 129.

More enigmatic evidence comes from the headquarters of the *Dux Britanniarum* at York. Hurried excavations in the late 1960s beneath the Minster, carried out as engineers fought to shore up its massive foundations, confirmed that the church was constructed on the site of the basilican hall in the Roman *principia* of the legionary fortress – a telling location in its own right. Material from the collapse of the hall, including a significant quantity of young-culled pig bone, was dated to the later fourth or early fifth century. Analysis of finds from the waterfront in the *colonia*, the veteran settlement on the opposite, south-west bank of the River Ouse, showed that a substantial Roman building there was repaired, refurbished and rebuilt several times after 375–400.[26] Fifth- and sixth-century cemeteries have long been known from the peripheries of the Roman town, and the establishment of a royal church here – the first in Anglian Northumbria and the precursor of the Minster – by King Edwin in 627 reflects the propensity, as at Carlisle, for former Roman towns to attract royal and ecclesiastical investment – another thread of continuity.

South of the frontier zone in the less militarised Tees Valley, David Petts has assembled a raft of seemingly circumstantial evidence to paint a picture in which novel expressions of power display a geographical, regional logic. Here, military control was exercised along the line of Dere Street at the eastern periphery of the Pennines. The major settlement on this line was the walled town at *Cataractonium* (Catterick), halfway between the headquarters of the *dux* at York and the River Tyne, guarding access across the Pennines through Stainmore Pass and Swaledale.* To the east, the broad valley of the Tees encompassed low-lying, well-watered fertile soils, long cleared by prehistoric agriculturalists. The northernmost villas in the Roman Empire are to be found here: the country seats of urbane local officials and worthies. If fort commanders adapted to new, challenging realities by investing in relations with communities dependent on them for protection, villa owners seem to have adapted in much the same way. Villa-style buildings are now known at Old Durham, Faverdale near Darlington, Holme House in Piercebridge, Quarry Farm at Ingleby Barwick, at Dalton-on-Tees and at Leeming Bar; possibly also at Brotton near Redcar.[27]

The site at Ingleby Barwick, only recently discovered as a result of housing developments, provides a model. This was a second-century wing-corridor

---

* Across the lower reaches of the dale, a series of transverse earthworks may be evidence of attempts to block that passage in the Early Medieval period. Fleming 1994.

villa where, sometime in the late fourth century, grain-drying kilns were inserted into the bath house *caldarium*. An aisled barn and a large circular stone building, other examples of which are known in the region and beyond, look like equivalents of Birdoswald's timber granary/hall conversions. The small sunken-floored structures or *Grubenhäuser*,* so diagnostic of fifth-century settlements further south in England's eastern counties, have also been recorded here. 'Anglian'-style pottery was found in a fire pit, and a late fourth- or early fifth-century crossbow brooch – indicative of a military or civil office-holder – was found at the site.[28]

At Catterick, sited on the south side of the River Swale some 5km east of the spectacular waterfalls at Richmond from which it may derive its name,† frustratingly little of the town is accessible to archaeologists – much of it lies beneath Catterick racecourse and the tarmac of the A1. Peter Wilson has assembled all the evidence for late Roman and early 'Anglian' Catterick[29] and notes that in later centuries it retained a high status in Northumbria – the site of royal weddings in 762 and 792,[30] and Bede mentions the *Vicus Cataracta* in a passage relating to the early seventh-century Christian conversions.[31] *Catræth*, the Brittonic form of the name, seems to appear in the most famous early Northern poem, *Y Gododdin*, which tells of a great battle beneath its walls. A British force which had assembled at *Din Eidyn* (Edinburgh) had marched to its defeat here at the hands of the Angles of Bernicia and Deira some time in the late sixth century.[32] A number of excavations, often piecemeal over many years, has revealed tantalising hints of the town's sub-Roman fortunes: a 'theatre' space with flagged floor, cut into by the sunken floor of a *Grubenhaus*; another *Grubenhaus* lying within a ditched enclosure; post-pits filled with 'Anglian'-style pottery and large quantities of animal bone; burials inserted into the latest buildings in a nearby fourth-century roadside settlement. Wilson argues for occupation of at least part of the town into the fifth century and beyond but acknowledges that the record from Catterick is at best partial.

Even so, Catterick's location provides a focus for looking at the Tees Valley as a whole *cultural landscape*. Since the publication of Nick Higham's landmark survey of Early Medieval Northumbria[33] some thirty years ago, scholars in

---

* The German term for a distinctive type of small structure of the period built over a pit dug into the ground. They are sometimes known as 'sunken featured buildings' (SFBs).

† Wilson offers an alternative, equally evocative derivation: *Catu-ratis*: 'battle-ramparts'. Wilson *et al.* 1996, 6, following Rivet and Smith 1979, 304.

historical geography, place-name studies and territorial evolution have fashioned new conceptual tools that reveal complex interactions between land use, settlement and cultural identity.³⁴ For Northumbria, Brian Roberts drew on the work of Joan Thirsk, who observed that British cultural landscapes have emerged from different balances of three types of landscape zones: the open pastures of 'wet and windy' uplands and lowland pastures of fen and marsh; a *bocage* patchwork of savannah lands, with small and large woodlands, copses and wood pastures; and the land that has, over millennia, 'experienced the plough'.³⁵

Plotting the presence and density of woodland from *Domesday Book*, Old English and Scandinavian place-names reflecting current or former woodland and the incidence of commons and moorland from the Land Utilisation Survey of the 1930s,³⁶ Roberts highlighted, in negative, core areas of long-time settled and husbanded land: 'Cleared, stone-picked, manured, drained by ditches, ploughed, harrowed, cropped, and effectively warmed by human care.'³⁷

In Northumbria these husbanded areas are to be found in the broad plains of river valleys and where fertile, well-drained, accessible soils are to be found. Maps 3 and 4 on pages 26–7 highlight these areas: in and around the lower Tweed Valley; along Northumberland's coastal plain and the Tyne Valley; around the head of the Solway Firth, in the Tees Valley and South Durham; along the Vale of York and in Ryedale, the Vale of Pickering and the Yorkshire Wolds.

Roberts has termed these husbanded zones 'cultural cores', reflecting an idea of cultural, social and economic unity, of shared resource and identity. He emphasises that at a local scale there may be a mix of all three landscape types – a patchwork in which localised climate, soil, access, flooding patterns, winds and river courses may all act counter to the general trend, but at a regional scale there are zones within which one of these types predominates. The sources he was able to use to derive the cultural corelands are patchy – north of Yorkshire, there was no Domesday survey – and he restricted his 2010 mapping to the lands south of the Anglo-Scottish border. To reconstruct the corelands of a greater Northumbria, including lands now in Scotland, we have used a comparable suite of evidence: place-names from three separate studies; the incidence of Anglian-style crosses and inscribed stones; primarily arable land as mapped on the Land Utilisation Survey of the 1930s, and a small number of regional analyses. The result is a speculative extension of corelands into Lothian and Dumfries and Galloway.* At its

---

* Professor Roberts has very kindly suggested a broad framework for this exercise.

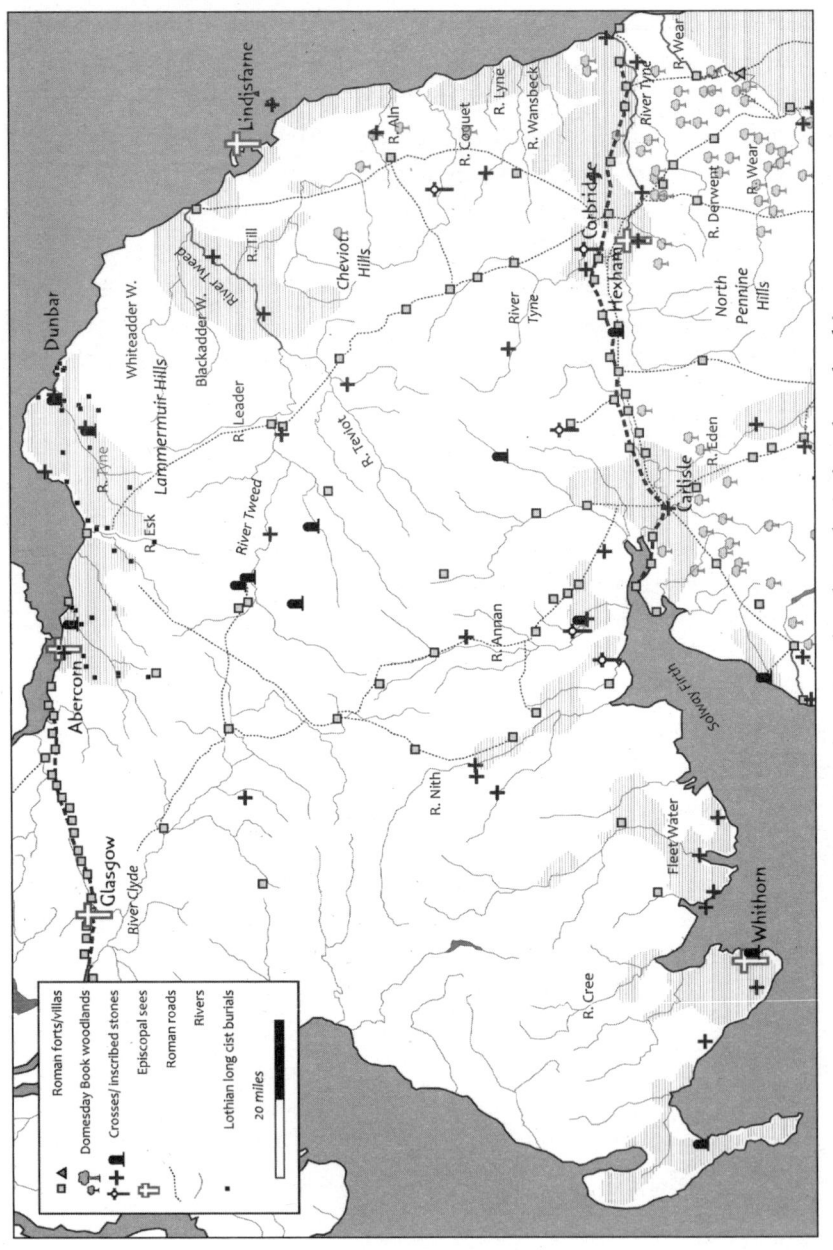

Map 3 Northern Northumbria: the 'cultural corelands'

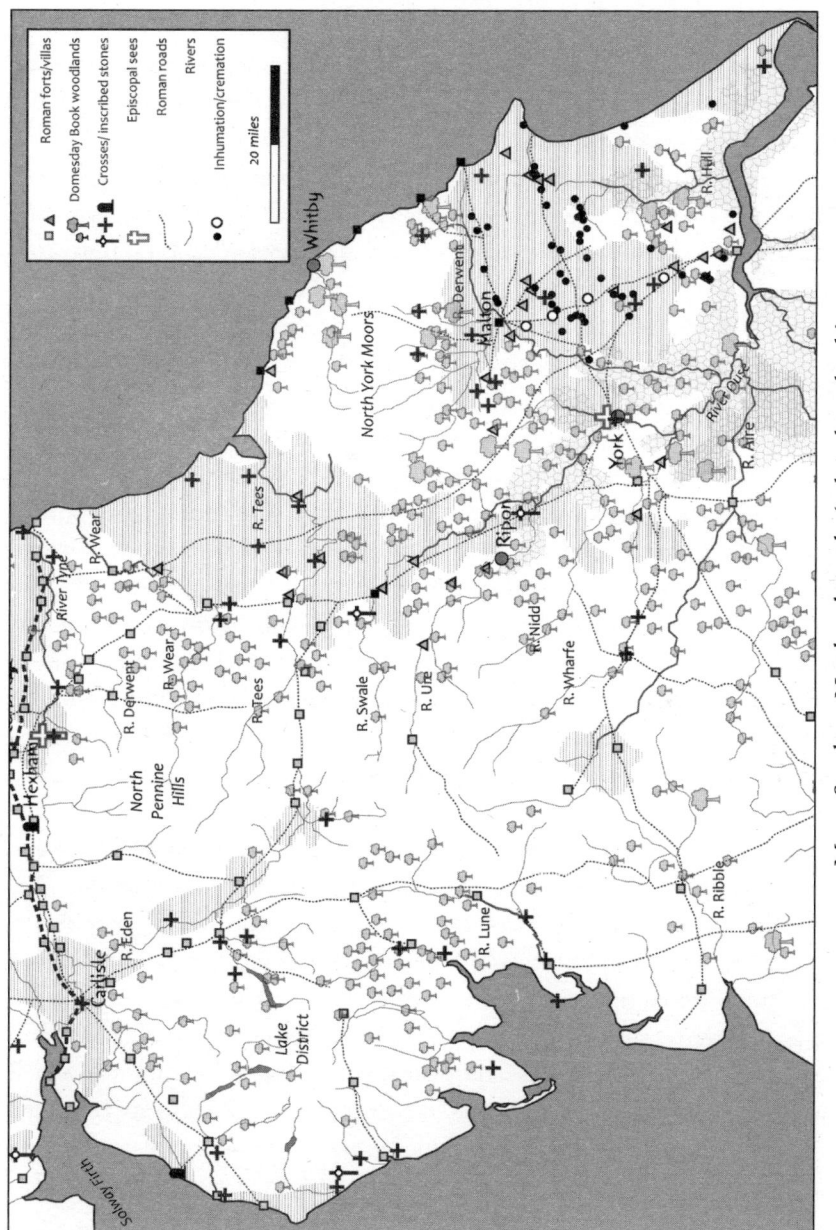

Map 4 Southern Northumbria: the 'cultural corelands'

heart lie markers for what is sometimes called an Anglian or Northumbrian 'takeover', on the basis of the occurrence of metalwork and sculptural styles, distinctly Anglian names and historical references to active Northumbrian ecclesiasts outwith Bernicia and Deira.

With some confidence we propose cultural cores for the Rhinns of Galloway and Luce Bay; the Whithorn peninsula; the watersheds of the Fleet and Urr rivers and parts of Nithsdale and Annandale. In Lothian a coastal concentration of these markers emerges along the River Tyne* and, west of the River Esk, along the coastal plain of the Forth estuary, while Roberts's Tweeddale coreland might tentatively be extended as far upriver as Melrose.[38]

The coherence of his scheme is striking. When independent evidence for the emergence of local power centres in the fifth and sixth centuries is plotted onto these corelands, it becomes clear that there is some fundamental relationship in play. The names of some regional polities further south in England – the *Tomsæte* (dwellers along the River Tame in Staffordshire), *Arosæte*, *West Willa* and others, offer a strong hint at how tribal affinities might concentrate in lands that shared a physical and topographic, as well as cultural, unity. In the case of the drainage basin of the River Roding in Essex, Steven Bassett has shown that its eight Medieval parishes – known collectively as The Rodings – are fossils of a small Early Medieval polity formed of a number of contiguous *vills* – the fundamental units of territorial lordship.[39] For the *Rodingas* and other groups like them, the river was both a magnetic focus for their identity and a portfolio of self-sustaining resources: water meadow, pasture, tilled fields and woodland.

The Romano-British landscape had been intensively managed: for grain, wool, meat, timber and minerals such as salt, iron, lead, tin and copper. The concentration of villas and productive rural settlements in the Tees Valley, Ryedale, the Vale of Pickering and Yorkshire Wolds indicates a high level of agricultural production. Along the lower Tyne, Northumbrian coastal plain and Solway Firth, a similar pattern of intensive settlement and agricultural enclosure, including hundreds of farmsteads of 'native' form, shows how well the regional economy was integrated with the Frontier Zone, supporting its garrisons with an active, growing workforce and economic activity: in transport, construction, services to the military and food production. Pollen

---

* Confusingly there are two River Tynes. The Lothian Tyne runs east into the North Sea just north-west of Dunbar.

evidence for woodland clearance and a rise in grass and arable weeds in the hinterland of the Wall during its heyday is more or less consistent.[40]

That these corelands are fundamental to the landscapes of the North, and not merely a function of Roman imperial investment in its Atlantic province, is proven by the settlement and environmental record, which shows not just an acceleration of intensive land use in the Roman period; but that the trend had already begun before the legions arrived.[41] Even beyond the frontier, in the apparently harsher landscapes of the Cheviot Hills, rich, well-drained volcanic brown earth soils were so fertile that much woodland clearance for intensive pasturing and small-scale cultivation began in the centuries before Roman influence was felt, and prehistoric settlement evidence across the Cheviots shows higher levels of rural population than the land supports today.[42]

Environmental evidence for the impact of the political, social and economic upheavals of the fourth and fifth centuries is gradually accumulating. Woodland, particularly of birch, alder, oak and hazel, regenerated in the hinterland of the Wall and elsewhere. The evidence is locally inconsistent: in some areas a more open landscape was maintained and cereal cultivation continued. But the overall picture is of land less intensively utilised rather than abandoned, and with much local variation. The regeneration of hazel, for example, might indicate land tumbled down to scrub, then woodland; but it is also the primary utility tree of farming communities, providing a wide range of small-bore, pliant materials for walling, roofing, fencing and light construction, when coppiced on a regular eight- or nine-year cycle. If less meat, wool and grain were being consumed – and therefore produced – much of the land whence they came may have been managed with a lighter touch as wood pasture: a mix of managed trees, small-scale cropping and low-intensity grazing of the sort still practised in parts of Continental Europe.

Cooler, wetter conditions rendered some lowland areas uninhabitable: the Humber Levels above the confluence of the Trent and Ouse; parts of the Vale of York and Vale of Pickering, for example. On the south side of the latter, strips of land roughly 2km wide, stretching from the River Derwent up to the high, open pastures of the Wolds, had been demarcated since the late Bronze Age by burial mounds and earth banks or dykes. At more or less regular spacings along the north-facing scarp, small defended enclosures, like Staple Howe in the parish of Knapton, suggest that a form of territorial lordship enabled élite families to control and consume the surplus of these strips. In the adjacent parish, West Heslerton, very large-scale excavations over several decades have revealed, beneath layers of windblown sand, a landscape occupied from the

Late Paleolithic and intensively from the Neolithic period onwards, replete with field systems, settlements and trackways, burial mounds and cemeteries.

In the Roman period, with a major military fort at Malton half a day's travel to the south-west, native so-called 'ladder' settlements lined a road linking the fort, and York beyond, to the coast at Filey. By the fourth century the lower lands in the Vale were increasingly prone to flooding; the string of settlements was more or less abandoned in favour of new sites on higher, drier land. Here, at West Heslerton, a much-visited prehistoric and Roman shrine complex, complete with bread ovens to feed its pilgrims and piles of discarded oyster and mussel shells, stood where a precious Wold spring emerged from the chalk scarp.[43] A densely occupied settlement covering some 16.5 ha grew up below it and on both sides of the stream during the fifth and sixth centuries; and, almost uniquely, its cemetery has also been excavated, albeit bisected by the A64 trunk road.

Some 400m to the north-east of the settlement, the cemetery in which the early inhabitants of the settlement were interred was only the latest in a palimpsest of ritual structures including a Neolithic hengiform monument and Bronze Age barrows, partly bounded by an Iron Age pit alignment and occupying the east side of the stream as it flowed out into the flatlands of the Vale.[44] It seems as though some at least of the prehistoric barrows were still visible. Broad phases of burial have been obtained from the 100 or so graves, which yield sufficiently distinctive finds – brooches, dress pins, beads and other ornaments; knives, girdle hangers, shields and spear and a single sword – to assign them to roughly fifty-year bands. A significant number of metal finds preserved the patterns of textiles – tabbies, twills and tablet-woven bands – in their corrosion products: the largest corpus so far from Northumbria.[45]

Burials were predominantly inhumations, with little evidence of intercutting, suggesting that markers were employed to identify them. The cemetery seems to have been organised polyfocally, and this indication of possible traditional family groupings has been reinforced in recent years by DNA and isotope analysis of some of the individuals, showing familial associations. The headline from these analyses is that a minority of the population had probably been raised non-locally, perhaps in Scandinavia – including males, females and juveniles.[46] At any rate, the pervasive idea that the cultural affinities of grave goods is an indicator of ethnic origin rather than group identity is untenable. Locals and non-locals alike were buried with 'Anglian'-style artefacts. A more recent, much larger study looking at DNA from well-provenanced sites from the east of

Britain, including West Heslerton, suggests that a much higher proportion – both male and female – of the burial population in the Early Medieval period may have moved from homelands on the Continent, albeit over a long period.[47] A more refined understanding will, doubtless, emerge with each new study.

Because of the size and longevity of the West Heslerton community one might also expect to find evidence of territorial lordship emerging, or re-emerging here. But it is hard to see any sign of hierarchy among West Heslerton's organised clusters of houses, workshops, craft areas and animal pens huddled below the former shrine – of one large house or central hall. The rectangular hall-type dwellings are of almost identical size.

In death, as well as in life, West Heslerton's population seemingly belonged in family groups of more or less equal status. For archaeologists writing the narrative of Early Medieval lordship, of its kings and queens, bishops, thegns, abbots and abbesses, West Heslerton might look like an exception; an anomaly. But local and regional diversity – different, perhaps less visible manifestations of lordship; areas of stronger or weaker affinity; communities bound by less hierarchical codes or able to maintain stronger traditions of independence – all have their place in the Early Medieval mosaic.

Territorial lordship emerged at different times in different places and at varying scales, both before and after the withdrawal of Roman administration from Britain. In the lands north of the Humber it is first visible to archaeologists at forts, towns and some villas. As generation gave way to generation, centres of local power extended control over more settlements and resources, in a process that only becomes transparent with the earliest recording of land transfers to the church in the seventh century. Larger territorial units came to be organised from a central lordship site and, as these emerge, they show consistent signs of having been arranged on a duodecimal basis – that is to say such units, as they become visible in the historical record, often come in multiples of six or twelve – townships or *vills* – under the collective term 'shire'.[48] This *extensive* form of territorial lordship required a different order of management and exploitation. A home farm – fort, town, villa – might draw all requisite foodstuffs and labour services from its immediate hinterland; but extensive lordship required that the lord – a former garrison commander, local civic dignitary or native aristocrat – move to where he could consume those taxes in kind: the origins of itinerant kingship (see Chapter 2).

The politics, economics and social interplay that gave rise to what looks uncommonly like a 'system' in the seventh century evolved over 200 years – a dozen generations of human life. If historians are to take anything from the very uneven and problematic sources at their disposal, it is the sense that lordly poetry and battle cry were accompaniments to social and economic upheaval, conflict and hardship. Three principal documents are in play for the North, long ago gleaned of much significant material but nevertheless still subjects of fierce debate and widely varying interpretation. Like the archaeology, the history begins, it seems, on the Wall – perhaps even at Birdoswald.

> I, Patrick, a sinner, quite uncultivated and the least of all the faithful ... had as my father the deacon Calpornius, son of the late Potitus, a priest, who belonged to the town [*vico*] of *Bannavem Taburniae*; he had a small estate [*villula*] nearby, and it was there that I was taken captive.[49]

Patrick, the patron saint of Ireland and author of the only first-person account of life – and slavery and Christianity – in fifth-century* Britain, belonged to what passed for its middle classes. He was taken in a slave raid at the age of sixteen and suffered a long period of captivity in Ireland; eventually escaped and after many adventures returned to his family; then went back to Ireland and spent the rest of his life there as a bishop, preaching and converting. The name of the town near which his patrimony lay, *Bannavem Taburniae*, has caused much scholarly ink to be spilled. No such place is recorded from Roman Britain. Charles Thomas, the historian of Early Christianity in Britain, proposed a scribal error by a cleric who did not know the name but who miscopied an earlier *Banna Venta Burniae*. A *Bannaventa* is known to have existed: Whilton Lodge, near Daventry in the central Midlands along the line of Watling Street. Thomas thought this an unlikely place for Irish raiders to be operating in the early fifth century and instead proposed *Banna* – that is to say, Birdoswald.[50] *Banna* is a credible Brittonic word for a horn or spur of land, such as that on which Birdoswald perches above the gorge of the River Irthing. *Venta* is a known Latin word for a market or meeting place. *Burniae* suggested to Thomas *Berniae*, a pass or gap such as exists at nearby Greenhead on the line of the ancient Tyne–Solway

---

* The dating of his *Confessio* and, therefore, of his floruit, is a matter of debate; but a date in the middle or late fifth century for his death seems plausible, given that his father was both a deacon and a decurion (as we find from his other surviving text, the *Letter to Coroticus* (Letter, X)). For a summary of the debate see Thomas 1981, 307ff. Various annal dates for his death are discussed by Dumville 1993, 29ff; they centre on the 450s.

trans-Pennine route – and the name was, he believed, transmitted to the later kingdom of Bernicia, 'land of the mountain passes'.* Raiders penetrating inland from Carlisle, less than 20 miles away along Stanegate, is a highly credible context for that period; and Patrick's supposed sphere of operations in Ireland is northern.

If nothing else, Patrick's story offers telling information about territorial lordship in the fifth century after local power supposedly devolved to the *civitates*, the tribal councils. His father held office as both a deacon and as a decurion – the latter a civic position likely to have been based in Carlisle. He owned a small estate – a *villula* – which shows unequivocally that territorial lordship in the first half of the first post-Roman century was still being exercised within a Roman civic and Christian milieu, alongside the military lordship so tellingly exposed by excavations at Birdoswald and elsewhere. Carlisle, Catterick and Lincoln are all good candidates for former *civitas* capitals re-emerging as the centres of post-Roman political and territorial entities.

Patrick's background is unlikely to have been exceptional. Memorials to Brigomaglos at Vindolanda; to Latinus, the descendant of Barrovadus at Whithorn in south-west Scotland; to Vetta, the daughter of Victorianus on the Cat Stane at Kirkliston on the south edge of Edinburgh – all speak of literate, Latin-using communities in the fifth century. In the sixth century Carutanus, son of Cupitianus, in Liddesdale; Coninia in Manor Water, Peebles; Nudus and Dumnogenus, the sons of Liberalis, on the Yarrow Stone, were all commemorated in Latin inscriptions. The western part of the Brittonic-speaking world – south-west and south-central Scotland; the Isle of Man; Wales, south-west England and northern Brittany – continued to participate in the common culture of the late Antique West with at least occasional, and possibly enduring, contacts.[51]

The *Confessio* offers telling detail, too. Slavery was a feature of raiding across the sea and beyond the frontier in the fourth century. That Patrick was enslaved 'with so many thousands' implies that it was a common enough fate. That his return to Britain after six years was facilitated by a ship's captain who asked no questions and who deposited him and others on an unpopulated shore away

---

* Some philologists are uneasy about Thomas's assumption that the 'e' in *Berniae* transmitted as *Burniae*. The original argument that Anglicised Bernicia and Brittonic *Bryneich* is the 'land of the mountain passes', referring directly the trans-Pennine route through Greenhead, comes from Kenneth Jackson (1953, 704–5).

from a harbour or port suggests a lucrative trade in people smuggling. That Patrick was, after another period of some years in captivity, able to return to his family implies that they, and their family estate, remained intact despite the disruptive and no doubt tragic effects of raiding on those communities.

Two other native narrative sources purport to record events and political trends in fifth-century Britain. *De Excidio et Conquestu Britanniae* is a three-part sermon by a Latin-educated Christian cleric known as Gildas. It consists of a pseudo-historical account of fifth-century events and an unflattering portrait of contemporary rulers and clerics.[52] Like Patrick, Gildas's life and, therefore, his text, float in chronologically muddy waters, with proposed dates for the composition of the *De Excidio* ranging from about 500 to about 540.*

Gildas seems to draw on flimsy oral history for much of his reconstruction of events in the generations before his birth. He has a notion of Scottish and Pictish raids on, and the subsequent recovery of, the frontier that might be a folk-memory of the Barbarian Conspiracy of 367; but he mistakes Hadrian's Wall for the Antonine Wall and dates both to the end of the fourth century or the beginning of the fifth – evidence, he says, of the Romans leaving the North Britons to defend themselves.[53] He knows of Magnus Maximus but cannot place him coherently in his narrative of impiety, ill faith and tyranny.

Gildas records that after the final departure of Roman forces 'foul hordes' of Picts and Scots appeared in the North, and lazy Britons failed to defend against them. Then: 'Our citizens abandoned the towns and the high walls . . . and resorted to looting one another.'[54]

A petition sent by the 'miserable remnants' to the senior Roman commander in Gaul, perhaps during the political crisis of the late 420s and 430s, contained this complaint: 'The barbarians push us back to the sea, the sea pushes us back to the barbarians; between these two kinds of death we are either drowned or slaughtered.'†

The call for help being unanswered, the British nevertheless won a victory that stemmed the assaults of their enemies for a while; but famine followed; then peace for a few years during which Britain was flooded with luxurious foreign goods. Licentiousness followed, then a plague – divine retribution straight out of the Old Testament. Now, all the members of a council – surely

---

* Adams (2021a, 200) reviews the evidence and favours a date in the last decade of the fifth century.

† For a detailed discussion of the date and identity of the recipient, see Adams 2021a, 139f.

the tribal governors of former Roman *civitates* – along with the 'proud tyrant' (*superbus tyrannus*) recruited three boatloads of Saxons, notoriously competent and predatory sea-going Channel raiders, to beat back Britain's enemies in the North. Gildas's understanding was that political governance on a national level survived in at least parts of the province, even if their ill judgement had fatal consequences. These mercenaries – the standard late Roman term for such forces is *foederati* – were granted monthly allowances. Gildas uses specific terminology for these payments: *epimenia, annonae* and *munificentia* – monthly rations; renders in kind from local farms; and cash. Inadvertently he thus shines a light on a distinct type of territorial lordship at work, paying mercenaries by allotting them lands from which to draw renders, along with a hard-cash bonus.

In time, those allowances and the right to render from those lands – and one wonders whose lands they had once been – proved insufficient. The Saxons rebelled: raiding, burning, laying low the great towns. 'There was no burial to be had,' Gildas says, 'except in the ruins of houses or the bellies of beasts and birds.'[55] His account is thin on detail, almost completely lacking in geographic specifics, and its internal chronology is virtually non-existent before the well-known denouement of his historical section. In it, a native leader named Ambrosius Aurelianus – whose parents had 'worn the purple' – led the Britons to a great victory at Badon Hill, some forty-four years before Gildas's own birth.

If Gildas's nostalgically independent Britain had functioned under a sort of national government, in his own day Britons were ruled by kings – five of them: 'but they are tyrants'. Their geographies are equally vague, although the consensus among historians is that they, like Gildas himself, belong in a western milieu. The same goes for the shameless fools who make up his contemporary priesthood. That a British diocesan church survived into the late fifth century seems evident from Patrick's account – he was summoned from Ireland to Britain by his diocesan masters to account for himself. A diocesan church required funds, either in the form of land grants (the right to render) or donations from wealthy patrons such as those whose generosity seems to have compromised Patrick's standing among fellow bishops. In either case, functioning territorial lordship is implied: priests and kings alike were supported by food surpluses generated from land holdings. Indeed, as a clerical class re-emerges into the relatively bright historical daylight of the seventh century, it is clear that monastic entrepreneurs, and the bishops who administered their dioceses, were a sub-species of territorial lords (see Chapter 4).

Whatever else continues to fascinate and frustrate in Gildas's sermon, nothing of what he purports to tell historians about the fifth century has a direct bearing on Northumbrian affairs. His sermon against kings and priests is generalised and providential: bad things were visited by God on those who failed in their Christian duty. His purpose was not to write history, but to preach.

The testimony of a miscellany first compiled in the early ninth century by a British historian sometimes known by the name Nennius ostensibly offers much more direct information about the North. It is formed of three parts: the so-called *Historia Brittonum*; a section on the Cities and Wonders of Britain; and the *Annales Cambriae* or Welsh Annals. The first part is a narrative history which amplifies Gildas's account, showing some impressive knowledge of fourth-century emperors in Britain, setting the Saxon rebellion in Kent and giving names to both the 'superb tyrant' (Vortigern), whose ill-fated invitation to Saxon mercenaries initiated the final destruction of Roman Britain, and the leaders of the mercenaries (Hengest and Horsa). This political account ends with Section 46, when Vortigern cedes territory in Essex, Middlesex and Sussex to the Saxons.

Legendary episodes follow involving St Germanus, Arthur and St Patrick. They seem to be interpolations cut and pasted, so to speak, into the main narrative, which ends with a single-paragraph account of large-scale migration into South-east England from Germany under Saxon kings 'until the time when Ida reigned, who was the son of Eobba. He was the first king in Bernicia, that is, Berneich.'[56]

The milieu switches suddenly to the North. There follow genealogies of Bernician, Kentish, Mercian and Deiran kings and extracts from king lists interpolated with records of Northern battles, to the end of Section 66; then a brief but potentially enlightening Chronography. Lists of the Cities and Wonders of Britain follow and the miscellany is completed by the Welsh Annals, a very terse list of events dating between 447 and 954. Because of the political context and very late date of its compilation, and a frustrating lack of corroborative support, historians' trust in 'Nennius' has waxed and waned over the decades. As a miscellany it cannot be dismissed out of hand, despite grave reservations about the weight of interpretation that it will support – not least by Leslie Alcock, who championed it as a narrative history of the Arthurian period in his brilliant 1971 synthesis *Arthur's Britain*[57] but who, in a second edition published some thirty years later, had become a critical sceptic.

Necessity being the mother of invention, Northumbrian historians still cautiously trawl these opaque waters to provide some sort of political outline for the century and a half between the withdrawal of Roman imperial control in the first decades of the fifth century and the middle of the sixth century. If nothing else, the name Ida, son of Eobba, fires a starting gun for the narrative history of Northumbria. But the idea of Northumbria, as it emerges into history as a single entity, is by no means straightforward.

2

EARTH-HALLS: 451–616

Bede's Northumbria – Boundaries and
frontiers – Deira – Burials – Kingship and
the food render – Northumbria's first kings

In the beginning were the people. When Bede wrote of Northumbria, he referred to 'the people of the Northumbrians', *Nordanhymbrorum gentis*.[1] And as with the Northumbrians, so too the Bernicians and the Deirans also appear in Bede's writings as peoples, *gentes*,[2] or peoples of a kingdom r*egnum Deirorum* and *regnum Berniciorum*[3] or a province – *in provincia Berniciorum; in provincia Deirorum*.[4] Understood as a unified political entity, Northumbria emerged out of a conflict between the ruling dynasties of the two sub-units at the beginning of the seventh century, when Æðelfrið of Bernicia achieved dominance. Nevertheless, as late as the 670s, his grandson Ecgfrið (671–685) ruled in Deira through a sub-king named Ælfwine. There is no evidence of a Deiran king or sub-king after the death of Ælfwine in 679, but if the Northumbrian kingdom was by then a political reality, the province of the Bernicians apparently still retained an identity in people's minds in 731 when Bede used the present tense of his verbs to explain that 'Whithorn, as it is commonly called, belongs to the province of the Bernicians', *Qui locus, ad provinciam Berniciorum pertinens, vulgo vocatur Ad Candidam Casam*.[5] Only in time did a geographical definition of a territory come also to define the people.[6]

Bede had found it necessary to explain that the Northumbrian people was that people who lived 'on the north side of the river Humber'.[7] For a geographical definition of the kingdom, rather than a social or political one, the one marker was the River Humber, fixed in the name itself, and as long ago as 1948 the historian Peter Hunter Blair set himself the task of defining first the southern boundary[8] and then the internal boundary between Bernicia and Deira.[9]

His reading of the Northumbrian southern boundary takes it from the Humber estuary to the confluence of the Rivers Ouse and Trent, then skirting around the south and west sides of the marshlands of the lower reaches of the Rivers Idle, Don and Aire, the route marked by the Roman road from north of Lincoln, through Doncaster and on to Castleford. Between these marshlands to the east and the Pennines to the west, this route crosses some 11 miles (18km) of open country and here is a linear earthwork surviving in fragments, the Roman Ridge (or Rigg), running parallel to the River Don, on the opposite side from the Roman road; this is possibly a post-Roman defensive work. As the line approaches Castleford, it gains access to the trans-Pennine route along the Aire Valley, not firmly in Northumbrian hands until the middle of the seventh century, and thence across to the River Ribble, which formed the Northumbrian–Mercian boundary west of the Pennines, and on towards the Irish Sea.

To trace the boundary between the two sub-kingdoms, Hunter Blair began with two sources from the twelfth century, only to find inconsistency between Reginald of Durham, who placed the boundary along the River Tyne, and Richard of Hexham, who cited the Tees. The lands between Tees and Tyne had been, in Reginald's understanding, wilderness inhabited only by wild beasts.[10] Bede's attributions of named places to one or other of the kingdoms did not resolve the matter and so Hunter Blair then developed a circumstantial argument from two points of evidence.[11] First, the account of the murder of King Oswine in 651[12] places the events within a triangle bounded by Piercebridge, Greta Bridge and Scotch Corner, that is the south side of the Tees: it is likely that the conflict was somewhere within the boundary zone. Second, that on Bishop Wilfrid's expulsion in 687, his Northumbrian diocese was split into a Deiran diocese centred on York and a Bernician diocese centred on Lindisfarne; the latter was later further divided between Lindisfarne and Hexham.[13] For Richard of Hexham it was traditional knowledge that the southern boundary of the Hexham diocese, that is, where it marched with York, lay along the River Tees.

In the seventh century, diocesan geographies had tended to match that of the kingdoms they served. On these two points, then, Hunter Blair concluded that the Tees was the boundary line and not the Tyne. The archaeological study of burials appeared to support the idea of the Tees as the internal boundary. As Rosemary Cramp observed in a wide-ranging review, the total lack of cremations north of the Tees and west of the Pennines is striking; the large community inhumation cemeteries of Deira are not found in Bernicia.[14]

But the discovery and excavation of a community cemetery with 117 inhumations and three cremations on the north bank of the Tees at Norton prompted Cramp to suggest that the whole valley, and not just its south side, was Deiran territory.[15]

Peter Hunter Blair's work to define the Northumbrian kingdom and its two sub-units by reference to their boundaries became generally accepted, though subject to some points of critique. In a view from the Mercian side, Nicholas Brooks used the names of peoples in the tribute list known as the Tribal Hidage* to sketch the extent of Mercia. He considered that the general locations of these peoples could be agreed but that it is not possible to define their boundaries. His main challenge to Hunter Blair was to assert that the border implied in the name Mercia was the Welsh border and not the Northumbrian.[16] David Rollason worked broadly within Hunter Blair's model but he stressed the uncertainties of limited evidence and evidence derived from later periods: given the disruptions of the Viking era, the definition of the Ribble as the boundary on the west rests on 'a slim basis of evidence indeed'; and he questioned the idea of coincidence between diocesan and political boundaries. He made a telling observation, especially in respect of the southern boundary, that it is better considered as a frontier *zone* rather than a line, within which the degree of control exercised by Northumbrian kings fluctuated over time, even in such an apparently clear-cut case as the Humber itself.[17]

Eventually, Nicholas Higham addressed Hunter Blair's southern frontier head-on. He emphasised the fluidity of boundaries through time: the distinction between a 'Northumbrian' north and a 'Mercian' centre in England emerged from the royal politics of the seventh century and was then entrenched from 735 with the creation of a Northumbrian archdiocese.[18] The Roman Ridge, still undated by excavation, is a somewhat erratic feature with two bank-and-ditch alignments a kilometre apart. It is not comparable with Offa's Dyke. A pre-Anglian date is perhaps more likely, and it is unsafe to attribute it to the eighth century.[19] There is thus no reason to claim the course of the Don as the boundary. Control of the wetlands and its routeways is likely to have fluctuated with the fortunes of individual

---

* A list of kingdoms and subordinate territories with assessments in hundreds or thousands of hides, generally attributed to the eighth century, generated at either the Mercian or Northumbrian court. See Adams 2021a, 235ff.

kings. Even after the loss of Lindsey* in 679, Northumbrian kings conducted business south of the Don: King Aldfrið was present at the synod held under his protection at Austerfield in 702.† This argues for a boundary on the same line, or approximately so, as the Domesday boundary between Derbyshire and Yorkshire's West Riding, that is well to the south-west of Hunter Blair's line.[20] West of the Pennines, the boundary is the River Mersey and not the Ribble. Mercian control over Lancashire south of the Ribble was a development of the tenth century.[21]

Brian Roberts cut through these problems of boundary definition in his radically different approach, already described in Chapter 1, of defining cultural corelands.[22] He identified a Deiran core within the East Riding of Yorkshire, that is the Wolds and Vale of Pickering, and a Bernician core in the lower-mid Tyne basin. The lower Tyne is, perhaps, the best place to get a visual sense of these corelands. Crossing one of Newcastle's seven spectacular bridges and looking west from a height of about 80 feet above the River Tyne, one sees the broad valley until it becomes enfolded in gentle, fertile hills towards Hexham. Between and separate from the Tyne and East Yorkshire cores is *Catræth*, named from the Roman centre at Catterick, in the lower Tees Valley, extending in a ribbon south towards Aldborough along the valley of the River Swale and the line of the Roman road, and north into the eastern side of County Durham. In the lower Tweed basin and along the Northumberland coast is the core of Bamburgh-*Din Guaire*. A core around Carlisle on the south side of the Solway and stretching south into the Eden valley is, more controversially, Rheged, still ruled by a 'British' dynasty into the early seventh century. Among other small core units is that of the 'British' kingdom of Elmet, east of Leeds between the Rivers Ouse and Aire.

The frontier between the two sub-kingdoms of Bernicia and Deira, as they had emerged by the seventh century, is thus the tract of woodland across northern Durham; neither the Tyne nor the Tees can be held as firm boundary lines. This explains Reginald's twelfth-century characterisation of the zone between these rivers as wilderness inhabited only by wild beasts.[23] This landscape-based analysis allows a more geographically nuanced approach to

---

* An ancient kingdom centred on Lincoln, bounded on the west by the River Trent and on the east by the North Sea coast. Lindsey was an object of disputed overlordship between Mercia and Northumbria.
† See Chapter 7 and Map 17 on page 199 for the distribution of Aldfrið's coinage south of the Humber.

people and their areas of settlement, and thus to the emergence of the kingship which developed during the seventh century, than does the Bernicia–Deira duality. This is derived from the historical writings of the eighth century and is predicated on the sometimes violent dealings between two ruling houses. The territories over which kings ruled did not have fixed borders but were fluid entities, reflecting the extents over which any one king could command authority.[24]

The cultural corelands model offers a geography to knit together the three elements that make up a kingdom: people, their kings and the territories within which relations between people and kings are played out. For people, a new archaeological signature comes early and strongly in the Deiran core in the form of burials around the edges of the Wolds of the former East Riding of Yorkshire.* The outcrop of chalk that forms the Wolds emerges north of the Humber estuary in a narrow band between Brough and Hessel, running northwards and then broadening as it sweeps east, crescent-shaped, towards the coast at Flamborough Head. The scarp slope, rising to more than 200m above sea level, overlooks the Vale of Pickering to the north and the lowlands of the Derwent Valley to the west as the river emerges from the Vale of Pickering, to flow south towards the Humber. The dip slope faces east and south towards the lowlands of the River Humber and beyond, to the peninsula of Holderness in the extreme south-east.

Dry valleys dissect the dip slope, opening up spaces with sands and gravels laid over the chalk and affording good terrain for settlements: Kilham; Garton and Driffield around the headwaters of the River Humber; Middleton; South Dalton and Bishop Burton. Higher slopes are often described as being marginal lands, but a geomorphological study at Cowlam Well Dale, 4km east of Sledmere, showed that fertile soils occur as down-slope deposits resulting from erosion brought on by both natural processes and human actions in the past.[25] The Great Wolds Valley, running from west to east, carries the Gypsy Race. This is the only near-permanent watercourse through the chalk massif; it is ephemeral in its upper reaches around Duggleby but from Rudston down to the coast at Bridlington there is usually a continuous flow.

Most of the Wolds burials are inhumations, and they mark this area as having developed its own cultural traditions, distinct from those across the Humber in Lincolnshire, where large cremation cemeteries are the norm. The earliest burials, however, are cremations dating to the fifth–sixth

* See the map of Southern Northumbrian 'corelands' on page 27.

centuries. Sam Lucy shows four locations on high ground along the western edge of the Wolds, more or less along the line of one of the Roman roads, overlooking the valley of the Derwent. They feature prominently in the landscape in a way that suggests they acted as boundary markers for a new community.[26] Two of these, Birdsall and Huggate, are single-burial sites; Langton may have had multiple burials, but information rests on chance finds made without systematic record in the mid nineteenth century.

At Sancton there is a more secure corpus of information, derived from both chance findings and archaeological investigations made from time to time between the late nineteenth and mid twentieth centuries. Some 250 or more urns have been reported – in one estimate the cemetery contained between 250 and 450 cremations; it is the only Deiran cremation cemetery on a scale comparable with those of Lincolnshire and East Anglia. Depending on the duration of use, this could equate to a community of 100 adults over a period of 150 years. A second cemetery site (Sancton II) is also known, some 800m from Sancton I, at the edge of the present-day village. This has both cremations and inhumations and continued into, or belonged to, the sixth century, a little later than the cremation cemetery.[27] The large corpus of cremation urns and grave goods from Sancton I lends itself to analysis and comparison with other groups. Kevin Leahy has identified a first-phase pottery style common to both Sancton and Lincolnshire cemeteries at Cleatham and Elsham, and further away at Elkington in Northampton, while the metalwork has Frisian affinities. This perhaps reflects a time before a clear Deiran identity had developed from a wider Anglian tradition in eastern England. But if so, Deira as it developed did not become isolated from wider influences: Leahy identifies a potter whose products are known from Lincolnshire, Nottinghamshire, Leicestershire and Norfolk.[28]

As time progressed, from the early stage of burials in the fifth–sixth centuries, through the late sixth–seventh, and on to the late seventh–eighth centuries and the end of the furnished* burial traditions, inhumation became the dominant burial rite, with some cemeteries containing a relatively small number of cremations, and burials becoming more widely spread around the area. Few of them were established high up in the Wolds after the early cremation set, and these tended to be smaller cemeteries and of the later stages of use,

---

* 'Furnished' is the term used to describe interments accompanied by personal adornments, such as brooches and dress pins, and weapons such as swords, spears and shields.

rather than the larger cemeteries of the late sixth–seventh centuries which favoured the dry valleys and the lower slopes coming down from the Wold tops. A striking feature of the distribution is that the valley of the Derwent to the west is without burials and, with some few exceptions, so too is the Holderness peninsula, both likely to have been marsh areas at this time. Further west, into the Vale of York, only around the edges of York itself have burials been identified.[29] Striking also is a string of cemeteries around and below the 200m contour overlooking the Vale of Pickering to the north – including that at West Heslerton – and cemeteries on both sides of the gap through which the headwaters of the River Derwent break through from the Vale of Pickering between the higher ground of the Wolds and the Howardian Hills to the west.

The Yorkshire Wolds is one of the richest archaeological landscapes in England, revealed in Cathy Stoertz's comprehensive delineations from air survey of cropmarks and extant earthworks.[30] Settlement foci, monumental features, trackways and linear boundaries from different eras of the past all feature in her densely populated maps. Yet, as Chris Fenton-Thomas observes, this form of presentation does not address a point of chronology, that in the long-term development of the landscape, features of a visible past have come forward into new presents for re-working and re-imaginations of their meanings.[31] The emerging Deiran cultural identity was formed in part by ways in which burial rites integrated communities into elements of an inherited visible landscape of linear boundaries and burial monuments of the past, in particular the round barrows of the Bronze Age and, to a lesser extent, the square barrows of the pre-Roman Iron Age that are distinctive to the Wolds.

Linear boundaries criss-cross the Wolds, some many kilometres in length, along and between the terrain's dry valleys; their densest concentration is in the central Wolds between Driffield and Millington, first studied and mapped by the antiquarian investigator J.R. Mortimer.[32] Most take the form of a single ditch, which can be as much as 2m deep, with flanking banks of chalk rubble. Several have three sets of bank and ditch running in parallel; Huggate Dykes is exceptional in having six. Some are long axial lines defining broad swathes of territory, while others delimit enclosed parcels of land; there is no single function attributable to them. They are difficult to date, but several cases are reported of these boundaries incorporating already-standing barrows of the Bronze Age in their line. Over how long they were under construction is impossible to say, but some remained visible features of the landscape into historic eras forming township boundaries and, in some cases, boundaries of the larger Medieval units of hundreds and wapentakes.[33]

There are hints that Deiran communities acknowledged the significance of these boundaries by setting burials into them.* In the extreme north-west of the Wolds, at Vessey Pasture, Mortimer observed a point at which a linear boundary cut directly through the centre of a standing barrow and here an Anglian burial was inserted into the mound – the Old English kenning 'earth-hall'† neatly evokes a sense of propriety, almost of homeliness.[34] In the central Wolds, between the villages of Huggate and Fridaythorpe, a cremation urn was set into the bank of Huggate Dyke.[35] Green lanes following the lines of linear earthworks define both the north and south boundaries of the township of Garton. The north boundary, Sledmere Green Lane, proceeds along a dry valley and over open ground. At the watershed, a monument was raised in the mid nineteenth century in memory of Sir Tatton Sykes. Its construction damaged part of the linear earthwork, and Mortimer excavated here in 1866. The earthwork was made of three banks with two ditches in between. Set into the central bank was an Anglian inhumation cemetery with more than forty bodies laid out along some 60m length (see the plan on page 46). Further excavation in 1959, 200m east of Mortimer's and on the south bank of the monument, revealed a continuation of the cemetery, with burials into the eighth century.[36] Along the south boundary, at Garton Gatehouse, Mortimer excavated twenty-six graves and a single cremation urn running west from a round barrow, set into the north ditch of a double-ditched linear boundary. In the following year, 1871, he excavated another thirty burials, probably eighth century in date, in the ditch extending east from the barrow.[37]

John Robert Mortimer (1825–1911), a corn dealer from Driffield, and William Greenwell (1820–1918), a Durham canon, were the leading excavators on the Wolds in the second half of the nineteenth century. Both were prolific barrow diggers and, to a great extent, a Deiran Anglian-era archaeology first emerged in their excavations in the form of secondary burials inserted into Bronze Age burial mounds. Sam Lucy's catalogue lists twenty-five such cases, many with multiple secondaries, with a cluster around Driffield, another on the highest part of the Wolds at the north-west corner, and a scattering of others mostly on the high interior of the Wolds.[38] Driffield is tucked in at the foot of the Wolds dip slope, where the headwaters of the River Hull rise. A mound at King's Mill Road, levelled in 1893, contained a

---

* As the excavated cemetery at West Heslerton, on the edge of the Vale of Pickering immediately north of the Wold massif, appears to show.
† *Eorðreced* – from line 2719 in *Beowulf*.

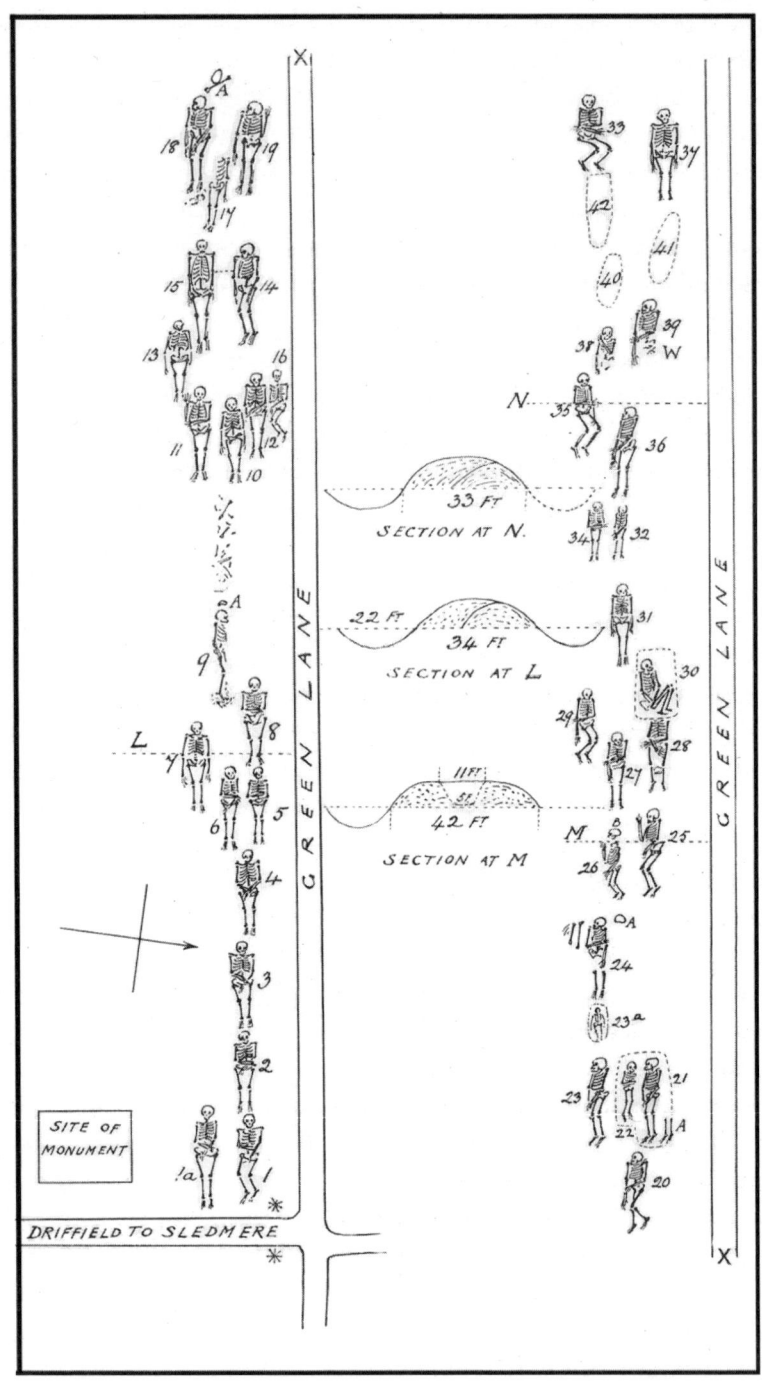

Map 5 J.R. Mortimer's plan of burials along Sledmere Green Lane

Bronze Age inhumation, with twelve secondary inhumations and Frankish pottery also recorded.[39] Also within the present urban area, Moot Hill revealed a burial with a sword when part of the mound was dug away in 1858. A little to the east of the town, the mound known as Cheesecake Hill had been partly quarried away in 1845 for material to fill in some hollows; this brought burials to light, and a sort of rescue excavation followed. Then, in 1871, Mortimer re-examined what was left, finding two small pits without any contents, eleven Anglian inhumations and one cremation. Grave goods associated with these included annular and cruciform brooches, strings of beads, knives, buckles and a spear and shield.[40] Immediately east of the town, at Kellythorpe, Lord Londesborough opened a barrow in 1851. As well as the primary Bronze Age burial in a cist, there were ten secondary inhumations. Mortimer then reinvestigated in 1870 and 1872, finding twenty-seven more Anglian inhumations, and in 1887 workmen discovered another thirteen.[41] One and a half kilometres west of this, at Kirkburn, a large cruciform brooch found in Mortimer's barrow number 137 is probably from a secondary inhumation.[42] Two kilometres north-west of here, also in Kirkburn, four secondary burials were placed in the partly silted fill of a barrow ditch.[43] This is a little to the south of the prehistoric linear boundary between Kirkburn and Garton townships at the point where Mortimer excavated the cemetery, referred to above, extending both east and west from a barrow. Further west of here, on the Kirkburn side of the boundary, Mortimer recovered an Anglian burial in his barrow C46.[44]

Mortimer knew of the tradition of Iron Age chariot burials on the Yorkshire Wolds: he referred to six and cited other doubtful cases.[45] However, he was apparently not aware of the wider Iron Age tradition of burial within square barrows. These were no longer visible features in the landscape but have come to light more recently though the medium of cropmarks.[46] At least some of these may still have been visible in the Early Medieval era, for excavation within the extensive square-barrow cemetery at Garton Station, bounded on the south side by the linear boundary already discussed, recovered forty-three individuals from thirty-five graves of this period.[47] This is the only known case of such an association, but there could be an archaeological recovery bias at play here: if more sites were dug, more cases might be known.

Anglian burials in Deira have come to light over the years through their association with monumental features in the landscape. Settlement locations of this period are much more tenuous, with no remains visible on the surface, and so an archaeological study of settlement has been slower to develop. One line of approach is to ask whether places of settlement during the Roman period continued in use thereafter. The Roman fort at the River Derwent crossing at Malton attracted civilian settlement outside each of its gates. On the south side, between the fort and the river, occupation extended over 20ha; a circuit of walls defended part of this area in the third and fourth centuries. Occupation continued beyond AD 400, but for how long is uncertain.[48] The problem here is one that bedevils the archaeological study of the fifth century more generally. During the Roman period, the supply of dateable coinage to the army and civil administration underpins its archaeological chronology, and ceramic types are dated by association with coins. No Roman imperial coinage reached Britain after AD 402. How long the existing coin supply remained in use is an open question and all that can be said of features or layers of ground of the fifth century that contain Roman coins is that the coins give a date *after which* the feature or layer was formed. A pottery industry with a production centre at Crambeck, 7km south-west of Norton, developed a new type of ware during the fourth century, known from its surface colour and texture as Parchment Ware. This supplied a market in the northern military zone, and it continued in production beyond the end of the military occupation, but its duration is not known.[49]

Roman villas on the Howardian Hills, on the Wolds near Driffield and around Brough-on-Humber, were in use at the end of the fourth century, but for how long is subject to the same problems as those encountered at Malton. No Anglian settlements on or close to villa sites are known from south of the Vale of Pickering. It may be that the central villa complexes had been abandoned, or that Anglian settlements were deliberately sited away from the older centres. But it does not necessarily follow from this that the landed estates themselves and their tenurial structures had collapsed.[50] Not all Roman-period settlements were villas.

While the linear boundaries, visible on the surface or detected as cropmarks, give some insight into the broad divisions of land in the Anglian period, air photography has not been so revealing of settlement sites.[51] Stoertz has, however, drawn attention to a set of eight enclosure complexes that are curvilinear, in contrast to the more numerous rectilinear cases, with traces of internal features including, possibly, a *Grubenhaus*. Five of the eight lie in the Great Wold Valley.[52]

At a Romano-British settlement on the north bank of Gypsy Race about 1km east of Rudston, a scatter of Anglian pottery occurred above a late-Roman feature, and near to this lay the pit of a *Grubenhaus* and another small pit from which excavators recovered more pottery and a girdle hanger, an item that normally occurs with female Anglian burials. Across the river, 1km south-west from here, postholes revealed rectangular building with a floor area of 7.5m by 4m. From within posthole fills came an iron knife blade of a form dated by typology within the period AD 450–700 and animal bone with a calibrated radiocarbon date of AD 690–980. All these items and features occurred within the narrow confines of an excavation along a gas pipeline. But geophysical survey at the second location showed that the posthole building stood at the southern edge of a wider settlement area.[53]

Intensive fieldwork around Wharram Percy, at the north-west edge of the Wolds, led Colin Hayfield to think that some of the Roman-era farmstead settlements survived into the Anglian period, but with a longer-term trend for outlying farms to be abandoned and settlement concentrated in central places.[54] Whether this result can be extrapolated right across the Wolds has been a matter of debate.[55] From a study of the place-names, Margaret Gelling observed that the names around the Wharram area are typically of the later Anglo-Saxon period, from the late ninth century;[56] this accords with an earlier gap in the pottery record from the Wharram excavations. There had been, she suggests, a fall-off in the number of people living in the northern part of the Wolds, with levels not beginning to pick up again until the eighth century. Place-names might be a more reliable indicator of early Anglian settlement locations than the few visible archaeological remains. The key observation is that the earliest name-types are to be found around the edges of the Wolds. These include topographical names: Kirkburn, Eastburn, Southburn, Elmswell, Driffield and names in *-ham* and *-ingaham*: Goodmanham; Yedingham, Everingham, Brantingham, Wintringham, Harpham; *vill* names in the drier central Wolds tend to be Scandinavian, with only Sledmere and Fimber having early names.

The location of burials is not necessarily a reliable proxy for settlement: the burials on the high Wolds tend to be those placed in Bronze Age barrows, making claims for links to an ancestral past. Anglian-period settlement was, Fenton-Thomas suggests,[57] most likely to have been 'on the wold-edges, in areas with ready access to surface water where they also had land locally available for a full range of livestock and crop-related agriculture'. The revelation of intact late Roman and Anglian landscapes beneath wind-blown sands at West Heslerton and Sherburn demonstrates this.

* * *

By the time that Deira first appears in the historical record, in King Edwin's reign (616–633), it is already an emergent kingdom. Foundation myths, which in time became embedded in genealogies recorded in the *Anglo-Saxon*

Chronicle, accounted for the origin of kingdoms by evoking war-band leaders who claimed descent from the god Woden and who arrived with small groups of men to establish their rule. Bernician kingship is traced to the arrival of Ida at the coastal stronghold of Bamburgh in 547. He was the son of Eoppa, son of Esa, son of Ingui, son of Angenwit, son of Aloc, son of Benoc, son of Brand, son of Bældæg, son of Woden, son of Freotholaf, son of Frithwulf, son of Finn, son of Godwulf, son of Geat. The first reference in the *Chronicle* to the Deiran line is under the year 560, when Ælle is said to have succeeded to the kingdom of Northumbria. Ælle was the son of Yffi, son of Uxfrea, son of Wilgisl, son of Westerfalca, son of Sæfugl, son of Sæbald, son of Sigegeat, son of Swedbæg, son of Sigegar, son of Wægdæg, son of Woden.

The *Historia Brittonum* gives a suggestion of state building with the note that Ida was the first king in Bernicia; that he 'held the countries in the north of Britain'; that he joined *Din Guaire* (the Brittonic name for Bamburgh) to Bernicia.[58] It also implies that *Din Guaire* was under threat during the time of Ida's son Theodoric when Urien of Rheged, in alliance with three other British kings, besieged him on the island of Lindisfarne. The Welsh heroic poem *Y Gododdin* tells of the defeat of the Britons at *Catræth*.* These source texts for people and events date from long after the foundation-era events they describe and, as David Dumville has remarked, they give no clear sense of the structure of political authority or of its historical context.[59]

Both Bede and the *Anglo-Saxon Chronicle* – following Bede – date the line of Bernician kings from the year 547 by back-calculation.† But where did they come from? There is no burial tradition in Bernicia of the sort that characterises the Deiran heartlands: cremation cemeteries that may reflect immigrant communities; the re-use of prehistoric burial mounds. There is a persistent, nagging thought that the similarity of the Old English name Lindisfarne, for the island known in Brittonic as *Medcaut*, to the folk name of the English population of Lindsey or *Lindissi*, the *Lindisfaran*, is more than coincidental. Caitlin Green has reviewed the evidence and presented a convincing case that there was, indeed, a genuine link between the two.‡ The

---

* See below in this chapter; for the text of *Y Gododdin*, see Koch 1997.
† See below in this chapter for problems with this date, and a suggested solution.
‡ Green 2012, 235–65. Coates and Breeze (2000, 254) offer an alternative derivation for name Lindisfarne, from an Archaic Irish expression meaning the 'domain of Lindis', where Lindis refers to a small river, as suggested by Symeon.

etymological derivation is credible and allows for the migration of part of a folk-group, the *Lindisfaran*, to an island off the north-east coast, giving the name *Lindisfarnae* or *Lindisfarena ea*: the island of the *Lindisfaran*. It is conceivable that these Lindisfaran were migrants or refugees or that they were imported as *foederati* – mercenaries under the leadership of one Ida. Were they *mearc-weardas* – border-watching 'wolves' established to protect the region from other predatory forces?

Green makes another intriguing observation: that several other apparently early Northumbrian folk-names, preserved in settlements at Billingham, Spaldington and Jarrow, also have obvious links to names preserved in Lincolnshire or Fenland territorial polities: *Billingas*, *Spalda* and *Gyrwe* – each one corresponding neatly with one of Roberts's Northumbrian corelands. If those links are historically credible, they may have a bearing on later relations between Northumbria and the kingdom of Lindsey – a precious and frequently contested prize in the long-running rivalry between Northumbrian and Mercian kings.

The source texts purporting to preserve traditions about state formation offer no sense of how kingship emerged as an Early Medieval institution. It is treated as a given, whereas it is an emergent status, contingent on the sort of lordship implied by the post-Roman hall at Birdoswald and made evident in the writings of Bede and other authors. The interrelationships between people, kings and territory are much more effectively shown in the workings of food renders and the royal circuit, as Thomas Charles-Edwards explained.[60] This was the glue that held together the economic and social foundations of the kingdom. Bede wrote of King Edwin (616–633) travelling to his *villa regia* of *Ad Gefrin*, the present-day Yeavering, where he and his court spent thirty-six days.[61] The Great Halls of this royal *vill* came to light in Brian Hope-Taylor's archaeological excavations in the 1960s.[62] King Edwin also travelled to centres near Catterick and at *Cambodunum* in Elmet. Bishop Wilfrid's biographer, Stephen of Ripon,* was describing the same sort of circuit when, waspishly, he wrote of King Ecgfrið and Queen Iurminburh going about through towns, fortresses and villages every day in the 670s and 680s, rejoicing and feasting in worldly pomp.[63] Both refer to the king's circuit, in which he and his court travelled between royal centres. In this way, the king established himself as a visible presence across his territories and made it possible for people to approach the court.

---

* Stephen is known in older literature as Eddius or Eddius Stephanus.

One such was the young Wilfrid (633–709), suitably kitted out from home with fine clothes, weapons, horse and companions, who presented himself to King Oswiu's queen, Eanflæd. Wilfrid had social standing as the son of a thegn who had received the king's companions in his house. Oswiu's brother King Oswald (634–642), dining on Easter Sunday, had made himself available to poor people who had arrived seeking alms (see Chapter 4).* In their halls, the king and his court received food renders collected together as a service owed from his people in the areas around and about to the king, whose lordship gave protection and honour. King and court travelled to their food, engaging in the conspicuous consumption of the wealth of the land. The law code of King Ine of Wessex (688–694) lists the produce in the food render: bread, honey, ale, wethers (castrated rams), geese, hens and cheese.[64] The monasteries that the kings endowed in the seventh century also became part of the circuit and food render: Wilfrid, when granted a set of estates in the Pennines at the dedication of his church in Ripon in about 672, provided three days and nights' feasting, although in the more austere setting of Lindisfarne, King Oswald and his men had to be content with plainer fare.[65]

The circuit introduces the territorial dimension of kingship. Charles-Edwards suggests that we can distinguish between the core and periphery of the king's territory, with regular iterations in the core, but only occasionally at the peripheries.[66] What is the core and what the peripheries probably depends on the home base of any king; Edwin's core territories were likely to have been around Deira. *Ad Murum*, along the River Tyne 12 Roman miles from the coast, from where King Oswiu conducted his political diplomacy during and after the 640s,[67] was probably peripheral for Edwin. His progress to Yeavering, 130 miles north of Malton, and to Littleborough on Trent in the kingdom of Lindsey, was to make himself visible in areas that came under his sphere of influence only after his defeat of King Æðelfrið.

Beyond the core and peripheral areas lay a zone in which the king had no established circuit, regular or occasional.[68] These were areas which a king subdued, possibly for just a short period of time, and from which he exacted tribute.† Tribute was of a different order from the food renders to the king in his core and peripheral territories. It implied subjection and there was no honour in providing it, for the king extracting the tribute had no hall here at

---

* Bede *HE* III.6.
† In a study of kingship among the Scots in the tenth century, Neil McGuigan refers to such areas as predatory zones. McGuigan 2015, 157–8.

The claustrophobic intimacy of the seventh-century crypt at Ripon belies the extravagant feast that accompanied its dedication

which the chief men of the area could share in the king's hospitality and companionship. Here the king did not come to the food, but the food went 'on the hoof' to the king's halls in his own territories: the tribute of livestock.

Cattle raiding and cattle tribute accentuated the subjection and humiliation of the people and their leaders compelled to pay such tribute. The other side of the coin is that a king who could exact such tribute enjoyed a heroic reputation. In Welsh poetry, a successful king is 'a driver of cattle', and a poem in praise of Cadwallon, who eventually killed Edwin, declares that his cattle had not bellowed before the goads and spear points of Edwin's men: he had succeeded in denying Edwin's demand for tribute.[69] In Irish literature, a raid on a prize bull at Cooley was fit subject matter for an epic poem, the *Táin Bó Cúailnge*.[70]

Along with the tribute of cattle, successful raiding brought a king bounty in the form of material wealth and slaves who could be traded into English and

European markets and material wealth such as the Staffordshire Hoard of gold and gems from sword fittings and other military equipment; this is likely to be battlefield loot, in this case from successful raiding by a Mercian king, perhaps into Northumbria.[71] Such loot oiled the wheels of patronage within the king's court where service in battle could be rewarded with its spoils. The Old English kenning 'Ring-giver' for a king says much of what was expected of them by their followers, celebrated and approved by the *Beowulf* poet. A king needed armed men in his service. Bede records of Oswine, sub-king in Deira (d.651), that 'everywhere the most noble men flocked to his service from almost every kingdom'.[72] 'A single man in possession of a good fortune, must be in want of a wife'; serving in the warband of a successful raider was the route to that fortune.

What, then, is the geographical definition of the kingdom of Northumbria, or is any definition possible? At the height of their power in the mid seventh century Northumbrian kings exercised lordship over an area between Humber and Forth, from east coast to west. Beyond these bounds, Edwin is said to have ruled over all the inhabitants of Britain, English and British alike, except for Kent; King Oswiu (642–671) subjected the greater part of the Pictish people to English dominion.[73] These are cases of the over-kingship or *imperium* that Bede attributed to seven English kings. But these are not cases of territorial aggrandisement with administrative and military occupation, in the way in which European powers carved up Africa in the nineteenth century. When King Ecgfrið won a victory in Mercia in 674 he did so with a small army, killing innumerable people, driving out the king and subjecting that kingdom to tribute.[74] This was not an attempt to occupy and govern territory in the long term; it was a raiding party to win booty, just as his army later came back with slaves as booty from a raiding trip in Ireland.[75] The extent to which Northumbrian kings projected their power over other kingdoms depended on their success as predatory raiders.

The English kings' genealogies, with their claims of descent from Woden, were retrospective constructs serving in the seventh century and beyond to validate a contestant's claim to the throne, with no necessary relationship to biological reality.[76] But, as Ian Wood observed, there is a threshold after which they do appear to refer to historically verifiable individuals.[77] This comes in the third quarter of the sixth century, a generation after the twin catastrophes of the 530s – a series of volcanic eruptions followed by a Europe-wide plague – and a generation before Augustine's mission to Kent in 597 and the subsequent development of written records. This is the horizon from which kings and kingdoms come into focus as tangible entities. For Northumbria, this brings us to Æðelfrið and Ælle.

Bede apparently knew little of Ælle. In the *Ecclesiastical History*, he appears only once in the context of a traditional story told of Pope Gregory.⁷⁸ Seeing fair-haired boys in the slave market in Rome, the pope asked about them and was told that they were English, that they came from Deira and that the name of their king was Ælle. This encounter motivated Gregory to send a mission to convert the heathen English. The *Anglo-Saxon Chronicle* and the *Historia Brittonum* between them add little: a genealogy making him the son of Yffi and father of Edwin; that he became king in Deira in 560; that he died in 580 to be succeeded by Æðelric, who reigned for five years. Of Æðelric, the sources have nothing to add. This date of 580 for Ælle's death is inconsistent with the chronicle which Bede attached to the end of his 725 work *On the Measurement of Time*, that is a few years before the *Ecclesiastical History*, in which he noted that Ælle and Æðelfrið were kings in Northumbria at the time when Pope Gregory's mission arrived in Kent.⁷⁹

The Deiran kingship of the late sixth century is inextricably mixed in with the kingship of Æðelfrið of the Bernician line descending from Ida. Here again, there is chronological and dynastic confusion which will presently need careful unpicking. Bede, however, does establish to some extent a historical context for Æðelfrið, even though his understanding of him as a historical figure is limited and one-dimensional. For Bede, he epitomises warrior kingship – the epithet used, with two adjectives in their superlative form, is *fortissimus et gloriae cupidissimus*: 'very strong and very greedy for glory' – the one who ravaged the Britons more than any other English ruler.⁸⁰ For the writer of the *Historia Brittonum*, he was *Flesaur*, 'Twister'.⁸¹

The regnal list appended to a very early copy of Bede's *Historia*, and known as the Moore Memorandum, records the names and regnal lengths of Northumbria's kings from the date of its compilation in about 737 all the way back to a semi-legendary Bernician progenitor, Ida.⁸² From that list Bede calculated that Ida ruled for twelve years from the year 547:* the founding date of Northumbrian history. In this list King Æðelfrið is allotted an impressive twenty-four years and, back-calculating from Bede's contemporary, King Ceolwulf, he must have begun to rule in the year 592/3. The date of his death in 616/7 is independently attested; so, on the face of it, this regnal scheme is a consistent and credible source. In fact, it is the bedrock of a continuous political narrative on which much else depends.

---

* Bede was the first historian to popularise the so-called Dionysian dating system, originally calculated from the supposed date of Christ's incarnation by Dionysius Exiguus in the sixth century.

A few preparatory words of caution are required here. Early Medieval kingship was a complex, negotiated status, not a zero-sum game. Frequent evidence from elsewhere in Britain of co-rulers, rival rulers and partial rulers is concealed in Northumbria by such simplistic, retrospective linear sequences; dynastic editing was a key political tool. There may have been many more 'kings' competing for dynastic success than we know of. The descendants of the winners got to tell the tale. Some rival dynastic lines that appeared in the eighth century traced their line back to Ida – either genuinely or spuriously – and there is enough evidence of fraternal rivalry to suggest a more nuanced narrative lying unseen beneath layers of streamlining. And then, regnal years are always given in whole numbers, but kings are unlikely to have lived such convenient lives. This creates uncertainties which can cumulatively lead to inaccuracies. Historians are generally able to calibrate regnal lists against other, independently corroborated events; but some dates are more secure than others. And one must compare the purpose of a regnal list with that of a genealogy. One is a list of the winners and how long they held the reigns of power for; the other is a list of sons who succeeded their fathers as kings, and with no attempt at counting the lengths of their reigns – it's a generational record, meant to be recited at a feast or tribute-taking ceremony. Finally, the question of when the Early Medieval chronographers' year began and ended has been much debated. Bede's dates are generally regarded as being at least a year too early for the late sixth and early seventh century.

The Moore Memorandum regnal list conceals other nagging inconsistencies, betrayed by an awkward British tradition and by sporadic entries in the *Anglo-Saxon Chronicle*, which expose serious flaws in Bede's confident chronology. The list runs as follows: Ida *xii annos*; Glappa *i annum*; Adda *viii*; Æðelric *iiii*; Theodoric *vii*; Freodwald *vi*; Hussa *vii*; Æðelfrið *xxiiii*. Working back from 616, these give approximate *Anno Domini* dates as follows:

Ida	547–559
Glappa	559–560
Adda	560–567
Æðelric	567–571
Theodoric	571–578
Freodwald	578–585
Hussa	585–592
Æðelfrið	592–616

In a Bernician genealogy first written down at the beginning of the ninth century, the *Historia Brittonum* offers the names of twelve sons of Ida.[83] Of these, Adda, Æðelric and Theodoric appear successively, immediately after him in the same source in a regnal list that excludes Glappa's one-year reign;[84] but he is a minor inconvenience. Now, Ida's second son, Æðelric, reigned four years after the death of his presumed brother Adda in 567. But an *Anglo-Saxon Chronicle* entry under the year 588 records the death of King Ælle and the succession of a King Æðelric, who reigned after him for five years. The phrasing of these events suggests, perhaps, Ælle's deposition or murder by the latter. King Ælle belongs to the genealogy of the Deiran kings; so the Bernician Æðelric, turning up after a gap of seventeen years (571–588) in a rival kingdom, suffers both a chronological and a geographical dislocation. There is no reason to think there were two Æðelrics: in all surviving Deiran genealogies Ælle is followed by his impeccably attested and dated son Edwin, not a Deiran Æðelric. Edwin ruled over all Northumbria after defeating Æðelfrið in 616/7, so there is certainly some sort of discontinuity in the Deiran dynastic succession: of twenty-four years, in fact, after 592/3 when, according to the *Chronicle*, Æðelric died.

As for King Æðelric's son, Æðelfrið *Flesaur*, he only succeeded his father in Bernicia after a gap of some twenty-one years, during which time his father apparently enjoyed a brief reign of five years in Deira. To confuse matters further, the *Historia Brittonum* records that Æðelfrið reigned twelve years in Bernicia and twelve more (*alios*) in Deira, and twenty-four in both.[85]

Doubts about the Bernician regnal list are increased by a gloss in the *Historia Brittonum* against the reign of Freodwald, whose dates should be 578–585 but during whose reign, so the gloss goes, Pope Gregory sent a proselytising embassy to Kent. That event, otherwise known as the Augustinian mission after Canterbury's first bishop, bears a rock-solid date of 597, most unlikely to have been mistaken by any historian in Early Medieval Britain. A scribal error – or another anomaly requiring a rethink of the regnal list?

Conventionally, counting back twenty-four years from his known death in 616/7 places King Æðelfrið's succession from Hussa in Bernicia to 592/3. The event that marks Æðelfrið's unification of Bernicia and Deira as a single *imperium*, Northumbria, neatly dividing his reign into the two twelve-year segments described by the *Historia Brittonum*, is dated by Bede to 604. In that year a great battle was fought in which Æðelfrið was the victor. Bede says that

Áedán mac Gabrain, king of the Scots that dwell in Britain, being alarmed by his [Æðelfrið's] success, came against him with a great and mighty army, but was defeated and fled with a few followers; for almost all his army was cut to pieces at a famous place, called *Degsastan*...[86]

Ironically, for such a celebrated site, *Degsastan* has never been identified, but by common consent the battle was fought in what later became the borderlands north of the Solway Firth, perhaps near Liddesdale in Roxburghshire. Áedán mac Gabrain was king of Dál Riata – roughly modern Argyll, with a principal fortress at Dunadd or Dunollie – between about 574 and 609: so the geography of the campaign is wholly northern. It does not fit with the idea of a campaign in which Æðelfrið, having already ruled over Bernicia for a dozen years, conquered Deira and united the lands north of the Humber into a single kingdom; especially since the *Anglo-Saxon Chronicle* dating of Æðelric's career in Deira would much better suit Æðelfrið succeeding him *there* in 592/3.

Suppose, then, that the orthodox reading of Æðelfrið's career, succeeding Hussa in 592/3 in Bernicia and then, twelve years later, adding Deira to his portfolio, is a misreading. A single, modest inversion allows a more congruent sketch to be drawn. And while several other solutions to the problem have been advanced over the years, the application of Occam's razor – let the simplest solution win – is adopted here.

Suppose, instead, that Æðelfrið succeeded his father, Æðelric, in Deira in 592–3 (to agree with the *Chronicle* entry) and ruled there for twelve years – doing no disservice to the *Historia Brittonum* entry. At that time (604) he was sufficiently powerful that, perhaps on Hussa's death or precipitating it, he could tilt for the throne of Bernicia, his birthright. His bid provoked Dál Riata into the fateful encounter at *Degsastan* which propelled Æðelfrið to lordship over all the North, for another twelve years.

What follows? The dates of all the Bernician kings prior to 604 have to be shifted forward by twelve years, so:

Ida	559–571
Glappa	571–572
Adda	572–580
Æðelric	580–584
Theodoric	584–591
Freodwald	591–597
Hussa	597–604

The result is that Hussa is ruling in Bernicia in 604; Freodwald dies conveniently in 597, the year made memorable by the arrival of the Augustinian mission in Kent; Æðelric is deposed by his brother Theodoric in 584, just four years before he reappears in Deira, having (one infers) killed or deposed Ælle and sent Ælle's son Edwin into the nearly thirty-year exile so dramatically described by Bede. As it happens, the *Anglo-Saxon Chronicle* provides further corroboration for this scheme. In its entry for 604 it describes how, in the battle at *Degsastan*, Æðelfrið's brother Theodbald was slain with all his retinue; and then it says: 'Hering, son of Hussa, led the host thither'. The implication is that in the aftermath of an Æðelfriðan coup against Hussa, the latter's son invited Áedán mac Gabrain to join with him in a counter coup – a plot that failed spectacularly in the remote and forbidding natural fortress of Liddesdale. 'From that time,' wrote Bede, 'no king of the Scots has dared come into Britain to make war on the English to this day.'[87]

Bede had no great interest in solving chronological problems concerning King Æðelfrið's early career. He had his own particular reasons for remarking that after *Degsastan* in 604 no king of the *Scotti* would wage war on the English; but it is nevertheless a credible marker for the attainment of English overlordship over the north British kingdoms that would endure at least until the end of the reign of Æðelfrið's grandson Ecgfrið in 685. But the British historian, and the poets of the British tribes who encountered Northumbria's sixth-century kings, had much to say about the tribal interactions through which Bernician and Deiran warlords and their Brittonic-speaking antagonists to the north and west, defined themselves as distinctly separate peoples. In the British version of the Bernician regnal list recorded in *HB* 63, Theodoric (whose amended dates are now 584–91)

> fought bravely against that Urien together with his sons. At that time sometimes the enemy and sometimes our countrymen [*cives*] gained the victory, and he [Urien] penned them in for three days and three nights in the island of *Medcaut* [Lindisfarne]; but whilst he was on this expedition he was murdered, at the instance of Morcant, out of envy, because he possessed so much superiority over all the kings in military science.

The apparently long-running campaign between Theodoric and the legendary British King Urien of Rheged is, in the amended chronological scheme and by virtue of this entry, dated to the years before 591.

There is no circumventing a third, very obvious, flaw in the British historian's order of events, because a gloss against the reign of Hussa (now dated 597–604) records that four kings fought against him: their names were Urien (who should have been dead before 591), Rhydderch Hen, Guallauc and Morcant. Urien is associated with Rheged, west of the Pennines; Ridderch Hen belongs in the genealogy of the British-speaking kings of *Alt Clud* – Dumbarton Rock in Strathclyde. Guallauc appears to have been a king of Elmet – roughly West Yorkshire; Morcant may have been a king in southern Pictland or among the Gododdin. Urien, Guallauc and Morcant could trace their line back to a single progenitor, Coel Hen – the Old King Cole of nursery rhymes.[88]

Urien's improbable resurrection after his betrayal and assassination by Morcant is at least consistent with his and other famed British leaders' legendary appearances in a range of undateable poetic settings in which he floats in Brownian temporal motion. The most celebrated of these is the battle elegy – or collection of elegies – associated with Aneirin: *Y Gododdin*. Here at least are broadly identifiable geographies: a Gododdin homeland in Lothian, with a fortress base at *Din Eidyn* – Edinburgh; and the locus of a great and tragically ill-fated raid or war against *Catræth* – sometimes explicitly seeming to mean the walled Roman town of Catterick, sometimes also apparently the polity of *Catræth* centred on the Tees Valley.

The enemy of the Gododdin are the heathen men of Deira or, more loosely, Saxons or *Lloegrwys*. Their allies are men of Gwynedd in North-west Wales and Anglesey; Elmetians; men of Aeron (roughly Ayrshire) and Ridderch's men of *Alt Clud*. The allegiance of the men of Bernicia – in its Brittonic form *Bryneich* – is less clearly defined; and in other poetry Bernicians appear as allies of the *Gwyr y Gogledd*, the Men of the North. Perhaps Æðelfrið's British moniker *Flesaur* – Twister – reflects a change of allegiance, deplored by one-time British allies. In any case, Anglian Deirans are always the enemy. Among the heroes named are Madawg of Elmet; Cynon of Aeron and Yrfai, lord of Eidyn. Urien is frustratingly missing from *Y Gododdin;* but in the elegies of Aneirin's fellow poet, Taliesin, he is the lord of *Catræth*[89] and of *Erechwydd* or Rheged – that shadowy kingdom which seems to have lain around the Solway Firth, in the Eden Valley or West Pennines.

If the British historian knew that Æðelfrið's moniker was the unflattering *Flesaur*, then Taliesin knew another leader of an invading army of Bernicians as *Fflamddwyn* – Flame-bearer. He appears as the aggressor against the Men of the North in a poetic account of a battle at the unidentified *Argoed Llwyfain*, perhaps in the region of the River Lyvennet in what is now

Cumbria.⁹⁰ *Fflamddwyn* might be identified with Theodoric, against whom Urien and his sons fought in the years after Æðelric's short reign among the Bernicians; but he might equally be Æðelric himself.

If *Catræth* was a contested region, it overstretches the diaphanous evidence of the poetry to propose just a single battle there some time in the late sixth century, giving rise to so many poetic glories and anachronistic participants. More likely, tribal polities in East Yorkshire, the Pennines, the Tyne Valley and Lothian found the rich lowlands of the Tees Valley a region worth fighting for over a long period – generations. Andrew Fleming's analysis of a series of probable Early Medieval linear earthworks that cut across Upper Swaledale west of Catterick shows how tangible evidence of such political tensions might play out on a landscape scale.⁹¹

It is a moot point whether Britons were always, and only ever, the antagonists of Anglian Northumbrians. In the *Annales Cambriae* an apparently important battle fought at *Arfderydd* (Arthuret, near Longtown in coastal Cumbria) pitted Gwenddolau son of Ceidio (a descendant of the legendary Coel Hen) against the sons of Eliffer. These men, named elsewhere in the *Annales* as Gwrgi and Peredur, were said to be cousins of Urien. It seems that internecine warfare was rife. If tribal affinities were defined by geography, language, warrior tradition and loyalty to warrior lords as cult figures embodying the fortunes of the *tribe*, it is much riskier to project backwards from Bede and the British historian, and forward from Gildas, to create a milieu of undiluted ethnophobic rivalry. It is true that tribal affinities can be reinforced by othering, a sense of who the 'countrymen' – *cives* in Latin, *cymry* in Brittonic or the *gens Anglorum* in Bede – were not. But convincing evidence of cultural hybridism counters the idea. Northumbrian kings had Irish, British, Mercian and Pictish mothers and wives; were sometimes fostered at each other's courts. The north Northumbrian landscape was littered with settlements that bore equivalent English and Brittonic names, frequently attested by Bede. Several Northumbrian kings were at least bilingual, if not positively polyglot. In metalwork, architecture, memorial and territorial management, British and Anglian influences were as cross-bred as their royal patrons. Briton and Angle were likely as often allies as rivals. And in the extraordinarily rapid adoption of Christian worship and a powerful ideology of Christian kingship in the first half of the seventh century, British and Irish Christian traditions are as prominent and influential as those of Rome – more so, in fact, in the North and West. In Bede's narrative of the conversion, Æðelfrið the heathen and British and Irish Christians play a catalytic role.

King Æðelfrið, whose birth must be placed no later than about 573–5, had first taken a wife named Bebba.[92] He was said to have given her the fortress of *Din Guoaroy or Din Guaire* – a Brittonic name with the proposed meaning 'Fort of the theatre/amphitheatre', with a connotation of perhaps an assembly site, even a racecourse.[93] It became known as *Bebbanburg*, later Bamburgh after her.* Her issue may have been the son called Eanfrið, whose own son Talorcan would become king of the Picts. On this basis some historians have assumed that Bebba must have been British; but it is no more than speculation. The likely date of that union is during Æðelric's reign in Bernicia between 580 and 584. Æðelfrið either repudiated her or she died sufficiently early that Æðelfrið married again – this time to Acha, daughter of the Deiran King Ælle whom his father succeeded – perhaps killed – in 592. This marriage conferred legitimacy in both Bernicia and Deira on his children by her – at least six, perhaps eight of them. The birth of their oldest son, Oswald, in about 604 suggests that the marriage to Acha took place in the years immediately preceding the battle at *Degsastan* – it seems likely to have been a matter of expedient alliance. The cost of this alliance to Bernician security was the threatening survival of her brother, Edwin Ælling, who spent most of his first thirty years in itinerant exile at the courts of Gwynedd, Mercia and East Anglia.

The second battle which Bede describes was fought at the opposite end of Æðelfrið's sphere of interest, at the place he calls the City of the Legions, *Legacæstir*,† against the Britons of Gwynedd (North Wales) in 615/6.[94] Bede allows his hostility to the Britons to show through in writing of the cowardice of the British warlord Brocmail and his men who turned tail, thus allowing the slaughter of monks from the monastery of Bangor who had come to observe the battle. The battle had prophetic interest for Bede, but again the historical context is one of Æðelfrið fighting to establish Northumbrian overlordship beyond his core territories.‡ Here, however, the result was not so clear cut. The raid on Northumbria by Cadwallon of Gwynedd in alliance with Penda of Mercia in which King Edwin was to die in 632/3, and Cadwallon's subsequent ravaging of the kingdom, shows that dominance

---

* *HB* 63. Such eponyms are a common feature of the semi-legendary entries in early annals, often used spuriously to explain a place-name of otherwise unknown derivation.
† Known to the Britons as *Caerlegion*, probably Chester.
‡ Chester may have exercised control over valuable brine deposits in Cheshire whose salt was a highly prized commodity.

would still be contested.* A mass grave discovered at Heronbridge, just south of Chester, is a rare case of a battle cemetery, identified by the type of wounds inflicted on the bodies and evident on the skeletons. Dating from the late sixth to early seventh century; it is almost certainly from Æðelfrið's battle.[95]

In a dynastic sense, Æðelfrið's marriage to Acha was highly successful. Except for the reign of Edwin, their descendants kept hold of the Northumbrian kingship through three generations into the eighth century. Æðelfrið's rule over both Bernicia and Deira is usually taken as the beginning of the unified kingdom of Northumbria from the two sub-kingdoms; but matters were not quite so straightforward. There were sub-kings in Deira down to the death of Ælfwine in 679. However, and notwithstanding his long-term dynastic success, Æðelfrið failed to kill off possible challengers from the Deiran male line completely and this cost him his life. His attempts to have Edwin, son of Ælle, murdered while he took refuge in King Rædwald's court in East Anglia were foiled by Rædwald's queen. In 616 Æðelfrið met his death at the hands of an East Anglian army in a battle near the River Idle, and Edwin took the Northumbrian kingship. The precise location of the battlefield is unknown, but the armies must have met along the Roman road that skirts the wetlands on the south side of the Humber.

---

* Alex Woolf (2004) has raised objections to the identification of this Cadwallon with the son of Cadfan of Gwynedd, instead identifying him with a prince of the Strathclyde Britons; but Adams (2013, 102) accepts the traditional identification.

3

EDWIN: RING-GIVER 616–633

The exiled prince – Edwin's overlordship
– Tribal Hidage – Expansion into Elmet
– Conversion to Christianity – Yeavering
and *villae regiae* – West Heslerton

His early years were more than usually difficult for Edwin, son of Ælle of Deira. With Æðelfrið's dominance, his life was at risk and he took refuge among the Britons of Gwynedd in North Wales; it might well be that the Battle of Chester was Æðelfrið's attempt to hunt him down. He had by then married Cœnburh, daughter of King Cearl of the Mercians, and they had two sons, Osfrið and Eadfrið.[1] If there is a political dimension behind all this, it seems that a Mercian-Welsh alliance was forming and exploiting Bernician-Deiran dynastic infighting in response to Æðelfrið pushing beyond the southern edges of Northumbria.[2] King Æðelfrið's victory at Chester forced Edwin to move on elsewhere and he fled to King Rædwald's court in East Anglia.* But this did not put him beyond the reach of Æðelfrið's agents, who almost managed to bribe Rædwald to betray him into their hands; the queen's intervention saved him. This episode gave Rædwald an opportunity to intervene in Northumbrian affairs. He raised an army, defeated and killed Æðelfrið in 616 at the Battle of the River Idle and installed Edwin as king.[3]

With this turning of the tables, it was no longer the Deiran line at risk, but the sons of Æðelfrið. At the centre of the crisis stood Acha. Her husband's death and her brother's accession now endangered the Bernician line, her children. There could be no reconciliation between brother and sister; she immediately fled with her children, among them the future Kings Oswald and Oswiu, far from Edwin's

---

* Rædwald (c.599–c.625) had a royal complex at Rendlesham in Suffolk on the River Deben on whose lower banks the celebrated Sutton Hoo burial ground, where he may have been interred in his ship, is located.

reach to the kingdom of Dál Riata. With them went young men of the élite, displacing the top layers of the Bernician patronage system and thus opening the way for Edwin to establish his lordship.[4] Irish Annals record the names of two Bernician æthelings, Ælfred and Osric, fighting on behalf of Dál Riata in a battle in Ireland in 628. They are likely to be from the post-Æðelfrið diaspora, but Acha was relying on a deeper history of connections, for Bernicians are known to have been present in Dál Riata before the beginning of the seventh century.[5]

Edwin numbered among the seven kings who, according to Bede, exercised overlordship over others; he ruled over both English and British kingdoms to a greater extent than any had done previously, even bringing the islands of Anglesey and Man under his dominion.[6] He must, by implication, have had a navy under his command. In all probability these were shallow-draughted, clinker-built boats or hide-covered, wooden-framed currachs, propelled primarily by oarsmen-warriors owing military service to Edwin – perhaps partly drawn from tributary kingdoms like Rheged. They may have been able to step a mast carrying a single, square-rigged sail for use in favourable winds. The 23m-long, fourth-century Nydam boat, discovered in 1863, provides a basic model of which there must have been many local and regional variations. Such little evidence as we have for Early Medieval navies suggests that coastal sea voyages were common – more than fifty such journeys are mentioned in Adomnán's *Life of St Columba* (Colm Cille). Navigable rivers were used extensively as routeways, and the incidence of Tarbet-type names* in Scotland suggests that hauling boats overland across short distances between bodies of open water was possible. As a rough guide to crew size, the tenth-century *Senchus Fer nAlban* – 'The History of the Men of Scotland' – speaks of a boat with seven benches, two oars to a bench, while an eighth-century vessel belonging to Failbe of Applecross was said to have had a crew of twenty-two, accommodated on ten benches with two steersmen.[7]

We have little detail of what a wider Edwinian hegemony really means and how he achieved such dominance; it needs some careful unpicking. At the beginning of his reign he was beholden to King Rædwald and one might suppose that his capacity for independent action was constrained until Rædwald's death in 624/5, especially in any dealings south of the Humber. The kingdom of Lindsey, whose internal narrative history is quite unknown, was frequently disputed between Northumbria and Mercia before the late

---

* Gaelic *tairbeart* 'isthmus', literally 'carry across', in place-names often appears to indicate portages.

670s. North of the Humber, and around the edges of the Deiran core, King Edwin might well have had a freer hand.

The unique document known as the Tribal Hidage, and an early poem from the north of Ireland, provide two of the few clues to how overlordship was exercised. The former comes in an eleventh-century manuscript containing a list of thirty-four peoples and territories, assessed in numbers of hides and seemingly owing tribute to an unnamed overlord. It is by no means in its original form, but by general consent it belongs to the seventh or eighth century. If it belongs to the eighth century it is likely to be a Mercian list – for this is the century of Mercian *imperium*. If it belongs in the previous century, it seems likely that it was drawn up at the court of King Edwin, perhaps by one of the few literate clerics in his entourage.

Mercia, rated at 30,000 hides, begins the list – one reason why Nick Higham, arguing for an Edwinian origin, believes it to be Northumbrian – Mercian kings are hardly likely to have exacted tribute from their own lands. Wealthy East Anglia was rated the same as Mercia. Middle-ranking kingdoms like Lindsey, Essex and *Hwicce* were rated at 7,000 hides – a number that resonates with the size of the legendary Beowulf's kingdom.[8] By far the largest tributary value is placed on Wessex, rated at 100,000 hides – surely a punitive assessment and another reason for Higham to propose it as a list drawn up in the reign of Edwin – for he had every reason to exact such an enormous tribute from the kingdom which had sent an assassin to his court.* We cannot know what rate of tribute was applied per hide – but it was probably measured in head of cattle and perhaps weight of gold and silver. The smallest polities, rated at no more than a few hundred hides – the size of the most generous royal land grants in that period – belong on the edges of the fenlands, their tributary value almost nominal, but cumulatively amounting to another 7,000 hides. If nothing else, the Tribal Hidage provides us with the most basic outline of a political geography in the period when larger kingdoms were beginning to swallow smaller, less powerful kingdoms and semi-dependent chiefdoms. Bede's information that Edwin's Irish Sea conquests of Anglesey and Man had known hidage values (960 and 300, respectively) suggests that such assessments of tribute were applied by Edwin, if not his predecessors.

In the Early Irish Airgíalla Charter Poem† we catch a glimpse of relations between an overlord, king of the Northern Uí Néill,[9] and his tributary

---

* See below in this chapter. Higham 1995.
† Much of the following section is based on material in Adams 2021a.

neighbours, among them the confederation of tribes called the Airgíalla of Clogher. Circumstantially it seems to have an early eighth-century origin and may contain material from as early as the sixth century. The poem recalls the far-off days when the Airgíalla and their superior neighbours had been kin. In the interests of preventing potential feuds, they agreed rules covering compensation, rights of access, the behaviour of their animals and mutual hospitality.[10] Itinerant warrior lordship required additional rules governing the nature and delivery of renders, military service, the judgement of offences and the honour due from lord and dependant to one other – material almost completely unavailable in the English sources.

In the Charter Poem the Airgíalla are keen to stress the honourable nature of their relations with the Uí Néill. They enjoyed a seat of honour beside the High King of Tara during assemblies held at Tailtiu – Telltown, in County Meath. Their military service was limited to twenty-eight days (two fortnights) every three years and, at least in theory, they did not have to bring their armies into the field during sowing and harvest time in spring and autumn. They were entitled to an exceptional level of compensation for their losses in battle and to a generous share of booty won as the spoils of war. Their status gave them immunity from claims made against them during war and peace. Whether all these privileges were acknowledged by their overlords is another matter; but the Airgíalla felt entitled to claim them: they had earned those rights by virtue of historical alliance and through shared kindred.

Airgíalla's lawyers acknowledged, in return, the rights of their overlords. The Uí Néill kings were entitled to 'rising' – that is, they expected that their subkings and dependants would rise when they entered hall or chamber. More functionally, Uí Néill overlords were entitled to the military services of their underkings in order to prosecute wars of expansion against historic antagonists, the Ulaid, in north-east Ulster. As territorial lords they were entitled to expect entertainment and hospitality on their progress through dependent territories and to a range of renders, both from their own clients and from their underkings. In practice, this meant that some of the renders collected by the kings of the Airgíalla on their own behalf must be passed on to their Uí Néill overlords, diminishing their own potential for accumulating wealth.

The arrangements by which Edwin exercised lordship over subordinate peoples and their kings are unlikely to have been very different. Tributary kings aside, the reign of Edwin sees the beginnings of the Deiran kingdom extending beyond its core territory. The *Historia Brittonum* records that Edwin occupied Elmet and expelled its king Ceretic, a fact which itself militates against the Tribal Hidage being an eighth-century Mercian list because by then Elmet (rated at a paltry 600 hides) had long been a Northumbrian province.[11] The invasion may well have been an act of retribution, if Ceretic is the same man that Bede named as Cerdic, for Edwin's nephew Hereric had taken refuge at his court and was murdered there.[12] We are told nothing of the circumstances, but the finger of suspicion points to the Bernician king Æðelfrið as the reason why Hereric had to flee his home. Just as Edwin in his youth had been a fugitive from Æðelfrið, so his kinsman Hereric was also on the run. Hereric was not so fortunate as Edwin in his choice of protector. To avenge a murdered kinsman may have been Edwin's immediate motivation, but in his taking over Elmet, there was a deeper rationale at play.

* * *

Even today, the former East Riding of Yorkshire seems to be only tenuously connected to the road networks of the rest of England. This was so much more the case in the seventh century, before extensive land drainage, when the wetlands around the lower reaches of the rivers feeding into the Humber estuary impeded movement out of Deira and between the lands north and south of the Humber. Roman military engineers, needing to connect Lincoln and York, had addressed this problem with a road running from Lincoln in a wide loop north-west, crossing the Rivers Trent at Littleborough, Idle at Bawtry, Don at Doncaster, Aire at Castleford, Wharfe at Tadcaster and on to York. This follows the drier land of the narrow belt of limestone, keeping away from the edges of the former glacial lake deposits on the east side. Between the Don and Aire, this road crosses through the post-Roman kingdom of Elmet. Edwin thus secured access to this route. The defeat of Æðelfrið at the battle on the River Idle, and Edwin's own death in battle at Hatfield some sixteen years later, show how important this road was for the movement of armies, and when we find Paulinus in the king's retinue preaching at Littleborough, it shows Edwin's route into Lindsey.[13]

Elmet was a Brittonic kingdom, occupying the south part of Yorkshire, with a name meaning perhaps elm wood.[14] As mapped by Glanville Jones, its outline is diamond-shaped, with a tip at the extreme south of the historic county, south of Sheffield.[15] Its east-side boundary follows the River Don to the Humber estuary and, on the west, the boundary of the modern county, which in the main follows the east-west watershed of the Pennines. The River Wharfe defines its northern boundary, and north-west it marches with the small Pennine kingdom of Craven.[16]

There is little in the archaeological record to define an Elmetian population. But a grave slab from the church of Gard Sant at Llanaelhearn on the Llŷn Peninsula in North Wales carries the Latin inscription ALIORTUS ELMETIACO HICIACET: 'Here lies Aliortus a man of Elmet'. He was evidently a Latin-speaking British Christian. This is consistent with a group of three burials at Parlington Hollins, some 11km east of Leeds, which had been set into the infilled terminals of a ditched enclosure of the late-Roman period. From the manner of burial and the form of the graves, these would, as the excavators commented, have been interpreted as being late Roman but for radiocarbon dates indicating the post-Roman period. If, as this case implies, there is little to differentiate fifth/sixth-century burial styles from those of the Roman period, then, without radiometric dating, the post-Roman population is effectively indistinguishable through burial archaeology.[17] Other features from activity here, a set of nine post holes possibly defining a small rectangular structure, are not chronologically diagnostic in themselves without the radiocarbon determination AD 348–560. A pit cut through the fill of a Roman-period enclosure ditch could, from its radiocarbon dating of AD 268–560, be from the Roman or post-Roman period.[18]

Elmet's identity is defined mostly by Brittonic place-names. This is in marked contrast with the coreland of Deira, where any pre-English stratum of names has disappeared, except for the river names of Derwent and Hull. The Elmet name has survived at Sherburn- and Barwick-in-Elmet, and in Medieval times another six places carried this affix, all towards the eastern edge of the territory. A geophysical survey undertaken to the east of St Hilda's church in Sherburn revealed a very substantial settlement with scores of *Grubenhäuser* and a horseshoe-shaped enclosure containing grain-drying or malting ovens dating to the late seventh century.[19] Blair suggests that such settlements may be the precursors of later *burh* sites.

Names formed in *brettas*, such as West Bretton, *cumbra*, as in Cumberworth, and probably *walh*, as in Walton, refer to British speakers whom the Deirans encountered in Elmet and, along with British speakers, a functioning British Christian church survived, indicated by place-names containing the element *eccles*. This has come into modern English from the Latin *ecclesia*, by way of a version *eclēsia* spoken in Roman Briton; thence as *eglēs* among British speakers and adopted into Old English name forming as *eclēs*.* Its meaning, in a general sense, is church, but Alan James has shown

---

* The asterisk * before a name denotes a reconstructed form.

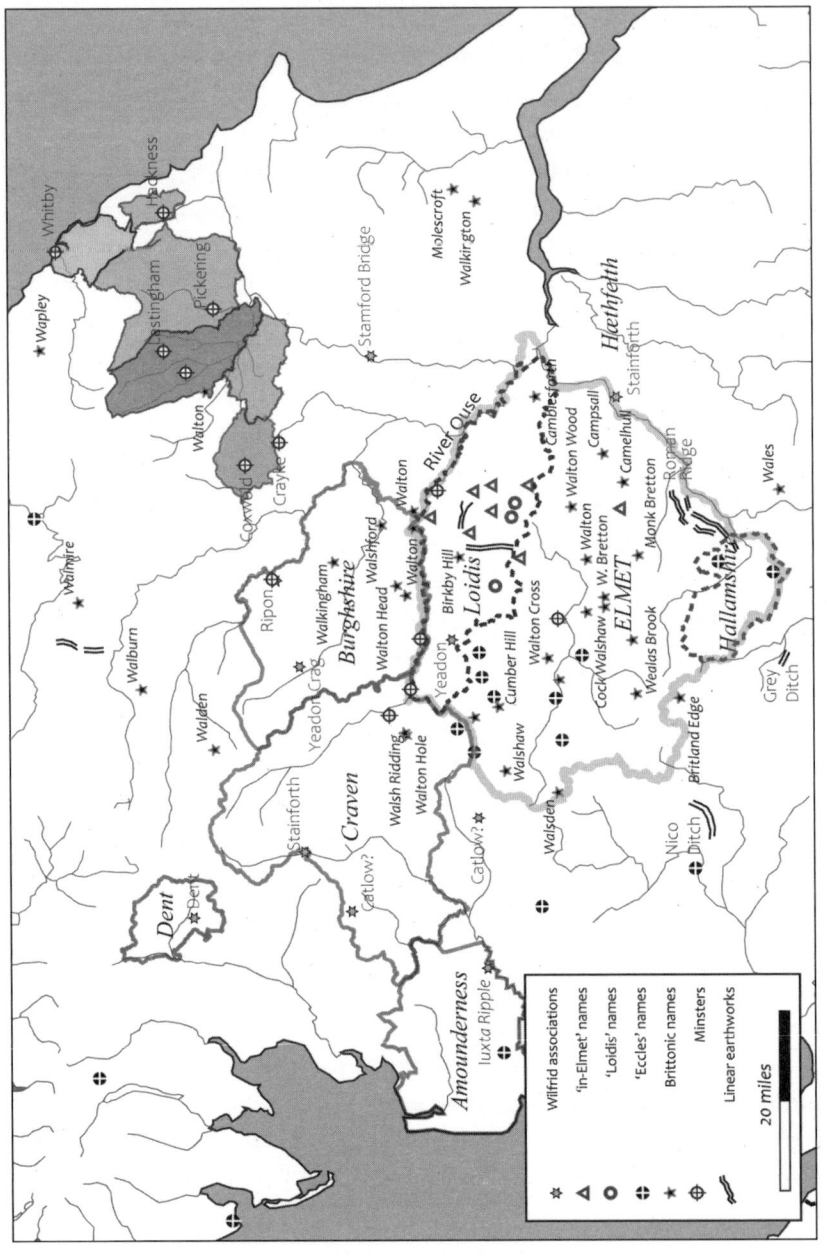

Map 6 The kingdom of Elmet reconstructed

that this is not limited to a physical church building but refers to landholdings of the British church. From the late fifth century, a pattern of landholding developed in which the church enjoyed the renders, dues and privileges of lordship over a wide territory, much as a Northumbrian secular lord did in the seventh or eighth centuries. Northumbrian English-language speakers recognised these landholding patterns; they adopted the word into their own language, understanding it to refer to the landholding as a unit; and they integrated these units into the emergent kingdom.[20] A cluster *of eccles* names in the western part of Elmet between the Rivers Aire and Calder suggests a church territory reaching up to the Pennine moorlands. In the south, west of Sheffield, Ecclesall and Ecclesfield indicate a British church territory later reorganised into the civil territorial unit of Hallamshire.[21] On a broader regional scale, *eccles* names can be used in conjunction with other place-names to construct a picture of Northumbrian expansion into Cumbria in the eighth century (see Chapter 8).

A set of churches and wells dedicated to St Helena, the mother of Emperor Constantine, also marks Brittonic Christian observance.[22] A later stratum of place-names formed in the Old English language to describe woodland; and woodland clearance clusters densely in the western half of Elmet, west of Leeds and Wakefield and especially between the Aire and Calder Valleys; in contrast, the limestone belt is almost devoid of such names.[23] Bede knew of a monastery in the wood of Elmet, though the location of neither is now known.[24]

Edwin established a *villa regia* at a place Bede names as *Campodunum* and a church nearby. These were burnt down in the destruction following his death and later a replacement was built in the *regio* of *Loidis*.[25] A *regio* is a sub-unit of the kingdom and the name *Loidis* has survived as Leeds, the city on the north bank of the River Aire, and in Ledston and Ledsham, just north of Castleton and by the Roman road. Working back from the evidence of estate structures of the post-Conquest period, Glanville Jones has reconstructed this sub-unit as the land between the Rivers Aire and Wharfe, corresponding to two of the later Medieval territorial units called wapentakes,* along with the ecclesiastical parish of Leeds on the south side of the Aire. This makes it the northernmost part of Elmet.[26]

---

* A Norse term introduced after the ninth century in Northern counties and roughly corresponding with the Southern *hundred*, a theoretical grouping of 100 *vills*.

The location of *Campodunum* has been much debated. One opinion places it at Dewsbury.[27] This equates the name with *Camboduno* of the Antonine Itinerary, a listing of routeways from the Roman period, in which it is said to lie 20 Roman miles (29.6km) from *Calcaria* (Tadcaster) on the road between *Calcaria* and *Mamucio* (Manchester). However, the text describing this route is, as it survives, incomplete and inaccurate: the given distance of 20 Roman miles (30.3km) from Tadcaster does not equate to Dewsbury, and there is no known Roman-period site at that point; the figure of 38 Roman miles (56.2km) given for the distance between the two end points is well short of the correct 53 Roman miles (78.4km). These are problems enough to conclude that the Antonine Itinerary is not reliable for secure identification of *Campodunum* as Dewsbury.[28]

There is a case to be made for Leeds, which Margaret Faull and Steve Moorhouse identify as 'probably the major early Anglo-Saxon site in West Yorkshire'.[29] Although Bede's *Loidis* applies to the wider territory of a *regio*, this does not preclude the possibility that the name referred also to a settlement, perhaps originating as the capital of a sub-unit of the Brigantes, and its hinterland – as Catterick seems to have been the caput of the *regio* of *Catræth*.[30] However, Bede's text implies that the second *villa regia*, the one in *in regio Loidis*, was built not at *Campodunum*, but elsewhere. Nevertheless, there is a good argument for a pre-Anglian Leeds, even if this is not *Campodunum*.[31] *Camboduno* is a Brittonic name meaning 'fort at a bend (in the river)'. This led Rivet and Smith to suggest a fort location on the north side of the River Aire at the confluence with Sheepscar Beck close to where the Roman road crosses the river.[32] A recent analysis from historic maps supports the idea of a fort, but on the south side of the bend in the river, in the wedge between the Aire and Benyon Beck, with an area of 0.6ha, comparable with others of the Flavian era; there is, however, no archaeological confirmation for this.[33] Also on the north side of the river, immediately north of the city's core area, is Quarry Hill where antiquarian scholars saw the earthworks, now quarried away, of a hillfort which might well be the *-dūn* that gave rise to the name.[34] Here, possibly, is a context for a Brittonic centre continuing in use into the post-Roman period.

East of Leeds is Grim's Dyke, an east-facing ditch-and-bank earthwork running directly north from the river on the eastern edge of the city for 5km and then curving north-west for about another 3km. In its best-preserved section, alongside Bullerthorpe Lane near Colton immediately south of the road to Selby, its bank rises to 2.3m above the surrounding ground and excavation shows its ditch to have been 1.2m deep.[35] Further east, around Aberford, are three dykes: Becca Banks running east–west along the north side of Cock Beck; South Dyke for a shorter length along the beck's south side; and The Rein running south-east from an intersection with South Dyke.[36] All these dykes, it is suggested, were dug together as a succession of defensive lines to protect the Brittonic capital on Quarry Hill in response to the encroaching Deiran kingdom.[37] Other commentators have questioned whether Grim's Dyke should be associated with the Aberford set: The Rein was not a defence, but more like the boundary dykes of the East Riding; South Dyke, which is north-facing, could be a defence for Elmet, but the south-facing Becca Bank is a Northumbrian defence against Mercian incursions.[38] Dykes such as this are notoriously difficult to date by archaeological methods: finds from ditch siltings do not securely date the construction episodes; those from within or beneath an embankment offer a *terminus post quem* (*TPQ*) for construction. In principle, this should differentiate between, for example, late-prehistoric and post-Roman dykes, but neither the excavation at the Aberford set, nor those on Grim's Dyke, managed to determine any *TPQ*. Review of the problem led the excavators back to one of the earlier opinions: that the Aberford dykes were a response to the advance of the Roman army in the first century AD.[39] It is all still more a matter of opinion than of evidence.

A third view places *Campodunum* somewhere along the River Don, possibly at Doncaster itself or, as Jones suggests, a little further upstream at Conisborough.[40] The Old English translation of Bede's *Ecclesiastical History* renders *Campodunum* as *Donafelda*, implying a location around that river, and Conisborough, whose name means 'the king's stronghold', later emerged as a local central place. At Domesday it drew resources from twenty-eight dependent manors.[41] It is not on the Lincoln–York road, but on one running south-west from Doncaster along the east side of the river, at the downstream end of a wide bend in the river. If, as suggested, gaining access to the Lincoln–York Roman road was Edwin's strategic aim, a centre on or close to the road, rather than a location further west, makes sound tactical sense; Leeds would fit the bill as the later replacement, after Edwin's death, in the former Brittonic stronghold.[42] A small hoard of five gold objects from the seventh–tenth centuries found in Leeds includes a fragment of an item of cloisonné work with a date assessment of AD 600–660. This piece is consistent with the idea of Leeds as a high-status centre from some time in the seventh century.[43]

In his study of the Norman Conquest of the North, William Kapelle drew attention to a significant number of Yorkshire's Domesday manors whose dependent berewicks (small outlying holdings) and sokelands (core *vills*) are recorded in, or close to, multiples of six and twelve.[44] He notes that 'Twelve villages make a shire above the Tees; a soke centre with eleven berewicks and sokelands make a soke in Yorkshire.' Sherburn, a defining component of Elmet, and Ripon both conform to a model of large shires, having twenty-four dependent *vills* each. If, as we infer, this duodecimal system goes back into the seventh century and beyond, then King Edwin's progress through Bernicia and Elmet and his control over their vast resources would have been eased by his administrators' familiarity with such a system; alternatively, he may have introduced it as a tool of Deiran administration.

* * *

The death of his patron, King Rædwald, in about 625 allowed Edwin a freer hand in dealings with other English kingdoms. The first sign of this is a marriage to Æðelburh, daughter of King Æðelberht of Kent. This brought him into contact with Roman orthodox Christianity, for her mother, the Kentish queen Bertha, was a Christian princess, daughter of the former Merovingian king Charibert (561–567). She had brought her faith and her chaplain, Bishop Luidhard, to the then-pagan kingdom and this afforded a point of contact for Augustine and the missionaries sent by Pope Gregory in 597, who secured the conversion of the court. A generation later, her daughter found herself in much the same position as her mother, in a pagan court with her chaplain, in this case Paulinus, who had come from Rome with the second set of missionaries in 601.

The conversion of Edwin and his court, with subsequent mass baptisms of people by Paulinus, is central to Bede's account of his reign, almost to the exclusion of other themes.[45] In this narrative, Bede paints a dramatic picture of a failed assassination attempt by Eomer, an agent of Cwichelm, king of the West Saxons. Edwin is in his hall by the River Derwent with his followers about to receive the assassin in the guise of an ambassador. Eomer approaches the king and suddenly lunges with a poison-tipped sword, but the king's quick-thinking thegn, Lilla, throws himself in front of his king and takes the sword-thrust, which kills him. A general brawl ensues; Eomer is killed along with another of the king's men, Forðere.[46] Lilla's Howe, a standing stone on Fylingdales Moor, preserves the loyal thegn's memory. Bede presents this episode as a stimulus which moved a hesitant Edwin towards conversion. The trauma of the occasion tipped the pregnant queen into premature labour and, following the safe birth of her daughter Eanflæd, Edwin, in thanksgiving and as a pledge of his intent, agreed to her baptism.[47] We are left to puzzle over why the king in

Edwin: Ring-giver 616–633

York's minster: founded in the ruins of the Roman fortress by Bishop Paulinus in 627

Wessex should have sought Edwin's death. A possible explanation is that Edwin was already achieving some dominance. His lightning raid of reprisal, in which he killed Cwichelm, suggests that he had enough muscle to march his army across Mercia and back without hindrance; a dominant Northumbrian king now in alliance with Kent could have looked very threatening from a Wessex perspective. In this context the 100,000-hide assessment for Wessex in the Tribal Hidage makes political sense.

The marriage to Æðelburh and the acceptance of her Roman bishop and his strand of Christianity began to turn Edwin's political focus beyond the north- and west-facing view-point of the Bernician kings, towards the European continent and Rome; Edwin and his queen were themselves recipients of letters direct from Pope Boniface.[48] Paulinus established his bishopric in York as a stage towards the fulfilment of Pope Gregory's plan for the English church, that there should be Metropolitans, that is archbishops, in London and York, each with twelve bishops under their authority.[49] Circumstances in the seventh century, however, dictated that Canterbury became the seat of the southern archbishopric from the time of Bishop Augustine's elevation to archbishop in 601, and here it remains to this day. Once the Northumbrian conversions had been made known in Rome, Pope Honorius (625–638) wrote to King Edwin with the information that he was sending to Paulinus the pallium, a band of white wool, to confer on him the rank of archbishop.[50] In the aftermath of Edwin's death York lost this status, eventually regaining it in 735.

The *Historia Brittonum*, however, records an alternative tradition that both Rhun, son of Urien of Rheged, and Paulinus baptised Edwin.[51] Whether this story is credible or not divides the opinions of historians,[52] but it calls to mind the tradition that Edwin as a young boy had taken refuge among the Britons of Gwynedd.[53] If Bede knew the story of Rhun's involvement, he glossed over it as incompatible with his view of Paulinus as God's agent in bringing about Edwin's conversion.[54] Edwin had probably already experienced a degree of *Romanitas* while an exile in East Anglia. The contents of the ship burial discovered beneath Mound 1 at Sutton Hoo in Suffolk in 1939, if this is indeed Rædwald's tomb, speak of a king who adorned his feasting table with silverware from the Byzantine world, possibly acquired as a diplomatic gift from Frankish courts or possibly gained directly by military service in the east,[55] along with the thirty-seven gold coins in his purse; he presented himself as a Roman ruler with military insignia – helmet, shoulder-clasps and belt-buckle – derived ultimately from the late-Roman army; and as symbols of his authority, he carried the staff of a consular governor and an emperor's standard.[56] Bede caught a sense of this when he wrote of Edwin in majesty in his kingdom, with banners carried before him in battle and in peaceful progress and a standard bearer walking before him in procession.[57]

Eventually Edwin over-reached himself and the Gwynedd-Mercian alliance that had been at play against Æðelfrið now turned against him; Edwin's raiding of Anglesey may have been a motivating factor.[58] In 632 Cadwallon of Gwynedd and Penda of Mercia engaged Edwin in battle, defeated and killed him at *Hæthfelth*. If this is Hatfield Chase, as generally supposed, this is in the wetlands on the south side of the Humber, between the lower reaches of the Don and Trent in the same general area as the 616 battle at the River Idle. There is, however, a suggestion that the 632 battle site is further south at Edwinstowe, in present-day Nottinghamshire.[59] *The Life of Pope Gregory*, written at Whitby, refers to Hatfield (*Heðfeld*) as a *regio*, a small territory occupying a narrow strip of ground in the wetlands in between Elmet and Lindsey, on both sides of the River Idle and reaching south to the catchment area of the small rivers that make up the headwaters of the Idle.[60] Two of

Edwin's sons from his first marriage to Cœnburh were involved in the battle. Osfrið was killed; possibly Edwin had appointed him as a sub-king in Bernicia.[61] Eadfrið survived the battle but seems to have been taken hostage by Penda, who later murdered him. Penda's motivation is comprehensible: both, as half-Mercian princes, were eligible for the Mercian kingship. The immediate outcome of Edwin's death was that Æðelburh, now a widowed queen, fled with her children to her people in Kent accompanied by Paulinus, who had collected up church plate as an emergency cash reserve. Such church personnel and infrastructure that Paulinus had built up collapsed, with just one deacon, James, holding on somewhere near Catterick.[62] There followed a year so troubled that it was, according to Bede, later struck from the record in the system for calculating regnal years, before Oswald son of Æðelfrið arrived.

The extensive lordship model outlined in Chapter 2, hinted at in King Edwin's progression from one royal *vill* to another, has a satisfying logic to it, revealed in a Bedan aside and reconstructed across a century of scholarship from Frederick Maitland and J.E.A. Joliffe to Geoffrey Barrow and Glanville Jones and beyond. Bede says that when Paulinus was converting the Northumbrian nobility, he and the king spent thirty-six days at the royal vill of *Ad Gefrin* – Yeavering in Glendale on the north edge of the Cheviot Hills. Yeavering lies some 20 miles inland from the Bernician ancestral seat at Bamburgh.[63] Bamburgh was a very large shire as late as the sixteenth century – large enough, perhaps, to support the royal household across three or four of the coldest and wettest months of the year when travel was undesirable. Bede hints that *Catræth*, the old territory with its royal *vill* at Catterick, may have fulfilled a similar role further south; and the hinterland of Malton may have acted as a Deiran winter quarters.

The length of the royal stay at Yeavering, thirty-six days, was not arbitrary, or a function of ceremonial, but the tenth part of a year: that is to say, that the hinterland of Yeavering, which we might call *Gefrinshire*, rendered sufficient food and services to the royal *vill* there that the king's household might be maintained for the tenth part of a year: it contributed some 10 per cent of the king's annual *feorm*.[64] *Gefrinshire*, as reconstructed, consisted of a topographically logical land unit reaching up into the fertile upland pastures below Cheviot, along the drainage basin of the River Till to the boundary of Norhamshire – eventually a possession of Lindisfarne. Its dependent *vills* included Chatton at a key crossing of the River Till; Ford and Chillingham; Lowick on the Devil's Causeway; Wooler, Fenton and Branxton. To the east, *Gefrinshire* abutted Islandshire; to the south-east Bamburghshire; to the south a Cheviot foothill estate, *Bromic*.* The Roman Devil's Causeway ran north to south through *Gefrinshire*, offering rapid access for mounted troops and messengers heading south to Corbridge or north to Tweedmouth. Norhamshire, *Bromic* and Islandshire were thus peripheral to core Bernician territories and could, later, be gifted to the nascent Northumbrian church without harm to the royal *feorm*. But they nevertheless belonged firmly within a logical scheme of extensive territorial lordship. Even a long-exiled prince like Oswald, Edwin's successor, knew what lands were his to give away or to keep: part of the store of customary tribal knowledge held by men who had known Bernicia in the days when Oswald's father, Æðelfrið, was the greatest warlord in the North.

* * *

It has long been known that *Ad Gefrin*, Edwin's *villa regia*, is Yeavering, on the northern edge of the Cheviot Hills, where a prehistoric hillfort crowns the summit of Yeavering Bell; and in 1949 an aerial survey revealed the precise location and the features of the complex as cropmarks on a raised terrace above the river and at the foot of the Bell. Then in one of the classic excavations of British archaeology between 1953 and 1962, Brian Hope-Taylor revealed the main features of the site, establishing it as the definitive reference for a site of early English kingship.[65]

Yeavering's great halls were the grandest of grand Northumbrian designs: reconstructed Viking Age hall at Fyrkat, Jutland, Denmark

* The early form of Breamish – that is, a river name in origin, used here as a territorial identifier.

At its heart is the sequence of four large rectangular hall-type buildings, each replacing its predecessor in the same position, with massive wall timbers and floor areas of more than 250m². As in almost all buildings known from this period, the upper timber structures have not survived, and the floor levels and ground surfaces of the day have been lost to erosion and the effects of plough cultivation. The surviving evidence is thus the austere imprint of the foundations that the builders had dug into the ground and in which they set their timbers. Interpretations of the structures depend on extrapolating from the evidence in the foundations; understandings of how the buildings were used depend on these extrapolations.

In the first two halls, most of the interior was a single open space suitable for a large gathering of people (see Map 7 on page 80), with a withdrawing chamber partitioned off at one end in the first hall (A2) and at both ends in its successor (A4). Both had four doors, set midway along the side walls and the end walls. These buildings, immediately on their discovery, attracted attention as actual examples of the sort of feasting hall described in the poem *Beowulf*.[66] The third and fourth halls, A3(a) and A3(b), show a change in architectural form whereby, in each case, the main rectangular space was compartmentalised into three almost-equal divisions, with only two exterior doors, again set midway along the long sides. At each end stood a rectangular annex, accessible only from within the building. These features imply a change in the use of the building and in the way in which the king and queen presented themselves: no longer the large open hall, but now smaller spaces with access more controlled, offering the precious regal commodity of privacy.[67] In the cases of A4, A3(a) and A3(b) a smaller building (A1) was associated with the halls at the opposite end of a fenced compound, perhaps as a more private domestic space. North and west of this central complex are other buildings, similar in form and structure with floor areas in the range of 70m² to 110m², small in comparison with the main buildings but nevertheless larger than most of the buildings known from this period.

West of the central complex is a feature still unique in the archaeology of this period, a wedge-shaped structure built from nine construction trenches in concentric arcs. This is a tiered seating area, an outdoor auditorium or theatre, capable of holding some 320 people, on the excavator's estimate.[68] At the apex of the wedge a set of postholes supported a dais from which a speaker or performer could address the seated audience; Hope-Taylor suggests there was a throne here. Behind the dais is a single large standing post. Postholes mark the positions of screens that form a semi-enclosed space wrapping around behind the dais and post and at the sides towards the

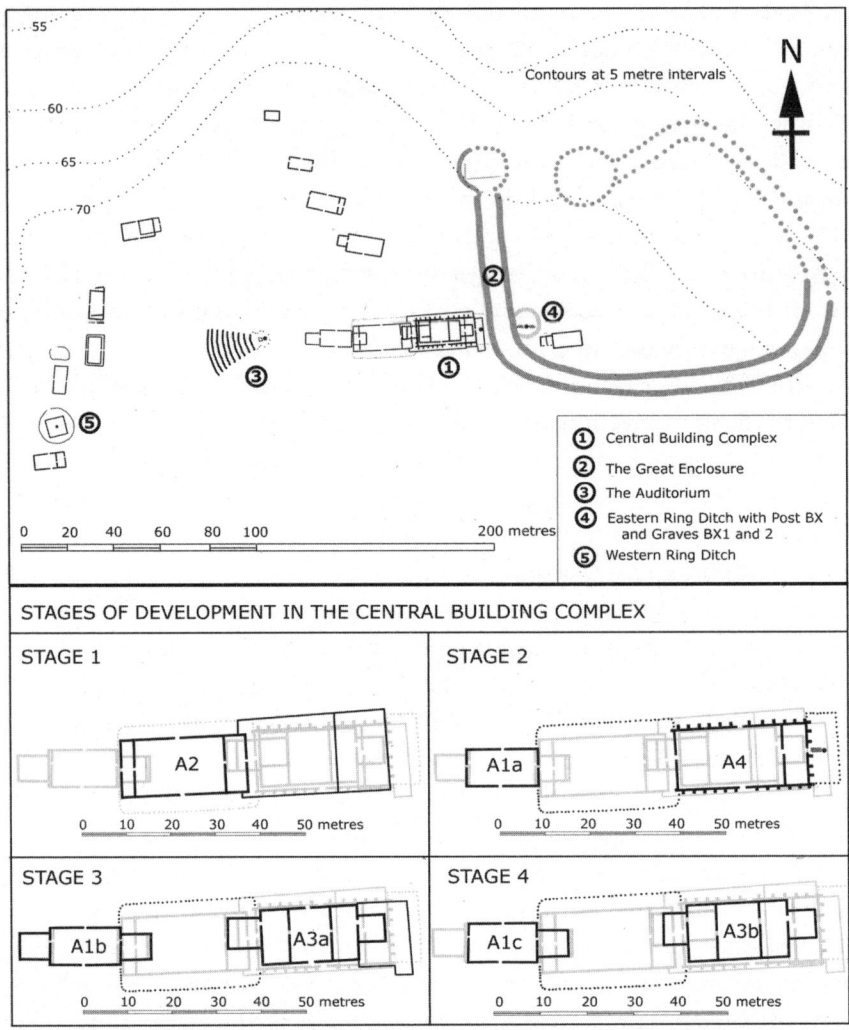

Map 7 The royal township at Yeavering, first identified from the air and confirmed as Bede's *Ad Gefrin* by Brian Hope-Taylor's excavations

seating. These screens would allow for processional entry and ceremonial approach to the dais, and also for movement of performers within the space, while the protagonist occupied a fixed position on the dais. Hope-Taylor thought this structure was modelled on a theatre of the Roman world: the wedge is a segment of the Roman semi-circle. Extending this idea, Paul Barnwell understands the single post behind the dais as a *staffolus*,[69] drawing on Frankish models, where the king's justice was proclaimed. In such a setting as this, the king could present himself to a much larger set of people than in the hall where he feasted his retainers. On his arrival at *Ad Gefrin*, the king might make formal procession to the auditorium and the *staffolus* to make his proclamations in much the same way that a Roman provincial governor might have processed into the theatre on his arrival into a town.

Yeavering was also a site of burials, with two sets, west and east of the main halls. Bone preservation in the acidic soils was minimal, but careful excavation revealed the impressions of skeletons as shadow features. On each side, a monument from the prehistoric past provided a focus for burials of the post-Roman period, suggesting to Hope-Taylor that there was ritual continuity in burial from the Bronze Age onwards. On the west side was a circle of standing stones (Western Ring Ditch) in which a cremation burial had been laid beneath a stone at the centre. A new cemetery developed from this with graves set out first in a radial arrangement from the central stone and within the circle. On the east side was a small ring ditch and barrow mound (Eastern Ring Ditch). Here a post was erected in the centre of the mound (Post BX); on each side of the post, west and east, a grave was dug into the mound on a radial alignment (Graves BX1 and 2). The alignment pointed directly to another post (Post AX) 20 metres further west and thence along the main axis of Hall A4. At the threshold of the east end door of A4, between Post AX and the door, was Grave AX[70] in which an individual was buried, legs flexed and holding an item formed of a long wooden staff with metal fittings. The excavator pondered its significance;[71] a ceremonial staff of some sort seems possible.

The positioning of these graves extending from the east ring ditch, with alignment along the main axis of Hall A4 and the very special positioning of the threshold burial, suggests that in some way the integration of hall-building and burials was fundamental to the planning of the whole complex. Graves on the east side laid-out rows – 'string graves', in the excavator's terminology – are thought to represent a war cemetery and, in the final stages of use of the site, a much more extensive community cemetery developed on the east side. Associated with these burials is a rectangular timber building with annex, which the excavator understood as a Christian church.

The final feature in the suite making up this complex is the one known as the Great Enclosure. This is a palisaded compound positioned at the edge of the terrace above the river which, on Hope-Taylor's analysis, went through several stages of development culminating in a massive double palisade with bracing and elaborate entrance terminals enclosing some 1.6ha. It is, in its first stage of development, the first post-Roman feature on the site, drawing inspiration for its form on a regional tradition of palisaded enclosures that reaches back into the pre-Roman Iron Age.[72] Its primary purpose, however, was not military but public and communal for seasonal musterings of cattle and periodic markets and festivals.[73]

Hope-Taylor understood Yeavering as a place of culture contact, where a new élite engaged with a native population and a 'vigorous hybrid culture' emerged, with the Great Enclosure as the key to understanding why this became a site of kingship.[74] In certain respects, his thinking has been called into question: on continuity of burial; on an evolution of building technique from indigenous British traditions; and on the primacy of the Great Enclosure.[75] And yet his underlying idea that here kings of the seventh century engaged with an ancestral landscape is still secure. The re-use of prehistoric burial monuments can be read not as continuity, in the way Hope-Taylor thought, but as the *invention* of tradition to harness the power of ancestry, just as royal lineages developed genealogies to show descent from the god Woden.[76] The feasting-halls and the open-air auditorium at the foot of the hill carry forward the functions of assembly and governance once served by the tribal hillfort on the top.[77] Brittonic place-names indicate what Mark Wood called 'linguistic domination' within the shire of Yeavering.[78] Hope-Taylor's analysis of Yeavering within a Forth–Tyne regional context receives support from Sam Lucy's review of the burials and her conclusion that they fit more comfortably into a northern British context than to a southerly Anglo-Saxon one.[79]

The immediate landscape context for the royal *vill* at Yeavering is highly evocative: at the foot of its now grassy whaleback the River Glen, in which Paulinus baptised Edwin's *comites* and their followers, runs east towards the River Till and its confluence with the Tweed. Behind it, the sacred massif of Yeavering Bell with its great Iron Age enclosure looks down with ancestral oversight; to the west and immediate north sensuous mammiform hills are topped with Bronze Age burial mounds. Today's visitor will see, in summer, the outlines of Edwin's halls marked out by cut grass and, in the last few years, it has been possible to see some of Hope-Taylor's trenches, the posthole outlines of his buildings, thrillingly exposed in excavations by Sarah Semple and Roger Miket – testing, often revalidating, Hope-Taylor's evidence.

In this regional sense, Yeavering is one of a number of centres associated with Bernician kingship of the seventh and eighth centuries along with Dunbar, Coldingham, Bamburgh and Yeavering's successor site of Milfield, in which the place-name is derived from a name in the Brittonic language: *Gevr-vrinn, *Dynbær*, *Cær Colud, *Din Guaire* (before King Æðelfrið re-named the place in honour of his wife, Bebba), *Mælmin*; the *dyn-* and *cær-* elements refer to fortified central places. Linguistic, archaeological and historical strands of evidence all point to the idea that Bernician kings adopted places, including fortified sites, which were already focuses of leadership in the precursor states.[80] This analysis allows for an understanding of Yeavering as the centre of a territory which Æðelfrið brought into the Bernician sphere of influence in much the same way that Edwin expanded Deiran power into Elmet.

Bede recorded that after the time of Edwin the Northumbrian kings abandoned Yeavering and built another centre at *Mælmin*, modern-day Milfield, 3.5km to the north-east.[81] If it is correct to take this at face value, it seems to be a move to relocate in the wider space of the Milfield Basin, around the confluence of the Rivers Glen and Till where a wide valley floor with gravel terraces has long been a favoured area for settlement and ceremonial as far back as the Neolithic era.[82] *Mælmin* was also discovered in air survey. Tim Gates's transcription of the cropmarks[83] shows a central complex of buildings within fenced compounds and surrounding this a massive double-palisaded enclosure of some 12ha. At its south-eastern edge, and on the terrace edge above the River Till, an oval palisade encloses some 0.5ha. North of the whole complex, scattered about are the small sub-rectangular outlines of the pits dug into the ground for *Grubenhäuser*.

In Yeavering and Milfield we recognise the features that characterise a *villa regia*, the shire centre to which the king processed on his circuit and where renders were collected for his periodic consumption. With this observation, we can look 16km west to another set of cropmarks that shares in these features at Sprouston, on the south-east side of the River Tweed,* almost opposite the town of Kelso.[84] Towards the centre of the complex are the footprints of two large rectangular buildings – one appears to have been re-built – each with an annex at both ends, closely comparable to Yeavering A3(a) and A3(b) and the central building at Milfield. Ian Smith, who transcribed and analysed the cropmarks, recognised three phases of development (see the plan on page 84).[85] The first refers to the prehistoric past of the Neolithic era. A broad ditch dug in segments describes an arc hard against the river edge, and south of this is a building. Phase 2, attributed to the Romano-British or early historic period, has two lines of palisades forming a small oval enclosure, with land boundaries extending from its edges. The third phase has the annexed buildings already mentioned and scattered around them others

---

* The river here flows from south-west to north-east.

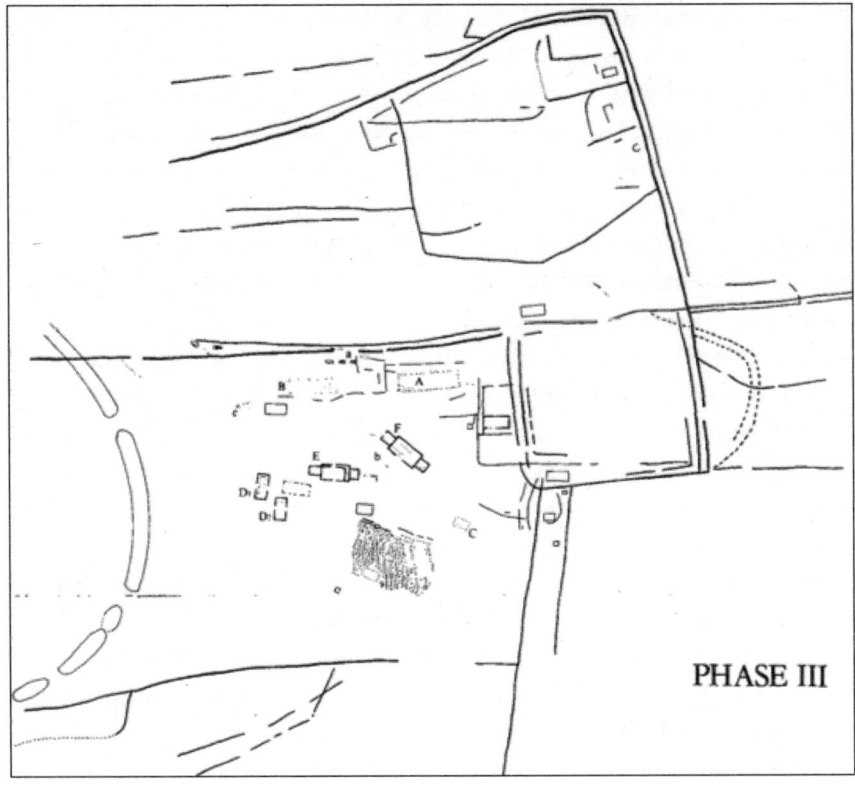

Map 8 Sprouston, on the south bank of the River Tweed, identified from air photographs. Ian Smith's plan of the layout

with wall trenches and individual postholes. East of the building complex is a double-palisade enclosure of much the same size as Yeavering's Great Enclosure. South of the buildings is a cemetery with at least 380 graves, tightly packed in rows laid out with reference to a rectangular building close to the south-west corner of the group. Without excavation it is not possible to define a chronology for this phase of activity, but the comparisons with Yeavering and Milfield argue strongly for a seventh-century date, the status of *villa regia* and another centre on the king's itinerary in the extended Bernician sphere of interest.* The shire territory associated with this centre may well be bounded by the Tweed on the north-east side, with Lindisfarne's landholdings *ultra Tweoda*, 'beyond Tweed', on the other side of the river, and the same monastery's Carham estate to the north-east.

* See Chapter 10 for a suggested historical context for Sprouston.

As a centre of kingship in the seventh century, Yeavering, and then its successor Milfield, came within the itinerary of the king's circuit as the central place in a shire territory of some 230km², operating within the systems of lordship and render described in Chapter 2.[86] But archaeologists of Early Medieval Bernicia are frustrated in their efforts to frame the social geography to go with Bede's intimate account of its politics by what seems an inexplicable paucity of settlement evidence: the residencies of Edwin's or Oswald's *comites*, or the lower ranks of thegns whose military service and renders supported these great overlords. We know much more about the geography of early monasteries than we do about their secular élite counterparts. Until relatively recently only one settlement contemporary with the ruling dynasty of the Idings had been both identified and excavated: Thirlings, in the Milfield Basin, identified through air photography and excavated between 1973 and 1981 by Roger Miket and Colm O'Brien.[87]

This is a flattish, low-lying landscape of light, tractable glacial soils lying in a triangle between the Rivers Glen and Till and densely utilised from the Neolithic period onwards for settlement and ceremonial. Some time in the sixth century a group of rectangular buildings was constructed here, forming a settlement unenclosed by major boundaries within an hour's walk of Yeavering. The larger, more apparently formal buildings – hall-type dwellings of a form familiar from right across central and southern Britain – were constructed on an east–west alignment using timber posts in-the-round, set in holes within continuous trenches. Two central doorways opposed each other, and gaps between posts, set about a yard apart, were infilled with vertically set planks. Walls appear to have been given extra support, or perhaps a broad covered eave, by external posts. Two of the buildings, A and P, were enclosed within stoutly fenced yards (see Map 9 on page 87). Building A seems to have been the focal household of the settlement, within a rectangular enclosure with an auxiliary building and compound P attached to it; it has been reconstructed as the 'hall' at Jarrow Hall, the open-air museum on the banks of the Tyne close to Bede's monastery church. It is one of five buildings of very similar dimensions, apparently conceived on a double-square plan. One larger structure, Building C, had been provided with an annexe (perhaps a stairwell) at its east end and may have functioned as a storage barn with an upper storey; even so, it is dwarfed by the great halls at Yeavering.

A series of apparently ancillary buildings, laid out at right angles to the 'halls' and constructed using thick squared offset planks, complete the major structures, with many other agricultural or craft structures that may be inferred from various clusters of postholes and stake-holes across the site. Further north, beyond the excavated areas, lies a scatter of sunken-feature buildings. Analysis of the ground plan suggests that the settlement as excavated comprises four main households, with household A-P holding the highest status. Within a shire hierarchy this looks like a second-order settlement under a minor lord – Bede might have called him a *comes* – with dependants beneath him, to whose residence food renders from a *vill* or *vills* were brought for consumption. If several generations of the same family lived here, they may have owed successive military services and render to Æðelfrið, then Edwin, then Oswald.[88]

Two other sites have more recently emerged during 'rescue' excavations in advance of gravel extraction in the Milfield Basin: at Lanton Quarry and Cheviot Quarry to the north and west of Thirlings. Three rectangular post-built 'halls' dating from the late fifth or early sixth century, severely truncated by later land-use practices, were excavated at Cheviot Quarry in the early 2000s.[89] Excavations at Lanton Quarry have not yet been fully published, but interim reports show a site that may be contemporary with the apogee of the township at Yeavering and which may yield evidence of its most obvious missing component: craftspeople, at the lower end of the social hierarchy.[90] Eight sunken-featured buildings or *Grubenhäuser* were constructed and used as workshops producing textiles, ground cereals, perhaps glass-making. The collection of Early Medieval pottery sherds, more than sixty of them, may seem modest – but it is very large by Bernician standards. Elsewhere, *Grubenhäuser* are rarely encountered in Bernicia – the first to be recognised was identified from a cropmark at New Bewick in the Upper Till Valley.[91] Excavation here in 1986 confirmed Tim Gates's impression that sunken-featured buildings could be detected from air survey of cropmarks,[92] and since then he reports another seven locations in which they have been observed.[93] It is difficult to know whether this concentration is unusual or to what extent there is a recovery bias against areas less conducive to cropmark formation.

King Edwin may have invested hugely in the palace complex at Yeavering but his dynastic corelands lay in Deira, from York on the River Ouse, north and east along the River Derwent, around the former Roman fort at *Derventio* (Malton) into the Vale of Pickering, and on the wide-open pastures of the high Wolds. Where was Deira's Yeavering? Despite much speculation, the site of Edwin's hall by the River Derwent, the scene of Bede's dramatic Easter assassination story,[94] is not yet positively identified. The former fort at Malton is a likely location for one of the royal centres of a Deiran

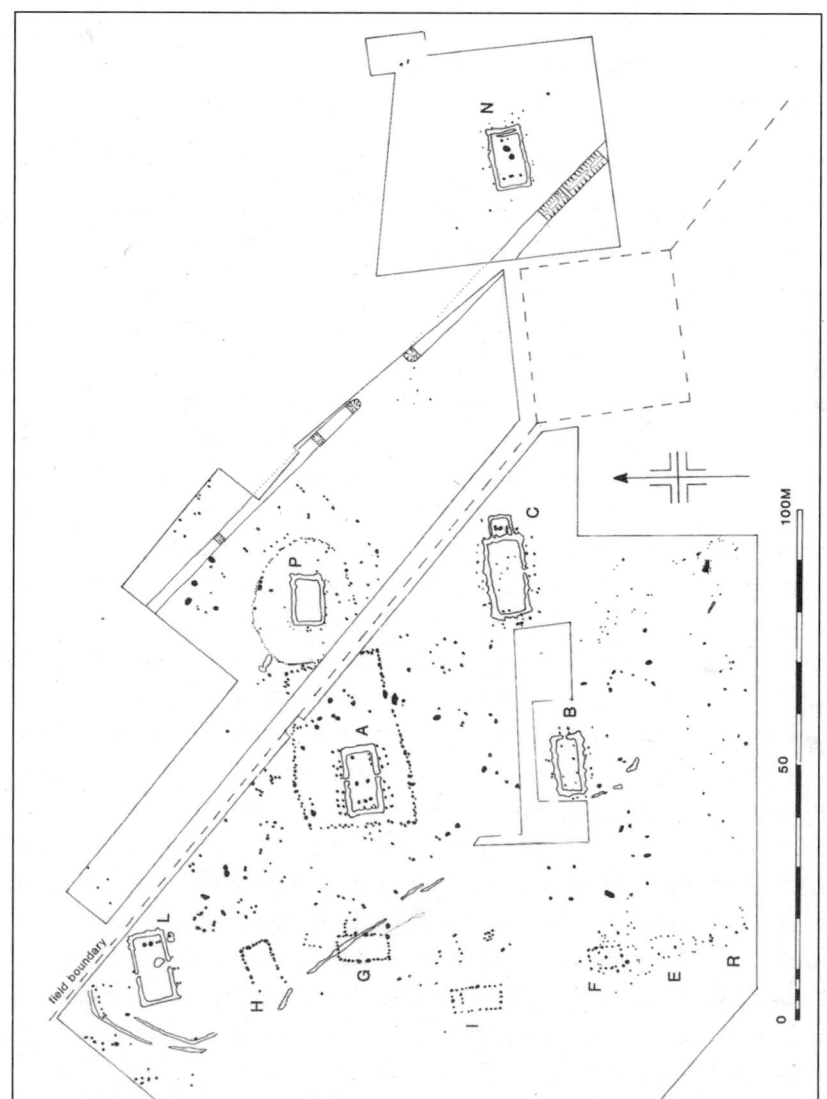

Map 9 The excavated settlement of a *comes* at Thirlings, in the Milfield Plain, Northumberland

circuit around the Wolds, along with Beverley, later the site of a monastery, and Driffield, the probable royal *vill* where King Aldfrið died in 705. Malton has a pivotal location at the mouth of Ryedale and the Vale of Pickering, the navigable Derwent giving access to the Humber via the River Ouse, and with a connecting road along the south side of the Vale of Pickering to putative beach markets on the coast.*

An upland, perhaps summer, hall on a Wolds circuit might be identified as the large timber hall set inside a Bronze Age ringwork on Paddock Hill, 2km west of the small village of Thwing. The site overlooks the valley of the Gypsy Race from the north, a few miles north of Driffield and close to a concentration of Roman villa sites in the central Wolds. Without proper publication, the detail is sparse; but occupation had certainly begun here by 700 and continued into the ninth century, judging by the presence of diagnostic *styca* coins. Finds included metalwork, ceramics, lava quernstones – a marker for trade with Continental Europe – and animal bone. A contemporary cemetery containing at least 130 burials was also excavated outside the ring work and the site's excavator, Terry Manby, interpreted the Early Medieval phase as a royal estate centre.[95] Like Yeavering, it may only have been occupied for short periods during the year.

An eighteenth-century chance discovery of the partial remains of an opulent Roman villa site at Hovingham has drawn Dominic Powlesland's attention to the site, which has yielded a number of Anglian sculptures, including crosses (see Chapter 5). The place-name might derive from an Anglian tribal name, the *Hofingas*; or from *hof*, a small hill. But Victor Watts has also raised the possibility that it derives from Old English *hof* meaning an enclosure, a temple or house – with the implication of a royal centre.[96] Hovingham lies 11km west of Malton along a Roman road that hugs the north-facing edge of the Howardian Hills overlooking Ryedale – a perfectly suitable site for an Early Medieval royal *vill* on a circuit that extended into Ryedale, where later church territories (discussed in Chapter 5) perhaps map the itinerary.

In any case the hinterland of Malton was well-populated and productive throughout the seventh and eighth centuries, as the epic campaign of

---

* Represented by the place-name element 'Wyke' – a specialist or dependent farm or trading place. Watts 2004. West Heslerton's excavator Dominic Powlesland agrees that these are probable beach market sites, and the following discussion owes much to conversations with him, for which we are most grateful.

excavation and survey carried out in the 1980s and 1990s in and around West Heslerton has shown. The prehistoric and Anglian cemetery here has already been discussed (see Chapter 1). From the fifth century, a densely occupied settlement covering some 13ha grew up below the late Roman shrine that had grown up around a spring flowing north into the Vale of Pickering from the Wold edge.

In contrast to the sprawling, shifting Early Saxon settlement excavated at Mucking on the Thames estuary, West Heslerton was carefully zoned into domestic, craft-and-industrial, and livestock management areas (see Map 10 on page 90). Coin evidence, material culture and radiocarbon dates show that the settlement, expanding from the shrine, saw an economic heyday in the eighth century and continued well into the ninth: spanning the entire period covered by this book, while the cemetery went out of use in the seventh century. A later cemetery has so far evaded detection. Material and structural evidence for butchery, metalworking, textile production and grain malting was concentrated in the north-west area of the site where more than 100 *Grubenhäuser* were excavated. Along with a probable horizontal turbine water mill, these are indicative of a productive community with access to a suite of key resources, from high Wolds summer grazing to scarp woodland, arable fields and water meadows, while the River Derwent was almost certainly navigable to this point. West Heslerton's inhabitants, or their lords, benefited from coastal and riverine access to overseas markets, from where high-quality imports such as Niedermendig lava querns and glass drinking vessels were acquired. The distinct functional zoning of the site, increasingly also recognised in sites further south from the late seventh century onwards, speaks of productive surplus rather than mere subsistence. With final publication a more refined chronology for the site will allow archaeologists to nuance its development and to portray with increasing confidence the communities and economy that underpinned Northumbrian kingship from the seventh century onwards.

King Edwin's overlordship of much of central Britain was predicated on powerful, existing institutions enabling him to draw wealth from, and administer, vast tracts of land through a well-established customary system of extensive territorial lordship. His late, almost reluctant conversion to Christianity prevented him from exploiting the full benefits of the new, rational form of kingship exploited by his successors. But he bequeathed to them an almost unshakeable idea of Northumbrian supremacy, the political capital of which they spent with great energy and imagination.

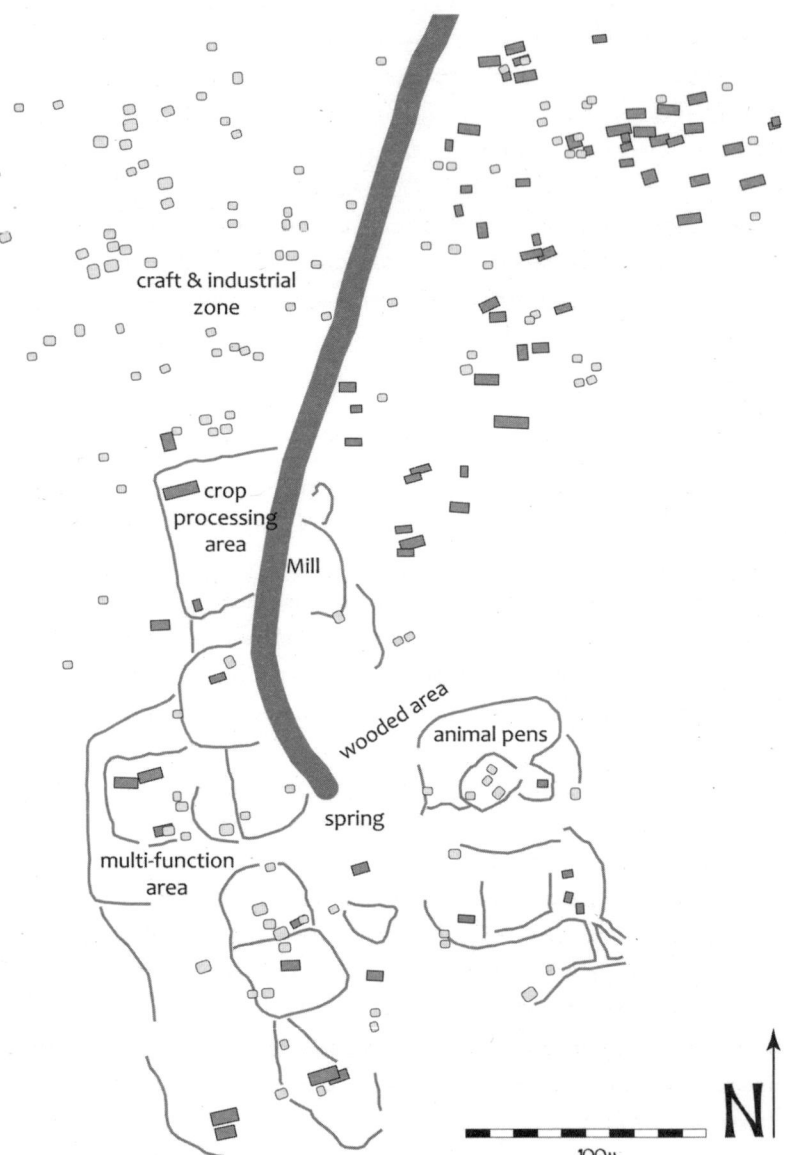

Map 10 West Heslerton, East Yorkshire: the most thoroughly excavated Northumbrian settlement

4

OSWALD: HEAVEN'S FIELD 633–642

Dál Riata, Colm Cille and Iona – Heavenfield and Lindisfarne – The Bernician shires – Thegn and ceorl – Oswald, Aidan, Bede – Oswald's Tree – Bede's providential kingship

If King Edwin fashioned his kingship as a hybrid between tribal and Roman models, his nephew and successor Oswald, son of Æðelfrið, took inspiration from the traditions and heroic myths of the Gaels. From the age of twelve to twenty-nine, Oswald was exiled in Gaelic-speaking Dál Riata along with his mother, Acha, and his younger brothers and sisters. Dál Riatan kings like Eochaid Buide (c.608–629), under whose lordship and protection Acha and her sons spent some dozen years, were kings of Argyll, Kintyre and the Inner Hebrides; but they also interested themselves in the politics and culture of the north of Ireland. Dál Riatan protégés, including exiled princes like Oswald and his younger brother Oswiu, fought in their wars there.

The cultural corelands of three Dál Riatan *cenéla* or kindreds – the Cenél nGabráin in *Corcu Réti* (Kintyre), Cowal, Bute and Arran; the Cenél nÓengussa on Jura and Islay and the Cenél Loairn in northern Argyll and Mull – are identified in a tenth-century document, the *Senchus Fer nAlban*, which reveals something of the ancient mustering arrangements of their amphibious warbands.[1] Their seat lay at one of the rocky fortresses, Dunadd in Kilmartin Glen or Dunollie on the rugged coast of Argyll. Excavations at Dunadd have revealed a wealth of artefactual material that includes glass, pottery and other exotica from as far away as Continental Europe.[2] The west coast of Scotland and Inner Hebrides were connected, as much as they were isolated, by the sea. Dunadd, like Whithorn, the Isles of Scilly, Ireland's east coast, Man and the South-west peninsula of England, was known to traders and ecclesiastics throughout the Irish Sea, on the Continent and in the Mediterranean for its mineral wealth and trading opportunities.[3]

In the later sixth century Dál Riatan kings had patronised a celebrated holy man, St Columba – Colm Cille, in Irish – himself an exile from political rivalries between the Cenél Conaill of Donegal, among whom he was eligible for the kingship, and their regional rivals. Colm Cille founded a monastic settlement on Iona, off the south-west corner of the island of Mull, in the 560s and over the next three decades established a *paruchia* of daughter houses scattered throughout the Western Isles.[4] He anointed Dál Riatan kings; approved their heirs and brokered political alliances between them and their sometime Irish allies and enemies.

The monastery on Iona, the subject of many campaigns of piecemeal excavation over the years, was enclosed by a rectangular *vallum*, a ditch and bank that demarcated the spiritual from the profane, on the sheltered east side of the island overlooking the Sound of Iona and 'mainland' Mull. A 'great house' provided for the community to gather en masse. A cemetery, Relig Odhran, was the burial site for later Scottish kings and at least one Northumbrian king. Iona became, and remained throughout the seventh century, a wellspring of ecclesiastical power, sculptural excellence, spiritual inspiration and intellectual endeavour. A lost Iona Chronicle underpinned much of the chronology of contemporary Ireland and northern Britain; its abbots' continued interest in Northumbrian affairs ensured lively, if intermittent, contact between their churches. The *Vita Colombae* was written by one of his successors as abbot of Iona to record episodes, particularly miracles, from his life.[5] It was from the *Vita* and from the visit of its author, Adomnán (628–704), to the Northumbrian court in the days of King Aldfrið (685–704), that Bede learned much about Iona and its role in converting the Northumbrian princes, Oswald and Oswiu, to Christianity.

King Edwin had been introduced to the idea of an intellectually rational form of kingship by Paulinus and in letters written to him and his queen by Pope Boniface, to which Bede had access through his contacts in Canterbury.[6] The model was Roman and imperial, literate and monumental, underpinned by the idea that an everlasting place by God's side was on offer to good kings who embraced the eternal, universal and exclusive church – at least through Bede's idealised lens. But Ireland and its churches had never been so directly influenced by Rome or its popes. In the Gaelic model that informed a new generation of Christian Northumbrian kings, there is a sense of power held at arm's length; of kings and holy men mutually supportive; mutually threatening; their relations always contingent. Its social contract was forged by the imaginative and moral power of the desert fathers, such as St Anthony, under dynamic tension with the sacral, tribal potency of Ireland's warlike kings. Even so, the model was underpinned by arrangements for the tenure of land.

Despite evidence that he both wielded political power and ruled over substantial island territories, Colm Cille's role as a territorial lord has received little attention.[7] Hierarchical lordship was a cornerstone of Irish and British society in the first millennium. By virtue of their loyalty and service to a king, secular lords held land for a life interest – his or theirs. That is to say, they were given the right to exact taxes in kind – food, materials and labour, including military service – from those who lived on a defined parcel of land. Within that territory lords maintained a household of free and unfree dependants, fostering networks of relations with their kin and other allies. The contract relied on a two-way system of patronage that exchanged the labour and oath-sworn loyalty of its tenants for protection and gift-giving, in a spirit of unbreakable reciprocity.

Lordship was essentially competitive, so the wealthier and more powerful lords also maintained a warband, a sort of fictive family of companions – in Latin *comites*; in Old Irish, *céilithe* – who rode with them on cattle raids, feasted and drank with them in their halls and swore loyalty to them unto death – the society recalled in the Airgíalla Charter poem.[8] The *comitatus* was fed and maintained from the renders of the lord's estate.[9] Its ranks were drawn from the same dependent client families, reinforcing inalienable bonds of hospitality, debt and gift. The more successful a lord, the more followers he attracted, the more land he might rule over, the more generous he might be – and a lord's generosity was highly valued.

That model also applied to monastic entrepreneurs. As early as the third century AD, pioneers of the monastic movement in the Holy Land, some of them former soldiers in the imperial army, had come to see themselves as *milites Christi*, soldiers of Christ; and their followers were, rather like the secular *comites*, soldierly comrades.[10] As their communities grew through endowment by sympathetic patrons and wealthy followers, so the saintly leaders of these communities began to behave, sometimes reluctantly, like territorial lords. Instead of martial glory, they won an eternal place in heaven by virtue of their miracles, humility and wisdom and through the sound management of their resources. The more 'successful' of them spawned imitations which, like their secular counterparts, owed loyalty to the founder's house. In Ireland, monastic patronage had long been dominated by two great cult figures: Patrick, the fifth-century British bishop and supposed founder of religious houses; and Brigid of Kildare, whose reputation as a saint and monastic entrepreneur ensures her rank alongside Patrick and Colm Cille in Irish religious history.[11]

When the earliest Irish abbots and abbesses were given lands on which to found religious communities, they became a type of specialised lord, gathering the needs of their holy *comitatus* from the lands over which they had been given rights; maintaining their fictive family of priests, monks and lay supporters and, ideally, winning for their communities an enviable reputation for discipline, humility, hospitality and good works. Like secular lords, spiritual masters attracted followers, usually from among their own extended kin, bound into the community by ties of mutual loyalty and their shared veneration of the great holy man or woman.

Colm Cille, who died in 593, four years before St Augustine's mission arrived in Kent, was first granted the island of Iona as his *territorium* by Conall mac Comgaill (c.558–574), king of Dál Riata.[12] That patronage continued under Conall's powerful successor, Áedán mac Gabráin (574–609), whom Colm Cille anointed and whose heirs he endorsed in a solemn prophecy.[13] Dál Riatan kings claimed rights over peoples on both sides of the North Channel, involving themselves with Irish kings sometimes as allies, often as antagonists. Colm Cille's cousin, Áed mac Ainmirech (d. 598), was a contemporary ruler of the Northern Úi Néill in what is now County Donegal; it was natural, therefore, that Colm Cille should act as a broker between the two kingdoms.* In return, he seems to have been granted lordship over other lands on which to found subordinate religious houses, expanding his territorial holdings and his *paruchia* just like any secular lord. His hagiographer Adomnán gives little detail on these other houses, but he certainly founded a monastery at Durrow in County Laois and at least two daughter houses of Iona were founded on islands in the Inner Hebrides: at *Mag Luinge* on Tiree and on the as yet unidentified *Hinba* – perhaps Canna or Colonsay. The Columban scholar Brian Lacey has shown that, despite strong traditions associating it with Colm Cille, the monastery at Derry was founded by a holy man called Fiachra. But he also suggests that a number of other early monastic sites – in Donegal at Gleann Cholm Cille, in the Hebrides, on Skye and on the western Scottish mainland – may have been founded by Colm Cille or his immediate followers, echoing a secular model of extensive lordship.[14]

What can we say about how Colm Cille acted as a territorial lord? Adomnán tells us that he was able to gather materials such as timber from a

---

* At the so-called Convention of Druim Ceatt (near modern Limavady) in 575.

hinterland that was larger than Iona – including parts of the Isle of Mull and mainland Ardnamurchan. He appointed abbots, probably from among his own people, to run his other monasteries. He intervened in and judged disputes; was able to seek protection for a fellow monk from a king in Orkney. In the Great House within the *vallum* on Iona he entertained both his holy companions and large numbers of visitors – his, as it were, religious clients.

In one very significant way, however, Colm Cille's lordship differed from that of his secular peers. Iona's community held its lands in perpetuity, passed down through a line of abbots who were, by and large, drawn from Colm Cille's own kin. They were thus able to invest in such cultural marvels as a scriptorium, a sculpture workshop and a mill. They seem also to have experimented with various strains of crops to improve their yield.[15] Such capital investment gave them a substantial advantage over potential religious and secular rivals and protected them, by and large, from predatory kings. They were to an extent insulated from the high stakes of tribal politics: the monastic institution survived the death of a king – up until the late eighth century when Scandinavian raiders began their predations. Abbots set themselves up as dispassionate mediators; as peace-brokers; in time Early Medieval kings would see them as something like civil servants, keeping the machinery of society functioning through chaotic times. The written word – the preserve of clerics – came to stand for unchallengeable legal truth.

It is evident from Adomnán's *Vita Colombae* that Prince Oswald enjoyed a close relationship with Iona's fifth abbot, Ségéne (623–652). His conversion to Christendom in the monastery of Iona was genuine and he is said to have related to the abbot, in person, the vision with which his triumphant return to claim the Northumbrian kingship was marked in the year 634.[16] In Adomnán's account the site of that vision is not named and there is no mention of the cross that is so central to the Bedan version; but St Columba's appearance in the vision which Oswald experienced the previous night was the ætheling's inspiration for victory. Subsequent events show that the Iona community and the court of the Dál Riatan kings saw Oswald as a protégé worthy of their investment.

By the universal rules of lordship and hospitality, Oswald and his brothers owed King Domnall Brecc (629–642) their support as his allies in Northumbria, providing a powerful counter to the ambitions of the British kings of Strathclyde at Dumbarton. Equally, Iona ensured that it had a stake in the fortunes of these converts: they would, if successful in reclaiming their father Æðelfrið's patrimony, found a new Iona in the North-east.

A late Welsh source hints that Ionan and Dál Riatan backing for Oswald's military campaign was more than spiritual. One of the triads in the collection called the Red Book of Hergest, in lamenting the death of Cadwallon at Oswald's hands, refers to the 'plotting of strangers and iniquitous monks', a reference, it would seem, to armed contingents, some of them monks, supporting Oswald's own warband – fellow exiles from Bernicia battle-hardened by their martial training in Ireland.[17]

The arrival of Oswald, son of Æðelfrið, marks the restoration of the kingdom to the Iding dynasty of Bernicia. Cadwallon had ravaged the kingdom during a year of anarchy, looting and burning royal estates. Northumbrian overlordship collapsed. Deiran rule devolved first to Edwin's son Eadfrið, who sued for peace but was later murdered by King Penda, perhaps in collusion with Oswald;[18] then to Edwin's cousin Osric who, according to Bede, apostatised, likely under pressure from a compromised nobility unimpressed by the fruits of Edwin's conversion.[19] Osric was able to raise an army sufficient to besiege Cadwallon in an unnamed fortified town (*oppido municipio*) which might mean York but was, perhaps, more likely the ancient Brigantian *civitas* capital at Aldborough: *Isurium Brigantium*, where the Roman road running along the east edge of the Pennines crosses the River Ure.[20] In the spring of 633 Cadwallon's forces broke the siege and destroyed Osric's army, killing him and effectively ending the royal line of the Deiran kings descended from Ælle.

In Bernicia, Æðelfrið's eldest son, Eanfrið, was chosen as king. Almost nothing is known of him, but the fact that he was the father of Talorcan, a later king of the Picts, has suggested to historians that he may have been the son of Æðelfrið's British wife, Bebba, and that he had been in exile among the Picts. At any rate he returned to Bernicia and, according to Bede, came to Cadwallon to make peace, 'unadvisedly' accompanied only by twelve chosen thegns. Cadwallon 'destroyed' him.[21] Given subsequent events the location of this Bernician catastrophe may be tentatively identified with the former Roman town of *Coria* – Corbridge, where Dere Street crosses the River Tyne.

Enter Oswald, the exile who, on receiving news that his half-brother had been killed, returned to Bernicia from Dál Riata with a small army to try his luck against Cadwallon. In Adomnán's account, Colm Cille appeared to Oswald as in a vision, adjuring him to be strong and to act manfully; to go out in the night from the camp with his army and fight; that God had granted him victory against Cadwallon, the slayer of Edwin and pillager of Northumbria. Here, Colm Cille is echoing God's words to Joshua, deliberately identifying Oswald with the assistant of Moses who led the Israelites back into the land of Canaan. 'Hearing these words the king awoke, and described his vision to the assembled council. All were strengthened by this, and the whole people promised that after their return from battle they would accept the faith and receive baptism.'[22]

Bede painted a set-piece scene in which Oswald set up a cross and invoked God's help in his just cause at the place whose very name *Caelestis Campus* (Heavenfield) announced its divine significance.[23] Visitors to the post-Medieval church here will note that it stands on the edge of a north-facing scarp with magnificent views as far as the modern Anglo-Scottish border some 50 miles away; approach from the south gives a strong impression of elevation – perhaps this was, topographically, a literal 'field in the sky'.

Heavenfield lies immediately north of Hadrian's Wall, a mile or so east of its crossing of the North Tyne at Chollerford and 3 miles west of Portgate, where Dere Street runs north from the Tyne crossing at Corbridge and intersects with the Wall: a key entry point into the Roman-controlled province. It seems likely that Cadwallon and his army were camped at Corbridge, the former Roman town that controlled access to both the eastern forts along the river and routes north and south along Dere Street – the modern A68. It also marked the west-bound departure point for the Stanegate, the Roman road that linked the Tyne Valley with the Solway Firth at Carlisle. The Welsh army was, it seems, anticipating an approach from Oswald, perhaps to sue for peace. But they seem not to have calculated for the possibility of the dawn raid implied by Adomnán's account.

From Bede's account of the raising of a cross at Heavenfield an audience familiar with Christian history is likely to have seen echoes of the career of the Emperor Constantine, who gained victory fighting under the sign of the cross at Milvian Bridge in the year 312. Bede's informants about the site were monks from the nearby monastery of Hexham, who had by then adopted Heavenfield as a place of pilgrimage and healing. Down to Bede's day, people were in the habit of cutting splinters from the cross, soaking them in water which they drank or gave to their beasts in the hope of effecting a cure for some ailment.[24] It is unlikely, despite Bede's account, that Oswald did raise a cross at Heavenfield. Interest in the cross in Western Christendom was stimulated by the discovery said to have been made by Pope Sergius (687–701) of a fragment of the cross of Christ and his instituting a liturgy for the Feast of the Exaltation of the Cross. The Northumbrian church was in touch with these developments: monks from Bede's own monastery were in Rome during the Easter celebrations of 701,[25] and Acca, who became bishop of

Hexham, was with Wilfrid on his Roman journey of 704–5.[26] The great high crosses of Northumbria – at Ruthwell, Bewcastle and Hexham – are an eighth-century development and the placing of a cross in memory of Oswald, the Northumbrian Constantine, at his battlefield site probably occurred within this context and under Acca's influence.[27]

Over the years, the battle that reasserted Bernician kingship has attracted the interest of historians drawing more on imagination than evidence. Heavenfield is a suitable place from which to launch an ambush on a complacent army camped inside the old town at Corbridge: it lies 5 miles to the north-west, hidden by the ridge of high ground along which the Wall runs. But Heavenfield itself has come to be understood, mistakenly, as the site of the fighting – even modern Ordnance Survey maps repeat the error. The Welsh Annals record the battle site as *Cantscaul*, which may derive from the Brittonic translation for *Hagustaldesham* – Hexham. But Bede placed it at *Denisesburn*, and Adomnán's account has Oswald advancing from his camp to the battle site. The name *Denisesburn* has disappeared from record but Canon Greenwell in 1862 had cited a charter of 1223 to associate this burn with the Devil's Water, a tributary of the Tyne flowing from the hilly ground to the south with an outfall between Hexham and Corbridge. From this, Tom Corfe was able to name *Denisesburn* as the Rowley Burn, which joins the Devil's Water 6km south of the Tyne, and to give a credible reconstruction of an early-morning march from the overnight camp at Heavenfield, 11km south and across the Tyne crossing at Corbridge to the site of a rout at Rowley Burn where, according to Bede, Cadwallon was killed and his army destroyed.[28]

The victorious Oswald then turned to his patrons in Dál Riata, inviting the monastery of Iona to send a mission to his kingdom. After a false start under a missionary who found the Northumbrian people 'intractable, obstinate and uncivilized', Bishop Aidan arrived and set up a monastery under the king's patronage on the tidal island of Lindisfarne. A close working relationship developed between king and bishop, through which new forms of governance and a religious infrastructure began to emerge.[29]

Bede's account of how Aidan was selected for the mission may not have captured the full truth of the matter. He was apparently in attendance at a 'meeting of the elders' held on Iona to address its failure. He criticised the unnamed bishop for being too hard on his intended converts – for failing to offer them a simpler, more sympathetic message. After careful consideration of his speech, the elders agreed to make Aidan a bishop and send him to instruct the Northumbrians. This rather makes it sound as though Aidan were drawn from

Modern statue of St Aidan on Lindisfarne

the ranks of Ionan monks. But a late Irish source, the *Martyrology of Donegal*, whose author seems to have had access to sources unknown to Bede or Adomnán, listed Aidan's first episcopal seat as *Inish Cathaigh*: Scattery Island in the estuary of the River Shannon in County Clare.[30] The monastery was founded in around 540 by St Senán and its bishops controlled three dioceses. We have permission to believe, then, that Aidan, said to have been descended from the same line as St Brigid, was chosen because of his existing pedigree as a churchman: it was very much in Iona's interest that his mission succeeded.

Bede paints a charming image of Aidan and King Oswald enjoying a personal friendship that extended to the king sitting at the bishop's side, translating his Irish into the vernacular for the king's ealdormen and thegns.[31] The mission to the Northumbrians was directly patronised by the king, through the gift of the island on which to found a church and through the endowment of estates, suitable to a man of Aidan's rank, from which to draw the renders necessary to support his new community and its pastoral ambitions.

Lindisfarne – Holy Island – was chosen by Aidan as Northumbria's Iona in the east: its first monastic church. The island lay within sight of the ancestral Bernician fortress of Bamburgh. The British had called it *Medcaut* – perhaps the 'charmed' or 'healing' island.[32] The prominent outcrop of hard Whin Sill bedrock on which the Tudor castle sits lies across a sheltered bay from the location of the Medieval priory, while the north half of the island is dominated by more recently accumulated sand dunes leading to the celebrated tidal causeway.

Nothing certain is known of the location of Aidan's church or its architecture. But the original land endowment can be reconstructed with some confidence from the later coastal and riverine holdings of Islandshire and Norhamshire.[33] Islandshire, an 8km-wide coastal strip, stretching some 21km from the south bank of the Tweed, abutting the royal shire of Bamburgh and including Lindisfarne, seems to have formed the core of the original Oswald endowment. With an estate centre at Fenwick and dependent farms at Goswick (perhaps specialising in raising geese), Cheswick (for dairy products), Elwick (for eels)* and Buckton (a deer farm), Islandshire came to function as a self-contained resource unit. The new territorial lord of Lindisfarne – that is to say, Bishop-Abbot Aidan – drew on this estate for the initial needs of the community, inheriting the rights and privileges of an earlier, unnamed and unknown lord who was either dead or displaced or was offered lands elsewhere as compensation by the new king. Many other estates across Bernicia and Deira are likely to have been apportioned by Oswald to reward the loyal *gesiðas* who had been in exile with him in Dál Riata.

We have argued elsewhere that in later decades, when Lindisfarne invested in the scriptorium that produced the Lindisfarne Gospels, an upland estate acquired specifically for the raising of calves, to be slaughtered young for use in vellum making, was added to the island's portfolio – *Bromic*, that is, the Breamish Valley which rises close to Cheviot and runs east towards the Till.[34] Norhamshire, inland along the Tweed from the coast, was certainly in the possession of the community by the middle of the ninth century and the *Historia de Sancto Cuthberto*, a tenth- or eleventh-century document purporting to record the fortunes of Lindisfarne and its landholdings, lists other estates acquired under successive bishop-abbots from successive royal patrons.

---

* Although it might alternatively derive from the personal name Ella. Diana Whaley pers. comm.

We can speculate that among the enthusiastic Irish who came over with Aidan and afterwards, a number of agricultural and technical specialists were recruited. Ionan monks seem to have had access to early-ripening strains of barley, for example;[35] and given that a tidal water turbine powered a monastic watermill at Nendrum on Strangford Lough from at least the second decade of the seventh century, it is possible, even likely, that a millwright came to Lindisfarne.[36] So far, attempts to identify a likely early mill site have proved fruitless although Waren Mill, where the Waren Burn – a boundary feature of the earliest Lindisfarne estates – empties into muddy Budle Bay, may have ancient origins. Other mills were historically sited on the outflow of the South Low River at Brock Mill near Beal; and at Fenham Mill, directly across the bay from the island. Early Medieval millwrights would have been spoiled for choice.

King Oswald did not arbitrarily carve out estates for his new bishop and thegns by a broad sweep of the royal arm. These were existing territorial units of great antiquity whose origins may belong to prehistory. Their extent and their boundaries were describable in topographic terms that are often still comprehensible. Section 4 of the *Historia* has it thus:

> And this is the boundary of the territory of Lindisfarne: from the River Tweed as far as the mouth of the Waren Burn, and from there upwards as far as the place where the Waren Burn rises next to Hepburn Hill, and from that hill as far as the river that is called Breamish, and from there as far as the river that is called the Till, and all the land that lies on both sides of the same river Breamish up to the place where it rises.[37]

On a local scale, this might be a suitable description of the bounds of a cultural coreland based on the drainage basins of the Rivers Breamish and Till.

The Lindisfarne first seen by Aidan looked very different to today's treeless mosaic of regular grassy fields with the panhandle of sand dunes leading to the modern causeway. Earlier causeways further south, running directly across the sands to Fenwick – the historical estate centre for Islandshire – are known from maps. The dunes seem mostly to have accumulated in the Medieval period.[38] Before the seventh century the island was covered largely by hazel and birch woodland. The Lough – the island's only standing freshwater – might have been a natural feature enhanced to provide either fish for the community or water for a mill – or even, as David Petts suggests, a site for 'devotional immersion'. The original harbour, now known as the Ouse, lying immediately east of the Medieval priory and its churches, was much more extensive than it is now. Seabirds, shellfish, coastal fish such as mackerel and herring and marine mammals – seals, dolphins, perhaps the odd whale – provided year-round hunting potential. Ongoing excavations by David Petts of Durham University in partnership with Dig Ventures are revealing a very complex sequence of activities – including the industrial processing of metal and other materials – dating to well before any monastic establishment: whatever Aidan found on his arrival on Lindisfarne in 635, it was not a greenfield site.

Nothing certain is known of the church or the community constructed by Aidan, although on his death he was apparently buried in a 'cemetery of the brethren' there.[39] A church constructed by his successor, Bishop Finán (651–661), another Irishman trained on Iona, was said by Bede to be suitable for an episcopal see. Nevertheless, it was constructed of hewn oak, thatched with reeds *more scottorum* – in the Irish fashion – and dedicated to St Peter.[40] To this church, perhaps constructed on the site where the later priory church of St Peter stands, Aidan's bones, and those of Cuthbert, born in the year of Oswald's victory, were brought in due course. The compiler of the much later *Historia de Sancto Cuthberto* believed that in the days of Bishop Ecgred (830–845) Aidan's original church was taken to Norham and rebuilt there. If that is true, the original must have been timber too; and must also, as John Blair argues, have been carefully curated over the intervening centuries – perhaps even encased within a stone church, almost as a shrine.[41]

Iona Abbey: the foundation of Colm Cille in the sixth century and mother house of the Northumbrian church on Lindisfarne

More obscure is the nature of the first monastic settlement, the size of the community or its make-up. By analogy with Iona it must have consisted of cells for the monks; a guest house is referred to by Bede in the context of Cuthbert; and more than one cemetery existed; perhaps also a writing hut for the abbot, like that possessed by Colm Cille on Iona.[42] A retreat and probably a small chapel lay on an islet just off the south-west tip of the island, later used by St Cuthbert.

As it happens, something more can be said about the wider contemporary community, following the excavation of a cemetery preserved in the sand dunes close to Bamburgh Castle, between 1998 and 2006.[43] The Bowl Hole cemetery was first noticed in 1817, in the shifting sands of a winter storm. It was relocated by test-pitting in 1996 and since then around half of the original cemetery has been excavated, producing the remains of about 120 individuals buried in graves cut through dune sand or the underlying clay. A number of radiocarbon samples date the burials to the seventh and eighth centuries, during the period of Bernicia's political dominance. They were laid out in rough rows, largely respecting any earlier graves and aligned broadly west to east. Around a tenth of the graves were shown to have been lined with one or more thin stone slabs set on edge – incomplete versions of the cist graves known from the early centuries AD in southern Scotland.

A variety of body positions, and the age and gender spread of the individuals – roughly equal numbers of males and females with a bias towards those over the age of fifty, but a third of them juveniles – indicates that these people belonged to a secular community – inhabitants of Bamburghshire. But only a minority had been born and raised locally: analysis of strontium and oxygen isotopes from the teeth of seventy-nine individuals showed that only seven of them were native to Bamburghshire. More than twenty came from an area broadly defined as western Scotland or Ireland; nearly thirty came from southern England or the near Continent; five were probably Scandinavian natives and seven came from southern Europe or the Mediterranean.

Pathological studies have shown that generally those buried in the Bowl Hole were of above average height for the period; they had terrible teeth (the consequence of a diet rich in sugars and starch) and a range of everyday injuries such as rib fractures and broken arms – generally healed well before death. Infectious diseases were present but within the lower expected range for the period, while evidence for nutritional stress was infrequent. A few of them showed signs of osteoarthritis. One young female suffered from a serious condition that would have adversely affected her quality of life, perhaps even killed her prematurely; but she had been afforded the same burial treatment as her peers.

Two exceptional individuals showed evidence of violent injury – conforming with an Early Medieval average of about 2 per cent in a cemetery population. One was an elderly male with a trauma injury to the front of his skull, which had healed; the other a young male aged between eighteen and twenty-four who had been fatally wounded by a series of bladed injuries down his left side, consistent with an attack by a right-handed antagonist. He had died elsewhere and been brought 'home' to be buried.

The majority of the individuals seem to have been buried clothed, with an unremarkable suite of knives, dress ornaments, combs and domestic tools. Their religious and indeed ethnic affinities cannot be assumed, although during and after Oswald's day (perhaps even before) they are likely to have been at least nominally Christian. The as yet only partially published evidence from ongoing excavations within the castle by the Bamburgh Research Project show that towards its north-west end, at least, metals processing, mortar mixing and animal butchery were carried out there – very much as archaeologists find at a wide range of lordship centres in this period.[44] Nearly twenty of the Bowl Hole individuals, most of them female, showed signs of activity-related pathology: squatting facies (the result of long hours spent squatting while working) and lower teeth notched by repeated drawing of either cord or thread – perhaps a function of mending fishing nets. The Bowl Hole community may have been the smiths, butchers, fisher folk, masons, woodworkers, herders and labourers required for the *vill* to function when the royal household was in residence, and to keep the fortress functioning when it was not.

Much has been made of the presence of so many non-local individuals, particularly those from western Scotland or Ireland, which naturally draws the inference that they may have been associated with Bede's statement that after the founding of the monastery on Lindisfarne 'many came from the country of the Irish into Britain'.[45] The overlordship established rapidly by Oswald, and the propensity for craftspeople, traders and slaves to move or be moved across the Early Medieval landscape, may explain the diversity of this community. Recent, wide-ranging studies of cemetery communities belonging to this period have shown a comparable mix of local and non-local populations in settlements bordering the North Sea and English Channel.[46] Plague, warfare, economic pressure and political instability ensured that this was an age of mobility. If cemeteries from the same period were located and excavated on Lindisfarne, or within Bamburgh Castle itself – where one might expect to find the élite members of the *comitatus* of the Bernician kings – the comparisons would be enlightening. The grave of no Northumbrian king has knowingly been identified. As it is, the population of contemporary Bernicia is poorly evidenced from burials; the only other cemetery of this size to be identified, at the probably royal township at Sprouston, is unexcavated. There is nothing in Bernicia remotely comparable with the graves and cemeteries to be found on the Yorkshire Wolds in Deira.

Bernicia's dead are, to say the least, discreet. However, recent discoveries from Eslington in mid Northumberland, reported under the Portable Antiquities Scheme, include a pattern-welded sword, folded for deposition, and a shield mount, comparable with items from high-status burial assemblages from southern and eastern England.[47] The site has been severely degraded by cultivation and its interpretation depends on finds recovered from the topsoil, but it is likely that there was a high-status male burial of the mid to late sixth or early seventh century with grave goods including a sword, a large knife, three spears, a belt knife, a shield, possibly harness fittings and other objects. Fragments of two square-headed brooches suggest female burials. Rob Collins and Sam Turner, who have studied this, suggest that the Eslington material marks a cultural shift in this part of Northumbria, with an increasingly stratified and militarised English aristocratic culture emerging in Bernicia in the late sixth or very early seventh century.[48] This burial site cannot be associated directly with Thirlings, some 20km distant, yet the two are complementary as evidence of a Bernician élite in the spheres of both settlement and burial.

Evidence of élite burial in Deira, a little later than Eslington, has come to light spectacularly in a late seventh-century cemetery of unique layout at Loftus in the Cleveland Hills (see Map 11 overleaf). Some 109 graves are known, with more than eighty set out in four neat rows, two of them double rows, to form an open rectangle, almost square, of 36m by 34m. Within the open area is a ditched mound, thought to be a mausoleum, some small buildings and – possibly the primary feature – a rarely seen case of an individual laid out on a wooden bed.* The rite of bed burial and grave goods, including a scallop-shaped pendant of gold and garnet, suggest a high-status female; a nearby grave, thought to be that of a male, may be associated with her.

---

* Sherlock 2012. Half a dozen other bed burials are known from southern England.

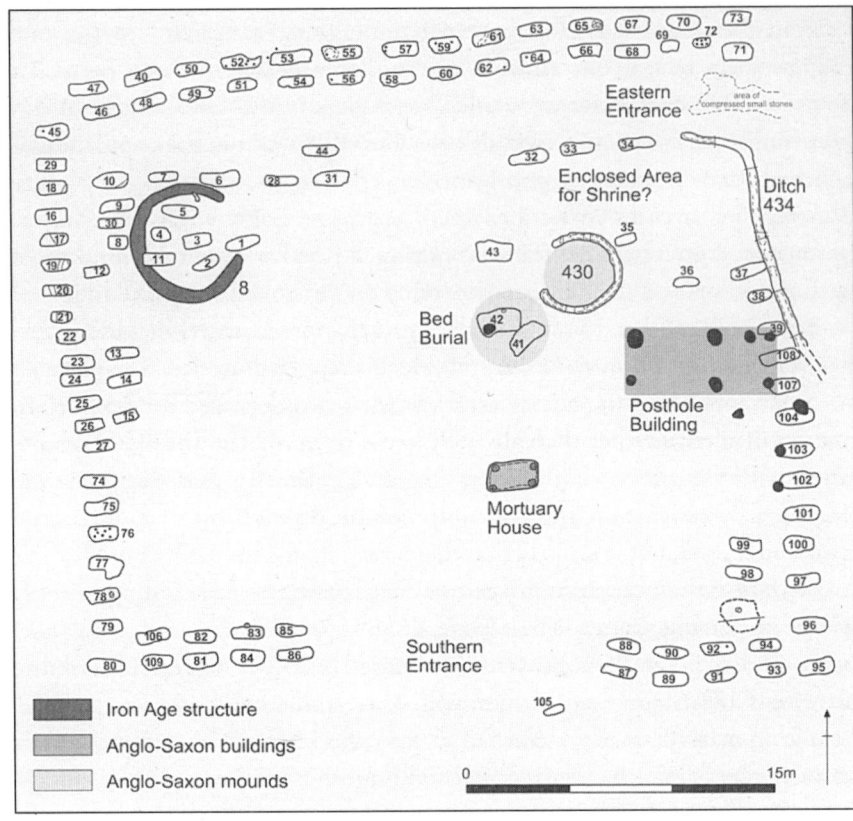

Map 11 Excavated features at the unique funerary complex at Street House, Loftus, in the Cleveland Hills

In the archaeology of settlement, the Milfield Basin (see Chapter 3) is exceptional in every way: rich in deep-time archaeology from the Neolithic period onwards; enjoying well-drained, tractable and fertile soils, attractive to successive generations of farmers, monks and tribal chiefs. The same glacial geology also makes the area attractive to quarry companies for its easily winnable gravels, rendering the archaeology susceptible to a range of detection techniques from aerial photography to geophysics. Is the Early Medieval settlement density of the Milfield Basin a function of detection, or was it always a heavily populated area in a sea of sparsely settled woods, pastures and unproductive moorland?

When Thirlings was abandoned, perhaps to make way for *Maelmin*, the seventh- or eighth-century successor to Yeavering mentioned by Bede,[49] the buildings seem to have been disassembled, the site emptied of reusable material culture and turned over to pasture. Finds from the site were sparse indeed – a few glass beads and a possible glass beaker; a very few sherds of pottery; a loom weight and spindle whorl. The layout and size of the settlement has parallels with sites further south such as Cowdery's Down in Hampshire and West Stow in Suffolk. Such establishments must have been common in Northumbria – whose political and social institutions are predicated on its minor lords. Their invisibility can be attributed to a range of factors: poor surviving material culture, especially of pottery; sites lying beneath permanent pasture which show poorly on aerial photography; the low level of commercial and industrial development through which many sites are first detected; and the likelihood that many of them lie beneath farms whose buildings still occupy the same sites more than a thousand years later.

Suspicion that the paucity of Early Medieval settlement evidence is a matter of silence rather than absence is reinforced by the 2006 discovery of an extensive sixth- to eighth-century settlement south of the hamlet of Shotton (see Map 12, page 108), just off the Great North Road in South Northumberland – in advance of surface coal mining. On the slopes of a south-facing ridge three sixth-century 'halls' appear to be the remnants of a larger settlement truncated by later ploughing. In the following century a series of ditched and fenced enclosures demarcated a number of compounds in which 'halls' and ancillary buildings – craft and agricultural workshops and storage facilities of various sorts – were strung out along the same slope. Again, material culture is scant; but there is evidence of metalworking and textile production. The enclosures, quite distinct from any other Bernician site, bear comparison with those at West Heslerton and sites further south.

The settlement here was long-lasting, occupied until at least the end of the eighth century, perhaps beyond – there are signs of buildings refurbished and repaired. The halls are of similar size to the buildings at Thirlings but there are no larger structures such as the annexed Building C. All the buildings were constructed of earth-fast posts. The absence of any hearth remains led the excavators to infer suspended plank floors. If Yeavering was the palace of Bernician kings, and Thirlings the estate centre of someone Bede might have called a *comes*, then Shotton's inhabitants belonged to the caste of *ceorls* – dependent farmers owing food renders and services to a thegn. In the Medieval period Shotton township was grouped with other dependencies of a *vill* at Plessey, whose manorial centre lay no more than a mile away from Shotton on the south bank of the River Blyth.[50] Plessey may in turn have been a component *vill* of Bedlingtonshire, first mentioned in the *Historia de Sancto Cuthberto*[51] and claimed as an estate in the possession of the Lindisfarne Community from the days of Bishop Cuðheard (c.900–915).

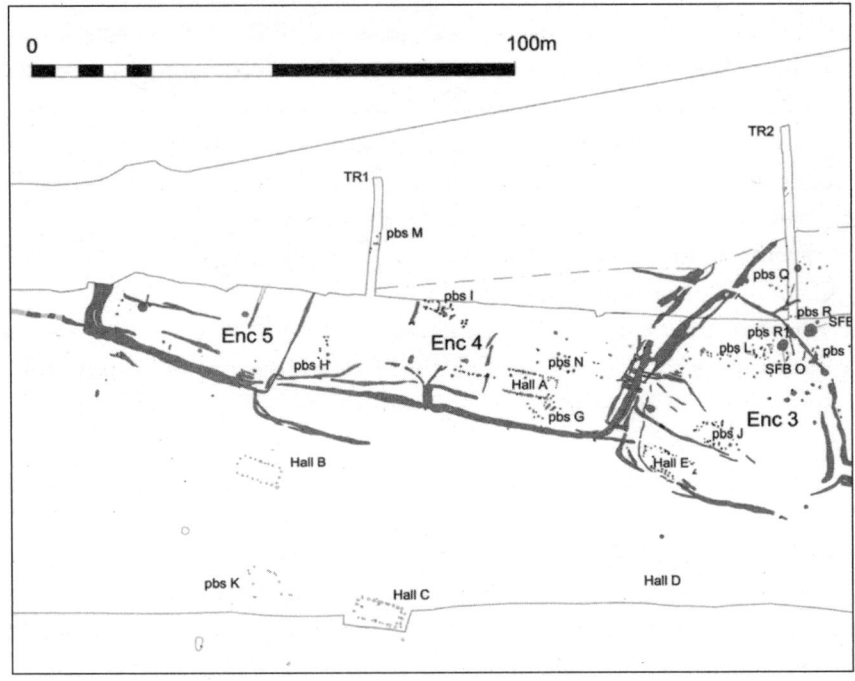

Map 12 Part of the excavated settlement at Shotton, central Northumberland

Even more recently, attention has been drawn to a site near Felton on the River Coquet, the estate centre of another Bernician shire, where previously unsuspected early Anglo-Saxon structures have been encountered during excavations centred on Scandinavian metalworking finds of the tenth century; and another site to the north of Felton where a watching brief 'strip and record' operation was carried out in advance of a housing development.[52] Here more than a dozen unenclosed timber posthole buildings hint at another contemporary settlement. Like Shotton, Felton lies close to the Great North Road, documented only as late as the thirteenth century but likely to be much more ancient in origin.[53]

The rural economy of sixth- and seventh-century Bernicia seems likely to have depended heavily on extensive pasturing of livestock, perhaps in the low-intensity form of wood pasture – but with access to open summer grazing on the higher ground of the North Pennines and Cheviot Hills. Oats, barley and bread wheat were cultivated at a small scale along with flax for its fibre. Milk and butter, wool and hide were important secondary products, among the renders named in the early seventh-century laws of King Ine (689–726) of Wessex.

Even if, as seems likely, the archaeology of seventh-century Bernician settlement and burial is drastically under-represented, there is nothing at all to suggest the sort of economy that began to emerge further south in Mercia in the eighth century. Here, coin finds and dramatic changes in settlement layout and density, in partnership with abundant, if lop-sided charter evidence, tell a story of agricultural expansion and specialisation; of productive trade and the resultant enrichment of monastic and secular settlements. For early sixth- and seventh-century kings like Oswald, economic enrichment was predicated on a successful career as the leader of a warband: raiding neighbours; rendering other kings tributary. Death in battle of members of the *comitatus* promoted the careers of younger warriors eager for glory and for land on which to settle, constantly recycling the pool of available estates to gift as reward for service.

King Oswald's portable wealth consisted of booty won in battle or surrendered as tribute by subject kings: weapons, martial finery, hoards of Roman coin and plate, horses, slaves and cattle on the hoof. As an Early Medieval king it was his honour and duty to distribute some of this wealth as gifts, in an eternal and unbreakable cycle of mutual obligation with his dependent thegns. He must also host feasts in his halls, at which the surplus renders of his estates were consumed, poets sang their verses and royal functionaries recited the genealogies of the king and his guests. The drinking horn at a royal feast must never be allowed to empty. In the days of Oswald's royal forbears, a priest like Coifi, King Edwin's former chief priest and enthusiastic Christian convert, would preside over sacrifices, auguries and propitiatory magic. In his capacity as the new king's chief priest, Aidan was obliged to fulfil that role in a Christian context.

Bede vividly describes a scene at one of King Oswald's feasts, held symbolically on Easter Day and attended by Bishop Aidan, at which a dish of silver – fine Roman plate, perhaps – filled with rich foods, was placed on the table before him. In good Christian fashion Aidan was asked for a blessing on the bread, when the feast was interrupted by a 'minister'. Bede says that this man's duty was to relieve the suffering of the needy – in effect he is an early example of what would later be called the king's almoner. He told the king that a 'very great multitude' of paupers had assembled from every district and were sitting in the precinct (*platea*) seeking alms (*elemosinae*). The king responded, much to the satisfaction of the bishop, by ordering that the delicacies be carried out to them; that the dish itself be broken up and the pieces divided among them. Aidan, delighted at this act of pious munificence, grasped the king by his right hand and said, 'May this hand never wither!'[54]

Aside from a very obvious distribution of small gifts to the poor which references Jesus's washing of his apostles' feet at the Last Supper and which has much later echoes in the distribution by a monarch at Easter of Maundy money, Oswald's gesture and Aidan's response may also have deeper symbolic Irish and Brittonic associations. As Bede says, Oswald's right arm remained incorrupt after his death and dismemberment in battle, fulfilling Aidan's prophecy. It was preserved and venerated down to Bede's own day in a silver casket held in St Peter's church in the royal fortress at Bamburgh. Now, there was an Irish tradition, recorded in the *Annals of the Four Masters*, that a king of the mythical *Tuatha Dé Danann*,* named Nuada, lost his right arm in battle and was subsequently regarded as unfit for the kingship. After receiving a working prosthetic arm magically crafted from silver he was restored to the kingship.[55] Nuada has a British counterpart in the god Nodens, a healing deity of the indigenous Britons and focus of cult sites at Lydney in Gloucestershire and further north in Cumberland. Nuada's epithet Airgetlám – 'silver hand or arm' – is equivalent to Oswald's own Irish nickname *Lamnguin* – 'bright blade or silver arm'.[56] Somehow, during his time fighting for the warbands of his Dál Riatan hosts, Oswald's right arm seems to have acquired something of a mythical reputation, drawn on by Aidan to mark the symbolic – but now decisively Christian – power of his act of generosity. Dare one suggest that Oswald's right arm had been injured in battle; that Aidan's gesture was ironic?

* * *

Oswald is one of those kings said to have exercised overlordship, ruling more widely than any of his predecessors had done among all four of the language groups that Bede had identified on the island: Britons, Picts, *Scotti* and English.[57] Yet Bede gives no insight into how this formerly exiled son of Æðelfrið achieved such *imperium* from the ruined kingdom that Cadwallon had left behind, and in such a short reign of only eight years. He describes Oswald as 'most holy and most victorious' and, elsewhere, 'a most Christian king' and, although he exercised supreme power, he was nevertheless 'always humble kind and generous to the poor and strangers' – hence the inclusion of the story about the Easter feast.[58] Such a characterisation sits uneasily with the information that, even in far-off Kent, so fearful was Edwin's widow, Queen Æðelburh, of Oswald's power that she sent her children to the protection of her kinsman King Dagobert in Francia, or that years later the monks

---

* A supernatural race of deities.

of Bardney would remember him as a hated conqueror.[59] Bede's focus is on the 'most Christian' dimension of Oswald's kingship and not the power play by which he attained dominance. The only episode he records of Oswald acting beyond his own kingdom involves King Cynegils in Wessex.[60] Oswald was present and sponsored him at his baptism; Cynegils then adopted Oswald as his son and gave him his daughter as wife; and the two kings set up an episcopal church in Dorchester-on-Thames for Bishop Birinus, who had conducted the baptism. Bede's comment that 'it happened that' (*contigit*) Oswald was in Wessex at this time seems either naïve or disingenuous: Oswald was there for a reason; he probably had his army with him. Did Oswald force this alliance on Cynegils at sword-point, or was it an alliance of mutual interest directed against a third party? We can only guess.

At any rate this campaign, literally and diplomatically outflanking the rising Mercian power in the Midlands, was conducted apparently without military interference from King Penda, through whose territories Oswald must have passed. Even if the West Saxon alliance was of mutual interest, Oswald taking the other king's daughter as wife was an act of submission on the part of the king of Wessex. As it is, Oswald's consort is the least visible of the Northumbrian queens in the seventh century. Historians must trust the dubious tradition of Reginald of Durham in the twelfth century that her name was Cyniburh.* She bore one son, Œðelwald.

After dealing with matters in Wessex and Kent, Bede returned to Oswald to record his death, killed in battle by King Penda of Mercia at *Maserfelth* in 642.[61] Clare Stancliffe's review of the evidence supports the traditional identification of this place as Oswestry – *Croesoswallt* in Welsh – in Shropshire.† The name derives from the grimly ironic 'Oswald's Tree': the stake on which his severed head was placed by King Penda. Both Oswald and his father fought in the marches between England and Wales or, in seventh-century geography, between Mercia and the Brittonic kingdoms of Gwynedd and Powys. Possibly their focuses of interest were the brine springs at Nantwich, Middlewich and Northwich in Cheshire, aiming to assert Northumbrian dominance of this important natural resource, or to try to prevent a Powys–Mercian duopoly of control.[62] Oswald's father, King Æðelfrið, had fought in the same region in

---

* Tudor (1995, 187) is sceptical: Cyneburh was also the name of one of Penda's daughters.
† Stancliffe 1995b. The *Annales Cambriae* name the place as *Bellum Cocboy* under the year 644.

616, the penultimate year of his reign. But here again, as with the Wessex episode, Bede made no attempt to elucidate the power politics that took Oswald to this area. Instead, he immediately recorded healing miracles said to have occurred at the site of his death and then miracles at Bardney, improbably far away in the kingdom of Lindsey (see Chapters 5 and 7).*

Bede recounts several stories relating to the origins of a widespread cult of Oswald. It seems that he was slain by King Penda in person; that the Mercian king ordered Oswald's head and hands to be severed from his body – a post-mortem insult not merely to his defeated enemy, but to Oswald's *patriae*, his homeland. A year later King Oswiu, Oswald's younger brother and immediate successor, came to the battlefield with an army and reclaimed them. By the twelfth century a legend had grown up that Oswiu had searched in vain for his brother's remains until a vision pointed him towards the place where a great bird – we are to understand that it was a raven, the harbinger of death – had carried the king's incorrupt right arm into an ash tree, symbolic, perhaps, of Yggdrasill, the pagan Norse World tree; the bird dropped the arm and where it landed a spring burst forth, signifying its owner's identity and sanctity.[63] Bede, reporting eighth-century traditions, says that Oswiu took the arm and hands and had them interred at Bamburgh, while he had the head buried on Lindisfarne – a somewhat back-handed gift to Aidan's community.[64]

The miracles associated with the site of Oswald's demise have been the subject of much academic discussion over the years because despite Bede's portrayal of Oswald as the type of a most Christian king, the stories he relates bear distinctly unchristian overtones, as does Reginald of Durham's tradition about the great bird identifying his arm.[65] The first of Bede's tales relates to a rider, travelling past the battlefield, whose horse was cured of a seemingly fatal spasm when it rolled in agony onto the very place where the king had met his end. He reported the miracle to an innkeeper, whose daughter had long suffered from paralysis. Her parents subsequently took her to the site, where she was cured.[66] A second story involves a Briton, also passing the site, who noticed a patch of ground greener and lusher than the rest of the battle-field. Suspecting that someone very holy must have died there he took some soil from the site and kept it in a cloth. Arriving that evening at a *vill* where the people were enjoying a feast, he joined them, hanging his precious cloth on a wall post. Late in the night, after much revelry, the roof of the hall caught fire, the guests fled and the hall burned to the ground – apart, that is,

---

* Bede here makes a jump in chronology and geography. Bede *HE* III, 9–13.

from the post on which the holy cloth had been hung.[67] Bede says that so many people came to the place seeking cures that gradually a hole was excavated to the depth of a man's height.

Such were the sorts of miracle through which early cult sites became folk-attractions and centres of healing and wonder. But as Alan Thacker has pointed out, Oswald's death, the distinctly pagan story of Oswiu's retrieval raid and the post-mortem miracles, together with the sites of many wells associated with Oswald's cult, are distinctly lacking in ecclesiastical associations; the horse recalls the sacral role of horses in kingship, while the role of a Briton in relating one of the stories suggests a British folk element to the cult's origins.[68] The multiplicity of Oswald's body parts available to cult impresarios like St Wilfrid in the later seventh century ensured that his cult became far more widespread than that of the undoubtedly very holy, but singular, remains of St Cuthbert.

Bede was selective in what he wrote. Nearly a century after Oswald's death, he depended on correspondents in monasteries in Lindisfarne, Hexham and Bardney and the royal centre in Bamburgh for information which he viewed through the lens of his own life as a monk. From such transmission and reception, as Clare Stancliffe has shown, Bede came to understand Oswald as king in a unique way.[69] There were kings who set aside their kingship to take up the religious life or to embark on pilgrimage; there were kings who died as murdered innocents at the hands of pagan warriors. But for Bede Oswald was unambiguously a saint, while also being a successful king, a 'soldier of Christ'.[70]

* * *

Much of what we know of the seventh century comes from Bede, but Clare Stancliffe has observed that when writing about Oswald, he exercised artistry in the selection and deployment of the material available to him.[71] He was skilled in deploying narrative techniques to carry the ideas he wished to convey, and he does not necessarily give a fully rounded view of the workings of kings. On his own admission, he wrote with moral purpose: if history records people's good deeds, then readers are encouraged to imitate the good; if evil deeds are recorded, the devout reader is encouraged to turn away from that which is harmful.[72] Although Bede saw nothing inherently divine about kingship, thinking of it as being morally neutral,[73] and although he recognised that the material prosperity of a people often rested on the king's prowess in war, he came to writing history from long experience as a commentator on the scriptures and, as present-day scholars have come increasingly to recognise, he viewed the history of his own people and its kings through the filter of his biblical studies.[74] Bede's method in scriptural exegesis was allegorical. An individual, place or event in the Old Testament could be understood as a type, referring to the New Testament, in which it was fulfilled, to the moral life of the church in the present and to the life hereafter.[75]

Bede developed his ideas on the emergence of a people and its kingship from three of his Old Testament commentaries, *On the Tabernacle* and *On the Temple*, both from the 720s, and an earlier work, on which he was engaged in 716, *On the First Book of Samuel*.*[76] The first two of these works concern the journey of the Israelites to the Promised Land and the building of the First Temple in the reign of King Solomon, and for Bede the building of the Temple references allegorically the founding of an English church: in the kingship of Israel he found a model for English kingship.[77] His study of his first three Northumbrian kings, Æðelfrið (c.604–616), Edwin (616–633) and Oswald (634–642), is a carefully constructed trilogy to show the emergence of a full Christian kingship out of pagan origins, determined by God's plan for the English people; this is what the philosopher of history, R.G. Collingwood called providential history.[78]

Bede knew of genealogical traditions concerning kings and he knew of the idea of descent from Woden: he had cited the Kentish ancestry of Hengist and Horsa back to that ancestral god.[79] But when it came to his own kingdom, his only reference to the beginnings of Northumbrian kingship was a brief mention of Ida in the year 547 in the chronological *aide memoire* he wrote at the end of the *Ecclesiastical History*.[80] In the main body of the work, Northumbrian history opens towards the end of the sixth century with King Æðelfrið, who is introduced as a warrior 'very powerful and most eager for glory', with the note that nobody had subjected more land to the English nation.[81] The two episodes of warfare, the battles at *Degsastan* and *Legacæstir*, are enough for Bede to set up his model of kingship. He reached back to his studies of the First Book of Samuel in comparing Æðelfrið to King Saul.[82] He was an ambiguous figure whose kingship had not found favour with God, and yet, as a great warrior, he protected God's people from the aggression of the Philistines. Thus Bede builds a set of correspondences, drawing his own people, the English, into the narrative of salvation which the Old Testament anticipates: Saul, understood as a type in exegetical terms, prefigures Æðelfrið, the pagan warrior king; Saul's people, that is God's people, the Israelites prefigure Æðelfrið's people, the English; the Philistine enemies of Israel prefigure the *Scotti* and the Britons. By

---

* This Old Testament book is now often known as the First Book of Kings.

extension, Saul's enemy in the kingdom of Israel, and his eventual successor, David, prefigures Edwin who overthrew Æðelfrið. In this way, Bede concluded the first of the five books of his *Ecclesiastical History* by setting the English people and its kings firmly within the providential history that began with the people of Israel in the Old Testament.

Book II opens with an obituary for Pope Gregory, placed here in its correct chronological place in the work. When he picks up the narrative again,[83] it is not where he left off with Æðelfrið. He takes us back to Pope Gregory's missionary, Archbishop Augustine, and to a bad-tempered meeting with leaders of the British church which ended in a stand-off. Angrily, Augustine denounced them in a prophecy: if they refused peace with their brothers, they would suffer war from their enemies; if they were unwilling to preach the way of life to the English people, they would suffer death at their hands. Bede adds the comment that, through the workings of divine judgement, all this came about. Then, with a sharp jump-cut, Æðelfrið is back slaughtering Britons and their monks at Chester: as the instrument of God's punishment, he fulfils Augustine's prophecy.

With King Edwin, Bede does not opt for a straightforward chronological narrative. He opens with Edwin already a great warrior king, and immediately he declares his determinist position by saying that Edwin's early power had increased as a portent that he would receive the faith and the heavenly kingdom.[84] The driving force of the rest of the Edwin narrative is the inevitability of conversion. It is a *tour de force* in narrative technique in which Bede has taken disparate elements, derived possibly from different oral traditions, and brought them together as a drama in three acts in which Edwin first resists the call to God, then in a flash-back scene of the time when his life was in danger while he was in exile he is reminded of his debt to his protector, and finally he accepts Christianity as the first of Bede's Christian kings.[85]

Æðelfrið, like Saul in the Old Testament, served God's people although he was not a Christian king; Edwin came to Christ during his kingship; Bede's kingly trilogy culminates with Oswald, who appears on the scene as the fully fledged 'most Christian king'.[86] Book II of the *Ecclesiastical History* concludes with a scene of devastation;[87] Book III opens a year later and, if anything, things are worse. The unified kingdom of Northumbria has unravelled, and its two puppet-kings have turned away from Christ; Cadwallon has killed both.[88] Into this desolation comes Oswald, son of Æðelfrið.[89] There is no introductory back-story; suddenly, he is here at Heavenfield where, as a new Constantine, he gives battle under the sign of the cross. To underline the providential significance of this event and this place, Bede immediately jumps to the present day, almost a century after the battle, with first-hand testimony from a monk called Bothelm of healing effected by a splinter cut from the wood of Oswald's cross.

Edwin had achieved greatness as a portent of his future conversion. Oswald gained from God a wider rule than any of his predecessors had enjoyed, over the four language groups of the island.[90] Yet in between the battle that brought him to power and the battle at *Maserfelth* at which he lost his life, Bede gives no insight into how Oswald achieved his dominance; instead, Oswald's story is that of the spread of Christianity. This sets up the narrative for the second battle, at which King Penda of Mercia killed Oswald, moving the providential theme to its culmination.[91] At Heavenfield, Oswald, under the sign of the cross, gained his earthly kingdom; at *Maserfelth* he attained the kingdom of eternal life. The signs of this are in the five chapters of miracle stories associated with the relics of Oswald and the sites of his two battles with which Bede concludes his account.[92] With Oswald, kingship among the English has now achieved full union with God.

PART II: 643–737

CHRONOLOGY II: 643–737

643 – King Oswiu goes to Oswestry and fetches Oswald's remains; inters his arms at Bamburgh in a silver casket and gives the head to Lindisfarne.

Record of a battle between Oswiu and the Britons (*AT*).

643–650 [?] – Periodic raids by Penda into Bernicia, as far as Lindisfarne (Bede *HE* III.24).

646 – Approximate date for the foundation of a monastery at Hartlepool (*Heruteu*) by Heiu, the first English abbess. Heiu soon retires to a dwelling at *Kælcacæstir* (Tadcaster) and is replaced by Hild (c.650), the great-niece of King Edwin (Bede *HE* IV.23).

647 – A possible date for the foundation of a monastery on the north bank of the River Wear (Chester-le-Street?) with Hild as its first abbess (Bede *HE* IV.23).

649 – A possible date for an attack on Northumbria as far as Bamburgh by Penda and a Mercian army 'during Aidan's episcopate' while he is living on Farne (Bede *HE* III.16). An attempt to burn Bamburgh is prevented by Aidan's prayers.

651 – A revolt by Oswine against King Oswiu; Oswine disbands his army but is betrayed and murdered (Bede *HE* III.14); Oswine is succeeded in Deira by Œðelwald aged ?16, to 655.

St Aidan dies in the church at [?] Yeavering on 31 August (Bede *HE* III.17). He is buried in the cemetery at Lindisfarne and succeeded by Bishop Finán.

Monasteries have by now been founded at *Mailros* (Old Melrose), Coldingham and Gilling West (by Eanflæd, in expiation for the murder of Oswine).

[?] Cuthbert becomes a monk at *Mailros* (Bede *Vit Cuth*).

652 – [?] Oswiu is forced by Penda to retreat as far as Stirling, and to sue for peace, with hostages including Ecgfrið. Possibly the same events as those recorded for 655.

Finán builds a church on Lindisfarne, of hewn oak thatched with reeds (Bede *HE* III.25).

653 – Peada of Mercia, Penda's son, marries King Oswiu's daughter Alhflæd and is baptised at *Ad Murum* by Finán (Bede *HE* III.21, 22): the beginning of the Irish mission to the Middle Angles. Oswiu's son Alhfrið (aged [?] seventeen) probably marries Penda's daughter Cyneburh.

Wilfrid (aged [?] nineteen) and Benedict Biscop make the journey from Northumbria to Rome (Bede *HE* V.19).

654 – Possible date for the foundation of Lastingham by Œðelwald in a remote part of the North York Moors, under Cedd's direction (Bede *HE* III.23).

655 – The 'Distribution of Iudeu' and the campaign against Oswiu by Penda on the Firth of Forth; Oswiu is forced to give up a huge ransom (*HB* 65; Bede *HE* III.24).

Ecgfrið, Oswiu's son by Eanflæd, is held hostage under Queen Cynewise of Mercia.

The Battle of the River Winwæd. Penda, King of Mercia, and thirty chieftains are killed. Œðelwold waits to see who will win. [?] Oswiu kills him. Oswiu achieves dominance over Mercia until 658 (Bede *HE* III.24). In thanks for victory Oswiu establishes twelve monasteries – six in Bernicia, six in Deira.

Oswiu subjects the Picts to his rule (Bede *HE* III.24) and hands control of southern Mercia, below the Trent, to Peada.

656 – Peada is murdered by treachery of Alhflæd (Bede *HE* III.24). Oswiu rules Mercia directly, to 658.

657 – Foundation of a monastery at Whitby under Abbess Hild; Ælfflæd is given into her care (Bede *HE* III.24).

658 – King Oswiu plunders Mercia (*AC*).

A rebellion by Mercian ealdormen expels its Northumbrian governors and sets up the Christian Wulfhere, son of Penda, as king (Bede *HE* III.24).

659 – Abbot Eata founds a monastery at Ripon, with Cuthbert as his guest master (Bede *Vit Cuth* VII); he is succeeded at Old Melrose by Boisil, Cuthbert's teacher.

660 – Wilfrid is given Ripon with thirty (*VW* 8) or forty hides (Bede *HE* III.25). Wilfrid expels the community of Eata including Cuthbert (Bede *Vit Cuth* VIII).

664 – A plague (after a July comet sighting): Archbishop Deusdedit dies.

The Council of Whitby (*Streanæshealh*) (Bede *HE* III.25) is hosted by Hild. Delegates include Bishop Agilbert, Colmán, Wilfrid, Kings Oswiu and Alhfrið. King Oswiu convenes the synod to determine which church to follow: Iona or Rome. He decides in favour of Rome.

Bishop Colmán abdicates from Lindisfarne and is replaced by Eata.

Wilfrid is appointed bishop of Northumberland at York and goes to Francia to be consecrated.

Cuthbert becomes prior of Lindisfarne.

[?] Alhfrið dies this year or soon after.

669 – The arrival of Theodore of Tarsus in England as archbishop of Canterbury, to 690 (Bede *HE* IV.1).

Wilfrid completes the restoration of Paulinus's church at York.

670 – King Oswiu dies of natural causes, aged fifty-eight (*ASC*). He is succeeded by Ecgfrið, his first son by Eanflæd.

Wilfrid builds a stone church and crypt at Ripon, probably financed by the plunder of British churches in the Pennines, which he has been granted (*VW* 17).

Queen Eanflæd retires to Whitby Abbey.

672 – The Synod of *Herutford* (Hertford): Theodore begins the process of dividing Britain into dioceses (Bede *HE* IV.5).

673 – The foundation of Hexham Abbey by Wilfrid on an estate given by ex-Queen Æðelðryð, who retires to her sister's monastery at Ely (*VW* 22; Bede *HE* IV.19).

King Ecgfrið marries Iurminburh of ?Kent or Francia.

674 – King Wulfhere of Mercia invades Northumbria and is repelled (*VW* 20).

Wearmouth monastery is founded by Benedict Biscop on land given by Ecgfrið (Bede *Hist Abb; Vit Ceol Anon*); Biscop travels to Gaul to bring back craftsmen in glazing and mortar. He brings Ceolfrið to Wearmouth as prior (*Vit Ceol Anon* 5).

675/9 – Possible date for the foundation or rededication of Bardney monastery by Æðelred of Mercia and Osðryð, daughter of Oswiu. They endow it with Oswald's relics (Bede *HE* III.11).

678 – Archbishop Theodore divides the Northumbrian see into four (Lindisfarne and Hexham in Bernicia; York in Deira and Lindsey) (*ASC* E 678).

King Ecgfrið briefly re-asserts Northumbrian control over Lindsey (Bede *HE* IV.12).

Wilfrid is expelled (Bede *HE* V.24; *VW* 24); he travels to Rome to seek intervention from the pope.

679 – King Æðelred of Mercia and King Ecgfrið of Northumbria fight a battle on the River Trent: Ecgfrið's younger brother Ælfwine is killed; Lindsey is lost to Northumbria. Theodore oversees a peace treaty.

Adomnán becomes the ninth abbot of Iona.

680 – Abbess Hild dies at Whitby (Bede *HE* V.24). Eanflæd becomes abbess of Whitby jointly with her daughter Ælfflæd. Hackness monastery is founded.

Wilfrid returns from Rome (*VW* 33) and is imprisoned in *Broninis* under the reeve Osfrið (*VW* 36); then at Dunbar under the reeve Tydlin (*VW* 38).

Bede enters Wearmouth monastery, aged seven.

Abercorn is established with a Northumbrian bishop on the Forth estuary.

A possible date for the translation of Edwin's relics to *Streanæshealh* – perhaps as part of a restorative deal after the Trent battle.

681 – Wilfrid is released into exile in Mercia.

683 – Death of Æbbe, abbess of Coldingham and 'uterine' sister of Oswald (aged possibly seventy-five).

684 – Ecgfrið despatches pre-emptive force to invade Ireland; attacks Brega.

Cuthbert visits Ælfflæd, sister of Ecgfrið, at Coquet Island; discusses succession (*Vit Cuth Anon* III.6).

685 – Cuthbert consecrated bishop of Hexham (Bede *HE* IV.28; *ASC*).

A monastery at Jarrow, founded by Benedict Biscop on forty hides of land granted by Ecgfrið (Bede *Hist Abb*; *Vit Ceol Anon* 11) is dedicated on the ninth Kalends of May (23 April) by the king.

Ecgfrið launches pre-emptive strike on the Picts.

Cuthbert visits Carlisle with Iurminburh and has vision of Ecgfrið's death (*Vit Cuth Anon* III.8).

Ecgfrið's army is slaughtered on 20 May at *Dún Nechtain* (*AU* 686; Bede *HE* IV.26): the Battle of *Nechtansmere*.

King Aldfrið (Ecgfrið's half-brother) succeeds as king. All Northumbrian conquests north of the Forth and Solway are lost. Rheged is retained.

686 – Wilfrid is restored to the see at York with his lands at Ripon and Hexham (*VW* 44).

Adomnán of Iona visits Northumbria and gives Aldfrið a copy of *De Locis Sanctis*. Aldfrið frees sixty prisoners taken by Ecgfrið from Ireland, at Adomnán's request (*AU*; *AT*).

An outbreak of plague; there are only two survivors at Jarrow. Abbot Eosterwine dies (Bede *Hist Abb* 10).

687 – The death of Cuthbert on Inner Farne; there follows a dispute between Wilfrid and the Lindisfarne monks; they are purged (Bede *Vit Cuth* 40).

688 – The date of Adomnán's second visit to Northumbria, perhaps to Wearmouth and Jarrow (Bede *HE* V.21).

690 – Archbishop Theodore dies and is succeeded by Berhtwald.

Benedict Biscop dies (Bede *Hist Abb* 14) aged sixty-two.

691 – Wilfrid is expelled by King Aldfrið and is given sanctuary by King Æðelred in Mercia.

698 – Beorhtred, at the head of a Northumbrian host, is killed by the Picts (Bede *HE* V.24; 699 in *ASC* E; *AU* 698.2).

Cuthbert's coffin at Lindisfarne is 'translated' and his body found to be incorrupt (Bede *Vit Cuth* 42).

c.700 – *The Anonymous Life of St Cuthbert* is written by a monk of Lindisfarne. A possible date for the production at Wearmouth-Jarrow of the *Codex Amiatinus*, the oldest known surviving copy of Jerome's *Vulgate* bible.

702 – Wilfrid is called to account at a church council at Austerfield, West Yorkshire. Archbishop Berhtwald excommunicates him. Wilfrid sets off for Rome again, aged sixty-nine (Kirby 2000, 121; *VW* 46–7).

705 – King Aldfrið dies at Driffield on 14 December. Eadwulf (of unknown parentage) usurps the kingdom of Northumbria.

705 – The siege of Bamburgh. Eadwulf is exiled after two months (*VW* 59). Osred (aged eight, son of Aldfrið) succeeds as king of Northumbria (to 716), is protected by Wilfrid and by Beorhtfrið of [?] Dunbar, who raises the siege (*VW* 60).

(Or 706) the Synod of Nidd *(VW 60)*: Wilfrid's lands at Hexham and Ripon are restored to him.

709 – Wilfrid dies at Oundle, aged seventy-five; his body is taken to Ripon (*ASC* E).

711 – Beorhtfrið attacks the Picts [?] in revenge for the deaths of his father and grandfather, at a battle in Manau between *Caere* (Stirling) and *Haefe* (Linlithgow) (*AU* 711.3; 710 in *ASC*).

714 – A probable date for the death of Ælfflæd, sister of Ecgfrið.

716 – King Osred is killed 'to the south of the border' (*ASC* E). He is succeeded by Cœnred, to 718.

Abbot Ceolfrið of Jarrow retires and sets out on pilgrimage to Rome carrying one of three 'pandects' – complete bibles – made at Jarrow and Wearmouth (*Codex Amiatinus*); he dies on the way (Bede *Hist Abb; Vit Ceol Anon* 23 onwards).

717 – King Eadwulf's death in [?] Dál Riatan exile is reported in Irish Annals (*AU*).

718 – Osric succeeds to the kingdom of Northumbria to 729/731 (*ASC*).

721 – Bede's *Prose Life of St Cuthbert* is completed.

c.725 – Bede writes *Concerning the organisation of time* (*De Temporum Ratione*).

729 – King Osric dies (731 in *ASC* A); Ceolwulf succeeds to the kingdom of Northumbria, to 737.

731 – King Ceolwulf is tonsured and imprisoned in a coup; he recovers the kingdom (*Hist Reg*).

The diocese of Whithorn is established under 'English' rule by now (Bede *HE* III.4).

Bede completes his *Ecclesiastical History of the English People*. The effective end of contemporary Northumbrian narrative history.

734 – Bede's *Letter to Archbishop Ecgberht* of York (brother of King Eadberht) on spurious monasteries and reforms to diocesan structures.

735 – The death of Bede at Jarrow.

Archbishop Ecgberht receives the pallium at York (*Hist Reg*).

737 – King Ceolwulf is tonsured and forced to enter the monastery at Lindisfarne (Bede *Continuatio*). He gives significant endowments to the monastery. Eadberht (brother of the archbishop of York) succeeds, for twenty-one years (*Hist Reg*).

'A great drought made the land unfruitful' (Bede *Continuatio*).

King Æðelbald of Mercia harries Northumbria (*ASC*).

5

OSWIU: GOD-FRIEND 643–670

Oswiu and Deira – Patronage – Oswiu, Penda and Mercia – Endowment of monasteries – The monasteries of Ryedale – Wilfrid and Ripon – The lower Tyne coreland – The Synod of Whitby and its aftermath

With Oswald killed in battle, his younger brother Oswiu, then about thirty years old, gained the kingdom, ruling for twenty-eight years until he died of natural causes in 670/1. Drawing on what Oswald and Aidan had begun at Lindisfarne, he developed an astute sense of governance and a church-state collaboration for his political diplomacy.

He was the last of the kings who, according to Bede, held overlordship over southern kingdoms; he held almost the same territory as Oswald had done and took tribute from the *Scotti* and Pictish peoples.[1] There is little record of his warfare. A passing reference to St Cuthbert, as a youth in army camps in the face of enemies, implies military campaigns early in Oswiu's reign and a note in the Irish *Annals of Tigernach* for the year 643 records a battle between Oswiu and the Britons.[2] This was perhaps the expedition to recover Oswald's remains from the battle site at *Maserfelth* (see Chapter 4).

As a youth, Oswiu had spent time in Ireland; he fathered a son named Aldfrið, known to the Irish as Flann Fína, from Fín, daughter of Colmán Rímid of the Cenél nÉogain dynasty in the north.[3] Aldfrið would succeed his half-brother Ecgfrið as Northumbrian king in 685 (see Chapter 7).* But

---

* James Fraser (2009, 217) doubts this parentage, suggesting that a dynastic link between the two houses 'is more likely to have been concocted by a pseudo-historian than to reflect Aldfrið's real heritage'. That Aldfrið had Irish connections is, however, secure.

at the time of his brother's death Oswiu was married to Rhieinmelth,* a princess of the ruling house of Rheged, with a son and daughter, Alhfrið and Alhflæd, probably aged about seven or eight years old.† This looks like the result of an alliance with the British kingdom, formerly hostile to Bernicia, either to build a position for the sons of Æðelfrið in preparation for Oswald's return in 634, or to consolidate Bernician hegemony in the North-west once Oswald had secured power. Alternatively, it was an initiative by Oswiu himself, to strike out independently of his brother: the tenor of their relationship is unknown.

As king, however, Oswiu sought a new marriage alliance in Kent. He dispatched a priest, Utta, to King Eorcenberht (640–664) to negotiate a marriage to Eanflæd, daughter of King Edwin and Æðelburh. This was a first-cousin marriage into the Deiran line, ensuring that Oswiu's children by Eanflæd would inherit legitimacy in both Northumbrian kingdoms through their father and mother. Such a dynastic strategy also, inevitably, placed his children by Fín and by Rhieinmelth in a subordinate position: they would be displaced as direct heirs.

Careful diplomacy was needed to work around difficulties. First was Rhieinmelth's position. If she is the *Rægumeld* whose name appears in the list of queens in the Durham *Liber Vitae*,‡ it may be that she had been persuaded to retire into religious life; her children, though, remained associated with Oswiu's court.[4] Then there was the legacy of historic hostility and suspicion between the families of Æðelfrið and Edwin. But Utta was skilled in the task and he duly returned with the bride. He was later rewarded with the abbacy of a monastery *Ad Caput Caprae*, at Gateshead.[5]

Bede lent his own weight of legitimacy and approval to this marriage by relating the story of a miracle which he had himself been told by a priest who had heard it from, as it were, the horse's mouth. Utta, he says, had gone to seek blessing for the mission from Bishop Aidan at Lindisfarne, informing him that

---

* *HB* 57: she was the daughter of Royth, son of Rhun, son of Urien (*HB* 63): an illustrious pedigree.

† It is not absolutely certain that these were children by Rhieinmelth, but their ages at their marriages in about 653 militates against their being children of Eanflæd. If Alhfrið was raised bilingual in English and Brittonic, it has implications for Oswiu's policy towards the kingdom of Elmet.

‡ The book of benefactors of Lindisfarne and its successor communities. Originally a ninth-century text. Rollason 2004.

they planned to travel to Kent overland but to return by sea. Aidan had commended the priest to the Lord and given him a flask of holy oil, knowing that the return journey, by sea, would be perilous. It duly happened that on the voyage home with the new queen and her entourage, their boat encountered stormy seas and was in danger of foundering when Utta, remembering the holy oil, cast some of it on the waves. The seas at once calmed and they proceeded safely on their way.[6] This was a sign of God's favour; but also of Lindisfarne's approval: an early example of ways in which the seventh-century Northumbrian church and state exercised mutual support – the royal gift of land at Gateshead for a monastic foundation being the material reward for that support.

King Oswiu needed a Deiran marriage for, in the early years of his reign, his position here was not secure. He ruled indirectly, with Oswine, son of the Osric who had ruled Deira during the year after Edwin's death, in place as his sub-king. But Oswine was a charismatic figure who built up a strong court around him. Eventually, in 651, he fielded an army against Oswiu at a place called *Wilfaræsdun*, which Bede places 10 miles north-west of Catterick. This is somewhere about the Scotch Corner of today, where the cross-Pennine former Roman road, now the A66, strikes out north-west from the Dere Street line of the A1. But, like the grand old Duke of York, Oswine marched his men back down the hill: he disbanded his army. He himself went into hiding but was betrayed and murdered at Oswiu's behest in an act which Bede called abhorrent to all (*detestanda omnibus morte*).[7] Thereafter, Oswiu brought Deiran kingship closer to home by appointing first his nephew, Oswald's son Œðelwald, and then his own son Alhfrið, although both eventually rebelled against him.

King Oswiu inherited from his brother a way of governing the kingdom in a partnership with Aidan, his Lindisfarne bishop, and he was able to build on this to use his church and its people in political diplomacy, although it seems that, on a personal level, he and Aidan had become estranged and that Aidan had attached himself to the Deiran court of Oswine.[8] To what extent Aidan had developed a monastic infrastructure by the time he died in 651 is not known in detail. Bede gives generalised statements to the effect that Aidan travelled widely around the kingdom and that many missionary priests came from Dál Riata; churches were built; land and other gifts were given by the king to establish monasteries; Irish teachers set up schools.[9] More specifically, Aidan encouraged female religious life. He consecrated Heiu, the first nun in the Northumbrian kingdom, who set up a monastery at Hartlepool on the coast just north of the Tees estuary[10] and he was responsible for

Dere Street, the Roman road linking York in Deira with the Tyne at Corbridge and the Antonine Wall at Edinburgh: a highway for the armies of kings and their enemies

starting Hild on her career path. A daughter of King Edwin's nephew Hereric of the Deiran royal household and recently widowed, Hild was on the point of joining her sister Hereswið, by then a widowed queen of East Anglia, in religious life at Chelles in the Paris basin. From a first small community, Aidan progressed her career to Hartlepool and then Whitby, both double monasteries for men and women similar to the East Anglian monastery of Ely. The latter enjoyed close connections with the double monasteries of Chelles and Farmoutiers in Merovingian Francia.[11] On the headland at Hartlepool, Robin Daniels' excavations have shown small rectangular timber buildings set out in neat alignments close to the present-day St Hilda's church.[12] They give tangible form to the 'small houses – *domunculae* – built for praying and reading' that Bede described in the monastery of Coldingham.[13] One of these Hartlepool cells is reconstructed, full size, at the Jarrow Hall Museum.

After Bishop Aidan's death in 651, Iona sent as his successor Finán who, if the genealogies are secure, was a brother of Fín, the mother of Oswiu's son Aldfrið (see also Chapter 7). Whether this appointment was at Oswiu's request, or whether an Ionan initiative, it brought a familial relationship into play to secure the Iona-Northumbria alliance into a new era. With Finán in post, Oswiu began using his Lindisfarne bishop as an agent in moves to establish an overlordship in the English Midlands, where a new, powerful confederation of small polities was coalescing around a Mercian coreland, probably somewhere along the Middle and Upper Trent Valley. King Oswald's nemesis, King Penda of Mercia, had risen inexorably to achieve overlordship in the Midlands from very obscure beginnings, since his first historical appearance in battle against the kings of Wessex in 628. His predecessor, Cearl, had married a daughter to Edwin during his exile – a very obvious threat to Æðelfrið which may have prompted his attack on Chester in 616. Penda himself married Cynewise, a daughter of the West Saxon King Cynegils (c.611–c.642). Mercia had also forged an enduring alliance with Welsh kings in Powys and Gwynedd, forming a powerful political and military bloc and a clear threat to Northumbrian dominance.

Penda's attitude towards Christianity was equivocal.* Bede paints him as a heathen and idolater, an implacable enemy of Northumbria; but admits that he had no intrinsic antipathy towards Christianity – only to those he regarded as hypocrites.[14] Some time in the 630s or 640s Mercian armies defeated East Anglian kings in battle and by 642 Penda was able to decisively defeat and kill Oswald. He married his sister to the apostate King Cenwealh of Wessex; Cenwealh later repudiated her, and Penda chased him into a three-year exile.[15]

The question of Mercia's geography has troubled historians over the decades. In Old English, Mercia means 'borderland' and in the Medieval period the Marches

---

* His geography is obscure but if, as seems possible, he was of *Hwiccan* stock, he may have been raised in a British Christian milieu. Adams 2025.

were the frontier between English and Welsh communities. From the Tribal Hidage *Myrcna landes*, assessed at 30,000 hides, is defined most easily by its neighbours – that is to say, by what it was not. To the north were the *Pecsætna*, dwellers in the Peak District of what is now Derbyshire. To the west, the *Wrocensætna*, the territory centred on Roman Wroxeter. To the south-west lay *Westerna* and *Hwicce* – the latter a kingdom based on the Severn and Avon Valleys and assessed at 7,000 hides. To the east, across the Trent, lay Lindsey and beyond that the Fenland territories of *Gyrwe, Spalda, Sweodora* and others. A host of other smaller polities, from Leicestershire to Bedfordshire and Northamptonshire, seem to have comprised the lands known as Middle Anglia, which Penda gave his son Peada to rule. Mercia, it seems, had originally been the lands either side of the Middle and Upper Trent Valley. Bede, writing ninety years after Oswiu's accession, understood that the kingdom was made up of two elements, northern and southern; his information was that the former was assessed at 7,000 hides; the latter at 5,000 hides.[16] If the boundary between the two was the Trent, then perhaps the Mercian corelands around Tamworth, Lichfield and Burton were the original Marches. Through the seventh century, increasingly powerful Mercian kings subdued its satellites, eventually absorbing them. The sons of their former rulers became more or less loyal Mercian ealdormen.

* * *

Christianity afforded kings a new form of patronage through sponsoring a client king in baptism, as King Oswald had found with King Cynegils of Wessex.[17] Oswiu, perhaps militarily weak in his first years and having to deploy such subtle tools of diplomacy, summoned King Sigeberht of the East Saxons to his hall at *Ad Murum*, there to be baptised by Bishop Finán.[18] In an even more ambitious move to pick off client kings around the edges of King Penda's Mercia, Oswiu also brought Penda's son Peada, who was sub-king in Middle Anglia and a friend of his son Alhfrið, to Finán and baptism at *Ad Murum*.* This was a condition of his marriage to Oswiu's daughter Alhflæd in a two-way marriage alliance, with Alhfrið married to Penda's daughter Cyneburh.[19] However insouciantly Penda might have viewed the baptism of his children, it was nevertheless an expression of Northumbrian 'soft' power, whose threatening message cannot have been lost on the Mercian king. From the mid to late 640s, for more than a decade, Penda waged an ongoing campaign of aggression against Oswiu.

By now, Oswiu had trained priests available to him. These were not only

---

* See the genealogies on pages xvii–xix of this book.

missionaries from Iona but, by the 640s, Northumbrian children who had been taught in Paulinus's churches during the 620s and had come to maturity. He sent four of them, Cedd, Adda, Betti and Diuma, along with Peada on his return to his own kingdom, with Diuma establishing a bishopric there – perhaps at Leicester in Middle Anglia. He then moved Cedd on to King Sigeberht, as bishop to the East Saxons, from where he regularly reported back to Finán.[20] In the post-imperial world of the second half of the twentieth century, players such as the International Monetary Fund and cultural bodies such as the British Council were the agents of the sort of soft power that Oswiu was now bringing into play. Cedd was one of four brothers trained in Lindisfarne, with Cynebil, Cælin and Chad (*Ceadda* in the Latin texts), who became bishop in Northumbria in the aftermath of the Synod of Whitby and later bishop of Mercia in Lichfield. Adda was the brother of the Utta who had negotiated Oswiu's marriage to Eanflæd.

With kingly sponsorship of monasteries, a new way opened for curating the memory of kings and thus for dynastic assertiveness. In East Anglia in pre-Christian and Early Christian times the ruling dynasty had achieved this through ostentatious burial rites and monumental features in the landscape at Sutton Hoo, as long-term visible memorials. There is no evidence from archaeology or texts that Bernician or Deiran kings had used such means. But the monastery now afforded institutional settings for demonstrative, and possibly competitive, display and post-mortem commemoration curated by members of their families – female members feature prominently – occupying senior positions in the monasteries.

Commemoration of Oswald had been complex and contested, with seemingly competing cult sites at Hexham (and nearby Heavenfield), Lindisfarne and Bamburgh, while the place of his death developed as a popular cult site, where the ground on which he fell was believed to have miraculous healing powers.[21] Long after his death, in the 670s, his niece Osðryð, then queen in Mercia, promoted his cult in that kingdom in monasteries at Partney and Bardney – where she had his torso and battle standard recovered from the battle site.[22]

Eanflæd, while she was queen, was instrumental in setting up a monastery with implications for the politically sensitive power relationships between the Bernician and Deiran dynasties, when she compelled King Oswiu to pay the blood-price for murdering her kinsman Oswine by endowing a monastery at Gilling. As widowed queen she joined her daughter Ælfflæd in the monastery at Whitby, and there Oswiu was buried, while his wife and daughter kept his memory alive. When Eanflæd died, she was buried alongside him.²³ While Eanflæd was still alive, Whitby became the burial place for her father King Edwin also, after his remains were recovered from the battlefield of *Hæthfelth* of some fifty years previously.²⁴ His granddaughter Ælfflæd, as abbess, took the commemoration a stage further, committing it to writing when she commissioned a *Life of Pope Gregory* which includes a section on Edwin.²⁵

If fragmentary inscriptions from a cross-head in Whitby and a cross-shaft at Hackness have been correctly interpreted, then it seems that Acha, Edwin's sister and Oswiu's mother, was also commemorated in Whitby, and Æðelburh, Edwin's queen, mother of Eanflæd and grandmother of Ælfflæd, was commemorated at Whitby's daughter-house in Hackness.²⁶ Ælfflæd was the curator of the post-mortem memorialisation of her family and in this she gave focus to the Deiran female line.

The writings from the eighth century present the kings as the driving force in the establishment of monasteries. But patronage is a two-way relationship requiring consent on both sides. In Bede's narrative of Edwin's conversion, we see a long-drawn-out process of Edwin coming to acceptance. From an early stage, he had told Paulinus that he would have to consult the members of his court, and it was only after a debate in council that he finally consented to baptism and was able to bring his people with him.²⁷ Thomas Pickles has argued that conversion in any region could only be achieved when local kin groups came to accept Christianity, seeing conversion as a strategy to stabilise their social position. Children whom Paulinus had baptised at court or in mass public baptism during Edwin's reign had by the 650s become adults and, from these, new social groupings could coalesce: what Pickles calls an 'ecclesiastical aristocracy'.²⁸

The beginnings of this aristocracy are apparent in Deira in association with Oswine's memorial at Gilling. Its founding abbot, Trumhere, was a kinsman of Eanflæd and Oswine; he was afterwards appointed bishop in Lindsey.²⁹ Ceolfrið joined Gilling at the beginning of his career. His brother Cynefrið and their kinsman Tunberht had previously been abbots at Gilling. Cynefrið left to travel to Ireland. Following an outbreak of plague in 661, Ceolfrið and Tunberht transferred to Ripon, with Wilfrid by then as its abbot.³⁰ Tunberht became bishop of Hexham in 681.³¹ Whether Wilfrid was related to Ceolfrið and Tunberht is not known – it seems likely – but he was from an élite family, with a father of sufficient standing to have entertained the king's retinue, and his association with sub-king Alhfrið suggests Deiran origins;³² when he gained a property on the Isle of Wight he installed Beorwine, a son of his sister, as abbot.³³ Ceolfrið, after his ordination as priest in 669, travelled to Kent and East Anglia to observe religious practice there and was then sent to assist Benedict Biscop, to whom he was related, in setting up the house of Wearmouth.³⁴ Here, in 680, he saw the admission of the seven-year-old Bede as a child oblate and he became Bede's teacher and mentor.³⁵

* * *

During the early years of his reign, Oswiu seems not to have been in a sufficiently strong position to challenge Penda openly. But his interventions in Essex and Middle Anglia were too much of a provocation for the Mercian king. In 649 or 650 Mercian forces raided as far north as Bamburgh, unrecorded by the *Chronicle*. For Bede the episode provided an opportunity to demonstrate Bishop Aidan's power to draw on divine intervention; it also, incidentally, provides fascinating detail that fleshes out our knowledge of Bamburgh's hinterland – perhaps even the dwellings and workshops of the individuals buried at the Bowl Hole. Bede says that since Penda could not take the rocky fortress by siege, he determined to burn it:

> He pulled down all the steadings which he found in the neighbourhood of the town and brought thither a vast heap of beams, rafters, walls of wattles, and thatched roofs, and built them up to an immense height around that side of the city which faced the land.³⁶

When a suitable offshore wind arose, the vast heap was set alight. Tongues of flame and a column of smoke rose from the fortress walls and was soon visible to the community on Lindisfarne, a few short miles to the north. In response, Aidan raised his hands to heaven, bewailing Penda's evildoing. At once, the wind veered to the opposite direction, saving the fortress and instead driving the enemy off. This incident must be dated before Aidan's death in 651 – an event itself invested with miracles.³⁷

In 654 Penda 'treacherously' killed King Anna of East Anglia – code for assassination rather than open battle.³⁸ His east flank secure, he now came north in force. According to Bede, Oswiu's first response was to try and buy him off with an offer of treasure, but for Penda this was more than an expedition for booty and he rejected the overture.³⁹ The *Historia Brittonum* implies that Oswiu did hand over treasure.⁴⁰ Kings of the Britons joined forces with Penda at a city called *Iudeu* and Penda distributed to them treasure taken from Oswiu, an event known as the 'Distribution of Iudeu'. This is likely to mean that Picts or Britons of Strathclyde, or both, saw an opportunity to kick back against Oswiu's overlordship and that Penda restored to them booty which Oswiu had previously taken in raiding.* Bede gives the information that Oswiu's son Ecgfrið was placed as a hostage into the house of Queen Cynewise in Mercia.† This and the 'Distribution' taken together suggest that a treaty, punitive to Oswiu, had in fact been reached, with a Mercian-Pictish/Strathclyde alliance forged to rein in his power and subject him to Mercian overlordship.[41] If so, it soon unravelled.

A year later, at a site by the River *Winwæd* (the present-day River Went) along the Roman road skirting the west edge of the Humber wetlands north of Doncaster, Penda's large army was caught unawares by a small force under Oswiu and Alhfrið, which trapped them in floodwaters after heavy rain. Penda and many of the Mercian élite were killed – Bede writes of thirty *duces regii*, sub-kings and provincial rulers – along with Æðelhere,‡ Penda's East Anglian client king, and British allies. Oswald's son, Œðelwald, the Deiran sub-king, had also apparently joined Penda's forces, but when the battle came he stayed on the sidelines.[42]

The outcome was transformative for Oswiu. It removed Penda and broke the Mercian aggression that had troubled Northumbria since the death of Edwin twenty years previously. It also put an end to any Strathclyde or Pictish incursions from the north and, above all, established Oswiu as the dominant force of the age.

As the victor, Oswiu had the power to dictate terms and he used the opportunity to develop and to consolidate the Northumbrian influence in the Mercian sphere that he had been building before Penda's attack. He reorganised Mercia into two broad divisions, ruling northern Mercia directly and placing Penda's son Peada as king of the southern part.[43] He appointed Diuma, one of the four churchmen originally sent to Middle Anglia with Peada, as bishop for Mercia, Lindsay and Middle Anglia. So, after 655, King Oswiu was directly or indirectly overlord of the whole of England north of the Thames. As king, he ruled directly in Bernicia and northern Mercia. Under his

---

* Northumbria's old allies in Dál Riata were by this time substantially weakened after defeats both in Ireland and, closer to home, by Picts and Strathclyde Britons.
† Penda's West Saxon queen.
‡ Bede, in an aside, tell us that King Æðelhere's brother Anna, whom Penda had killed, was 'the cause of the war'.

authority, he had sub-kings in place in Deira* and in southern Mercia. Finán, as bishop of Lindisfarne, had jurisdiction in Bernicia and Deira and bishops under his authority in Mercia and the East Saxon kingdom. This made him, in effect if not in name, a Metropolitan.† In a throwaway line, Bede also tells us that Oswiu subjected the greater part of Pictland to his dominion.

This huge power block was too extensive to last and Oswiu's settlement began to unravel to some extent when, in the following year, Peada was assassinated, supposedly through the treachery of his queen, Oswiu's daughter Alhflæd. Then, in 658, a faction within Mercia who had been protecting Wulfhere, a younger son of Penda, brought him out of hiding and set him up as king.‡ King Oswiu took an army into Mercia and raided there, but Mercian support for Wulfhere remained solid.[44] If this counter-coup curtailed Oswiu's power over Mercian kingship, Wulfhere nevertheless appointed a succession of Northumbrians as his bishop in Mercia (among them, Cedd's brother Chad) and so Lindisfarne retained its influence over the church south of the Humber.[45] Wulfhere and Oswiu jointly sponsored the completion of a new fen-edge church and monastery at *Medeshamstede*§ – restorative justice, perhaps, for Peada's murder and for the death in battle of Wulfhere's father, Penda.

* * *

While faced with Penda's threats, Oswiu had made promises: that, should he be victorious, he would in thanksgiving dedicate his infant daughter to God in perpetual virginity and that he would found twelve new monasteries. Once victorious, he then gave Ælfflæd into the care of Abbess Hild, who was at the time ruling the monastery in Hartlepool. Ælfflæd remained in Hild's care when they moved on to Whitby where pupil, in time, succeeded teacher as abbess, ruling at first jointly with her widowed mother, Eanflæd. Not only did she curate the memory of her father and grandfather, but she was to be active in securing her family's hold on the Northumbrian kingship when she intervened with leading churchmen at two moments of crisis to ensure the succession first to Ecgfrið and then to Aldfrið.[46]

The new monasteries of the second part of Oswiu's promise were founded, six in Bernicia and six in Deira, each with an endowment of ten *familiae*.[47]

---

* He placed his own son Alhfrið there after Œðelwald's failed alliance with Penda at the *Winwæd*.
† The archbishop of a province.
‡ He ruled 658–675, followed by his younger brother, Æðelred (675–704).
§ Later known as Peterborough.

This term is usually translated as 'hide' but for this era it is better understood as a family farm rather than a precise unit of area measurement. It was land to secure the livelihood and support the activities of the monks, in perpetuity. The families on those farms thus became tenants of the monastery, where they now owed service and render of produce, just as they had done on the king's estates, and the community enjoyed the rights and incurred the responsibilities of a landholder: their abbots were territorial as well as spiritual lords. Though these were smaller land transfers than the seventy *familiae* to Wearmouth and forty to Jarrow under King Ecgfrið a generation later, they were nevertheless grants on a significant scale. They mark the early stages of a process that would in time create an imbalance in the patronage relationships which supported the kings, as more land became alienated from the king's fisc to the church in perpetuity.

King Oswiu had previously endowed a monastery at Gilling as an act of reparation for his murder of Oswine.[48] Whether this was at Gilling East at the edge of the Vale of Pickering or at Gilling West near Richmond has been a point of debate.[49] His Deiran sub-kings also sponsored monasteries. His nephew Œðelwald had given a grant of land at Lastingham, on the southern edge of the North York Moors, for Cedd to build a monastery.[50] Oswiu's son Alhfrið, who was appointed sub-king after the battle at *Winwæd*, gave ten *familiae* at *Stanforda* and thirty at Ripon to support a monastery there.*

The names of Oswiu's twelve monasteries are not given and their locations are uncertain. Coldingham, where his sister Æbbe was abbess, and Utta's Gateshead might number among the six in Bernicia, but this is no more than a guess. In Deira, Richard Morris[51] has drawn attention to a cluster of religious houses in Ryedale around the edges of the Vale of Pickering, suggesting that some or all of the six might be concentrated here. This seems likely, for the intensity of royal interest here is striking, with no fewer than six kings between the mid seventh and mid eighth centuries known from texts to have had some involvement in religious houses: Oswiu and Oswine at Gilling, Œðelwald at Lastingham, Ecgfrið at Crayke, Eadbert and Æðelwald Moll at Coxwold and Stonegrave.[52] Hovingham, as we have noted, is suggestive of a royal estate centre (see Chapter 3). Evidence, other than text, for religious houses and their communities can come in the form of fragments of ecclesiastical sculpture such as crosses, often built into the fabric of later church buildings, or of structural remains recorded in archaeology; all these forms

---

* *VW* 8: see below in this chapter for the political significance of Ripon.

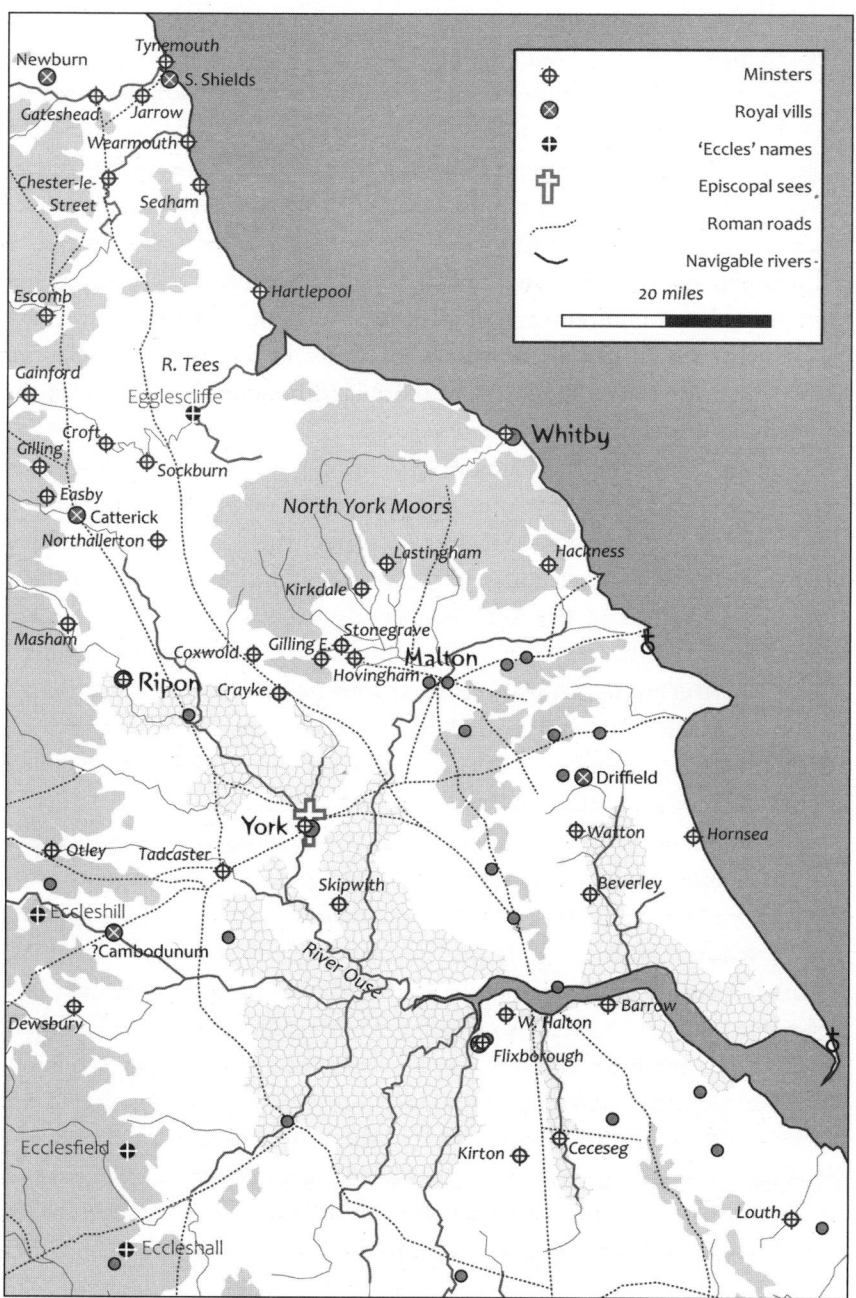

Map 13 Deiran monasteries and churches

are evident in the Ryedale set, though it is not possible from the material remains alone to give precise dates for their foundations, nor to understand precisely their status, whether they were houses of a monastic community, or not. But such strands of evidence point towards a tight cluster of foundations around the north side of the Vale and some outliers.

The north side of the Vale of Pickering is around the edge of the Deiran coreland of Brian Roberts' mapping,[53] extending beyond the ancestral homelands of the Deiran kings and available to them to grant out as *bookland* to the church. In the *Ecclesiastical History* Bede described royal *vills* (*villae regiae*) with surrounding territories (*regiones*). Sometimes these territories had names with a suffix *-ingas* which has the sense of 'the people of' the named territory: the territory is defined by its people. In Ryedale, *Læstingas ēa*, Lastingham as it became, *Piceringas*, Pickering, and **Hofingas*,* Hovingham, are examples. Many centres of religious communities known from the seventh–ninth centuries had emerged as mother churches by the twelfth, serving areas that were many times larger than a typical parish. This suggests that these communities were founded with large territories from royal endowments and that they had developed systems of pastoral care within their territories which, by the twelfth century, had become formalised as parishes. The pointers towards this are the cases in which seventh–ninth century sites of religious foundations re-emerged as estate centres with widely dispersed dependent *vills* and with the church at the centre controlling several parishes within the area of lordship.[54]

This interlocking of territorial lordship and parochial structure has enabled Thomas Pickles to reconstruct the geography of early royal territories transferred to the church in Ryedale and around the Vale of Pickering.[55] The Howardian Hills on the south-west side and the Tabular Hills on the north-west and north sides ring the west end of the Vale of Pickering in a horseshoe shape, with the Vale of York to the west and the North Yorkshire Moors rising north beyond the Tabulars. Here churches and church lands occupy strategic locations between the Deiran corelands on one side and the Pennine lands across the Vale of York to the west.[56] Roman engineers had earlier provided a road extending west from Malton along the north edge of the Howardians towards this gap. It is traced securely as far as Hovingham and is thought to have continued onwards.

---

* See Chapter 3 for the suggestion that the 'Hof-' element may have another derivation.

Sculptured frieze at All Saints' church, Hovingham, North Yorkshire

In the parish church of All Saints in Hovingham, a carved stone slab from a tomb-shrine was built into the eleventh-century tower and small-scale excavation within the interior revealed a length of construction trench and two courses of a stone building which the excavator speculatively interpreted as a small two-cell structure of nave and chancel. A charcoal sample from the fillings of the foundation trench has a calibrated radiocarbon date of AD 610–890, calculated at the 95 per cent probability level.[57]

These are tantalising results from keyhole work, hinting at an early church building. The stone slab, now placed behind the altar in the south aisle, is carved with an eight-panel arcade, each panel containing a standing figure and the theme of the set is Marian. At each end is an angel; three panels on the left side represent the Annunciation and three on the right the three women at Christ's sepulchre. It is a carving of the early ninth century, part of a tomb-shrine thought to have been prepared for the translation to Hovingham of a saint whose lifetime was during the seventh century; the set of figures in the carved stone slab suggest a female saint. In this respect, it compares with the shrine made at Lastingham after 750 for the second translation of the relics of Cedd.[58] Hovingham is known to have had a Roman precursor ever since the discovery in 1745 of a hypocaust, bath and mosaic floor. Recent geophysical survey confirms the presence of a large villa-type building, possibly the centre of an estate associated with Malton.[59]

In the Domesday survey of 1086, Hovingham held demesne lands in dependent *vills*, from Grimston in the west to Swinton in the east, suggesting that this estate represents the former large royal territory named from the people of one Hofer,* which itself probably emerged out of an estate of the Roman era. Pastoral care for its people came from Hovingham. Within the territory, the monastery at Gilling had a close familial bonding with the centre, and Stonegrave had a church presence by the ninth century, if not before; both eventually became centres of parishes.[60]

Beyond Hovingham, along the Roman road, Gilling East sees a break in the higher ground between the Howardian and Tabular Hills, forming a natural routeway out of the Vale of Pickering and onwards to the Vale of York and the main Roman roads. This site, at the edge of the Deiran coreland, seems the more probable location for an assertive and politically charged statement of Deiran kingship than Gilling West. Its church has a sculptural fragment built into the south chancel wall of the present church. Scroll moulding, minimal foliage and the rigidity of its medallions associate this stylistically with the eighth-century Acca's Cross in Hexham.[61]

At the west and east ends of the Gilling Gap lie Coxwold and Stonegrave, respectively, watching over the ways in and out and progress through the gap. Both feature in a letter from Pope Paul I (757–767) to the Northumbrian King Eadberht (737–758) rebuking him for having taken these monasteries from Abbot Forðred and given them to Æðelwald Moll (see Chapter 9).† By the time of the Domesday survey, Coxwold was the centre of an estate referenced in the fourteenth century as Coxwoldshire.[62] Stonegrave has ninth- and tenth-century sculptural fragments. Geographical proximity and the fragments of evidence, physical and textual, point to interconnections between Hovingham, Gilling, Coxwold and Stonegrave in the eighth century.[63]

On the north side of the Vale of Pickering, Kirkdale and Lastingham are sited at the edge of the Tabular Hills, in valleys where tributary rivers flow from the higher moors south towards the River Derwent. Kirkdale is known for an inscription recording the rebuilding of the church in 1060, but excavations have taken its structural history back to the eighth century. The church is sited at a point where the flat and steep-sided narrow valley follows a gentle curve. This has led Richard Morris to identify this as *Cornu Vallis*, where Abbot Ceolfrið, after leaving Wearmouth-Jarrow in 716, paused on his route through Yorkshire to await news of the election of his successor as abbot.[64]

---

* See Chapter 3 for the suggestion that the 'Hof-' element may have another derivation.

† These may have been thought to be spurious monasteries, such as Bede had denounced. Whitelock 1979, 830–1.

Burials and remains of a monumental structure of some sort, possibly a mausoleum, from the late Roman or post-Roman period underlie the remains of the church, which has developed through three structural phases before its present form. The earliest phase is tentatively suggested from limited excavation as a single-cell building with an apsidal east end 14.4m in overall length and 8m wide, corresponding closely to the width of the present nave but offset slightly; burials are associated with this phase.[65] Two grave covers of the late eighth–ninth centuries are incorporated into later fabric. One is fringed with a skeuomorphic representation of a pall, a textile used for wrapping a relic. The draping of a richly embroidered cloth over a free-standing tomb was a proclamation of sainthood, suggesting that this grave cover marked the translation of a saint's relics, as in the cases of Lastingham and Hovingham.[66]

Philip Rahtz and Lorna Watts, the excavators, think that this small church did not serve a full-scale religious community but was more akin to a mortuary chapel and that Kirkdale was a dependent settlement within a secular estate whose centre lay at Kirkbymoorside.[67] To understand why this part of the narrow valley of the Hodge Beck should have become a focal place for burials, and possibly the translation of a saint, the excavators turned to a phenomenological reading of the landscape. In dry seasons the water flowing in the beck disappears into a sink hole upstream from the church site, reappearing again some distance further downstream. In the words of one observer, to see 'the mouth of the cavernous feature' that suddenly appears in the spring and disappears later in the year 'is like peering into another world . . . this strange behaviour of an otherwise prosaic watercourse . . . made the valley in some way numinous'.[68] This association of a shrine with a watercourse emerging from the hillside recalls West Heslerton on the opposite side of the vale.

Cedd's monastery of Lastingham was also the place of his death and burial after his return from the East Saxon kingdom. Two carved stone panels, dated on stylistic grounds to some time after 750, are now known to be parts of a shrine for the translation of Cedd's remains. Lastingham shows a religious community engaging with the landscape at an immediate local level as well as within a wider regional setting. It is sited at an edge location, between the fringes of the Vale on the south side and high moorland to the north. This prompted Bede to describe the place as better suited to robbers and wild beasts than normal human habitation and he drew on an Old Testament text of Isaiah to say that because of the monastery, grasses, reeds and rushes grew where once dragons lay; Cedd made the place sacred through a long cleansing ritual at the foundation[69] and, as Richard Morris has shown, the cleansing extended out on to the moor. A door on the north side of the church leads out to a trackway up the hill. Climbing the hill, a pilgrim can see in the distance two of a set of four prehistoric burial mounds in the distance, known locally as the Three Howes.

At a small plateau part-way up the slope stands another burial mound named Ainhowe on which a cross, known as the Ana Cross, has been placed. From this point, the pilgrim now sees three of the four distant burial mounds, the Three Howes: at the Ana Cross the pilgrim gains a vision of a Calvary. The existing Ana Cross replaces an older monument. A fragment of a cross-head found by the church and dating from about 800 implies a monument that stood some 7.5m tall; a hint perhaps of the sort of cross that might originally have stood on Ainhowe. The church site itself may have been determined by an act of cleansing. It occupies a bluff above a fast-flowing watercourse, Ellers Beck, and a secondary small watercourse emerges from beneath the church. Architectural fragments of Roman date found here suggest a shrine of some sort for a water cult, re-adopted for monastic use in the mid seventh century.[70]

Lastingham's Medieval parish was a huge, elongated area stretching some 24km from the moorland tops into the Vale of Pickering. The original form of the name *Læstinga ēg*, 'the island of the people of the *Læstingas*', in which *ēg* refers to an island, cannot plausibly apply to the present village and church site, but Kirby Misperton, linked with Lastingham through sculpture, is precisely an island formed of glaciofluvial deposits rising dramatically from the wetland of the Vale, with the church towards the highest point.[71] Two fragments of cross-shaft of the ninth and tenth–eleventh centuries, one built into the north wall of the church nave here, have stylistic connections to Lastingham.[72] The parishes of Lastingham, Kirkbymoorside and Kirkdale have overlapping areas of jurisdiction along their borders suggesting they are divisions of a once-larger unit and by the mid nineteenth century Kirby Misperton and the southern part of the extensive territory had broken away into smaller parishes. In summary, the hypothesis is that Cedd's monastery was established and pastoral care provided in the extensive royal territory of the *Læstingas*; subsequently, Lastingham acquired estates at Kirkbymoorside, Kirby Misperton and Kirkdale where small church communities in time evolved into parishes as sub-divisions of the original mother parish.[73]

By 1066 the territory of the *Piceringas* had developed into a royal estate, loaned out to the Northumbrian Earl Morcar. The earliest hint of an ecclesiastical presence in Pickering is from tenth-century sculpture. Middleton, which clings to the edge of the sedimentary stone of the Tabular Hills immediately above the north edge of the Vale, has an eighth- to early ninth-century cross carved on a stone set into the church tower; it has features in common with a Lastingham cross-head and the cross carved on the Kirkdale grave cover; it may have been cut from a Roman sarcophagus.[74] The mother parishes of Pickering and Middleton interlock, suggesting they are divisions of a once-unified territory, though how and when two parish centres emerged is not known.[75]

Peripheral to the main set of sites, but possibly associated, are Crayke and Sherburn. Crayke lies south of Coxwold, in the Vale of York, where King Ecgfrið gave a property to the Lindisfarne community as a staging point on a route to York at a point where the steep conical hill commands an extensive view south along the Vale of York.[76] There are two fragments of a late eighth-century cross-arm, and Alcuin referred to Eccha, an anchorite who died here in 767.[77] An appraisal of the local landscape places the core of the monastic precinct on the south-east slope of Crayke Hill, tucked in beside the road layout, with the cemetery on the top of the hill and the church slightly downslope. A village green set out in the tenth–eleventh century clipped the south edge of this precinct and much of the rest became incorporated into a field when an open-field system was established. The parish boundary takes a roughly circular route around the now-enclosed fields and within this, road and land-boundary alignments trace an inner circuit; this is suggested as the boundary of the original monastic precinct.[78]

Sherburn, 5km east of West Heslerton along the south edge of the Vale of Pickering, lies on a ridge of glacial moraine projecting north into the wetlands of the Vale providing a natural causeway. Fragments of cross-shafts and grave covers survive from the ninth to eleventh centuries. Archaeological survey shows an extensive Early Medieval settlement and an industrial area with large cavity-floor buildings and a large-scale corn drier, for which there is a calibrated radiocarbon date of AD 605–674. This looks like a centre for receiving renders of produce, first for a royal estate and then possibly the lands of a religious house.[79] The adjacent parish of Heslerton provides some of the most abundant and well-understood evidence for Early Medieval settlement anywhere in Northumbria (see Chapters 1, 3 and 9).

* * *

The foundation in 659 of a religious community at Ripon on the east edge of the Pennines had lasting political and ecclesiastical significance.[80] Its first abbot was Eata, previously abbot of the monastery at Old Melrose on the River Tweed in the Anglo-Scottish borders. Here Cuthbert, later bishop of the Northumbrians, first entered the religious life in about 651. Bede's use of its Brittonic name, *Mailros*, allows the suspicion that this had been an earlier, British Christian centre, as does a spread of *eccles-* names in the area. Its dramatic location, in a tight loop of the River Tweed within a mile of the Roman fort at Newstead and the three peaks of the Eildon Hills, is best viewed from above, on Bemersyde Hill at Scott's View. The sense of exclusivity and isolation, of secular power held at arm's length, evokes the relationship between Lindisfarne and Bamburgh, Iona and Dunadd. It was from here that Cuthbert travelled south to Ripon with Eata and became his guest master.

A year after its foundation, Ripon was taken from Eata and given into the hands of Wilfrid, a young nobleman who had attached himself to the court of Alhfrið, Oswiu's half-British son and sub-king of Deira, with a new grant of an extra thirty *familiae** of land to support the monastery. Wilfrid, who had developed an early antipathy towards the Irish version of Christianity and resolutely pursued a more orthodox, Roman line, expelled Eata and his monks, including Cuthbert.[81] He also gained ten farms at a place called *Stanforda*. The location is uncertain: perhaps Stamford Bridge on the River Derwent, or perhaps one of two places called Stainforth.

Ripon's location and its royal patronage may be more politically significant than has been realised. It was sited on a spur of land within the confluence of the Rivers Skell and Ure, some 6 miles upstream from the former *civitas* capital and large Roman town of *Isurium Brigantium*: Aldborough, close to Boroughbridge at a crossing of the river by the Great North Road. At the time of the Domesday survey Ripon, Aldborough and Knaresborough were the centres of three interlocking estates, Ripon belonging to the archbishop of York and the other two to the king, in a large territory called Burghshire which is likely once to have been a single land unit held by the king.[82] To the south lay Elmet; to the west the small British kingdom called Craven; to the north perhaps *Erechwydd*, an eastern territory of the kingdom of Rheged along the valley of the Swale above Catterick. One can infer from Alhfrið's patronage here that royal power in these formerly British territories had been devolved to him. The obvious further inference is that Oswiu had given him control here as part of what we would call a hearts-and-minds diplomatic initiative: Alhfrið was half-British; is likely to have spoken his mother's tongue; may, as of right, have inherited land here. Now established in his own community under royal protection, Wilfrid was in a position to act on a larger stage. In the same year he was ordained as a priest at Ripon by Agilbert, Gaulish bishop of the *Gewisse* in Wessex.[83]

---

* Forty *familiae* according to Bede in *HE* III.25.

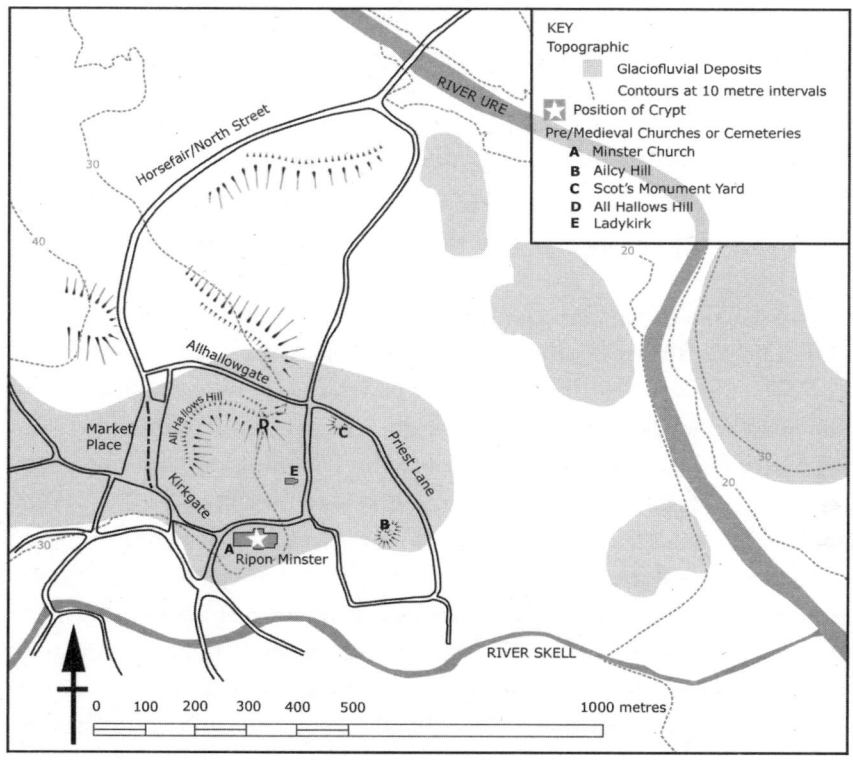

Map 14 The natural and ecclesiastical topography of Ripon

The Medieval minster church of Ripon is the successor building to Wilfrid's church of the seventh century. It stands some 200m south-east of the Market Place, prominent on a bluff which falls off sharply south to the River Skell, within the town which occupies the wedge of ground between the River Ure to the north and east and its tributary the Skell, a little over 1km from the confluence.

Five sites in the core of the town have yielded evidence of Medieval and/or pre-Conquest churches and/or cemeteries. These are Ailcy Hill, with burials of seventh–ninth centuries; Scot's Monument Yard, the site of a possibly thirteenth-century church and the find spot of a *styca* of the ninth century; All Hallows Hill with an undated cemetery; Ladykirk with a cemetery of perhaps eighth–ninth centuries and a possibly contemporary church; and finally, the minster site itself where the crypt of Wilfrid's church still survives. Four of these locations were on prominent ridges or mounds formed from periglacial deposits, and Ladykirk's excavator described 'a small gravel hill' here.[84]

The natural topography of the site, with these ridges and mounds, and on land above the flood plains, goes some way to defining an irregularly shaped area of some 10ha. In a study of the town, Richard Hall and Mark Whyman observed that the street pattern to some degree encompasses this area. Allhallowgate and Priest Lane describe an arc extending from the north-west to a backwater of the River Skell south-east; Kirkgate, leading west and north-west from the minster into the Market Place follows the edge of the scarp between the two; a continuation of that line would cross the Market Square diagonally to a junction with Allhallowgate at its intersection with Horsefair/North Street which leads out north and east to a river crossing.[85]

It appears then, that the urban street pattern has preserved the boundary line of an ecclesiastical precinct, carefully selected for its position between the two rivers, and with the periglacial features defining key points in a polyfocal layout. If so, the site selection is unlikely to have been Wilfrid's doing but an inheritance from the Old Melrose community.[86] The wedge of ground close to the confluence here does not quite echo the peninsula within the loop of the River Tweed at Old Melrose, but the sense of being in the midst of water is common to both. The chronology of the burials and structural remains seen in excavations is too imprecise to distinguish between the original layout of the precinct and Wilfrid's; the crypt is the only secure marker. But, as Hall and Whyman observe,[87] polyfocal and non-axial precincts are known from Merovingian Gaul at the time of Wilfrid's travels. Ladykirk has attracted interest as being possibly the church of St Mary referred to by Richard of Hexham in the twelfth century.[88] But even if that church was in Hexham – this seems more likely – a second church here in Wilfrid's Ripon is plausible.

* * *

King Oswiu conducted his political diplomacy from a *villa regia* named *Ad Murum*.[89] This is usually understood to be Walbottle, a fort site along the line of Hadrian's Wall towards the western edge of the Tyneside conurbation. But at 14 Roman miles from the coast as the crow flies, this is further inland than Bede's measurement of 12 Roman miles. A better fit would be either the fort of *Pons Aelius* in central Newcastle, measured at 11.5 Roman miles via an upriver journey from the bar at Tynemouth, or the fort of *Condercum*, now the west-Newcastle suburb of Benwell, 11.8 Roman miles by overland travel from a landfall at Tynemouth, direct to Wallsend and then along the line of the Wall. Two brooch finds are the only archaeological record for post-Roman activity in this now built-up area of Benwell: a bronze cruciform brooch of the sixth century and a Great Square-Headed bronze brooch of the early seventh century. A glass vessel is said to have been found along with the latter brooch but was broken up by workmen. These items were probably from burials, but their contexts are not known.[90] There is, however, an argument from place-names in favour of Benwell. Allen Mawer suggested that the earliest form of the name in English could have been *binnan wealle*, meaning 'within wall', a close fit for Bede's *Ad Murum*.*

In Newcastle there was certainly a population, of whom 679 individuals are known to have been buried within the fort walls in a cemetery used from about 700 until 1080 when the castle was built. No structures are known from the earliest stages of the cemetery[91] but there are traces of activity within the fort during some time which cannot be more closely dated than after the Roman period and before the cemetery burials began. These include a drain and water tank, a line of post holes which could represent a fence or the wall line of a building, and hints of a ditch terminal and counterscarp bank on one side of the fort.[92]

The archaeological evidence is circumstantial, but it does seem that Oswiu was using one of the former Roman fort sites as the location of one of his halls within the cultural coreland of the lower Tyne Valley. Add to this a concentration of monasteries founded during Oswiu's reign and that of his son and successor Ecgfrið (670–685), comparable with the Ryedale cluster (see map on page 150): then, as Ian Wood has shown, there is a strong focus of kingly interest here.[93] Abbot Utta's monastery of Gateshead sits at the point where the Roman road heading north reaches the River Tyne, immediately opposite Newcastle. The state of the Roman bridge at this time is unknown, but it is tempting to think that Oswiu placed his trusted diplomat here to manage this strategically and economically important element of infrastructure and that, whether or not the Newcastle fort was the site of *Ad Murum*, this key crossing point of a navigable river was under the eye of both church and civil authority. Excavations within this intensively urbanised part of Gateshead have not revealed any structures from this period, but the excavator has suggested that outlines of an Early Medieval precinct are fossilised in the street pattern.[94] The Medieval church of St Mary, standing almost directly overlooking the bridgehead and where Bishop Walcher was murdered in 1080, might well mark the position of a seventh-century monastery church.

* We are grateful to Diana Whaley for advice on this point. See also Mawer 1920, 18.

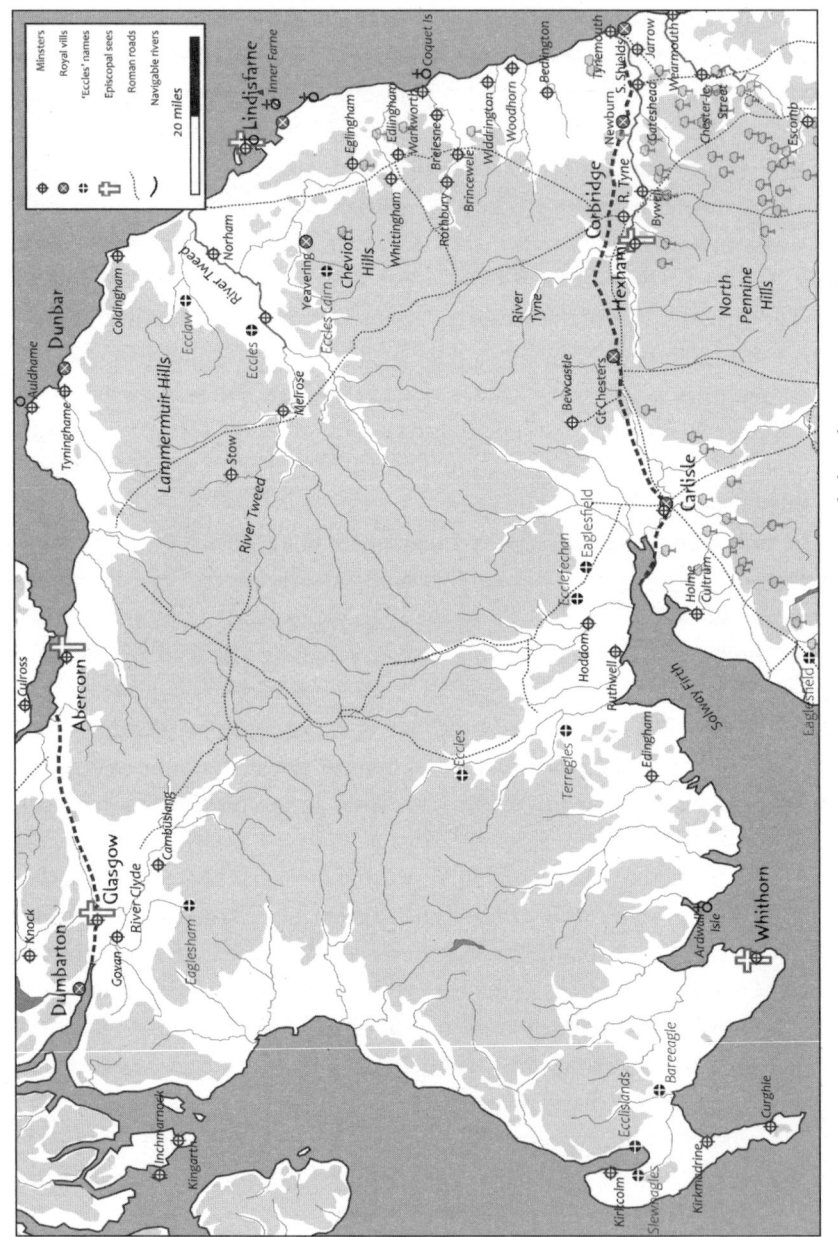

Map 15 Bernician monasteries and churches

At the mouth of the river, a Medieval tradition holds that the murdered king Oswine was buried at Tynemouth, on the headland where the ruins of the Medieval priory now stand proud, and the *Anglo-Saxon Chronicle* records that another murdered king, Osred, was buried here in 792. It seems surprising that the Deiran King Oswine should have been buried here and not at Gilling, the church founded in expiation of his murder by Oswiu; perhaps, as Ian Wood suggests, Oswiu made sure that the victim was taken away from the Deiran heartlands for political reasons.[95] But the Medieval monks of Tynemouth also claimed that Oswine was born at *Urfa*, identified as *Arbeia*, the Roman fort on the headland immediately across the river at South Shields. A collection of small finds of the seventh to ninth centuries from excavations here – a gilded copper-alloy mount, copper-alloy and bone pins, a pin beater, a stylus and some gaming pieces – lends some credence to the idea of a royal residence and certainly shows occupation within the former fort. In archaeological excavations conducted in 1963 at Tynemouth Priory, George Jobey identified foundation trenches of four rectangular timber buildings which, on stratigraphic evidence, he could say were later than the Roman period and earlier than the Medieval layers, with the tentative suggestion that these were monastic. Comparison with more recent findings, for example from Hartlepool, would allow a more confident identification than was possible in the 1960s.[96] The builders of King Ecgfrið's foundation of Jarrow, 4km upstream from *Arbeia*, were able to source stone from both *Arbeia* and the Roman fort of *Segedunum*, a further 3km upstream and across the river.[97] Between *Arbeia* and Jarrow lay another monastery, *Donamuða*, on the opposite side of the inlet of Jarrow Slake; both the monastery and the inlet became associated with King Ecgfrið.*

* * *

A single issue dominates Bede's account of the final decade of Oswiu's life, that of the correct date for celebrating Easter. This is a current running through the *Ecclesiastical History* from its first mention in Book II, Chapter 2 until the final resolution in Book V, Chapter 22, while the account of the Synod of Whitby of 664† in Book III, Chapter 25 is the centrepiece of the whole work. Here Bede brings it right down to the domestic level: King Oswiu, who had been

---

* Both discussed further in Chapter 6. Ian Wood (2008b, 19) considers this River Tyne tributary to be the Don of *Donamuða*, and not the Yorkshire Don. For the contrary view, see Parker 1985.
† A synod, strictly speaking, is a council of the church, but this conference called by the king has long been known as the Synod of Whitby.

schooled in the Irish customs of Iona and Lindisfarne, was celebrating Easter while Queen Eanflæd, who observed Roman customs, was still in the penitential season of Lent, observing Palm Sunday. This was not tolerable and so Oswiu called a meeting to resolve the matter once and for all. The meeting place was the monastery of *Streanæshealh* where Hild, teacher to Oswiu's daughter Ælfflæd, was abbess. This place-name has not survived. The name Whitby is of Scandinavian form and cannot have been coined before the ninth century, and we owe to Symeon, the Durham historian of the early twelfth century, the information that *Streanæshealh* was the earlier name for Whitby.*

Domestic harmony aside, this matter concerned Christendom as a whole. It mattered to Christian people that they should commemorate the resurrection of Christ, and it mattered that they should do so on the right day. But knowing which was the right day was easier said than done. The problem turned on reconciling the Jewish lunar calendar, which determined the feast of Passover, with the solar calendar in use in the West since Roman times. But since the solar year does not divide into a whole number of lunations, it was difficult to determine in advance which lunation would be the Paschal moon, defined as the one on which the moon is full – by convention on its fourteenth day – on or after the spring equinox. The task was to reach a calendrical solution to reconciling the astronomical realities, and the approach taken was to see if there was a cycle of a multiple of years across which lunar months and solar years would reconcile. The first point of argument at Whitby was that two such cycles were in use: Lindisfarne followed its mother house of Iona in using an eighty-four-year cycle, while Roman usage, which Wilfrid was now promoting in Northumbria, was a cycle of nineteen years. The second point of argument concerned the day within the month. Both parties held to the standard view that Easter should be celebrated on a Sunday and so there was a seven-day window within which the day could fall, but Lindisfarne accepted days 14 to 20 while the Roman rule was days 15 to 21. An added complication, though this was not raised in the debate as Bede presents it, was that there were two versions of the nineteen-year cycle and a rare disagreement between them was looming for 665. It is not obvious why the irreconcilable dates should suddenly have become intolerable to Oswiu when he and the queen had lived with this for some time; it may be that the forthcoming 665 discrepancy was the catalyst for the conference.[98]

---

* *Libellus* III.22. While Whitby has been generally accepted, there is an alternative view that the location was Strensall, north of York. Barnwell, Butler and Dunn 2003.

Bede writes a set-piece scene of a formal debate, a contest in three rounds, conducted in the presence of Kings Oswiu and Alhfrið. The protagonists were Colmán, bishop of Lindisfarne since Finán's departure in 661, speaking for the Iona-derived practices that the Northumbrian church had followed since Aidan first arrived at Lindisfarne; for the Roman practice Wilfrid, who was abbot of Ripon but who had yet to achieve great prominence, led on behalf of Bishop Agilbert, the head of delegation. At the conclusion Oswiu intervened to ask if it was true that St Peter has the keys to the kingdom of heaven; did Columba (Colm Cille) have the same authority? Colmán was forced to concede. Oswiu, wishing not to be turned away at the gates of heaven, decided the matter in favour of St Peter and Roman practice and against the Lindisfarne tradition that he had formerly followed. He had been a king for more than twenty years; he recognised power when he saw it and knew when to concede.

In the immediate aftermath, there was a shake-out at Lindisfarne. Colmán resigned; he and others in the community, unwilling to accept the new dispensation, left and returned to Iona. Tuda, educated in Ireland but a follower of Roman practice, was appointed bishop in Northumbria and Eata was transferred from his post as abbot at Old Melrose to the Lindisfarne abbacy; he was English, trained by Aidan.[99] Wilfrid, triumphant, was promoted to bishop of York and was sent to Francia for consecration at the hands of Agilbert. At Compiègne, he entered the cathedral seated on a golden throne carried by twelve bishops. But he tarried too long abroad and Oswiu appointed Chad to the neglected see. Wilfrid, on his eventual return, reverted to his post of abbot at Ripon.[100]

This arcane technical problem between two versions of the nineteen-year cycle may not have been of great interest to anyone outside of a clerical élite, but the fact of such a problem may have afforded Oswiu a pretext to bring to the surface a political undercurrent. When Wilfrid returned from Francia to find his see taken from him, the dog that didn't bark on his behalf was his patron, Alhfrið: he was written out of the script; neither Bede nor Wilfrid's biographer, Stephen, refers to him after Whitby. But Bede had already given a signal when he wrote in a brief summary introducing Oswiu's reign that Penda of Mercia, his nephew Œðelwald and his own son Alhfrið had all attacked him, with no further elaboration of Alhfrið's action.[101] The inference to be drawn here is that at Whitby a political drama was unfolding in parallel to the ecclesiastical. Alhfrið had been using Wilfrid and his continental connections as an ecclesiastical front for building a power base in Deira independent of his father and counter to his father's Lindisfarne allegiance. In calling the synod, Oswiu drew him into the open and, in a masterstroke of power play, Oswiu did not oppose his son, but instead adopted his cause as his own: cutting the ground from beneath Alhfrið's feet. Thus humiliated, Alhfrið had no choice but to take up arms and, as seems most likely, he was killed in the endeavour. No wonder Wilfrid stayed away.

The year 664 also saw a widespread plague in England, and during that year Deusdedit, the archbishop of Canterbury, died. Bede says that the plague 'raged far and wide with cruel devastation . . . laying low a vast number of people'.[102] In Ireland it became known as 'the Great Mortality'. In England it accounted not just for the archbishop but also, on the same day in July, King Earconberht of Kent; Tuda, newly appointed bishop of the Northumbrians; Cedd, one of the four priests sent into Mercia but now bishop of London; Abbot Boisl of Old Melrose and King Æðelwold of the East Saxons. A year later just a single bishop* ordained under Roman canons survived in England; and that is why Wilfrid had been forced, fatefully, to go to Francia for consecration as a bishop.[103] The East Saxon kings now apostatised.

At this stage in the history of the church, kings still had influence in the appointment of bishops, and Oswiu and Ecgberht of Kent decided between them that a priest named Wigheard should be the new archbishop just as, within his own kingdom, Oswiu had appointed both Wilfrid and Chad. Indeed, Oswiu's decision to align the Northumbrian church with Rome may have been given extra impetus if the decision was made after Deusdedit's death: he had enfranchised himself as an elector. Wigheard was sent to Rome but died there before the pope could consecrate him in that office. The matter now rested in the papal court and, after some delay, Pope Vitalian appointed Theodore, a sixty-six-year-old monk from Tarsus – present-day Türkiye.[104] This was an unlikely appointment, not only on account of his age, but also because he was a monk of the Eastern tradition. The pope also appointed Hadrian, an African abbot then in a monastery near Naples, to accompany Theodore, lest he should try to introduce Greek customs into England. Their departure was delayed while Theodore re-grew his hair so that he could be tonsured in the Roman manner. In an extraordinarily long reign of twenty-one years, Theodore transformed the institution of the English church, reorganising it under a diocesan structure, giving it a sound basis in Latin and Greek scholarship and enabling it to wield political and ecclesiastical power across the English kingdoms.[105]

---

* Wine, in Wessex. Wilfrid was now in Gaul. The other bishops were Lindisfarne-trained and ordained under Irish rites.

6

ECGFRIÐ: PEACE-WEAVERS 671–685

Overlordship and its loss – Deiran expansion
into the west – Trouble with Wilfrid –
Dunbar and a Lothian coreland – Monastic
estates and a lower Tyne focus of kingship

Ecgfrið, son of Oswiu, came to the throne in 670 in favourable conditions, achieving diplomatic and military success early in his reign. But losses in his later years, culminating in a disastrous campaign of 685 against the Picts in which he was killed, saw the end of Northumbrian dominance north and south of its core territories. In religious matters, however, the consequences of his father's decision at Whitby to adopt the Roman strand of Christianity bore fruit in spectacular developments initiated by Wilfrid and Benedict Biscop. A distinctive and especially vibrant micro-Christendom arose in Northumbria in the 670s and 680s. It nurtured Bede; it drew Northumbria into the learning and culture of Western Christendom; it transformed the Northumbrian countryside; and it flourished into the time of Alcuin in the eighth century.

It is difficult to achieve a well-rounded view of King Ecgfrið's reign because the written sources view him largely through the lens of his dealings with the principal church leaders of his time, Wilfrid, Benedict Biscop and Cuthbert; Wilfrid's biographer, Stephen, is an overtly hostile witness. Bede in the *Ecclesiastical History* has little to say about him; he generally down-plays, or at times even ignores, King Ecgfrið's successes; he makes no attempt to preserve his memory or to say where he was buried.[1]

As a boy, Ecgfrið was placed in the household of Queen Cynewise of Mercia as a hostage and bargaining piece in his father's dealings with King Penda.[2] Improbably, and in spite of Penda's death at the hands of King Oswiu's army in 655, he survived and returned home with insight, no doubt, into the realities of power politics, a good working knowledge of the Mercian court and perhaps friendship with Penda's sons, Wulfhere (658–674) and Æðelred (674–709), whom as king he would later encounter. Whether he acted as sub-king in Deira after the fall of Alhfrið is not known. He inherited a strong kingdom but was soon faced with a Pictish rebellion in 672.³ Irish chronicles record that the Pictish King Drest had been expelled. He was a son of the Dál Riatan King Domnall Brecc, with whom Oswiu had been allied. This looks like a shake-up in the balance of power in the north now that Oswiu had died, presenting the Picts with a chance to rise against their Northumbrian overlord.

Active on Ecgfrið's behalf in this campaign was a *sub-regulus* named Beornæð. He may have been a client king of Oswiu, holding a territory in Fife within the Pictish territory over which Oswiu had gained control. If so, the Pictish rebellion might have been an attempt, with Drest as a leader, to drive out Beornæð now that Oswiu was dead.⁴ Ecgfrið put down the rebellion. It may be that Bridei, who then emerged as the Pictish king, and Ecgfrið were related, and that Ecgfrið was using extended family networks to install a compliant sub-king. Whatever the case, Ecgfrið now wielded overlordship in southern Pictland, from Argyle eastwards to Aberdeen.⁵

South of his kingdom, Ecgfrið forged a strong position through marriage alliance. His queen, Æðelðryð, whom he married around 660, was daughter of King Anna of East Anglia and sister to Seaxburgh, who had married King Eorcenberht of Kent and whose son Ecgberht was king during the early years of Ecgfrið's reign. His Kentish connections were close also through church leaders. The Northumbrian churchman Benedict Biscop was in Rome at the time when the pope appointed Theodore as archbishop of Canterbury and he had accompanied Theodore to Kent. Early in Ecgfrið's reign, Theodore had quickly intervened in the church politics of Northumbria by restoring Wilfrid to the bishopric he had lost while absent in Gaul; perhaps Biscop had lobbied on his behalf. The Mercian King Wulfhere, also connected to Kent by marriage, had built up dominance south of the Humber after the collapse of Oswiu's post-*Winwæd* settlement; these competing interests led eventually to warfare and a battle in 674 in which Wulfhere was put to flight. King Ecgfrið subjected Mercia to tribute and imposed a Northumbrian bishop, Eadhæd, on Lindsey.⁶ The battle's location is unknown, but a place somewhere along the Roman road skirting the Humber wetlands would seem likely, given the incorporation of Lindsey into a now extended Northumbrian diocese.

Ecgfrið was now at the height of his power as a king and overlord, and a beneficiary of this dominance was Wilfrid, present at the battle against Wulfhere, who profited from the extension of his diocese across the Humber.⁷ But as well as being a bishop, Wilfrid was also an ecclesiastical entrepreneur in his own right. He already had a monastery at Ripon and now, in the 670s, he developed this asset. He constructed a new stone-built church and used its dedication ceremony to stage a highly theatrical display of power politics.[8] Assembling a cast that included King Ecgfrið and his younger brother, the *sub-regulus* Ælfwine, along with the élites of secular and clerical society, he draped the church's altar with textiles in the imperial colours of purple and gold and displayed a gospel book with gold lettering on purpled pages with its own gold and jewel-encrusted casket; this may have been the first time such a book was seen in Northumbria. This was Wilfrid's stage set and these his props for announcing deals agreed with the king over lands appropriated by violent suppression of British churches, which the king now granted to Wilfrid. These lands are described as *regiones*, a term which implies large administrative territories, and named as *iuxta Rippel, Ingædyne, Dunutinga* and *Incætlævum*, as well as *cæterisque locis* (other places) unspecified.

The locations are not absolutely certain and have been under debate, but there are some pointers. *Dunutinga* is identified as Dent, a village along the River Dee, one of the headwaters of the River Lune draining the west side of the Pennines, where a flat valley floor affords cultivable land to support the central place of an estate. The complete territory may have consisted of the Medieval parish of Sedbergh, some 215km² in extent, with the church at Sedbergh and the estate centre at Dent.[9] If *Rippel* refers to the River Ribble,[10] this too is on the west side of the main east–west watershed of the Pennines and suggests a territory corresponding to the Medieval hundred of Amounderness in Lancashire, with a centre perhaps at Preston at the head of the river estuary, or else higher up the river at the site of the former Roman fort at Ribchester. *Incætlævum* is identified at Catlow[11] and this could be a location in the Forest of Bowland, within the small kingdom of Craven or near to Nelson in Lancashire: both are west of the Pennine watershed. *Ingædyne*, with the meaning of 'steep hill', is identified as Yeadon.[12] Yeadon near to Otley, 11km north-east of Leeds, is associated with an estate later belonging to the archbishops of York, and this lends support to the idea that this is Wilfrid's site.[13] But Wilfrid's announcement of these donations at the Ripon dedication implies that they became his as proprietor of Ripon and not as bishop of York; another 'steep hill' further west may be more plausible.[14] Yeadon Crag, along the upper reaches of the River Nidd, just north of Pateley Bridge and 15km west of Ripon, is a possible location, though unlike the other *regiones*, this is east of the watershed. It is impossible to be sure, but a Pennine location seems likely in view of the other territories named.

The campaign that brought these lands into Wilfrid's portfolio seems to have been widespread, involving as it did 'other places'. Felicity Clark argues that these lay in the valley of the River Lune.[15] Five centres along a 20km stretch of the lower reaches of that river – Heysham, Lancaster, Halton, Hornby and Gressingham – stand out as having stone sculpture of the Anglian period indicating early monastic locations. Shared stylistic elements and motifs in the sculpture link these as an inter-connected set of locations, sharing characteristics with sculpture in Ripon, Northallerton, Jarrow and also Hexham, where the vine-scroll motifs on Acca's Cross are closely comparable with those on a cross-shaft at Lancaster. No other places in the whole of Lancashire have sculpture of this period. The Lune Valley had attained a territorial identity in Roman times named from a god *Contrebis* who is known from finds of three altars. After the Roman period this area of good-quality land is likely to have continued to support a population and it may have been the core of a small British kingdom, successor to *Contrebis*. The concentration of monasteries; the sculptural affinities between them and core Northumbrian churches, including Ripon and Hexham; and their location between the *regiones* of Dent and Catlow, together make a cogent case that these were church sites that Wilfrid established in the 'other locations' after the British clergy had been driven out.

The suppression of the British churches and the aggrandisement of Wilfrid's landholdings here extended Northumbrian interests into the Pennines beyond the watershed and on to the coastal plain of Lancashire north of the Ribble; we might see this as the third, and perhaps final, stage of consolidation of the Deiran expansion westwards following Edwin's move into Elmet in the 620s, and then Alhfrið's promotion of Wilfrid's interests in Ripon in about 660.[16] This analysis is seemingly at odds with Bede's statements that Æðelfrið had already subjected lands of the Britons to tribute and that Edwin had established a realm of peace from coast to coast.[17] But Felicity Clark has explored the idea of a frontier as a process that develops in several stages, allowing us to think of these western areas as being at first tribute lands where some degree of local autonomy prevailed under local rulers and local church organisation.[18] Deiran control then intensified through land taking and boundary setting, with new centres of lordship and new church sites established to replace what was now swept away. The three-day feasting that followed the church dedication mitigated the violence of the take-over as the king and people showed magnanimity towards their enemies – perhaps British leaders participated in the feast – to initiate the final self-shaping stage of frontier integration as the

Ecgfrið: Peace-weavers 671–685

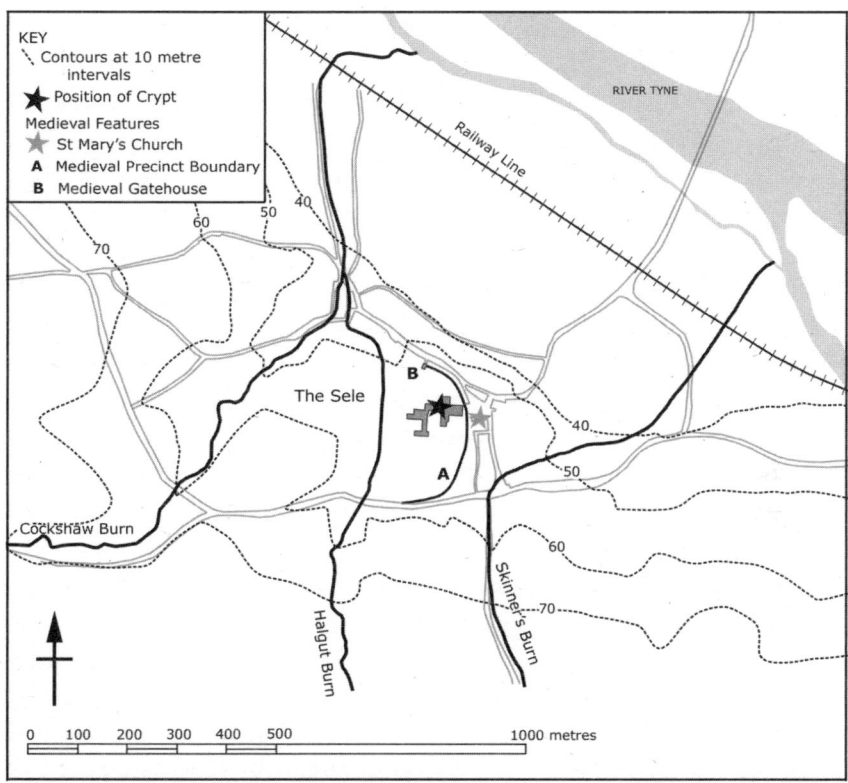

Map 16 Hexham: the abbey church dominated a hill overlooking the River Tyne

newly formed societies came to identify themselves as fully members of the Northumbrian realm. Wilfrid's domain was now huge.

In the early years of the reign, Wilfrid founded a new monastery at Hexham, in the middle reaches of the Tyne Valley. This came from the grant of a *regio* by Queen Æðelðryð.[19] If the Medieval Liberty known as Hexhamshire preserves the original extent of land granted, this was an estate covering some 300km² which the queen had received as dower on her marriage. The name is probably *Hagustaldes ēg*, with the *ēg* element, meaning 'island', referring perhaps to the bluff above the south bank of the Tyne on which the monastery, and the present town, are sited. *Hagustald* is usually a young warrior, and hence the estate is that which is given to the younger son.[20] From this etymology, Tom Corfe has proposed how it came into the holdings of the Bernician kings.[21] He notes that Heavenfield, the site of Oswald's arrival, and his battle site of *Denisesburn* are both within the territory and that in the *Historia Brittonum* and the Welsh Annals the battle site is named as *Cantscaul*, meaning 'the hero's enclosure', a similar meaning to the English *Hagustaldes*. Oswald's younger brother was Oswiu, the warrior hero holding the lordship of this estate through his marriage to Rhieinmelth of Rheged. It was a frontier zone between the lands of the emerging Bernician kingdom and the Rheged coreland of the Eden Valley in Cumbria. Through this marriage, this territory became consolidated into the Bernician realm. From Oswiu the estate passed to his younger son Ecgfrið and thence by his marriage to Æðelðryð as dower and on to Wilfrid.

Here at Hexham, Wilfrid embarked on a new building project.[22] Wall lines of stone from the principal church survive close to ground level within the footprint of the present parish church. Richard Bailey and his collaborators have painstakingly built up an understanding of the form of Wilfrid's church from observations made during re-building of the nave in the early years of the twentieth century, supplemented by their own small-scale archaeological interventions at different times since the 1970s. The church was of basilican form, with a nave of approximately 140–145 m^2 floor area and with a chancel and two side aisles of unequal widths, narrower on the north side. As at Ripon, a crypt lay beneath the chancel. A corridor led northwards from the eastern end of the north aisle, apparently linking the church to unknown buildings beyond. The east end wall of the chancel has not been observed: its position is inferred by reference to later fabric, and recent interpretations have modelled the west end by reference to the contemporary St Peter's in Wearmouth. They depend on extrapolating from limited observations, and two variants are currently proposed.[23] The main effect of the alternative models bears on the crypt. Eric Cambridge understands the main chamber to be aligned on the axis of the nave and chancel; Paul Bidwell has it offset south. In the former view, the two side entrances to the crypt begin outside the church; in the latter they are contained within the church.

East of the main church, and aligned on its axis, is a small structure, some seven metres long internally with an apsidal east end. It is not closely dated, but it is likely to have been built as a mausoleum in the seventh or eighth centuries.[24] Richard of Hexham and Ælred wrote in the twelfth century that there were two other churches in Hexham, dedicated to St Mary and St Peter, with the suggestion that Wilfrid himself built St Mary's.[25] The story from Wilfrid's *Life*[26] that St Michael in a vision extracted a promise from Wilfrid that he would make good his neglect of the mother of God by building a church in her honour lends credibility. Richard described it as a tower, almost circular, with four chambers projecting from it.²⁷ Fabric from the Medieval church of St Mary survives, visible at the backs of buildings on the south side of the market square. If this church preserved the site of its predecessor, this would place it some 80m south-east of the chancel of St Andrew's. Burials observed in the market square indicate a cemetery between the two churches. There is no corroborating evidence for the twelfth-century claim of a church of St Peter; Richard may have been referring to the St Peter dedication in Ripon.²⁸ The outer precinct boundaries of the monastery, such as those known at Hoddom in Dumfries and Galloway, for example,²⁹ have not survived in this urban setting. But there are hints in the topography. A cliff edge dropping down from below the 50m contour line to the valley floor sets a tight constraint on the north and north-east side of Hexham. On the east side, Skinner's Burn forms a natural boundary; on the west, the small Halgut Burn, some 80m west of the church, perhaps defined the edge of an inner precinct, with the open ground known as The Sele west of this as an outer precinct bounded by the sharply defined, narrow ravine of Cockshot; the limits south are less clear.³⁰

Wilfrid's monastery churches at Ripon and Hexham are distinctive in having reliquary crypts. Both survive as complete structures within the present-day churches. The two are remarkably similar in constructional detail and measurement units: products of the same mind, though Hexham shows refinements that suggest improvements made in the light of experience.³¹ In each case, there is a central barrel-vaulted chamber, with its long axis west to east, and two angled passageway corridors leading down from ground level, one on the south side entering directly into the chamber and one on the north leading to an entrance on the chamber's west side. Ripon's two corridors begin at opposite ends: the north corridor leads from east to west, the south from west to east. Both of Hexham's corridors lead down from east of the chamber. Hexham also has a third access, a steep set of steps leading straight down from the west. The north corridor and the west stairs meet in a well-articulated and fully vaulted antechamber, giving access to the main chamber. Ripon, without a west access, marks this position with a less emphatic half-vaulted widening of the corridor leading from the north. Niches are cut into the walls of both chambers. How visitor flow was managed at each, in liturgy or in pilgrimage, is a matter of speculation. Hexham's west stairs, descending from within the nave of the church, lend themselves to the idea of liturgical procession. As noted above, the main question at Hexham is whether the entrances to the two side corridors opened from within or outside the church.

Roman *spolia* from the town of *Coria* (Corbridge) deliberately embedded in the dim subterranean passage walls of Wilfrid's crypt at Hexham

The reliquary crypt is an idea and a structure deriving from the tomb shrines of saints, such as Wilfrid visited on his travels. There is no closely comparable example as a prototype for Ripon and Hexham. But, as Richard Bailey observed, search for a prototype in a strict sense may be unnecessary. Wilfrid could have identified elements seen in one or more cases and selectively transferred and adapted these to fit within the churches he was building.³² The significant point need not be architectural literalism, but evocation by alluding to particular features. The corridors, for example, could allude to the approaches to St Peter's tomb in Rome or, in a more tenuous way, to the catacombs.³³ Wilfrid's allusions possibly extended beyond Rome to the tomb of Christ within the church of the Holy Sepulchre in Jerusalem. Features known from this have been built into the Ripon and Hexham crypts: entry from the east side, with surrounding passages; a vaulted main chamber, higher than head height; a two-part structure with an outer chamber and an inner for the body itself; emphasis given to the north side of the chambers, the side on which Christ was believed to have been laid; a unit length of 7ft used in the chambers, as attested for Christ's tomb.³⁴ It may also be that the proportions of St Peter's church in Wearmouth echo those of the Temple of Solomon.³⁵

Wilfrid's biographer, Stephen, overcome by the magnificence of Hexham, exclaimed, 'we have heard of no other such building this side of the Alps'.³⁶ This is not strictly true: Wilfrid had seen churches more splendid in Lyons.³⁷ But this highly impressionistic comment captures for us the impact that these constructions were having in Northumbria: they put people in mind of Rome. Wilfrid deliberately played on this. In a landscape in which architecture was fashioned in timber and thatch across all levels of society, right up to the kings' great halls, stone walls and lead roofs assaulted the senses. Rome was a complex idea. In one way, it was a memory of a lost age of giants, now fallen into ruin.

> Splendid this rampart is, though fate destroyed it,
> The city buildings fell apart, the works of giants crumble.

The author of the poem called *The Ruin* may have been looking over the remains of Bath, *Aquae Sulis* of the Roman era.³⁸ But the ruins at Corbridge or York could prompt similar thoughts, or those of Carlisle, where Queen Iurminburh and Bishop Cuthbert took a guided tour in May 685 to see the Roman city wall and its water supply.³⁹ In another sense, some idea of Roman governance had survived, as illustrated by the way in which King Edwin had progressed around his realm with banners and a standard-bearer going before him.⁴⁰ He might have learned such display from his East Anglian hosts during his youthful exile: their warrior king buried in the ship at Sutton Hoo carried Roman-derived insignia and displayed Byzantine silver at his feasting table.⁴¹ Now, Wilfrid was re-imagining Rome in a material sense in

Northumbria. The crypt at Hexham is constructed entirely of *spolia*, building stone, recovered from Corbridge. While there is good evidence that the walling was rendered with plaster, possibly as a base for painting, some groupings of frieze-sections and some inscriptions may have remained deliberately visible.[42] The Ripon crypt was built of three types of stone, probably taken from the Roman fort of Aldborough, 10km to the south-east, and from a villa at Well, 5km north of Ripon.[43]

Before Æðelðryð's grant of Hexham, Wilfrid's Northumbrian interests had been centred in Deira. His arrival in Bernicia and into lands held within the Bernician ruling family could well have been seen as an undesirable and destabilising intrusion into the politics of the realm and to the family interests of the king.[44] It is certain that Queen Æðelðryð was a problematic figure, notwithstanding her value for Ecgfrið's diplomacy in the south; she was a reluctant queen and wife, unwilling to consummate the marriage. Bede recounts that he had discussed this point with Wilfrid who told him that he had proof of the queen's virginity.[45] The king, Wilfrid told Bede, had promised him lands and money if he could persuade the queen to consummate. In the event, and in collaboration with the king's aunt Abbess Æbbe, Wilfrid managed to extract her from the marriage and into religious life at Æbbe's monastery at Coldingham, from where she later returned to her own people, joining her sister Seaxburh in the family monastery of Ely as abbess. Ecgfrið's response to this is unknown except insofar as it gave him the chance of a second marriage and the siring of an heir. It seems likely that there was a negotiated settlement at the separation, and it may be that the Hexham grant was part of this, though the precise timings of events around the years 671–3 are unknown.

By the late 670s, relations between Wilfrid and the king had broken down. Ecgfrið was by then married to Iurminburh, whose name suggests that she was from the Kentish royal house. Stephen attributes this breakdown to Iurminburh's jealousy and claims that the king and queen bribed Archbishop Theodore to split up Wilfrid's York diocese.[46] The charge against Theodore is risible. He was engaged in re-structuring the English church and, sooner or later, he had to turn his attention to York where the diocese was as extensive as the entire kingdom of Northumbria. Wilfrid had not attended the church synod that Theodore held in Hertford in 673 but had sent representatives; it may be that he had suspected that the matter of dividing dioceses would be discussed and preferred to stay away.[47] Two of the decrees of the synod might be taken as direct challenges to Wilfrid's claim to Metropolitan status in

York: that no bishop should intrude into the sphere of another, and that none should claim precedence over another out of ambition; and the decree that more bishops should be created as the number of the faithful increased inevitably pointed to the division of the Northumbrian diocese. In 678 Wilfrid was expelled and his see was divided in two, with Bosa consecrated as bishop of Deira with his seat at York, and Eata as bishop of Bernicia centred at Lindisfarne or Hexham.[48] These were not priests from within Wilfrid's networks: Bosa was trained in Whitby;[49] Eata had been a protégé of Aidan and was one of the Old Melrose monks evicted from Ripon when Wilfrid took over. He was then abbot, first in his own monastery and then at Lindisfarne.[50] Wilfrid took umbrage and journeyed to Rome to appeal against Theodore's actions.

Iurminburh's opposition to Wilfrid is more credible. She pointed to his worldly wealth, his monasteries and his countless army of followers. The latter point certainly rings true: he had arrived back in England from his consecration as bishop with a retinue of 120 armed men.[51] Wilfrid was becoming over-mighty. It could also be that Hexham was a personal irritant for the queen. She might have expected that, on the dissolution of the king's first marriage, the dower lands of Hexham would have been returned to him and then passed on to her as the new wife.[52] But if there was personal animus, there was also a political context.[53] If Iurminburh was indeed Kentish, her marriage to Ecgfrið revived an alliance that had existed between Oswiu and his wife Eanflæd's kinsman King Ecgberht of Kent. In the 670s Kent came under pressure from Mercia, culminating in an attack by King Æðelred, brother and successor to Wulfhere. Northumbria and Kent had common interests against Mercia, while Wilfrid held monasteries there under the patronage of both Wulfhere and Æðelred.[54]

On his return from Rome, Wilfrid was imprisoned on Ecgfrið's orders, held first by a king's officer named Osfrið at *Broninis* – the location is unknown – and then in more severe conditions by Tydlin at Dunbar. Released at the request of Abbess Æbbe, Wilfrid then left Northumbria for some time.[55]

* * *

By the time of King Ecgfrið, the coreland on the coastal zone between the Lammermuir Hills and the lower reaches of the Firth of Forth was firmly within the Northumbrian civil and ecclesiastical sphere, with the king's authority centred on the *urbs regia* of Dunbar, and with an identity formed within the nexus of Anglian material culture. As late as the eleventh and twelfth centuries, Dunbar was recognised as a shire centre[56] and its territory underlies the historic county of East Lothian. As a coastal site and harbour, Dunbar was the northernmost link in the Northumbrian communications chain, along with Coldingham, Lindisfarne, Bamburgh, Warkworth, Tynemouth, Jarrow, Wearmouth, Hartlepool and Whitby.

But Dunbar represented a shift from the older territorial centre of the Gododdin on the great dome of volcanic rock that is Traprain Law, rising 120m from the valley of the River Tyne,* 10km inland.[57] Long the recipients of Roman largesse in the form of silver bullion, those who ruled from Traprain were able to display and deploy wealth in the form of the vessels, dress fittings and other ornaments and the hacksilver seen in the silver hoard discovered in 1919.[58] By the fourth and fifth centuries, the status of Traprain and its East Lothian territory as a lasting ally of Rome had provided the silver and the cultural context to fashion the massive silver chains that are known from Lothian and the southern edges of the Lammermuirs.[59] But some radical change occurred in cultural behaviour, marking the end of a close and long-lasting relationship with the late Empire that had characterised Traprain's territory and differentiated it from areas immediately to the south.[60] The great hoard of silver from Traprain and the massive silver chains were taken out of circulation and buried during the first half of the fifth century.[61]

Change was afoot also in the fifth century in the realm of burial traditions.[62] In place of a wide diversity of practices, emphasis lay on monumental graves and in particular the long-cist burials in which the body is laid out extended and aligned east–west, the grave lined with stone flags, set upright, and sometimes lidded and paved with stone.† These have a strong geographical focus in the Lothians and, to a lesser degree, extending north into Fife and Angus, with a scatter elsewhere in the north and west and along the east coast into Northumberland. The distribution overlaps with that of plain dug graves, but these are in a minority in the Lothians and are more typical south of the Tweed.

Another characteristic of burials of this period is the deliberate use of natural features in the landscape.[63] Small knolls formed from periglacial deposition are widely scattered throughout the landscape of the Forth–Tyne

---

* Not to be confused with the Northumberland River Tyne.
† The distribution of long-cist burials in Lothian represents an idea of settlement density up to the middle or end of the seventh century, before the overt expansion of Bernician influence here.

region, but it is a distinctive East Lothian phenomenon that these were selected for burials, usually of small groups of people, though two cases have about 100 burials. These glacial knolls are typically between about 7m and 17m in diameter. They can look like barrow mounds, but it does not seem that there was any confusion in the minds of those doing the burying. There is an observable contrast between use of glacial knolls in East Lothian and use of barrow mounds further south in southernmost Scotland and Northumberland where, despite just as great a density of the glacial features as in Lothian, these were not selected. Mortuary rites, as Adrian Maldonado observed,[64] can be stable over long periods of time yet change radically during times of social stress. Celia Orsini reads the knolls as providing a place for expressing community identity for populations vying to hold their claims in disputed lands in a contested landscape.[65] The fifth century saw radical change in mortuary rites; so too the seventh century. By its end monumental burial in its various forms – long cists, barrows, natural knolls – was disappearing in favour of simple, unfurnished dug graves. This is true also of the Anglo-Saxon furnished burial tradition.

The new, seventh-century focus of the East Lothian coreland, which had once been the territory of Traprain, was at Dunbar, re-imagined as an *urbs regia*. At Castle Park a small promontory was fortified by ditched defence lines in the late Prehistoric or Roman period.[66] After the defences had been levelled, a courtyard was set out over the former ditch lines with stone-founded and posthole features. A period followed devoid of activity until this location again came into use as small timber buildings of rectangular form appeared, comparable to examples elsewhere in Anglian Northumbria. Among these was a sunken-featured building, with loomweights scattered on the base of the pit, possibly from the building's collapse. A seventh-century belt buckle and fragments of a buckle plate broadly confirm the date and Northumbrian cultural affinities of this group. This small complex was further developed and brought within the protection of a palisade and rampart which, when projected beyond the excavated area, would have enclosed nearly 0.5ha. Later, a ditch-and-bank fortification superseded the palisade, taking in a wider area, and stone buildings replaced the earlier timber structures. A mortar mixer, similar to one found at the Wearmouth monastery,[67] is a residue of the craftsmen at their work. Finds of pins, needles, lace tabs and a strap end, and a comb carved from an antler testify in some degree to the day-to-day domestic life of this complex. Such is the archaeological evidence for the place in which King Ecgfrið had Bishop Wilfrid imprisoned.⁶⁸ There is no sign of any Yeavering-type hall which the *praefectus* Tydlin kept for the king – perhaps this stood on the edge of the promontory beyond the area excavated – but large amounts of animal bone, especially those of cattle, hint at the sort of feasting expected on a king's progress.

Dunbar sits on the south side of the estuary of the River Tyne. Around 10km further north, on the coast close by Tantallon Castle, is the small headland of Auldhame, now known from excavations to be the site of a monastic settlement that flourished between the mid seventh and the mid ninth centuries.⁶⁹ The appearance of human bones, disturbed in cultivation, prompted the excavations of 2005 and consequently this was the focus of investigation, taking in only a part of the headland. A broad ditch, at least 1.9m deep and set out in a curve across the neck of the headland from one side to the other, enclosed an area of about 0.6ha. This is likely to be originally the defensive work of a prehistoric promontory fort, though this is not confirmed archaeologically. But it was apparently still a current feature in the landscape in the middle of the seventh century, for it defined the south edge of a graveyard with at least 308 burials in situ; a smaller ditch marked the east edge. Graves, set out east–west, include long cists and earth-cut graves along with burials in coffins and some with pillow stones. A programme of radiocarbon dating has allowed the burials to be grouped into four phases, the first dating from 650–1000. The burials of this phase group around a small stone-footed chapel formed of two cells which superseded a timber-built oratory.

An entry from the Northumbrian Annals for the year 854 preserved in the *Historia Regum Anglorum* lists a circuit of ecclesiastical settlements claimed by the church of Lindisfarne between Tweed and Forth. This includes Auldhame, Tyninghame and Pefferham (thought to be Aberlady).⁷⁰ Tyninghame is close to Dunbar, across the Tyne estuary and a little way upstream where, 1km north of the village, a scatter of cropmarks of sunken-featured buildings suggests the presence of a settlement akin to those in the Milfield Basin.⁷¹ As yet, no early ecclesiastical remains have come to light, but the *Historia de Sancto Cuthberto* claimed for the Lindisfarne monastery 'all the land belonging to the monastery of St Balðere, which is called Tyninghame, from the Lammermuirs to Esk mouth'.⁷² This association of Balðere with Tyninghame, and his lifetime in the first half of the eighth century* do not easily reconcile to a traditional association with Auldhame and Bass Rock, but in the light of the Auldhame

---

* The Northumbrian Annals, which form a continuation to Bede's *History*, give the date of his death as 756.

excavation results, Alex Woolf suggests a solution along the following lines.⁷³ In much the same way that Cuthbert has come to be seen as Lindisfarne's saint although he was not its founder, so Balðere, though not the founder, came to be the premier saint and patron of Tyninghame and its dependencies. Auldhame, already 'old' at the time of the first written record, was the original small religious community, presumably adhering to the traditional, pre-Whitby, Easter observances. With growth and increased prominence, it was relocated from its clifftop confines to a more spacious lowland setting; the original site became a dependent cell, retained and valued as a locus of sanctity and continuing place of burial. A closely comparable case of relocation might be the shifting of *Caer Colud* from the exposure of Kirk Hill near St Abb's Head to the shelter of Coldingham;⁷⁴ perhaps that move came after the death of its abbess, Oswiu's sister Æbbe.⁷⁵

The *Historia de Sancto Cuthberto* claims a huge landholding for Tyninghame, equivalent to the whole of East Lothian. The textual evidence for the first really large landed endowments to Northumbrian monasteries comes from the time of King Ecgfrið. If this is the case here, Tyninghame looks like a house founded under royal patronage to pair with the *urbs regia* that was now operating from the former Brittonic fortress of *Dynbær*, in much the same way that Lindisfarne paired with Bamburgh. Secular and ecclesiastical authority may have been coterminous, exercised over the whole of the shire, but on the matter of who drew the revenue of render from where, it seems likely that the church could claim the land north of the River Tyne and the civil authorities the land to the south.⁷⁶

Further west around the coast, and just west of the town of North Berwick, the Medieval settlement of Eldbottle has been identified in archaeological evaluation trenches.⁷⁷ Radiocarbon dates point to occupation between about 400 and 1400, with a first phase of activity within the period 400–670. The few cut features seen in the narrow trenches do not allow for any detailed understanding, but an Anglian centre of some sort, as implied by the *-botl* element of the place-name,⁷⁸ seems to be confirmed. The English language dominates the place-names of East Lothian; Dunbar is exceptional in retaining its Brittonic roots. Among these are the *-ham* and *-ingham* names: Morham (where there is a sculpture fragment), Auldhame, *Pefferhame*, Tyninghame, Lyneringham, Whittingehame. These may indicate ecclesiastical estates, with *-ham* representing estates dependent upon a minster, and at least in some cases *-ing-* may indicate the group of people associated with a minster.⁷⁹ Once this territory from Lammermuir to Eskmouth came under the king's administration from the centre in Dunbar, the Northumbrian church developed an infrastructure from its principal house at Tyninghame.

The East Lothian area lay within the territory of the Lindisfarne diocese but the establishment in 681 of a bishopric at Abercorn, west of Edinburgh on the south side of the Forth, is testimony to an attempt to bring land within what is now Midlothian into the Northumbrian sphere of influence. Two sites known within the hinterland of Abercorn, each at a distance of some 8km, give some context.

On land which is now within the perimeter of Edinburgh airport, near Kirkliston, a long-cist cemetery was first discovered in 1860 and subject to limited investigations in connection with later development at the airport. At least forty-two long-cist graves were observed, set out in neat rows on a naturally formed knoll, though the full extent and the total number of burials is not known.[80] A focal feature of the cemetery is the rounded boulder standing 1.3m high above ground level, known as the Catstane. It is a prehistoric standing stone and inscribed on its east face is a pre-Northumbrian Early Christian inscription which can be read as IN OC T / MVLO IAC T / VETTA F / VICTR – 'In this tomb lies Vetta, daughter of Victorinus'.[81] The stone stood beside a road leading to a crossing of the River Almond at the boundary of the Medieval parish of Kirkliston, whose name combines Brittonic and Gaelic elements with the sense of 'domestic enclosure'. It appears, then, to be marking the entrance to the territory of a high-status residence and administrative centre.[82]

At Ratho,[83] west of Edinburgh, is another example of settlement being sited at a place of prehistoric burials with its focus a ring-ditched feature, within which were two cremation burials in urns. Features of the Early Historic period include a two-phase palisade enclosing a sunken-feature building whose remains held a large number of clay loomweights, and two rectangular post-in-trench buildings. There is not enough detail known of this site, nor of its wider context, to assess its status within a Northumbrian settlement hierarchy. Abercorn and Ratho could be seen in the context of frontier development, but Andrea Smith expresses an alternative view, that the bishopric might have been created to serve and regulate an already-established population of Bernician Angles living amongst the sort of British Christian communities implied by the Catstane cemetery. Whatever the case, the Anglian presence here failed to influence place-naming to any great extent and it may have been too short-lived following the withdrawal of the Abercorn bishop in 685.[84]

* * *

King Ecgfrið's relations with Benedict Biscop were not so fractious as his dealings with Wilfrid. Like Wilfrid, Biscop had travelled to Rome, but he enjoyed a more wide-ranging experience of Christianity, and its monastic forms in Western Europe, than did Wilfrid.[85] He thus offered Ecgfrið different possibilities for a Rome-facing church in Northumbria, enhanced by his close association with Archbishop Theodore and with John the Cantor, responsible for the liturgy in Rome, whom he accompanied to England in 679.[86]

With grants of land from Ecgfrið in 674 and 681, Biscop began building programmes first at Wearmouth, on the north side of the river, and then on the south side of the Tyne a few kilometres from the sea, at Jarrow. Rosemary Cramp's excavations in difficult urban settings while housing was being cleared from the sites in the 1960s and 1970s have gone a long way to defining the central complex in both cases. St Peter's church at Wearmouth had a nave of some 108m^2, a chancel of uncertain length, side aisles north and south, which may have been divided into small cubicles and, at the west end, an entrance porch beneath a tower and *narthex* (antechamber). The entrance porch and tower and the west wall of the original nave survive as part of the fabric of the present parish church. On the south side of the church was a graveyard whose beginnings preceded the building. Crossing this area was a corridor connecting the church with a rectangular building range aligned parallel to it. Enclosing walls bound the structures into a tight complex.[87] St Peter's stood above the Wear, closer to the river than is the case now that the topography is much altered from its natural state by ballast dumping and encroachment over the foreshore. It is at a point where a small headland projects forward. A stream course 160m south-west of the church partly defines a plateau and possible central ecclesiastical complex similar to that at Jarrow.[88] From here the river loops north-east for a kilometre to the coastal headland, though how much came within any wider precinct is unknown.

At Jarrow, two churches were built on the same axis. The larger basilican church of St Paul has a footprint almost identical to St Peter's,[89] though without the *narthex* and with a narrower north aisle – hinting, perhaps, that the Wearmouth chancel began short and was only later lengthened. East of this was a free-standing, single-cell building of some 50m^2 floor area. This structure, now rebuilt at its east end and with additional window openings, is the chancel of the present-day parish church. A tower of the late Anglo-Saxon period connects the chancel to the nave built in the eighteenth century over the remains of the demolished seventh-century structure. The relative positioning of the two seventh-century buildings here is similar to that of the two

Bede's church at Jarrow on the south bank of the River Tyne

structures at Hexham: this was an arrangement which both Wilfrid and Biscop are likely to have seen on their travels in Gaul – at Chelles, Autun and Lyons, for example.[90]

As at Wearmouth, there was a cemetery on the south side and, beyond the graves, two large rectangular buildings, probably residential, were set parallel to the church.[91] The steep slope down to the River Don on the south side was terraced, with some small structures and a building, possibly a guest house, at the foot of the slope close to the position of the present bridge. The course of the Don loops around the south and east sides hard against the plateau on which the church sits, with the now filled-in intertidal mudflats of Jarrow Slake on the east side. It may be that a palaeochannel north of the Don, detected in magnetometry survey running west–east 60m from St Paul's, formed the north side of a central ecclesiastical complex on a raised knoll,[92] with perhaps a more extensive outer precinct, bounded by the Tyne 600m north of the church.

1. Bamburgh Castle: ancestral seat of the Bernician kings from the sixth century.

2. Heavenfield, where Oswald raised a cross the night before battle. The original cross was revered in Bede's day for its healing properties.

3. Reconstruction at Jarrow Hall of the excavated Hall 'A' at Thirlings: the home of a minor Northumbrian thegn.

4. Reconstruction at Jarrow Hall of an Early Medieval sunken-floored building. Such structures seem to have been used as general-purpose workshops.

5. The church at Lastingham, founded by Cedd in about 654 on the edge of moorland: a 'place better suited to robbers and wild beasts', according to Bede.

6. The medieval churches on Lindisfarne, likely on the site of the original foundation of 635.

7. The ramparts of Old Oswestry hill fort, perhaps the site of King Oswald's final battle and his death at King Penda's hands in 642.

8. Stained-glass window at St John Lee near Hexham, depicting the scene at Heavenfield before the battle of Denisesburn as described by Adomnán and Bede.

9. Yeavering Bell: Iron Age hill fort and, below, the site of the royal township of *Ad Gefrin*.

10. The great enclosure ditch at Yeavering, re-excavated in 2023 to resolve questions posed by Hope-Taylor's interpretation of its date and function.

11. The Norman chancel arch and nave of St Cuthbert's church at Norham, where the Lindisfarne community relocated in the ninth century.

12. In a bend of the River Tweed, with the Eildon Hills behind, the site of Old Melrose monastery, where Cuthbert first entered religious life.

13. Escomb church, County Durham: a seventh-century foundation close to the Roman fort at Binchester, perhaps under Wilfrid's patronage.

14. The carved stone 'Frith' stool at Hexham Abbey – perhaps the episcopal throne of St Wilfrid.

15. Reconstruction drawing imagining Hexham Abbey as originally built in the seventh century.

16. Alcuin (centre): a nearly contemporary portrait of the Northumbrian and Carolingian scholar in his last years.

17. Whitby Abbey: the medieval ruins on the site of the probable royal monastic complex of *Streanæshealh* founded in the seventh century, where St Hilda hosted the momentous council of 664.

18. The Franks Casket, carved from whalebone, generally regarded as a product of eighth-century Northumbrian craftsmanship: 22.9cm long, 19cm wide and 10.9cm high.

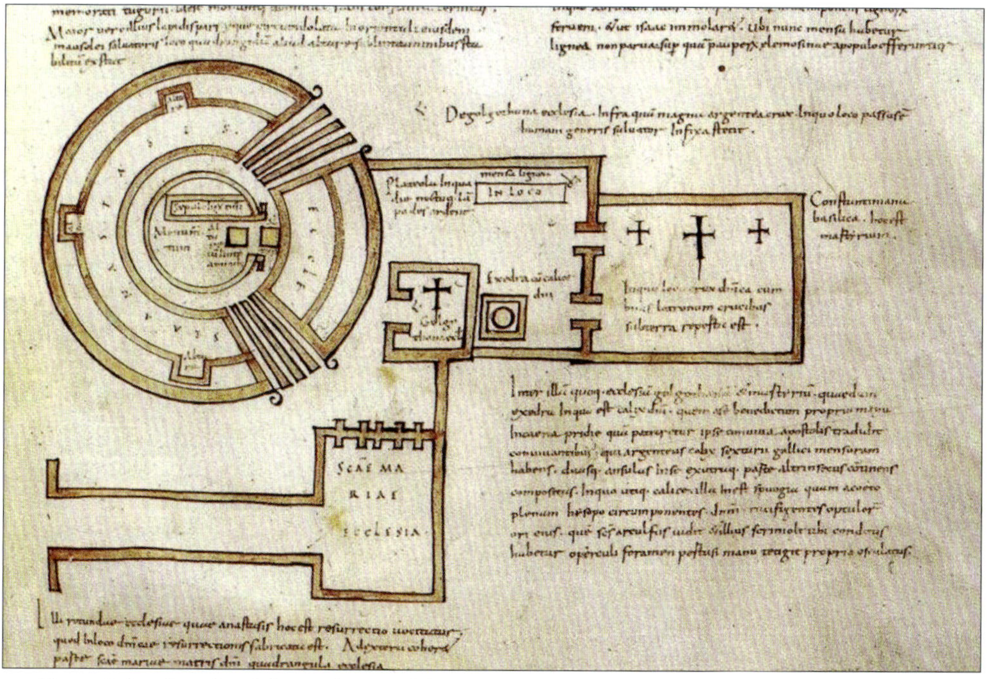

19. Plan of the church of the Holy Sepulchre, Jerusalem, from *De Locis Sanctis*, dictated by Arculf to Abbot Adomnán of Iona and copied in Northumbria.

20. (Above). The *Codex Amiatinus*: a complete Bible, produced at Wearmouth–Jarrow in 716 and taken by Abbot Ceolfrið on his final journey to Rome.

21. (Right). The so-called St Cuthbert Gospel – the oldest surviving intact binding on an English book – from the tomb of St Cuthbert.

To support their building programmes, Wilfrid and Biscop imported a package of materials technology and craft skills. Biscop brought stone masons and glass workers from Gaul because the skills were not present locally, and the glass makers passed on their knowledge to local workers.[93] Wilfrid returned from his consecration in Gaul with masons and 'artisans of almost every kind'.[94] The mortar mixer discovered at Wearmouth, evidence of their workings, was a technology already in use widely across Western Europe.[95] Numerous fragments of window glass have been recovered from the excavations at Wearmouth and Jarrow. Some have been re-set in an original window opening in the St Paul's chancel and some in panels in the Jarrow Hall museum. Colours are vibrant, in a range corresponding to forty-five colours in a standard reference chart.[96] The glass is a soda-lime compound, as opposed to a potash-rich mix which could have been harvested locally from seaweed, and it is cylinder blown. It appears to have come from the Mediterranean and Near East regions, imported as cullet for re-working on site.[97] Lead was a component of the window cames[98] and, beyond that, it was used structurally in the buildings. Wilfrid re-roofed the church in York with lead and Bishop Eadberht of Lindisfarne (668–698) renovated an early wooden church, covering both the roof and walls with lead sheet.[99] Lead fittings of various types come from Wearmouth and Jarrow: slivers, strips, plates and sheets.[100] Buildings at both of Biscop's sites were floored with *opus signinum*, the Roman 'concrete' formed from crushed tile or brick mixed into mortar.[101]

The builders at Wearmouth had limestone readily available to them, but nearby Roman sites provided most of the cut and shaped ashlar of the earliest phases for the round-headed doors, the window frames and quoins. At Jarrow, there is no source of building stone in the immediate vicinity and the small church which now forms the chancel of St Paul's was built almost completely of stones re-used from the forts of *Segedunum* (Wallsend), on the opposite side of the river, and *Arbeia* (South Shields) on the south side, just 4km to the north-east. The now blocked-in round-headed doorway on the north side appears to be a feature taken intact.[102] The same seems to be true also of the small two-cell church at Escomb on the south side of the River Wear near Bishop Auckland, 2.5km from the Roman fort of *Vinovia* (Binchester), where the squared stones that make up the walling are of typical Roman form: one, in the north wall, bears a legionary inscription, and the chancel arch is an intact feature re-used.

The tall, narrow chancel arch of the seventh-century church of St John, Escomb, County Durham

Once the monasteries were in place, the two founders resourced their architectural complexes with a wider support package which, in its totality, amounts to a complete religious–cultural programme. Biscop and his successor, Abbot Ceolfrið, gained papal decrees to protect both Wearmouth and Jarrow from external interference.[103] Wilfrid brought in singing masters to develop liturgical practice and claimed to have introduced double choirs to sing antiphons and responses.[104] Biscop returned from one of his continental journeys with the pope's liturgical specialist, John the Cantor, to teach Roman practice. Not only did John do this, writes Bede, but he left written instructions in a book in the monastery library.[105] Biscop collected vessels and vestments of all kinds for use on the altar and in the church,[106] as Wilfrid had done when he restored Paulinus's original church in York.[107] Relics were provided and distributed[108] and Biscop imported paintings with images of the saints and scenes from the Old and New Testaments. These he placed in the two churches so that they should serve as instruction for all, especially those who could not read.[109] To foster the intellectual life of the monasteries Biscop collected books for a library, and Ceolfrið doubled its size.[110] Not all the books were directly religious: Ceolfrið concluded a land deal with King Aldfrið in exchange for a book of cosmographies.[111]

From the library of the sixth-century statesman turned scholar Cassiodorus, who had set up a centre of learning at Squillace, in Calabria in the extreme south of Italy, Biscop acquired a single-volume bible known as the *Codex Grandior*. This was in the Old Latin translation which preceded Jerome's *Vulgate*, the translation that became the standard for Western Christendom. The lectionary used for liturgy at Wearmouth-Jarrow derived from southern Italy, possibly via a church in the Greek Quarter of Rome near the Palatine Hill.[112] Also from southern Italy, directly or indirectly, came a copy of Cassiodorus's commentary on the psalms, on which Bede drew for his own scriptural commentaries. Papal Rome was itself influenced by Byzantine Christianity and it has been argued that, when Ceolfrið was abbot, a Byzantine artist had come from Rome to the Wearmouth-Jarrow scriptorium to paint the portrait of Ezra in the *Codex Amiatinus*.[113] Although neither Wilfrid nor Biscop travelled to the Holy Land, knowledge of the tomb of Christ and other features and places associated with his life was circulating in the West.*

Christian entrepreneurs such as Wilfrid and Biscop were not attempting to simulate Rome in some re-creation; rather, as the great scholar of Early Christendom Peter Brown observed, centres in the West developed their own micro-Christendoms, each distinctive in its own way, derived from resources available locally or secured from elsewhere.[114] Nowhere within the former Roman province of *Britannia* was there such a wealth of material

---

* And see Chapter 7 for evidence of the wider circulation of a book from Iona, via Northumbria, to Continental Europe.

resources to hand from the Roman past than in the region of the frontier forts.[115] Here the Gaulish masons of the seventh century found familiar materials in familiar architectural forms.

All of this activity – religious, cultural, constructional – depended on the resources of the lands granted by the king: seventy farms in the case of Wearmouth and forty for Jarrow to begin with. Beyond this, the Wearmouth-Jarrow abbots seem to have been canny in land dealings so that by the time of Ceolfrið's death in 716, the double house had built up a holding of 150 farms, mostly within a strip of 8–10km wide between the rivers, and some to the south.[116] Much of this land now falls within the conurbations of Tyneside and Wearside and is difficult of access for archaeological or landscape research. But Brian Roberts has drawn on place-names, plan forms, historic maps, charters and other documentary sources to propose an interpretation of the landscape of *Werhale*; this gives a good case study of the internal structuring of an ecclesiastical estate.[117] He characterises the landscape as being a small *pays* within a great swathe of open pasture land and woodland that spread east from the Pennine foothills of County Durham to the coast. The terrain is a patchwork of two types of land: 'limited areas of arable and meadow, some in blocks, some in strips surrounded by a secure head-dyke, to protect crops from grazing animals . . . all set amidst a sea of waste comprising either wood pasture or open pasture, or a mixture of both'.[118] As late as 1600, it was still a patchwork of settled land dispersed among wastes.[119] Roberts worked back from c.1600 mapping and the charter evidence of farms carved from the wastes between c.1150 and 1350 to an experimental mapping of the landscape at about the year 700 in which the family farms, the *familiae* of Bede's texts, are represented by amoeba-like cells.[120]

In the ninth century these lands were transferred to the Community of St Cuthbert, the former Lindisfarne monastery, and thence in 1229 to Durham Priory management, and this allows a link to be made with the landholdings of the seventh–eighth centuries. Roberts' insight is to see that the holdings of between 30 and 52 acres (11–19ha), known as husbandlands on the priory estates, are essentially the same as the *familiae* of King Ecgfrið's grants.[121] This, referenced then to acreages derived from first-edition Ordnance Survey mapping, allows the estimate that the *familiae* constituted a resource of some 6,600 acres (2,400ha) of Roberts' first type of land: 'cleared, tilled, stone-picked, and perhaps manured arable land'. Some 5,000 of these acres lay between Tyne and Wear within a total area of 26,760 statute acres, meaning that there was some 20,000 acres (7300ha) of wastes.[122]

In the case of Wearmouth-Jarrow, not the least of the requirements from this land was the provision of calf skins for the vellum used in book production. Herd sizes are unknowable, but we can come one stage closer to placing the cattle in the landscape.[123] The *Boldon Book* of 1183 records the tenures, rentals and service obligations on the *vills* of the bishop of Durham's estates, and these include some within the former Wearmouth-Jarrow holdings. Boldon itself, to take just one example, renders a payment of 17 shillings for cornage (*de cornagio*) and one cow of metreth (*vaccam de metride*).[124] Here are two renders on cattle, both archaic survivals, in Medieval estate management. The cash payment for cornage is a commutation of what was originally the render of cattle on the hoof to the lord's household. The cow of metreth is the cow with her calf, still owed directly as a render in 1183 and not yet commuted to cash. The two payments refer to two types of cattle herds. Cornage was paid on the herds roaming the wastes, from among which bullocks could be rounded up and castrated for use as draught animals and heifers brought in to be put to the bull. This is the herd culled annually in the month of *Blodmonað* (November) when, as Bede records, 'the cattle which were slaughtered were consecrated to their gods'.[125] One such herd still survives in Chillingham, Northumberland, trapped since about 1630 when its grazing lands were emparked and enclosed by a stone wall.[126] The cow with calf was part of the herd managed for milk and for breeding and kept close to the settlements on the improved lands of the *familiae*. The requirements for vellum are the same as for dairying, that is a regular breeding cycle, except that calves intended for the vellum workshop are culled in their first spring, prior to weaning. Here then, on the 6,600 acres of *familiae*, were the cows whose calves yielded the hides for the books.

* * *

In 679 such overlordship as Ecgfrið had exercised in the Midlands unravelled in the aftermath of a battle fought against King Æðelred of Mercia, somewhere near the River Trent. One consequence was that Lindsey was lost to the Northumbrian diocese, and Bishop Eadhæd, who had been placed there after Ecgfrið's victory of 674, returned to Northumbria where Archbishop Theodore installed him as bishop in Ripon, newly established, though short-lived, as an episcopal centre.[127] Of more personal concern to Ecgfrið was that his younger brother, the sub-king Ælfwine, just eighteen years old, was killed in the battle. As his sister Osðryð was Æðelred's queen in Mercia, this death could have provoked a blood feud. But Theodore intervened as a mediator and negotiated an agreement for a payment of money in mitigation. Further bloodshed was thus avoided and relations between the two kingdoms stabilised.[128] But despite Ecgfrið's second marriage to Iurminburh, the succession was from this time uncertain.

Little is known of governance in Northumbria after the Mercian setback but if developments within the church are any guide, it was a period of re-structuring. In 681 the episcopal see of Bernicia was re-organised and sub-divided, as Tunberht took the bishopric in Hexham and a new diocese was created under Trumwine at Abercorn on the Firth of Forth for that part of the Pictish kingdom lying under Northumbrian overlordship.[129] Thus, there were now five diocesan centres, at York, Ripon, Hexham, Lindisfarne and Abercorn, where there had formerly been a single bishopric for the greater Northumbrian realm from Lincolnshire to Tayside.

In the same year, Ecgfrið made the grant of land to Biscop for the monastery at Jarrow. Bede is careful in his writings to present Wearmouth-Jarrow as a single monastery on two sites: 'the monastery of St Peter and St Paul which is at Wearmouth and Jarrow'.[130] But Ian Wood suggests that Bede has back-projected to 681 a unity which emerged only later in order to gloss over a much more troubled beginning for Jarrow.[131] The founding community, or at least part of it, was drafted in from Wearmouth with Ceolfrið as abbot, but Jarrow almost failed during the plague that struck in 685. Not only had Ecgfrið granted the land, as he had done for Wearmouth, but according to the author of the *Life of Ceolfrið*, he himself chose the site for the altar – presumably this means the main church. If this is more than a pious trope, it suggests that the king was taking a direct personal interest in the site; perhaps he intended it as the place of his burial and memorial. The inscribed stone commemorating the dedication of the main church in Jarrow on 23 April 685 can still be seen inside the present parish church. It marks the date as being in the fourth year of Ceolfrið's abbacy and the fifteenth of King Ecgfrið's reign; Biscop, who was away travelling in Rome, gets no mention.

It may well be that Ecgfrið was himself present at the ceremony. If so, this was probably his last public engagement in the kingdom before he embarked with his fleet that had been assembling on the inter-tidal mud flats of Jarrow Slake,* immediately beside the monastery, on his way to his death in battle.[132] Such a close association with King Ecgfrið left Jarrow exposed politically in the aftermath, and when it was on the point of collapse in the plague, it was expedient for a new régime to allow Wearmouth to absorb it. In certain respects, the two houses continued to operate as separate entities, each under

---

* Now filled in to provide parking for cars ready to be shipped from Nissan's terminal here. It was known to Symeon of Durham in the twelfth century as *Portus Ecgfridi*, Ecgfrið's Port.

their own abbot, with full unity achieved only when Ceolfrið became abbot of both following the death of Wearmouth's Abbot Sicgfrið in 688.[133]

Ecgfrið's Jarrow watched over his port on the mud flats of Jarrow Slake. On the opposite side of this 1.5km-wide inlet was *Donamuða*. This is possibly the monastery close to the mouth of the river to which Bede referred in the *Life of Cuthbert*, originally a house of monks but later converted to a nunnery.[134] Recording its destruction in a Viking raid in 794, the *Anglo-Saxon Chronicle* refers to it as *Ecgferthes mynster*. Perhaps Ecgfrið ordered the change in status when he set up Jarrow, transferring the monks there so that *Donamuða* should be a dower house and then burial place of Queen Iurminburh in the same way that Whitby served Queen Eanflæd.[135]

* * *

The final years of Ecgfrið's reign were troubled. The king's eventual succession was still in doubt and some among his advisors were disturbed by the military campaigns of 684 and 685. In 684 the king's half-sister, Abbess Ælfflæd of Whitby, travelled for a meeting with Cuthbert, who had resigned his post as prior at Lindisfarne and was then living as a solitary in the monastery's hermitage on the island of Inner Farne, not long before he was called to the bishopric in the following year. As the two *Lives of Cuthbert*, the Anonymous and Bede's, recount the occasion, Ælfflæd was worried about the succession and came to Cuthbert asking for advice; he reassured her by drawing her attention to Aldfrið, a son of Oswiu and half-brother to both king and abbess, who was living overseas.[136] For the authors of the *Lives*, the meeting was an opportunity for Cuthbert to display prophetic insight; but we might well read this in another way. It is less than convincing to suggest that Ælfflæd, who was keeper of her father's grave and his memory at Whitby, did not know of Oswiu's oldest son from his youthful liaison in Ireland. It seems more likely that she was taking the initiative in this matter, lobbying Cuthbert to build support for a move to contact Aldfrið and prepare for him to take the kingship after Ecgfrið's death. Her concern might well have been prompted by events of that year.

In 684 Ecgfrið sent an army into Ireland under a commander named Berctred, son of Beornæð of the Pictish campaign of 672, in an incursion that spared neither churches nor monasteries. Bede treats this with a sense of dismay, that they should 'wretchedly lay waste a harmless people who had always been most friendly towards the English'.[137] The context for the campaign may be a change in the balance of power in Ireland after 675 in which the Uí Néill of the north lost the high kingship, with the centre of power moving into the Plain of Brega and the Midlands. This had

Aberlemno II: battle scene depicted on the reverse of a shaped cross-slab – perhaps representing the Pictish victory at Nechtansmere in 685

implications for the Gaelic areas of western Scotland, offering the possibility of external support for subject kings of Ecgfrið who might wish to rebel.[138] Incursions into the western seaboard around the Clyde estuary from the Kingdom of Strathclyde based at *Alt Clud* (Dumbarton) were de-stabilising Northumbrian interests here. Meanwhile, sieges at Dunottar on the east coast near Stonehaven in 681 and Dundurn near Crieff in 682 show pressure building across the southern parts of the Pictish zone applied, most probably, by the Pictish King Bridei (671–692) against Northumbrian client states, among them that of Berctred, son of Beornæð, perhaps in Fife.[139]

Ecgfrið and his advisors saw the Irish expedition as a success and as a platform from which to reassert his overlordship of the Picts through a punitive campaign in 685. During his absence, Queen Iurminburh travelled to Carlisle to await the outcome in her sister's monastery, and there Cuthbert, now bishop of Lindisfarne, came to consult her and, no doubt, to visit the estate which Ecgfrið had granted to Lindisfarne. It was while queen and bishop were being shown around the city on a Saturday that Cuthbert had a premonition of the king's death. He advised the queen to leave and go as quickly as possible to Bamburgh and he would follow as soon as he was able.[140] The campaign of May 685 was a disaster: on 20 May Ecgfrið was killed in battle at *Nechtansmere*, usually understood as Dunnichen, near Forfar. A large cross-slab in the nearby churchyard of Aberlemno depicting a battle scene is thought to be a memorial of this encounter.

Bede thought that Ecgfrið had acted rashly and contrary to the advice of those around him, especially Cuthbert, who was by now bishop of Lindisfarne. He quoted the Roman poet Virgil in saying that from that time the hope and strength of the English realm began 'to ebb and flow away'. The Picts recovered possession of their lands, while the Irish in Britain and some parts of the British people recovered their liberty, says Bede. Many English were killed or taken into slavery, or else escaped, among these latter Bishop Trumwine, whose diocese of Abercorn was lost and who retired to the community at Whitby.[141] In other words, Northumbrian overlordship around and north of the Forth–Clyde collapsed. One wonders whether Aldfrið had any part in these events. Their outcome was that he did return and take the Northumbrian kingship. He restored the shattered state of the kingdom but, as Bede observed, 'within narrower bounds'. Northumbria was no longer an expansionist kingdom.

7

ALDFRIÐ: WORD-SMITHS 685–705

Alfridus sapiens – The Word and the
Book – Petrifying tendencies – Economics
– Thirty-four coins – On *Drifelda* – A
fashion for relics – Vested interests

The dramatic and prophetic account of King Ecgfrið's fall, the dynastic crisis it precipitated and the return of a Christian king from exile on Iona, reads like the reverse of a medal struck in another time – the heroic arrival of King Oswald in 634, after the anarchy of Cadwallon. For despite the new king's providential accession, Bede's Virgilian epitaph indicates that he, the historian looking back some fifty years, saw the end of Ecgfrið's reign as the beginning of a more general decline in Northumbrian fortunes.

Bede's generally cool attitude towards a king whom he described as *vir in scripturis doctissimus* – 'most learned in the scriptures' – relegates Aldfrið's twenty-year reign to the shadows cast by his illustrious predecessors.[1] King Æðelfrið's grandson prosecuted few wars, won no military victories, presided over a shrunken Northumbrian *imperium* and appears as a scornful, even petulant antagonist in the later, turbulent career of Wilfrid, the pre-eminent monastic entrepreneur of the age.

Aldfrið's Irishness, his questionable legitimacy, military diffidence and an unimpressive record of religious patronage were grounds enough for Bede's ambivalence. And yet modern historians and archaeologists are entitled to see, in the last quarter of the seventh century, the flowering of a Northumbrian cultural peak, an almost revolutionary economic dynamism and Britain's political and intellectual reintegration into the European mainstream.

It is true that a biographer of Aldfrið would have scant material to work with. If his mother's liaison or marriage to Oswiu dates to the period of his father's exile in Dál Riata before 642, then this forty-year-old 'bastard' son[2] was probably born between 640 and 645 and known in his youth by the Irish name Flann Fína mac Ossu.³ His mother, Fín, was the daughter of a king of the Cenél nÉogain of Inishowen.⁴ Ecgfrið and Ælfwine were his half-brothers; Bishop Finán of Lindisfarne may have been his uncle;⁵ Abbess Ælfflæd and Queen Osðryð in Mercia were his half-sisters.

In the Cuthbert narrative Flann Fína was living among the Irish at the time of Ecgfrið's disastrous campaign in Pictland. He was highly regarded in intellectual circles: a *sapiens*, of great wisdom. Even so, he may have been perceived as a political threat to Ecgfrið. It is conceivable that the ill-advised Northumbrian assault on Brega in 684 is connected with an attempt to remove him from the dynastic picture,⁶ alongside the political motivations outlined in the previous chapter. In any case, for Ælfflæd, seemingly the guardian of their father's dynastic interests, Aldfrið was the Iding dynasty's most assured hope of continuity after Ælfwine's death in the Battle on the River Trent in 679. Ecgfrið seems to have had a son, Oslac, by his second wife Iurminburh; but he would have been too young in 685 to secure the throne against rival contenders.*

Modern scholars suspect that a brief interregnum occurred between Ecgfrið's death and Aldfrið's arrival in Northumbria – perhaps as much as nine months.⁷ During this time senior surviving members of Ecgfrið's *comitatus*, along with bishops and collateral members of the family, are likely to have met in council. Any attempt to wrest control of the kingship by rival dynasts, or place the young Oslac on the throne, is unrecorded by Bede. The fear of a full-scale invasion from Pictland or Mercia may have concentrated Northumbrian minds in the aftermath of the crushing defeat at *Nechtansmere* under King Bridei. If Northumbria was now weak in martial strength, it still possessed formidable diplomatic assets; but the new king must deploy them with care. Where Ecgfrið had looked north to fulfil his ambitions, Aldfrið looked south.

Aldfrið's half-sister Osðryð was already married to the Mercian King Æðelred (675–704). Aldfrið himself married Cuðburh – named in the *Anglo-Saxon Chronicle* but not mentioned by Bede – a princess of the West

---

* The otherwise unknown genealogy for Oslac survives in *HB* 61. Charles Phythian-Adams believes that his progeny may have ruled as Northumbrian *subreguli* in Rheged – the last of the Idings who might claim partial descent, via Ecgfrið's mother Rhieinmelth, to the dynasty of Urien. Phythian-Adams 1996, 59–61.

Saxons, sister of King Ine and kinswoman of his friend Aldhelm.* It was not a successful union: the *Chronicle* entry for 718 records that they parted during their lifetimes.† His uncle, Oswald, had married a West Saxon and one can see in such alliances attempts to counter the rising power of the Mercian kings, in parallel with the cultivation of relations with Canterbury and with Wessex. The marriage seems to have been brokered – even suggested – by Aldhelm, abbot of Malmesbury Abbey and himself the son of a West Saxon king. He had known Aldfrið in earlier years – had probably been his spiritual godfather – and remained his friend.[8] Aldfrið had at least one son, Osred, whose existence is certain but who is unlikely to have been Cuðburh's child. He only reached majority in about 715, so he was a late arrival in the king's reign;[9] the identity of any second wife is unknown.‡ Bede's silence – perhaps discretion – on the matter obscures the background, the politics and the personalities.

Whatever the military and political weaknesses of the new Northumbrian régime, there is no record of warfare north of the Humber during the first twelve years of Aldfrið's reign. The outbreak of plague at the twin monasteries of Wearmouth and Jarrow in 685/6, which carried off Abbot Eosterwine and apparently left only two members of the community alive, does not seem to have been part of a wider event – it is not mentioned by any recension of the *Anglo-Saxon Chronicle*.[10]

In 686 the new king was visited by his friend Adomnán, abbot of Iona since 679, ostensibly on a mission to gain support for his plan to bring Iona into line with orthodox observances regarding, among other things, calculations for Easter and the monastic tonsure. Ulterior motives, unknown to or discreetly ignored by Bede, are suggested by the timing: two Irish chronicles recorded that during this visit the abbot requested the return of sixty

---

* He may have acquired his English name at the time of his accession, but Barbara Yorke, noting his relationship with his 'godfather', Aldhelm, offers the idea that the 'Ald' element was conferred in earlier times as a mark of respect to the great scholar. Yorke 2009, 9.

† Cuðburh retired to a life of monastic contemplation and became abbess of Wimborne (S1251a: https://www.esawyer.org.uk/charter/1251a.html retrieved 12.03.25).

‡ King Osric (718–729) is presumed to be a second son, although it is nowhere explicitly stated. A third son, Offa, is mentioned in the *Historia Regum* under the year 750.

prisoners, taken from Ireland during Ecgfrið's ill-advised raid on Brega in 684. They were duly delivered the following year.[11] Adomnán's stature in northern Britain and Ireland as a political, spiritual and political heavyweight is epitomised by his promulgation, at a synod held at Birr in County Offaly in 697, of the so-called *Cain Adomnáin*, or Law of the Innocents, the earliest explicit statement giving women, clerics and males under fighting age non-combatant status in war. Adomnán managed to secure as guarantors for his law more than ninety secular and ecclesiastical lords, including kings of Dál Riata and Pictland.[12]

Adomnán made a second journey to the Northumbrian court two years after the first, in 688. Among the gifts that the abbot brought for his friend, oiling the wheels of spiritual fraternity and international diplomacy, was a book which he had written, supposedly based on the recollections of a Gaulish bishop named Arculf who had visited Jerusalem; who had been cast by violent tempests on to the islands of Atlantic Britain on his way home; who had, after many adventures, been received by Adomnán on Iona. The abbot wrote these recollections down and Arculf had even drawn a plan of the church of the Holy Sepulchre on wax tablets for the abbot to copy. The resulting volume was called *De Locis Sanctis* – 'On the Holy Places'.[13] King Aldfrið graciously allowed it to circulate, for 'lesser folk' to read.* Bede saw a copy and was able to take substantial extracts which he included in the *Historia*.[14] He also says that he made an abridgement of the work. Both the original and the abridgement were widely copied and circulated across Europe. If the Ionan abbot also brought a draft of his new *Vita* of St Colm Cille, Bede did not record it. Adomnán, in writing of these two visits, recalled the devastation wrought by the plague: 'many whole villages on all sides were stricken . . . but, though I walked in the midst of this danger . . . the Lord delivered me.'[15]

From Malmesbury, Aldhelm sent the new king a more personal gift, an *Epistola ad Acircium*, a composite work including the letter itself (*Acircius* being Aldhelm's own epithet for the king), a treatise on numerology and various riddles. Only a man of the highest intellect could have regarded the gift as flattering. But this was a time when Northumbrian monasteries were also beginning to accumulate the precious treasures of a literate and artistic

---

* The exact date of the manuscript, now lost, and its arrival in Northumbria, are matters of speculation, and even Arculf's existence has been questioned. Yorke 2010. Bede *Vit Cuth* II.46.

European élite. Benedict Biscop had returned from his fifth and last journey to Rome in 679 with 'countless valuable gifts for the churches: a large supply of sacred books and ... sacred pictures'.[16]

Among the books with which he enriched the library at Jarrow was a work called *The Cosmographers*, which may once have belonged in the library of Cassiodorus.[17] After Biscop's death in 690 the king bought it from Abbot Ceolfrið for the price of eight *familiae* of land by the River *Fresca* – perhaps the Team, which flows into the Tyne a mile or so upstream of Newcastle, or the Deerness or Browney, which flow into the Wear upstream of Durham. It lay some distance away from Wearmouth and Jarrow, and may have been acquired because it held a particular resource – fish from the river; clean water for tanning and preparing leather; riverside woodland coppice for basketry or charcoal, perhaps.

The death of Cuthbert in his hermitage on Inner Farne in 687 at the age of fifty-three and the exhumation of his uncorrupted body in 698 prompted the Lindisfarne brethren to compile a *Vita*, on which Bede drew heavily for his own two works on the saintly bishop: a verse life and a prose life. At Whitby, something of a royal cult developed, curated by the dowager Queen Eanflæd and her daughter Ælfflæd, prompting the writing of a Life of Pope Gregory the Great and the acquisition of a grisly treasure: the head of King Edwin, Eanflæd's father, retrieved through miraculous prophecy and the dedicated searching of a priest among the age-old debris of the battle at *Hæthfelth*, some fifty years previously.*

By the time of Aldfrith's death in 705, Bede had produced his adaptation of Adomnán's book *On the Holy Places*, a short book *On Time*, his *Commentary on the Apocalypse* and the first version of his *Life of Cuthbert* in verse: the beginnings of a steady stream of scriptural commentaries and textbooks for students. His *Life of Cuthbert* in prose followed in c.720, along with a second version of the verse *Life*.[18] The Whitby *Life of St Gregory*, with its treatment of King Edwin, came some time between 704 and 714.[19]

Since the foundation of Lindisfarne as a daughter house of Iona in 635, the small grants of land on which holy men and women might found monasteries had been donated by kings on various pretexts: in grateful thanks for

---

* It is possible that the head was retrieved as part of the settlement brokered by Archbishop Theodore after the Battle on the River Trent in 679. Wood 2008b, 23; *Vit Greg Anon*, 18.

prayers leading to victory in battle; as an acknowledgement of miracles; in expiation of sins. Widowed queens retiring to the seclusion of monastic life might bring their dower lands and personal treasures with them: retaking marriage vows, in a sense, as brides of Christ. Enriched by the enlargement of their landed estates and driven, by circumstance or ambition, to behave like territorial lords, abbots and abbesses began to manage their portfolios constructively. With the benefits of earthly freehold, they were able to invest donated monies and sweat equity in new or improved technologies: higher-yielding breeds of livestock; more productive strains of grain; such wonders as watermills, perhaps. With the surplus labour of lay brethren, they were able to specialise in crafts: metalwork, sculpture and decorative textiles. It was only natural that they should also provide themselves with the means to produce books of their own, as analyses of the *Werhale* estates by Brian Roberts (see Chapter 6) and our own of the Lindisfarne estates (below) suggest.

Scriptoria are known from the direct archaeological evidence of the reparation of vellum in the monastery of Portmahomack, in north-east Pictland, and from the indirect evidence of the books that they produced.[20] Lindisfarne, Wearmouth-Jarrow, Whitby, probably also Whithorn in Galloway and Dacre in Cumbria produced manuscripts. The oldest surviving copy of Cassiodorus's *Commentary on the Psalms* was written in a Northumbrian monastery and is now in the Durham Cathedral library.[21] Wearmouth-Jarrow's output included three pandects, that is complete single-volume copies of St Jerome's *Vulgate* bible, edited under the direction of Abbot Ceolfrið, who introduced the highest standards of textual scholarship to the monastery's scriptorium.[22] One of these pandects, known as the *Codex Amiatinus*, is a triumph of Northumbrian scribal art.* Abbot Ceolfrið intended to take it to Rome as a gift for Pope Gregory II on his pilgrimage there in 716, but fate intervened. He died en route at Langres in Burgundy but some among his entourage continued on to Rome and presented Ceolfrið's gifts; the writer of the *Life of Ceolfrið* recorded the pope's thank-you letter to Abbot Hwætberht.[23] By the nineteenth century it had found its way into the library of the Abbazia di San Salvatore on Monte Amiata in Tuscany and is now held in the Laurentian Library in Florence. Weighing a monstrous 75lb, it consumed the skins of 515 beasts, bred specially for the

---

* Michelle Brown (2023) has recently demonstrated the likelihood that Bede annotated it and added marginalia.

purpose. Accounting for wastage, tic-ridden skins and sheets of vellum used for drafts and for other works, these three bibles in total indicate the existence of very substantial herds or flocks, raised under special management. Archaeologists have to ask themselves where such herds might have been raised.

The *Werhale* estates account for Wearmouth-Jarrow's scriptorial productivity, as discussed in Chapter 6. By the second decade of the eighth century the finest surviving insular Early Medieval manuscript, the Lindisfarne Gospels, had been produced in the scriptorium of the tidal island monastery just off the sea-torn coast of north Northumberland. We have proposed elsewhere that among the territorial acquisitions made by Lindisfarne during the seventh century were estates on the fertile, sheltered eastern slopes of the Cheviot Hills where calves, suitable for slaughtering at under two years of age to produce the high-quality vellum needed for such fine manuscript work, might be bred and husbanded.[24] In addition to specially raised calves, scriptoria consumed inks, dyes, wax tablets and exemplars from which to copy or take inspiration. Some of these might be sourced locally; others were high-value acquisitions from overseas.*

Prime among the assets of the élite minster foundations were their landed estates – the source of the renders that fed them and provided the bulk of their resources and, potentially, the means of accumulating profit. Initially modest grants formed cores that expanded according to the wealth produced by the monastic establishment and the generosity of their benefactors. The sale of *The Cosmographers* to King Aldfrið enabled Ceolfrið to acquire a new estate for Wearmouth-Jarrow, and it is evident that this was not land contiguous with the monastery.

In the construction, from the mid 670s, of new stone churches at Ripon, Hexham, Escomb, Jarrow, Wearmouth; investments in the written word and a professional intelligentsia; the production of the first Northumbrian coins to bear a king's name, a broader trend can be detected towards what has been termed 'petrification'.[25] In Bede's famous account of King Edwin's conversion, one of his chief men, carefully briefed by Bishop Paulinus and equally carefully précised by Bede, compares the life of (heathen) man on earth with the interior of the mead hall in winter: a

---

* The illustrations in the *Codex Amiatinus* are thought to be derived from the *Codex Grandior*, obtained, probably by Benedict Biscop, from the library of Cassiodorus. Gameson 2017, 1–2.

fire blazing at its centre, the king feasting his men while wintry storms batter the walls outside. A sparrow flies swiftly through the hall and for a brief moment, before it flits out again, the storm cannot touch it. What lies outside – allegorically, that is, before and after the brief span of human life – is dark, empty, unknown. Life, then, is fleeting and fluid; its pleasures and the comforts of comradeship, laughter and warmth are ephemeral, extinguished by exile, death and loss. Comparing this grim vision with the everlasting joys of the Christian faith, Bede contrasts dark with light, calm with storm, warmth with cold.

In parallel, we can see similar contrasts between the oral tradition of heroic poetry and the permanent oak-gall ink of the Latin script; the life-interest tenure of thegnly land and the in-perpetuity bookland of the monasteries; consumable render and the solidity of a king's coinage; wood and stone; the fluid time and truth of the regnal list and Bede's own *Anno Domini* computations. These superbly paired antonyms, reinforcing the universal, eternal bond between one people, the *gens Anglorum*, and the one church of Rome, were proof of the immensity of the cultural investment in the permanent and material. Bede saw this and brilliantly preserved the thought. For him, especially, writing concretised thinking.

Something of the same materialising process had already begun in Ireland, where investment in mill technology is vividly evidenced at Nendrum at the head of Strangford Lough. Here, in the early seventh century, a tidal horizontal turbine mill provided for efficient milling of flour and the generation of a saleable surplus, at the same time monumentalising the civilising and capital-intensive permanence of the monastic movement.[26] More subtle processes were also at work. In the graveyard at Cooley, near Moville on the west side of Lough Foyle, distinctive cross designs inscribed into stone grave markers show tapered points, fossilising wooden exemplars.[27] The same skeuomorphism was observed in church architecture by Charles Thomas in his survey of the Early Christian archaeology of northern Britain.[28] The surviving high stone crosses of Northumbria at Bewcastle and Ruthwell, with their runic inscriptions and intricate interlace, were monumentalised equivalents of the transition from oral to written text and imagery, probably copying earlier wooden versions – indeed, the runes carved on those crosses originated in a form of angular writing designed to be carved into wood, avoiding curved letter forms.

Incised cross grave marker from Cooley graveyard, Moville, County Donegal: a skeuomorphic representation of a wooden pointed-stake original

Petrifying tendencies are also on show in the crypt that Wilfrid constructed at Hexham, whose walls very deliberately incorporated large fragments of decorative masonry retrieved from a Roman mausoleum across the River Tyne near Corbridge. At Jarrow, stained glass, the first to be imported into Britain after the end of the Empire, was more than mere insulation against wintry storms: coloured glass transfixed fluid light; rendered it material. The mortar mixers excavated there, at Dunbar and at the monastery at Hoddom in Dumfriesshire, reinforced the idea of fluid materials solidifying. Bede had seen the Wearmouth mixer being worked in his youth and was so impressed that he remembered it and wrote of it in his commentary on the Book of Genesis.[29] Lime mortar's marvellous binding properties called to mind those of the universal and everlasting church. Stone churches built to last forever were like the foundations of King Solomon's Temple.

The church that Cuthbert, Aidan and Finán knew on Lindisfarne had been built of hewn timber, 'in the Irish fashion'.[30] The new stone foundations at Jarrow, Wearmouth, Escomb, Ripon and Hexham were projects driven by men – Wilfrid and Benedict Biscop – who had been to Rome, the eternal city. Those of an orthodox persuasion saw the ascetic Irish tradition as an embodiment of ignorance and material poverty, unfit for worship and reflective of antiquated, almost heretical views on Easter and various liturgical observances, whatever its romantic and aesthetic attractions. God's majesty was built into the fabric of stone churches.

Brian Roberts has drawn attention to a paradox. Benedict Biscop, under whom Wearmouth and Jarrow were first established, was able to bring or send back to his new foundations all manner of books, artistic treasures and fineries such as the two silk cloaks of marvellous workmanship with which he purchased three *familiae* of land on the banks of the River Wear. In reconstructing the early *territoria* of these establishments as *Werhale*,* Brian Roberts drew attention to the distribution of early monastic endowments and showed how they were often located around and beyond the edges of the cultural corelands. In this way kings did not alienate to the church properties from their ancestral lands but were using church magnates such as Biscop and Wilfrid as agents for economic development in the kingdom. At any rate, Jarrow and Wearmouth were not founded on prime real estate. So how did Biscop and his successors finance their treasure-gathering expeditions and other acquisitions?

---

* Described in detail in the previous chapter. Roberts 2008a.

Seventh- or eighth-century high cross with interlace decoration and runic inscription standing in the graveyard of St Cuthbert's church, Bewcastle, Northumberland

Biscop, like Wilfrid whom he had probably first met in Kent as they prepared to travel to Rome together in 653, was born into the Northumbrian aristocracy and, like him also, served in the king's army, subsequently being given lands on which to settle 'suitable to his rank'; but we do not know where they were. In any case these were the king's lands; Biscop could not sell them to raise cash. He travelled to Rome for the first time when he was twenty-five. Then, for a decade between 654 and 665, his whereabouts are unknown; he was on the Continent again between 665 and 667.

Roberts draws the circumstantial conclusion that Biscop was, or became, an itinerant trader and speculates that his admission to the clerical ranks by subjecting himself to the tonsure (in the monastery of Lérins on the French Riviera) may have been 'a necessary entrée into the world of trade'.[31] Much the same would apply to Wilfrid, whose own Continental travels seem to have enabled him to accumulate even more impressive wealth with which to 'purchase the friendship of kings and bishops'[32] and furnish his many monasteries with treasures and relics, leaving enough money on his death to make his antipathetic kings envious.

Contemporary texts, and the hard evidence of excavation, have enabled archaeologists to assemble an inventory of the sorts of goods being traded into and out of the Anglo-Saxon kingdoms from the second half of the seventh century. The careers of Biscop and of Wilfrid furnish us with books and skilled craftsmen, with silken cloaks, paintings, metalwork and jewellery, with exotic dyes and, in particular, with the precious relics of the holy martyrs. Bede and the annals also contain many references to slaves, of two sorts: those tied to the land as bonded labourers, and those captured in raids and battles – the profits of war. Bede reports that in his day *Lundenwic* was an emporium where the traders of many nations met; and he notes the presence of Frisian merchants in York. Trading ports facing England across the Channel and North Sea were well-known points of arrival and departure: Dorestad on the Rhine; *Quentovic* on the Canche; Boulogne on the Channel coast. Olive oil and wine, used in the Christian liturgy, had to be imported.

The stirrings of an insular economy, breaking out from the bounds of mere subsistence and consumed render, can be found in references to lime mortar, to the scriptoria, to lead- and iron-working, new strains of crops and fine linen for élite garments. Mercian charters from the 680s onwards often mention port facilities at London and the existence of royal officials, the *wicgerefa* and *thelonarius*, whose jobs were to extract tolls from, and cherry-pick as royal perquisites, the wares of arriving and departing traders. And place-names are increasingly yielding to scholarly scrutiny, with references to wharves, hythes and other riverine activity strongly hinting at increased arterial movement.[33]

The identification and excavation of newly established late seventh-century riverside trading settlements at *Eoforwic* (York), *Gipeswic* (Ipswich), *Lundenwic* (on the Strand and at Aldwych in London) and *Hamwic* (Southampton) has further expanded the known inventory of goods being traded: lava quernstones from Germany; glass vessels and recycled glass; salt; high-value metalwork and craft products made from bone, antler, leather and particularly wool.[34]

Before the reign of King Aldfrið, and accepting that the combined efforts of Wilfrid and Benedict Biscop are insufficient grounds to portray a thriving regional economy, evidence for wealth generation north of the Humber is scant, particularly in Bernicia. Between the Rivers Tyne and Forth very few settlements of the seventh to eighth century have been identified, let alone excavated. Yeavering was a seasonally occupied royal township whose economy seems to have been based on consumption: of timber, cattle and food renders. Excavations at nearby Lanton Quarry (see Chapter 3) show that it supported an artisan community, very likely entirely dependent on local, royal patronage rather than a regional or overseas trading economy.

The same probably goes for the élite coastal settlement at Dunbar, while the unexcavated site at Sprouston, on the edge of the cultural coreland of the lower Tweed, looks very like another royal township from the evidence of air photographs. The sole settlement in north Northumberland representing what one might call the squirearchy, probably the homestead of a *gesiða*, at Thirlings in the Milfield Plain, was likely dependent on the renders of its *vill* and on the gifts and patronage of its royal lords (see Chapter 4). In any case, it does not seem to have survived into the late seventh century.

Further south along the coastal plain recent excavations have begun to hint at elements of rural surplus. The settlement close to the River Blyth at Shotton was established by the middle of the seventh century (see Chapter 4). It shows an evolutionary sequence that would be familiar to many archaeologists working in the Midlands and East Anglia: unenclosed hall-type buildings succeeded by much more structured phases of occupation defined by ditched enclosures and fences strung out along a low ridge south of the river, with defined areas for the varying activities of farm and domestic production: of textiles, tool fabrication and maintenance, food processing and more.[35] Such investment in infrastructure and spatial organisation are indicative of a more organised interaction with the outside world. The River Blyth may not have been navigable at Shotton, but it may have lain close to a road with Roman or earlier antecedents, a day's walk north of the Tyne and within half a dozen miles of the coast.

Multiple phases of enclosure maintenance and redesign show that the settlement here consisted of three households, perhaps smaller than but analogous to the better-known 'village' excavated and reconstructed at West Stow in Suffolk. It was sustained over more than two centuries and the range of buildings of varying sizes supports the idea that Shotton was able to profit not just from consuming the crops (barley, oats, rye and bread wheat), fish, woodland and livestock of its hinterland, but from secondary products: wool, hides, cheese, perhaps salt.* The extremely modest material culture retrieved during excavation – a paltry nine sherds of pottery, a small amount of metalworking waste and no animal bone – is more indicative of the aggressively destructive soils on the site than of degrading poverty: the labour invested in the enclosures must be read as a proxy for a wider trend, from the mid seventh century onwards, for specialisation – and therefore trade – in secondary products. As John Blair has made abundantly clear in his magisterial survey of Anglo-Saxon England, the chances are high that many, if not most, of the successful settlements of the period are lost, or lie undetectable beneath the buildings and enclosures of later farms and villages.[36] The place-name evidence from Roberts's cultural cores is a terse witness to their presence.

A much denser pattern of minsters, hinting at a robust economy and regional and overseas trade may, like the royal townships, concentrate minds on the peak of a social and economic pyramid; even so, they are eloquent in speaking of an explosion in intellectual, cultural and economic activity. Between Hexham and the mouth of the River Tyne, at least six substantial monastic establishments are known from the seventh century – and there may have been several more. Hexham was founded on the dower lands of Queen Æðelðryð, on the edge of moorlands but embracing good pasturage and, perhaps, with access to the rich lead ores of the North Pennines. At Corbridge, although the presence of a minster is not proven, a watermill dating to the eighth or ninth centuries was identified and excavated in the

---

* The small hamlet of Saltwick lies less than 3 miles to the north-west.

1990s on the banks of the River Tyne, close to the old Roman town just downstream of its confluence with the Cor Burn.[37] The known minster at Gateshead (*Ad caput caprae*: the 'goat's head')[38] marks a transhipment point for vessels accessing the Roman road system connecting Bernicia with Deira and all points south. The inter-tidal mudflats of Jarrow Slake served as king Ecgfrid's port;[39] it would be a suitable place for a seasonal or 'beach' market. Tynemouth and *Arbeia* had oversight of ships entering and leaving the river; did one of these supply pilots to take a ship past the rocks and around the sandbanks of the river in its natural, pre-dredged state?

Jarrow and Wearmouth offer the best evidence for an integrated and productive Bernician economy. The intrepid travels of their abbots brought in and disseminated craft skills in building construction, decorative arts and book production. The systematic management of their large landed estates, to provide for what is likely to have been one of the densest concentrations of people in the kingdom – it numbered some 600 brethren at the time of Abbot Ceolfrið's departure in 716[40] – stimulated a productive farming regime and domestic economy. Bede paints a vivid picture of this in his biographical sketch of Wearmouth's Abbot Eosterwine. He 'took his share of the winnowing and threshing, the milking of the ewes and the cows; he laboured in bake house, garden and kitchen... putting his hand to the plough along the furrow, hammering iron into shape or wielding the winnowing fan.'[41]

The Tees Valley, so productive during the Roman period, has offered little in the way of clues to settlement density and economic productivity from the sixth century onwards. Whitby Abbey, perched on the cliffs beyond the high and unyielding massif of the North Yorkshire Moors and apparently isolated from the Northumbrian corelands, has produced a much greater wealth of material culture than its Bernician counterparts. A beach market seems to have existed a little further up the coast and the harbour, known by Bede as the Bay of the Lighthouse, was perfectly sited for coastal shipping. The large influx of visitors arriving here in 664 for the historic council meeting indicates a capacity to accommodate both ecclesiastical nobility and the royal court. Much analysis still needs to be conducted on the Whitby material, retrieved from several campaigns of excavation – in future the full picture promises much. Nevertheless, a very modest inventory of two coins, bearing the name of King Aldfrið and recovered from the abbey excavations, carry a considerably greater weight than mere quantity might suggest. They are the dispassionate, accidental testimony of an otherwise barely tangible economic revolution.

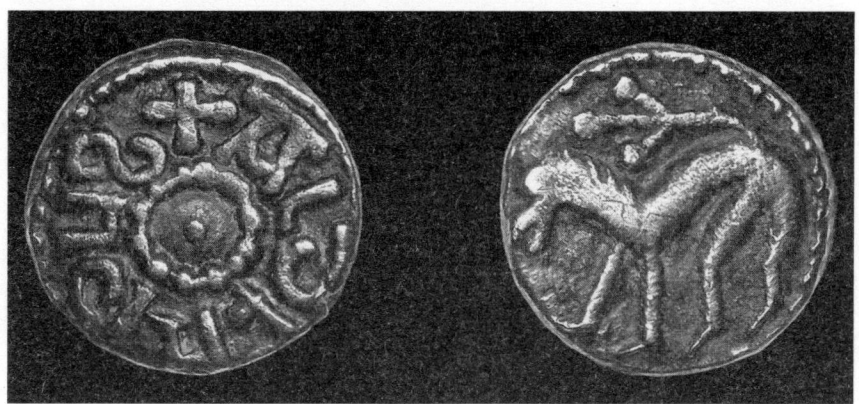

Obverse and reverse designs on a *sceat* of King Aldfrið

In total, thirty-four coins of King Aldfrið are now known.[42] In 2006, when numismatist Michael Metcalf produced the first modern analysis of them, he was able to identify only twenty-six: they seem to be turning up at a rate of one every two years. Compared to the nearly 800 high-quality silver pennies known from the reign of the Mercian overlord King Offa (757–796), this is a tiny number, hardly indicative of any sort of use as currency, let alone an economic rebirth. But numismatics has proved itself capable of demonstrating with a high degree of probability that a few surviving coins might represent very significant issues, while the distribution of coin find spots, even on such a small scale, is exceptionally revealing.*

Coins consist of a flan – a blank disc of silver alloy – laid on a metal die cut with a design which leaves a raised relief pattern on one side of the coin. A second die placed on top is struck with a hammer. The resulting coin has an obverse and a reverse: the side carrying the inscription and/or image of the king is regarded as the 'obverse'. Aldfrið's coins have a high silver content – something like 89 per cent – itself indicative of a productive economy and a ready supply of silver.[43] The coins, known as *sceattas*, are very light, no more than 1.25g each – at nearly twenty to the ounce, you can barely feel one in the hand. When Metcalf wrote, only twenty of the twenty-six coins were well-enough preserved to be able to compare die designs – the devil in the detail. Statistical logic suggests that if all the known coins in a series had been struck from the same obverse and reverse dies, a very small total coinage is indicated. But this is rarely the case. With every unique die or die pairing

---

* See Map 17 on page 199; Metcalf 2006.

identified, the number of likely strikings rises considerably, with a strongly mathematical probability. Each additional coin find thus carries considerable statistical weight. It is worth quoting, more or less in full, the argument that Metcalf adduces to calculate how many of these *sceattas* are likely to have been produced in the whole twenty-year reign of Aldfrið:

> a random sample of 20 specimens which yields very few die-duplicates implies that the original total of dies was considerably greater than 20 ... If there were, for example, just four non-singletons (i.e. specimens which are not the only representative of their die) among 20, or one-fifth, then the known dies will likewise represent about one-fifth of all the dies that were used – which takes us into the region of a hundred. Dies were quite high-tech in the late seventh century, and expensive to manufacture. Why make a hundred pairs, all with the same designs, in at most 20 years, unless they were needed? A pair of dies was technically capable of striking, on average, let us say 10,000 coins before it was discarded. If c.100 dies provided 19 per cent of the currency ... the total currency will have been roughly the equivalent of the output of c.500 dies. Even if half the output of the Aldfrið dies was exported, we should multiply 500 by 5,000, to reach a total of 2,500,000 *sceattas* ... Even allowing for margins of statistical error, it is sufficiently clear that a monetary economy ... was amply supplied with coinage. What happened in Aldfrið's reign was something quite new.[44]

Metcalf's conclusion is that Aldfrið's coins represent a much more substantial issue than those earlier series of gold or silver coins produced in such small numbers that they can only represent ceremonial or gift-giving. Aldfrið's Northumbria produced sufficient surplus from the land to support a genuine currency; and currency is the smoking gun of trade. None of the coins so far found came from hoards; each is a single find. Whitby has produced two; a site at North Ferriby, on the north bank of the Humber estuary, four; and a site at Lough in Lincoln also two.

If the total numbers implied are startling, the distribution map showing where these *sceattas* have been found is even more so. A single, unprovenanced example came from north of the River Tyne. The most distant came from *Hamwic*, the West Saxon trading settlement sited on the narrow peninsula between the River Itchen and Southampton Water in what is now Hampshire. Four come from Kent; one from near Dunstable, located where

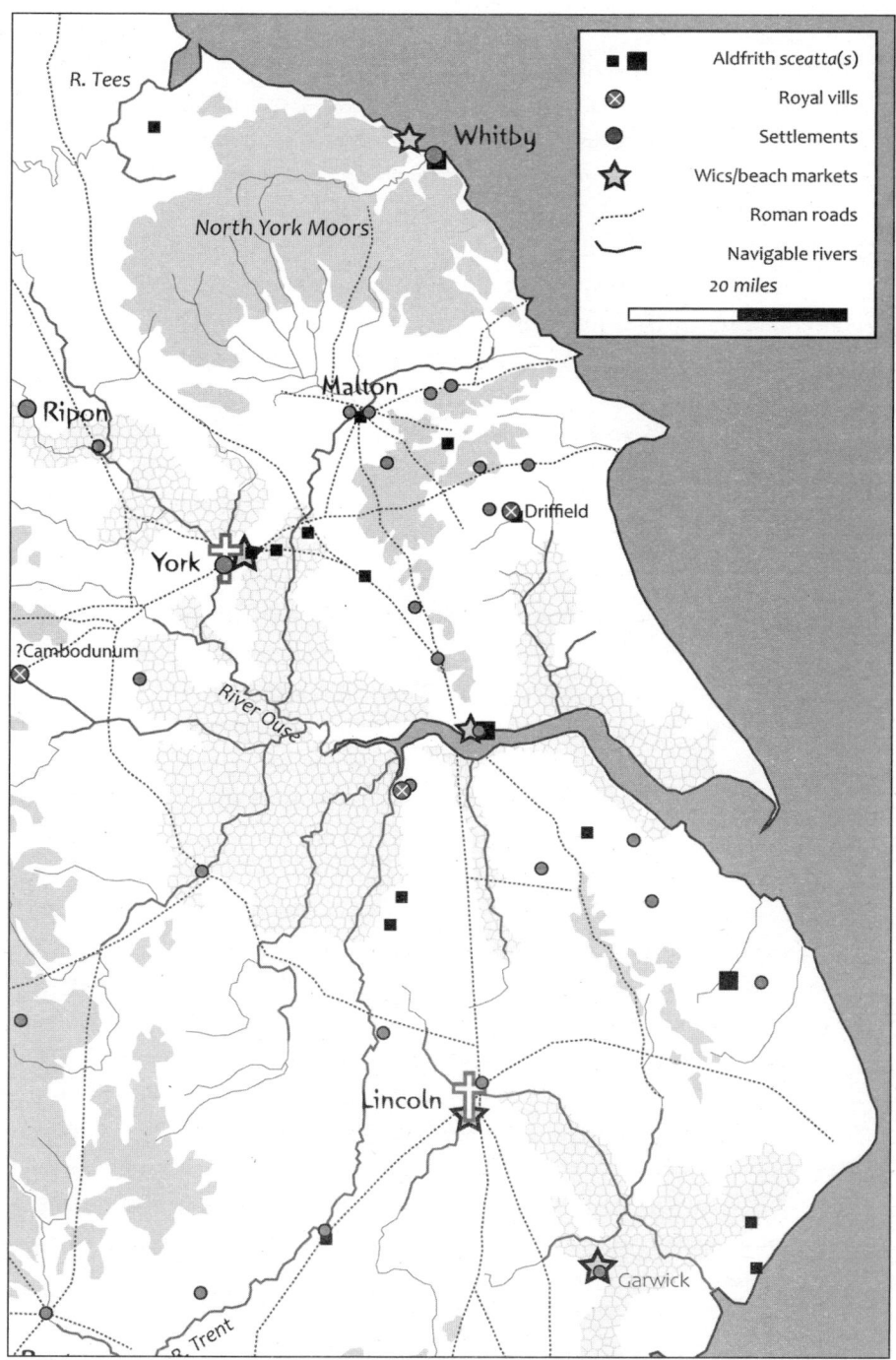

Map 17 Distribution of coins of King Aldfrið

Watling Street crosses the ancient Icknield Way; one from the East Anglian royal site and possible trading settlement at Rendlesham; one from Norfolk; another from Essex; two from close to the River Trent, one from near the River Idle and another Lindsey example from North Lincolnshire. The seven remaining coins whose provenance is known all come from the East Riding of Yorkshire, with a clustering along an axis between York and the Yorkshire Wolds. None has so far been found on the Continent, in London or in the Mercian heartlands. Any Northumbrian coins turning up in Frisian or Frankish ports are likely to have been recycled into local mints.

Coin finds from Aldfrið's reign will increase; they may one day amount to more than a hundred; but the pattern is unlikely to change dramatically. Each coin represents an accidental loss, one reason why archaeologists place such a high value on their distribution: they are disinterested witnesses. The coins found at riverine and coastal sites – at Whitby, on the Humber, in Kent, the Solent and along the Trent, are unmistakeable signs of water-borne trade. Coins from inland sites show that the economy represented by this trade was not exclusively based at the larger trading settlements: farming estates were receiving coin as currency, and in significant amounts. It is also noticeable that, with the exception of Whitby, which seems to have been located close to a beach market, none of these coins come from minster sites; so the otherwise strong case that can be made for minsters as commercial enterprises, for which evidence is now overwhelming in the eighth century, does not apply in Northumbria – at least, not during the reign of Aldfrið and not for some time afterwards. No more Northumbrian coinage was produced until the second quarter of the eighth century; Aldfrið's coins may have been in circulation for half a century.

In these decades no other English kingdom was issuing coins carrying a king's name.* The advantage for King Aldfrið in such a large issue was that he could ensure through his reeves and agents that at ports of entry into the kingdom – Whitby, North Ferriby and York, perhaps Tynemouth – only royal-approved trade might be conducted. That meant exacting tolls for goods entering and leaving and, in all probability, having a trading hall, or *sele*, of his own. The king could also ensure first pick of choice goods, and commission traders to look out for specialist items not available locally – hawks for hunting; furs; fine glassware.

---

* Naismith 2012, 90–1. King Eadbald of Kent (616–640) had issued a series bearing his name.

Why, one asks, did such commercial trade apparently not reach as far north as the Rivers Tyne and Wear, where capital was invested with such enthusiasm by monastic entrepreneurs like Biscop and Wilfrid and where, according to the testimonies of Bede and the other biographers, abbots were busy bringing goods and craftspeople in, invigorating the regional economy? Both geography and history imply an economic boom in the last quarter of the seventh century. Two possibilities emerge: one is that abbots were using alternative forms of 'currency' for their transactions – books, salt or woollen garments, for example. They may, at this time, have disdained the idea of 'trade', instead coding their economic transactions, in a very traditional Anglo-Saxon way, as reciprocal gift exchange. There is strong evidence for such a mentality in the correspondence between St Boniface in Frisia and his many contacts in England.* A second possibility is that Aldfrið's focus on the southern kingdom of Deira, in contrast to King Ecgfrið's more Bernician-focused interests, deliberately or otherwise excluded the northern part of the kingdom from his economic patronage. The same argument would apply to the equally coinless former kingdom of Elmet in the eastern Pennines. Surprisingly, although the political consequence of the Battle on the River Trent in 679 was the final loss of Lindsey and its tribute to Mercian control, Northumbrian coinage and, therefore, its economy, show that Lindsey's status was actually more fluid.

Several campaigns of fieldwork in East Yorkshire, and the notice of King Aldfrið's death in 705 at Driffield on the south-east edge of the Yorkshire Wolds, offer a focus for analysis.† The site discovered on Fishergate, on the east side of the River Foss in York in the mid 1980s, seems to confirm later written evidence of a thriving mercantile community – perhaps of Frisian traders – towards the end of the eighth century. The presence of a church here, founded by Paulinus under King Edwin and then completed under King Oswald, hints at a royal estate centre alongside the diocesan focus. In 735 York was established as Britain's second archdiocese after Canterbury. The stone-built, so-called Anglian tower, excavated in the 1970s, hints at a seventh-century refurbishment of part of the

---

* For example, a letter written to Boniface by King Æðelberht of Kent (c.748–754), accompanied by gifts of silver, a gold-lined drinking cup and two woollen cloaks in return (he hopes) for a pair of hunting falcons. *Boniface*, Letter 85, 155–7.

† West Heslerton, the most extensively excavated and impressive Deiran settlement site, has not produced any Aldfrið *sceattas* but eighth-century coins were found there in abundance. See Chapters 2 and 9.

late Roman defences.* The Fishergate settlement was established outside the Roman walled town some time in the late seventh century, broadly contemporary with the establishment of *Lundenwic* and *Hamwic*.

The 'Anglian tower' in York, perhaps part of a seventh-century refurbishment of the city's defences

* Its excavator, Jeff Radley, who was tragically killed by a trench wall collapse while excavating it, assigned the construction to the reign of Edwin. Later consensus suggests it may belong to the late Roman phases; but any date before the ninth century is possible. Palliser 2014, 21–2.

Anglian York looks as though it was polyfocal, with discrete areas under the respective control of the church, royal reeves and merchants. Who initiated the intensely active Fishergate site is a moot point, as is the case with the Mercian *burhs* in the eighth century – Frisian traders are the prime suspects. Kings and bishops benefitted from coastal and international goods exchange and probably, also, from the profits of crafts workshops, by creaming off perquisites and by controlling rights to extract tolls and other riverside fees. Evidence for their close interest in such matters comes largely from eighth-century Mercian charters.[45] The material evidence from the *wic* sites and their hinterlands hints at regional distribution, in the physical form of pottery which may have carried wine (Frankish Tating Ware pitchers, for example) and imported lava quernstones, reinforced by literary notices. Antler, bone and horn were all worked at Fishergate; textiles were being produced and cattle and sheep consumed in large quantities. Glass was being worked and fur prepared here for onward trade and regional distribution.[46] In Alcuin's day, at the end of the eighth century, York was a 'haven for ocean-going ships from the farthest ports,' able to penetrate far inland on the tidal River Ouse.[47]

York's traders and consumers were able to benefit from productive landscapes as far away as the Tees Valley, the eastern Pennines above Boroughbridge, the lower Ouse valley, from Ryedale and the Vale of Pickering and from the Yorkshire Wolds. Judging by the distribution of Aldfrið *sceattas*, Wold estates were driving production – as they also seem to have been during the Roman period, if the numbers of villas known from the Wolds is indicative.

Cottam, a deserted Medieval village, lies at the centre of the high chalk Wolds at the head of a typically dry valley, connected by an ancient droveway to the Roman road that linked York with the coast at Bridlington. By the end of the eighth century settlements in the immediate area were consuming high-quality metalwork and coins, examples of which have been recovered by metal-detecting in ploughsoil layers over the last twenty years or so. Formal excavations have revealed not clusters of houses, but complexes of curvilinear enclosures and pits characteristic of many crop-mark sites on the Wolds, often called 'Butterwick-type' settlements after the type-site. The probable presence of sunken-floored buildings at some of these sites hints at an Early Medieval date.[48] The enclosures and droveways indicate a pastoral economy, but a corn-drying oven excavated at Cottam also suggests a grain surplus; finds such as ceramic lamps, whetstones, some copper-alloy metal-working debris and tiny fragments of lead are indicative of craft workshops.

Animal bone remains evince a population of sheep or goat and cattle, of a range of ages which suggests both domestic consumption and production for trade. The presence of wool combs provides supporting material evidence for one major secondary product of this and other high Wold settlements, while the corn drier and quernstones hint, no more, at the extent of cereal production. So far, Cottam does not show signs of having consumed, or having had much access to, imported high-value goods.[49] But although the focus of activity was relocated in later decades, Cottam remained productive into the Anglo-Scandinavian centuries. The key question, perhaps, is: how dense were such sites on the Wolds; and how specialised was their production (names like Butterwick being suggestive of specialisation)? Eleven so-called Butterwick-type cropmarks have been identified so far.[50]

Very long-running excavations at the Wold site of Wharram Percy, about 12km due west and likewise situated overlooking a chalk valley, have revealed an extensive settlement spanning several centuries and developing into at least two Medieval manors. Wharram's inhabitants enjoyed the immense benefit of a small stream which was dammed, with one excavated feature interpreted as the remains of a mill or fish trap.[51] As at Cottam, sheep or goat bones dominate the animal assemblage. Quernstones fashioned from non-local material hint at the value of efficient cereal processing, while the lucky survival of cereal grains has allowed archaeo-botanists to demonstrate how free-threshing grain varieties gradually increased across the centuries. Non-ferrous metalworking was also carried out here, and finds of Tating Ware, associated with the Frankish wine trade, indicate that Wharram's lords had access to markets that their Cottam counterparts did not apparently enjoy.[52]

Some 10km south-east of Cottam, lying on the upper reaches of the River Hull, Driffield – Old English *Drifelda* – is the principal settlement on the Wolds, which here open out onto the flatlands of Holderness and the estuary of the Humber. Driffield is recorded first at the beginning of the eighth century: it was here that King Aldfrið was said to have died in 705.[53] Immediately before the Conquest of 1066 Driffield was the centre of a large estate consisting of four berewicks – outlying, dependent manors – with jurisdiction over ten further sokelands. By the time of the Domesday survey of 1086 it had been brought back into the king's portfolio. Chris Loveluck has suggested that this was a major royal estate – the Deiran equivalent of one of the Bernician shires, like *Gefrin* – belonging to King Aldfrið which passed, over the centuries, into the hands of the earls of Northumbria.[54] One of the component *vills* of this estate lay at Skerne, a low-lying settlement in a broad loop of the River Hull a couple of miles south-east of Driffield. Here, a wooden revetment for a jetty dating to the mid seventh century has been excavated.[55] Further downstream, at Watton* and Beverley,† minsters contemporary with the reign of Aldfrið are known; and sea-going ships are recorded reaching Beverley in the twelfth century.[56] The upper reaches of the Hull were canalised as far upstream as Driffield in the eighteenth century.

In his study of the Driffield estate Chris Loveluck suggests that iron-smelting and fisheries may have been important, profitable components of a wealthy and productive landscape.[57] Late seventh-century inhumations in the area contain large quantities of iron objects and an iron-working bloomery is known from excavations at a late Romano-British site at Elmswell, immediately west of Driffield. The natural mineral source may have been bog iron from the peatlands near Sledmere.

If, as seems very likely, Driffield was a core part of Aldfrið's lands, one might ask how he came by it, given the long exile of his youth. King Ecgfrið's focus had been northern and Bernician. But the Wolds are steeped in the monuments of Bronze Age and Iron Age; many burials of the sixth, seventh and eighth centuries were inserted into still-visible barrows; and the Wolds were densely occupied and industrially active through the Roman period. If Aldfrið made Deira his economic and personal core territory, is it too much to suspect the hand of his politically active and relatively local half-sister Ælfflæd, abbess of Whitby, in ensuring that this estate passed to the king in whose installation she had invested so much political capital? If so, he was able to make something of it, creating an economic powerhouse in Deira in spite of the loss of the kingdom of Lindsey to the growing hegemony of the Mercian kings.

Aldfrið may have seen York, the Wolds and the ancient coreland of Deira primarily in the context of what the Ouse and Humber had to offer: access to the Vale of York, the Trent, Lindsey and Mercia; to Frisian and Scandinavian ports and to Frankish and papal courts. In turn, his *gesiðas* and their families shared in the new wealth, enjoying the material fruits of contacts with the Merovingian world, able to lay their hands on a pitcher of wine every now and then; to bury their loved ones with amethysts, gold and silver brooches and glass vessels. The currents of power flowed along river and coast, connecting

---

* Probably Bede's *Vetadun*. Bede *HE* V.III.
† Bede's *Inderawudu*. Bede *HE* V.vi.

an enthusiastically Christian Northumbrian élite with its Continental neighbours. If Bede had little to say about Aldfrið's economic success, it may have been because, on the banks of the River Tyne, his otherwise splendid Jarrow was economically insulated from the Deiran honeypot.

* * *

The petrifying tendencies evident in stone buildings, in the products of scriptoria and in King Aldfrið's so-far unlocated mints are also conspicuous in the rise of corporeal cults. Travellers to the Continent had seen that the burial places of saints and the shrines of the Apostles were magnets for pilgrims and for royal patronage. In England a manifest example is the competition between the royal families of Mercia and East Anglia for 'ownership' of the Fenland site of St Guðlac's hermitage and shrine at Crowland, vividly portrayed in his eighth-century *Vita* by Felix.[58]

In 675/9 Mercian King Æðelred and his Northumbrian Queen Osðryð, half-sister to Aldfrið, had founded a monastery at Bardney on the River Witham in Lindsey. As a signal that they intended to found a royal cult centre there, they had retrieved the trunk and legs of the martyred King Oswald and sent them to the community as a gift, with initially unpropitious but ultimately miraculous results.[59]

This episode, improbable as it seems, should be seen in the broader political context of a long-running turf war between Northumbrian and Mercian kings for control of the province of Lindsey. King Oswald's body had been dismembered on the field of battle before the ancient ramparts of Old Oswestry in the Western marches. His head and arms had been retrieved on a raid by his brother Oswiu. The torso, legs and battle standard must have been kept in Mercia as battle trophies – and remained in the possession of Mercia's kings. After Penda's ultimate defeat and death in 655, Oswiu had asserted control over Lindsey, deploying his extensive political capital in the form of royal marriage and ecclesiastical patronage, before his proxies were expelled by Penda's sons. Ecgfrið had briefly reasserted control there in the 670s during the reign of King Wulfhere, according to Bede.[60]

Either shortly before or immediately after the Battle on the River Trent in 679 these gruesome relics were deployed as a sort of scent-marking of Mercian royal authority at a new royal cult centre, in lands that had once been claimed by Oswald's brother. King Æðelred and his Northumbrian consort – Oswald's niece – appear to have thought that this was good diplomacy. The monks at Bardney were appalled and had to be convinced to accept them by an apposite *deus ex machina* miracle.[61]

According to an entry in the *Anglo-Saxon Chronicle*, Queen Osðryð was murdered in obscure circumstances in 697 – another indication, perhaps, of how unwelcome overt Northumbrian influence was at the Mercian court. Her body was also interred at Bardney and the Mercian king joined them on his own death in 709.* The anonymous *Life of St Gregory*, written at Whitby, relates how, in equally grisly fashion, King Edwin's head was retrieved from the battlefield at *Hæthfelth* and taken to Whitby to invest a new royal cult there.[62] In 695, sixteen years after her death in the monastery which she had founded at Ely, Æðelðryð, former queen of Ecgfrið and patron of Wilfrid, was exhumed and 'translated' at the instigation of her sister Seaxburh.[63] She was taken from her wooden coffin and placed above ground in a stone sarcophagus retrieved from the deserted Roman town of *Grantacaestir*, according to Bede. Found to be incorrupt (a sure sign of virtue and heavenly favour), her relics became the focus of miraculous cures, and a thriving cult was born which evolved into that of St Audrey.

In 698, eleven years after the death of Cuthbert on Inner Farne, his remains were also exhumed and translated – partly as a response, one suspects, to the new Deiran cult of King Edwin at Whitby but also inspired by the miraculous state of Queen Æðelðryð's incorrupt body. The Lindisfarne community, at risk of being marginalised by the grand foundations at Hexham, Jarrow and Ripon, may already have felt some pressure to establish an institutional legacy, of which the *Anonymous Life of Cuthbert* is one material expression. Bishop Eadberht, Lindisfarne's abbot from 688 to 698, caused Finán's church of hewn oak and reed thatch, built 'after the Irish fashion', to be clad entirely with lead.[64] Perhaps a stone church would have been a step too far towards Rome. The material wealth that must lie behind the unknown source of such a large quantity of lead belies the community's otherwise unsullied reputation for asceticism.

Bede gives the fullest account of the translation: how Eadberht allowed his monks to place the holy man's bones in a light chest above ground, 'so that they might be worthily venerated'.[65] But the body was wondrously intact and whole, sweet-smelling and undecayed: 'more like a sleeping than a dead man'. A wooden chest was prepared to hold the relics – the same coffin, carved with figurative images of the apostles, whose fragments are still preserved at Durham Cathedral – and placed on the floor of the sanctuary. It

---

* The politics of the Mercian court at this time is addressed fully in Adams 2025.

is conspicuous that in later decades and centuries, when Lindisfarne monks recorded the history of their fortunes – gifts, thefts and significant events – that they referred to themselves as the Community of St Cuthbert: gifts were made to *him*; estates were stolen from *him*. His body became the spiritual and material embodiment of their fortunes, almost synonymous with the abbacy and bishopric of Lindisfarne. It is conceivable that, as we have suggested elsewhere, the monks of Lindisfarne had originally interred their holy man in a lead casket, with eternality in mind.[66] They certainly seem to have been able to lay their hands on sufficient lead sheets for such a purpose.

* * *

For the first time in Northumbrian history the king's prestige and wealth were driven less by warfare and raiding, supported by the tribute of bullion and livestock, than by cultural capital and by profits drawn from landed wealth. But at all times Early Medieval kings must negotiate a narrow path, balancing the interests of collateral members of regional élites against their potential threat to the dynasty. Increasingly, they must also maintain often complex diplomatic and intellectual relations with abbots and abbesses, bishops and distant but influential archbishops in Canterbury – themselves very largely drawn from powerful landed families.

Some of these powerful interests come onto the historical radar for the first time in the late seventh century. On King Ecgfrið's first expedition against the Picts in 671–3, he was accompanied by a 'brave *subregulus*', Beornæð.[67] The ill-advised expedition to Brega in 684 was led by a warlord named Beorht, according to the *Chronicle*. In 698 one Beorhtred, at the head of a Northumbrian host, was killed in battle against a Pictish army[68] and thirteen years later the *praefectus* Beorhtfrið attacked the Picts in Manau in revenge for the deaths of his father and grandfather.[69] In 706 the same Beorhtfrið, described by Stephen of Ripon as *secundus a rege princeps*[70] and as *praefatus regis princeps* – the 'king's chief man' – was the spokesman for King Osred, alongside Abbess Ælfflæd, at an assembly at Nidd called by the archbishop of Canterbury to resolve the long-running dispute with Wilfrid.

These men seem to have belonged to a powerful dynasty of alliteratively named *duces* – military allies and counsellors to three successive kings (see also Chapter 6). Two of them appear consecutively in the Durham *Liber Vitae*, between Kings Ecgfrið and Aldfrið. A notice in the *Annals of Tigernach* under 698 refers to the battle between Saxons and Picts in which *Brechtaidh* (Beorhtred), son of *Bernith* (Beornæð) was killed. If Aldfrið's south-facing policies relied on economic power, it seems that his northern flank – that is to say Bernicia – was delegated as a fiefdom to a great Northumbrian family. Their appearance in the Durham *Liber Vitae* suggests that they were important patrons of the Lindisfarne community – a signal of investment in an equally powerful spiritual fiefdom. We have followed James Fraser's circumstantial argument that the family held Fife as a tributary kingdom of Northumbria.⁷¹ But it is possible that their fiefdom lay closer to home in Lothian, or perhaps in an estate with a caput at the grand township at Sprouston, identified through air photography on the banks of the River Tweed.⁷²

Such great men were not the king's only secular representatives. We know of the names of two reeves, Osfrið and Tydlin, one of whom was entrusted with managing the royal estate at Dunbar; the other, Osfrið, at the unidentified *urbs* of *Broninis*.* In both cases they were responsible not just for the stewardship of the king's fiscal and estate management interests; they were also obliged to imprison the king's enemies. In 680 Wilfrid, returning from Rome and brandishing a papal missive in his attempt to win back control of the see at York, had been imprisoned in *Broninis*, then at Dunbar,⁷³ before being released into exile in Mercia, then Wessex, then Sussex before finding comfort there, finally, beyond the bounds of even King Ecgfrið's overweening *imperium*.

In the second year of King Aldfrið's reign, 686, on the advice and counsel of Archbishop Theodore, Wilfrid was allowed to return to Northumbria, and the king restored to him possession of the minster he had founded at Hexham in 674. Subsequently he was also restored to the see at York while Ripon, 'with all its revenues', was returned to him.⁷⁴ Wealthy and influential ecclesiasts like Wilfrid, with papal and archiepiscopal support, could not easily be dismissed like disloyal thegns – dispossessed or killed by the king's assassins. Church foundations, estates and treasures were inalienable; could not, at least in theory, be recycled to the royal fisc. Wilfrid was what these days might be called a disrupter, playing for the highest stakes and absolutely prepared to use all his considerable political capital to achieve his aims. Stephen, writing of Wilfrid's restoration, records that he 'drove the strange bishops out'.⁷⁵

Bede discreetly avoids mention of the aftermath in the *Historia*. But Wilfrid's return, the death of Abbot Eata at Hexham in 685 and of Cuthbert

---

* It might be an as yet unidentified site, perhaps near the mouth of the River Tweed. Durham has been proposed (Breeze 1999); but Alcock's suggestion that it refers to the natural mammiform hill on which Lindisfarne castle sits seems more credible. It may once have been called *Bebbanhlaw*, recalling the legendary name of King Æðelfrith's first queen. Alcock 2003, 212.

himself two years later, resulted in Wilfrid's de facto resumption as bishop of all Northumbria; and in the *Prose Life of Cuthbert* Bede alludes to something like a purge at Lindisfarne: 'so great a blast of trial beat upon the church that many of the brethren chose to depart from the place rather than be in the midst of such dangers'.[76]

Within five years, Wilfrid and his new king had fallen out: once again he was expelled from Northumbria, and this time he found a more settled exile in Mercia under King Æðelred.[77] But still he was not prepared to relinquish his historic claim on the see of York or his rights in the estates of Hexham and Ripon.

After the murder of Queen Osðryð in 697, and now in his sixties, Wilfrid's Mercian patron King Æðelred was in political, probably also physical, decline as a new century dawned. While the king retained a semblance of authority, the exiled bishop seems to have petitioned Archbishop Berhtwald to call an assembly to review his case. In 702 a council was duly convened on the diplomatically neutral border between Mercia and Northumbria, at *Atswinapathe*, or Austerfield, near Bawtry on the River Idle.[78] The sole account is Stephen's, and he paints a picture of furious arguments among the bishops who attended; a conspiracy against Wilfrid; spies among the Northumbrian contingent and eventual defeat, renewed exile and even excommunication, conceding him only possession of the monastery at Ripon. By the time that Wilfrid had, once more, travelled to Rome to petition the pope and returned brandishing another papal judgement in his favour, his world-weary Mercian sponsor had abdicated, retiring to the royal monastery at Bardney, where his late queen and the relics of the martyred Oswald lay.

The death of King Aldfrið in 704 or 705 presented Wilfrid with one final redemptive opportunity. Not for the first time, his friend Abbess Ælfflæd of Whitby, the pre-eminent peace-weaver, kingmaker and diplomat, was broker-in-chief. As far back as the beginning of Aldfrið's reign Archbishop Theodore had entreated her to intervene with her half-brother on Wilfrid's behalf.[79] In the months before Aldfrið's death Wilfrid, having returned from Rome to his monastery at Oundle on the River Nene in Mercia, had written once more to the king, requesting an interview. The request was rejected[80] but in his final sickness the king was said – by Abbess Ælfflæd – to have repented and to have requested that peace be made with Wilfrid after his death;[81] and Ælfflæd confirmed this to Stephen, the biographer.

On Aldfrið's death the Iding dynasty was left without a credible candidate to replace him: his son, Osred, was still a child. In his place the throne went to Eadwulf, whose ancestry is unknown. Wilfrid made contact with the new king's son, travelled north to Ripon and sent messengers to King Eadwulf. The king threatened to have him killed if he stayed. This was a year of high jeopardy in Northumbria. The ætheling Osred seems to have been besieged in the fortress at Bamburgh, under attack from Eadwulf but protected by his father's chief man, Beorhtfrið.* Within months King Eadwulf had himself been deposed and Osred installed, inferentially under the military protection of the northern warlord and the still-powerful influence of his aunt, Abbess Ælfflæd.

In 706 a synod was convened at Nidd in what is now North Yorkshire, a site whose obscurity belies the weight of the assembly. Stephen says that the synod was called by Archbishop Beorhtwald and that King Osred, his chief men, three bishops and their abbots attended. Ælfflæd, ever the diplomat and 'always the comforter and best counsellor of the whole province', testified to her late half-brother's deathbed contrition.[82] Beorhtfrið spoke too – at least according to Stephen's partial account:

> when we were besieged in the city called Bamburgh and surrounded on every hand by a hostile force ... taking counsel among ourselves, we vowed that if God granted our royal boy his father's kingdom, we would fulfil the Apostolic commands concerning Bishop Wilfrid.[83]

The archbishop 'took counsel' with his bishops and with Abbess Ælfflæd; Ripon and Hexham were restored to Wilfrid 'with all the revenues belonging to them'. But the greatest ecclesiastical entrepreneur of the age did not enjoy his last triumph for long: he died in 709 at his Mercian foundation, Oundle; his body was brought back to Ripon. Wilfrid had outlived his contemporaries. During the course of a long career he had scaled the heights and won the confidence of kings; he had also suffered catastrophic falls. Throughout, he had shown great resilience, but times had changed and his sort of personal ecclesiastical power building was no longer acceptable in the church as it had developed from Archbishop Theodore's reforms. At Austerfield in 702 he had faced a hostile council intent on bringing him down and took his case to the pope in Rome. But he still had influential friends, not least among them Abbess Ælfflæd. At the synod of Nidd a more humane attitude prevailed and he was afforded some dignity in retirement. Though he had been a contentious figure, he inspired great personal loyalty on the part of his followers.

---

* Unrecorded by Bede or the *Chronicle*; Stephen is the only source for this event. *VW* 60.

8

THE ANGELCYNN: 706–737

Decline and fall – Bede's last kings – Greater Northumbria – Whithorn and Hoddom – Cumbria – The rise of Mercia – Beneath the radar – The end of history

Bede's judgement, that after the reign of Ecgfrið Northumbria's strength began to 'ebb and fall away', may have been premature; but successive historians have generally accepted that the Battle of *Nechtansmere* marked the high spring tide of Northumbrian hegemony, never to be emulated in later decades. Northumbrian ambitions to render tributary the Pictish kingdom north of the Forth–Clyde isthmus and the kingdom of Mercia south of the Humber were never again fulfilled. Eighth-century annalists recorded no great military victories over its neighbours, and there is no evidence that Northumbrian kings again enjoyed the supremacy of the early and middle seventh century.

Bede says very little of his contemporary secular lords – they seem not to have lived up to the soaring reputations that he established for their celebrated Iding predecessors Æðelfrið, Edwin, Oswald and Oswiu. Bede's death in 735, four years after the completion of his masterwork, the *Historia Ecclesiastica*, seems not only to mark a final cultural decline but almost to signal the end of history: he had no successor as narrative chronicler of the *gens Anglorum*, and subsequent Northumbrian dynasts are mainly deeply obscure.

Eighth-century English history is dominated by the rise of a dynasty of very powerful, long-lived and politically significant kings in Mercia. The reigns of just two of them, Æðelbald and Offa, span the eight decades between 716 and 796. During that time at least eleven kings reigned in Northumbria and several of them met violent ends. The great political, cultural and economic achievements of that century are for the most part Mercian, with London emerging as an international emporium, and the navigable reaches of the Trent, Severn, Nene and Thames as highways spanning an increasingly productive Midlands landscape. Offa's Dyke; the basilican church at Brixworth; a fine silver coinage to match and be copied by Carolingian mints; Europe-wide diplomacy; exuberant sculpture and evolution bordering on revolution in Anglo-Saxon royal administration: all are Mercian achievements. And yet no Mercian chronicle survives from the court of Æðelbald or Offa; instead, a wealth of charters affords fascinating glimpses into an increasingly sophisticated machinery of government and patronage, a buoyant economy and a self-conscious secular and spiritual élite exploring the limits of power.

After Bede, Northumbrian historians must rely on the more Southern-focused *Anglo-Saxon Chronicle*, on sparse notices in a Northern Annal* whose last record was entered in 802; and on the so-called *Continuatio Bedae*, a miscellany thinly covering events between 732 and 766. A small collection of dubious land grants poses more questions than it answers; there are no authentic surviving contemporary Northumbrian charters.

A lack of detailed genealogies means that the dynastic fortunes of eighth- and ninth-century Northumbrian kings are at least partly speculative. Much more is known about the deaths of Wilfrid in 709 at Oundle, of Aldhelm in Malmesbury the same year and of the hermit Guðlac at Crowland in 714, than of the secular politics of these decades. Unrecorded by Bede, Beorhtfrið fought a battle of vengeance against the Picts in 711. But he does recount how, in 716, the Pictish King Nechtan mac Derilei, having assiduously studied ecclesiastical writings and having corresponded with Abbot Ceolfrið of Monkwearmouth and Jarrow, ordered that the Northern church should henceforth follow orthodox Roman practice in the tonsure and in calculations for the date of Easter.[1] Iona, too, was brought to orthodoxy under the guidance of a Northumbrian cleric, Ecgberht.† Where military arms failed, the power of rational argument and ecclesiastical authority succeeded in extending Northumbrian influence beyond its frontiers.

King Osred, succeeding his father, Aldfrið, after the short-lived coup by Eadwulf in 705, survived long enough to attain his majority in 715, but was

---

* The York annalist behind 'northern' entries in the *Historia Regum* up to 802; see also pages 277 and 281n.
† This appears to be the same Ecgberht to whom Bede addressed his famous letter of 734 and who became bishop, then archbishop of York – from an allusion in Bede *HE* V.22.

killed a year later.* The 'E' recension of the *Anglo-Saxon Chronicle* recorded that his murder took place 'south of the border' – that is to say, in Mercia, whose King Ceolred died in the same year 'in a frenzied fit', according to St Boniface.² Otherwise, his reign is unremarked.

That same year, 716, saw the departure of Abbot Ceolfrið on his final journey to Rome, carrying in his baggage train the great *Codex Amiatinus*, and perhaps also the completion of Bede's *Verse Life of Cuthbert*. Osred was succeeded by Cœnred who, according to an entry in the *Annals of Ulster* under the year 718, was a son of the otherwise obscure Cuðwine. Cœnred may only have survived two years but this left-field notice allows him to be placed in a dynasty recorded in the Anglian Genealogies³ and the *Anglo-Saxon Chronicle* for 731 as a brother of the later King Ceolwulf, to whom Bede dedicated his *Historia*. The genealogy records their distant descent from Ocg, son of Ida, placing them both in the most illustrious – and legitimate – line of Bernician kings, although one is here suspicious of a political fiction. King Cœnred died in unknown circumstances and was succeeded by Osric. Alliteratively, and on the authority of Symeon, he is likely have been a brother of Osred and, therefore, a younger son of King Aldfrið.†

As with all the kings after Aldfrið, Bede gives Osric's eleven-year reign short shrift. The last book of the *Historia* is concerned with miracles and ecclesiastical events, the exploits of overseas missionaries and the final resolution of the Easter controversy. Into that annalistic void, ironically, historians place the creation of Bede's treatise *De Temporum ratione* – 'On the Reckoning of Time' – which he finished in 725. Drawing on both ancient scholarship and his own computations and observations, he painted a rational view of God's creation: of a spherical earth, of latitude and its effect on daylight length; of the moon's influence on tides; of the calculation of dates from the incarnation, which he popularised; and with detailed instructions on how to calculate the correct date for Easter. In a modern translation the work takes up more than 240 pages.⁴ His *Chronica Maiora*, or Greater

---

* What appears to be the notice of Eadwulf's death in Irish exile in 717 is recorded in the *Annals of Tigernach*, where his father is said to have been Eouilb. His descendants became Northumbrian kings.

† Kirby (2000) raises the possibility that he was a son of Alhfrið and, therefore, probably the grandson of Oswiu and Rhieinmelth. *Hist Reg* II.42. For a full reconstruction of Northumbria's eighth-century kings, see the Northumbrian regnal list section of this book.

Chronicle, was compiled at the same time. If Bede was also working on the *Historia*, several theological commentaries and his *Prose Life of Cuthbert*, it is perhaps understandable that the affairs of his secular contemporaries were of decreasing interest.

King Osric died in 729 and was succeeded by Ceolwulf *Cuðwining*, brother of the short-lived Cœnred. In a few laconic, if portentous lines, Bede précises his reign as follows: 'Both the beginning and the course of his reign have been filled with so many and such serious commotions and setbacks that it is as yet impossible to know what to say about them or to guess what the outcome will be.'[5]

It is not very helpful. Of the undercurrents to which he alludes only one has any material trace. In 731 the king was 'taken captive, tonsured and sent back into his own kingdom'.* Bishop Acca of Hexham was also driven from his see,† and the two events may be connected; but subsequently, in unknown circumstances, Ceolwulf was restored and ruled another six years. A year after the abortive coup he was secure enough to be able to appoint his cousin Ecgberht to the see of York, and in 735 negotiations with Pope Gregory III succeeded in elevating York to metropolitan status. Two years later Ceolwulf retired, this time apparently voluntarily, to monastic seclusion.[6] He joined St Cuthbert's community on Lindisfarne and endowed it with suitably regal gifts: the *vill* of Warkworth and its dependencies and other estates in southern Bernicia.‡ Archbishop Ecgberht's brother, and the retiring king's cousin, Eadberht, succeeded him and ruled for twenty-one years. Dynasty stability had been restored to Northumbria.

It seems, then, that in the first half of the eighth century two principal dynasties were able to compete for power in Northumbria. It is tempting to think of Aldfrið's line – Osred and probably Osric – as having Deiran affinities, and the Lioualdings – Cœnred, Ceolwulf and Eadberht – as having Bernician affinities. The reality may have been more complex: political

---

* This enigmatic phrase implies that Ceolwulf was considered something of an outsider, but which kingdom he was sent back to is only implied by his later retirement to Lindisfarne – he is likely to have been a Bernician. It suggests he was effectively imprisoned in a monastery.
† *Hist Reg* 732, correctly 731.
‡ The only eighth-century land grants recorded in the *Historia de Sancto Cuthberto* – but of more than passing interest to historians and archaeologists. See Chapter 11. O'Brien *et al.* 2018.

undercurrents, the material remains of monuments, place-names and two further surviving genealogies combine to sketch a more fragmented and nuanced territorial picture. The first genealogy, in the *Anglian Collection of Royal Genealogies*, records a son of Ida, named Eadric, giving rise to six generations ending in Alhred, who ought by dead-reckoning to be a contemporary of Ceolwulf. None of the names in that list appear anywhere else but there is no reason to suppose it is entirely fictional.[7] An otherwise obscure fourth Bernician line, recorded only in the *Historia Brittonum*, was supposedly a branch descended from Ecgfrið's brother Ælfwine, who 'begot Oslac, begot Aldhun, begot Æðelsige, begot Ecca, begot Oslaph'.[8] Again, none of these men appear in contemporary sources; none of them issued coinage that survives. And then, there is that powerful Northern dynasty – we might call them Beornings – able to muster armies sufficient to attack Pictland and broker secular power in the North but not, apparently, eligible to vie for the kingship. Of the few hints at the political careers of these peripheral royals, the most convincing occurs in Stephen's notice of the founding of Ripon during the 670s. Among the dignitaries invited to its dedication ceremony were King Ecgfrið and his brother Ælfwine 'together with the abbots, the reeves and the sub-kings (*subreguli*)'.[9] In Mercia the careers of such men come increasingly into focus in the eighth century, when they appear frequently as signatories to royal charters. They were regional hard men, perhaps the descendants of those who in former times had been petty kings in their own right. They learned to serve their overkings and to enjoy the fruits of regional power and prestige; and by and large they seem to have remained loyal.[10]

Such unsatisfactory historical sources, ostensibly tracing Northumbria's entropic politics, are belied by the geography of a greater Northumbria slowly coming into focus during the last few decades of research through the idea of cultural corelands. Leaving aside questions of ethnic affiliation, military conquest and kingship for the moment, the evolution of those corelands – areas of concentrated human settlement, investment in agriculture, monuments and territorial control – must pre-date the age of Northumbrian overlordship. Before the aggressive Northumbrian expansion under King Æðelfrið and his successors, the Lothian lands must have lain under the control of Gododdin lords of Traprain; but the Cuthbert community believed that in the eighth century all the land from Tyninghame to Inveresk belonged to Lindisfarne:[11] an example of Northumbrian soft power wielding its *imperium* over an 'outer' Northumbria. Several strands of this *imperium* may be suggested. Firstly, the extension of orthodox spiritual and pastoral provision to areas already nominally Christian was itself an acculturating force. Second, the territorial power wielded by bishops, abbots and abbesses was Anglian territorial power, backed by the patronage and at least the theoretical protection of the king's *comites* or his *subreguli* at Dunbar or elsewhere. Thirdly, the investment in monumentalising the landscape with buildings and sculpture, probably also in new technologies such as mills and in more intensive livestock and crop management, reinforced the identity and economic fortune of Lothian's ancient cultural core. If the material remains and place-names of that period bear Anglian affinities, who can say how the inhabitants saw themselves?

Lothian is not as isolated from the rest of Bernicia as the historical Anglo-Scottish border has made it. Among the earlier sections of the *Historia de Sancto Cuthberto* are claims to a twelve-*vill* estate centred on Bowmont Water, immediately west of the Cheviot Hills, donated by King Oswiu or his son Oswine,[12] and the (once-British) monastic estate of Old Melrose 'and its dependencies',[13] formerly belonging to Abbot Boisl. And the bounds of the territory of Lindisfarne as described in the *Historia* continued beyond the River Tweed 'from the place where the Blackadder rises in the north as far as the place where it flows into the Tweed and all the land that lies between that River Blackadder and another that is called the Leader'.[14]

In reviewing the claimed possessions of the Cuthbert community, Alex Woolf has followed a suggestion by Alan James that many, if not most, Anglian names of *-ham* and *-ingham* form in south-east Scotland may have been applied to church sites. If the Lindisfarne *mansiones* or estate possessions listed in the various texts were not all minsters, each may at least have been the site of a church and a dependency of the diocese.[15] The process of acquisition may have been spread over a century and a half: they are not all likely to have been in the possession of Lindisfarne during the seventh century.

Something of the process of acquisition is revealed in the *Historia*: rewards for miracles and for victory in battle; and as the dowries, so to speak, of royal personages retiring to monastic communities. The terms of these gifts reveal the solid materiality of existing territorial units: *vills* 'and their dependencies' – the former estates of military retainers dying without issue or dispossessed or, like Cuthbert, having served their time under arms and making the transition, as so many others had, from king's *comites* to *milites Christi*.

In the texts of the two *vitae* of St Cuthbert lie further clues to Northumbrian territorial lordship north of the Tweed. In his youth Cuthbert tended his master's flocks on the hills above the River Leader, which flows south into the Tweed at Melrose.[16] A *praefectus* of King Ecgfrið named Hildmer possessed a *villa* near Melrose,[17] by which must be meant an estate centre or township. Hemma, a *gesiða* of King Aldfrið, possessed a *villula 'in regione Kentis'*, somewhere in the Tweed basin,[18] and a *vicus* belonging to another *gesiða*, of King Ecgfrið, lay on the banks of the Tweed. That these lands had, in recent times, been contested is suggested by a reference in the *Anonymous Life* to the days when Cuthbert, as a military retainer, was 'dwelling in camp with the army, in the face of the enemy'.[19] The implication is that there existed beyond the Tweed 'structures of authority' through which Bernician kings were able to invest in patronage in élite families, both secular and spiritual.[20]

It may be significant that a number of Brittonic place-names containing the element *Caer* occur in the lands between the Tweed and Forth. Conspicuously, these are mostly peripheral to the corelands that we have identified. Likewise, a number of *Caer* names have been identified in Cumbria[21] and, again, they are largely peripheral to the corelands identified by Roberts. Geoffrey Barrow, in a ground-breaking and highly influential paper, suggested that these names may identify shire centres – the sorts of *vills*, that is, where the *comites* and *praefecti* of kings might be based.[22] If they seem peripheral, it may be the case that they identify defensible upland sites inhabited during transhumant summer pasturing. Might the two *Caer*-names* along the upper Tweed and the Leader identify the *vills* and *halls* of men like Hilmer and Hemma?

A much broader geographical argument must be made for a 'Northumbrian' Galloway. This is an extensive promontory bordering the Solway Firth and northern Irish Sea to the south and the Firth of Clyde to the west. The Rhinns of Galloway are the closest point of mainland Britain to Ulster. Over the years broad, sheltered Luce Bay has produced material evidence of beach markets, and natural harbours exist at several sites. Good arable land is scarce here, but discrete cultural cores facing onto the Solway Firth can be proposed on evidence analogous to those suggested elsewhere. Prominent defended settlements at Trusty's Hill, Cruggleton, Tynron Doon, Burnswark, Mote of Mark and elsewhere all have either prehistoric origins or demonstrably Brittonic names. Dunragit and Rhionydd, even if they lack obviously defensible sites, bear names with kingly associations. Names featuring the Latin element *eccles*, for *ecclesia*, are not now thought to indicate the precise locations of churches

---

* Cardrona, 4km north-west of Innerleithen; and Carfrae, 6km north of Lauder, on a spur overlooking Dere Street.

but to reflect centres of territorial estates belonging to the British church, preserved through later assimilation into 'Anglian' control.[23] Their incidence is uneven in these proposed corelands; but distributions of late Latin-inscribed stones and the presence of fifth- to sixth-century exotic pottery, glass and metalwork from sites along the Solway coast reinforce the picture of a strong pre-Anglian cultural milieu. In this context the concentration of Anglian settlement names, Anglian-style crosses and minsters point firmly towards deep-time continuity, rather than to *de novo* English settlement.

In a sweeping historical account of Oswald's triumphant reconquest of Northumbria, his recruitment of the Irish Bishop Aidan to found an 'Iona in the East' on Lindisfarne and the proselytising mission of Colm Cille to the lands of the Northern Picts, Bede introduces the figure of Bishop Ninian, 'a Briton who had received orthodox instruction at Rome'. Bede says that Ninian's see was celebrated for its church, dedicated to St Martin of Tours, where his body, and that of many other saints, lies. He goes on: 'the see is now under English rule. The place which is in the kingdom of Bernicia is commonly called Whithorn, the "White House" [*Candida Casa*] because Ninian built a church of stone there, using a method unusual among the Britons.'[24]

At the close of his *Historia*, summarising the state of ecclesiastical provision in the early 730s, he records the installation of Bishop Pecthelm 'in the place called Whithorn, where the number of believers has so increased that it has lately become an episcopal see with Pecthelm as its first bishop'.[25]

Although modern scholarship tends towards the view that a British Ninian has been confused with Finnian of Movilla, an Irish holy man and mentor of Colm Cille, a largely conventional late eighth-century Life of Ninian, the *Miracula Nyniae Episcopi*, promoted a cult of the alleged British saint, co-opting him as an adoptive Northumbrian. The Whithorn peninsula is a lacuna in the geography of 'Eccles' names; even so, surviving traditions of an episcopal church at Whithorn in a late or sub-Roman milieu indicate that Anglian ecclesiasts were reviving an ancient institution.

Two other concentrations of sub-Roman church investment can be identified along the Solway/Gallowegian coast: on the Rhinns, with its three 'Eccles' names, and where Latin memorials at Kirkmadrine record the *sacerdotes* Viventius and Mavorius, while a lost Latin inscription from Curghie[26] recorded the presence of a *subdiaconus* named Ventidus; and along Annandale, with a suspected centre at Hoddom, with its high cross and local 'Eccles' names. If Whithorn was the episcopal centre and yet lacks 'Eccles' names, we can tentatively suggest that these names mark estates peripheral to the episcopal core.

Given Bede's notoriously anti-British sentiments, it is surprising, on the face of it, that he credits the foundation at Whithorn to a British saint. His motivation may be found in the tradition that Ninian had been instructed in the faith in Rome and was, therefore, an orthodox, canonically invested bishop under Rome's authority. He was, as such, a worthy precursor to Pecthelm and legitimised the refounding of the Whithorn diocese.

Orthodoxy mattered, especially in a historically Brittonic landscape with links to Ireland and the Welsh kingdoms. Wilfrid's quasi-military land grab among the British communities of the Pennines shows how hard 'soft' power might be.[27] Cuthbert's elevation to the bishopric of Lindisfarne in 685 may have been partly intended by Ecgfrið as a diplomatic gesture in exercising Northumbrian authority over Carlisle and its territories – Cuthbert's sensibilities and reputation may have smoothed ruffled waters, and his presence there in that year of crisis, with Ecgfrið's queen, looks pointed.[28]

Abercorn, the short-lived diocese on the Forth estuary west of Edinburgh, might belong to the same tradition of appropriating native diocesan centres for the expansion of the Northumbrian church in Lothian, while the royal monastic foundation at Carlisle, which became part of the Lindisfarne diocese, looks as though it must have formed part of the old alliance fostered between Rheged and Bernicia by King Oswiu's marriage to Rhieinmelth, great-granddaughter of Urien.

Whithorn had no such Lindisfarne connections. The diocese of Hexham, established in 678, was predicated on Wilfrid's overtly Romanist foundation there and his successors were scrupulously orthodox. For twenty years after Wilfrid's death in 709 his acolyte Acca was bishop of Hexham. Whithorn's first bishop, Pecthelm, had been a member of the Malmesbury community under Aldhelm – impeccably orthodox but with Irish connections. If Whithorn's absorption and episcopal revival was a Hexham initiative, it would not be a surprise.

Archaeologists take an understandably intense interest in Whithorn, the site of a twelfth-century priory and Medieval royal *burh*. It lies at the heart of a peninsula known as the Machars, between Luce Bay and Wigtown Bay and some 4km from the sheltered east coast. At the south-east tip of the peninsula sits the Isle of Whithorn, a rocky islet now reachable from the mainland but probably once separate. A Medieval chapel dedicated to St Ninian stands on the point, overlooking a narrow, rocky and sheltered deep-water harbour. A natural routeway along a low ridge connects it with the town.

Across Wigtown Bay at the mouth of the Water of Fleet lies Ardwall Island, site of an Early Christian chapel and burial ground excavated by Charles

Whithorn Priory stands on the site of the monastic church and settlement called *Candida Casa* by Bede

Thomas;[29] and excavations on a prominent hill overlooking the estuary of an Iron Age multivallate defended site, Trusty's Hill, have revealed evidence for élite occupation in the sixth and seventh centuries: animal bone, metalworking debris and imported pottery. The fort was razed, probably early in the seventh century, and the excavator has laid the blame on Northumbrian military expansion.[30] An idea that Trusty's Hill was a focus of Rheged kingship has, we think, been oversold; but its relationships to Whithorn, the Mote of Mark and Ardwall are significant of a long-established Solwegian cultural core.

Much closer to Whithorn, a stone with an incised cross motif bearing a very irregular Latin inscription, '(*Hic est L*)*oci Petri Apostolis*', was discovered on farmland to the south of the present town in the eighteenth century and in 1890 a Latin-inscribed stone was discovered 'on the site of the Priory'.[31] In a very worn and degraded script below a now-faded chi-rho monogram, it records the deaths of Latinus and his daughter, descendants of one Barrovadus – an apparently Irish name.

Whithorn's Early Medieval core is now hidden behind the formal, sober houses of George Street. The ruined priory stands on a knoll just to the west. The Machars seem otherworldly, cut off from the modern world; a fossilised cul-de-sac. But across the many centuries during which the Irish Seaboard was a highly interconnected routeway, Whithorn was far from isolated. It could boast links with trading centres and ecclesiasts across the late Latin world. Even so its underpinning archaeological narrative has been hard-won.

Excavations on the priory site in the 1890s revealed a stone-walled building to the east side of the Medieval church crypt. Over the years various inconclusive campaigns of small-scale excavation took place around the Medieval priory. From 1984 to 1991 investigations concentrated on the open area excavation of a small field south of the priory site in advance of proposed development, and in the Museum Gardens. Peter Hill's excavations established the existence of a group of bow-sided, light-walled structures, a shrine or shrines and graveyard, all predating the eighth century. A short section of ditch has been proposed, by the excavator, to form part of a monastic *vallum*. These earliest phases yielded a significant array of imported pottery and glass – the type of assemblage known from other prominent coastal sites along the Irish Sea, from the Scilly Isles and from Tintagel in Cornwall: all evidence of trade and exchange contacts with the late Latin Mediterranean world.[32] Metalworking crucibles and moulds indicate, as they do at another Solwegian coastal site, Mote of Mark, the recycling and distribution of fine decorative objects. If sub-Roman Whithorn developed as a cult centre and episcopal see, it also functioned as a site of lordship, consumption and distribution.

A period of major ecclesiastical investment in the early and mid eighth century materially ties the excavations into the establishment of Pecthelm's see. Two axially aligned oratories were constructed over a pre-existing shrine, and a stone-walled rectangular burial enclosure was constructed on the same alignment to the north-east. The enclosure provides the most secure dating evidence for this transformation, with a coin from the floor: a J-series *sceat* dating to between 715 and 730 – unique west of the Pennines.* Dendrochronological samples from the first buildings in this phase corroborate an early

---

* J-series *sceattas* have a distribution along east-facing rivers, and a concentration either side of the Humber; mints have been proposed at York or in Lindsey. Naylor 2006.

eighth-century date. A putative early church is proposed to the north, outside of the excavated area and in the vicinity of the later priory church, while two timber 'halls' were excavated to the south-east, axially aligned to each other.

Sometime in the later eighth century the two timber oratories were combined into a single church, enclosing a stone monument apparently focused on the site of the former shrine and with an altar at the east end – a unique bicameral building. The walls were constructed of timber posts set on stone plinths, with centrally opposed doors. A range of 'halls' was constructed to the south-east, and formal separation between the two zones was created by the construction of a stone wall with a cleared terrace on the south-east side. The vast majority of coin finds from the site, dating to the eighth and ninth centuries, were concentrated in that space and it is tempting, as Hill suggests, to associate their deposition with pilgrims arriving at a shrine and either being relieved of their money in return for souvenirs or leaving them as offerings in the hope of salvation, a cure for disease or, like the lead tablets from the Roman temple complex at Bath, accompanying curses. A major fire seems to have swept through the complex in about 845. As it happens, an episcopal list names five successor 'Anglian' bishops of Whithorn after Pecthelm – the last of them, Heathored, from the mid 830s onwards. Here, archaeology and history seem to complement each other perfectly.

A further ecclesiastical concentration with Northumbrian affinities might be identified in a small coreland around the lower reaches of the Rivers Annan and Nith on the north side of the inner reaches of the Solway Firth, where there is strong evidence of Northumbrian development at Hoddom and at Lockerbie. Two 'Eccles' names survive in Eaglesfield and Ecclefechan, suggesting to Alan James that there had been a large Northumbrian *eglēs* territory extending east from Hoddom and the River Annan and possibly also taking in Ruthwell.[33] A Roman road connected the region, perhaps known as Lochmaben, to the crossing of the Eden at Carlisle and all points east, south and north.[34] A Gallowegian bishop or an abbess of Carlisle might journey by road to visit their counterparts in Lothian along a more or less direct route without travelling east through the Tyne-Solway Gap. The Iron Age hilltop-defended site of Burnswark looms over the dale from the north-east, close to the modern town of Lockerbie, where excavations have revealed a sequence of Anglian-type rectangular timber halls dating broadly to the first half of the seventh century, with opposed central openings lying close to much earlier, Neolithic buildings.[35] They are not quite on the scale of the largest halls at Yeavering or Sprouston, but this looks like a high-status centre – the administrative caput of a secular territory, neighbour to the church territory of Hoddom.

The magnificent high cross at Ruthwell belongs firmly in the eighth-century tradition of Northumbrian high crosses at Irton, Hexham and Bewcastle. Quite apart from their exuberant design and technical brilliance, they evoke a productive landscape and focused spiritual and territorial lordship. They are the currency of intellectual sophistication, unshakeable faith and territorial ecclesiastical power.

The now-ruined church at Hoddom, lying in a loop of the River Annan a little to the south-east of Ecclefechan, once boasted its own sculptural tradition. Three Latin-inscribed stones, wholly secular in nature, come from close by: one is a dedication slab of the *VII Augusta* and *XXII Primigenia* legions. Their presence here indicates not sculptural continuity but the retrieval of Roman *spolia* from a nearby fort at Birrens. The use of such *spolia* in the construction of the Hexham crypt is well known. Early Medieval Christian sculptural fragments have also been found in the local area across the last two centuries – many of them now lost or destroyed but all presumed to come from the site of Hoddom's early church. The presence of fragments of a high cross here, with symbolic and design elements recognisable from those at Bewcastle and Ruthwell, indicates a high status for the church, as do two fragments of croziers, strongly associated with episcopal authority.[36] The Early Medieval church has not been located, although it almost certainly lay within the earthwork enclosure in which the post-Medieval church and graveyard sit.

Excavations in advance of quarrying in 1991 confirmed the presence of a substantial settlement sitting within the earthwork enclosure of some 9ha identified in cropmarks. Nestling against the inside of the north perimeter are five industrial/agricultural building stances that were occupied over several centuries, beginning around the middle of the seventh century. Individual clusters of structures were separated from each other by generous space – at least partly because of the risk of fire spreading from one industrial or agricultural building to another. None of the structures displays any domestic character, even if they otherwise conform to the ideal double-square, rectangular, earth-fast post construction style so familiar further east and south. The buildings were set within, and close to, the curving ditch and palisade boundary that follows the line of the river terrace, well apart (more than 150m) from the putative church site.

Detail of the carved interlace relief and runic inscription on the high cross at Ruthwell Kirk, Dumfriesshire

The earliest buildings so far identified were a barn and a kiln-barn; subsequent structures included more kilns of quite sophisticated stone construction within timber buildings, a smithing site and a tannery. Fortuitous conditions on site favoured the retrieval of charred grain and wood, so although the site was aceramic and yielded just two coins (both of the mid to late ninth century), a picture emerges of Hoddom as the central place in a productive landscape. Black oats were the principal crop with barley, rye and – especially in later decades – bread wheat also being processed here. Drying grain makes processing and grinding easier; helps to preserve it in damp conditions and kills pests. Barley can be malted in the same sorts of kiln, for use in brewing. If oats lack the prestige and cash value of wheat, they tolerate poor, wet soils characteristic of the area and, evidently, what oats lacked in nutritional punch they made up for in quantity: the output of the various kilns would have been sufficient to keep a mill – so far unlocated – very busy. Oats would have fed both a substantial monastic community and been used as winter feed for cattle and sheep. A wide variety of extensively, rather than intensively, managed woodland resources was available to the community: oak, ash, hazel, birch, alder and willow were all used, either in construction or in fuelling kilns and forges. Fragments of turned wooden bowls show that a lack of ceramics did not mean that the community lacked utensils or storage containers.

Hoddom is a rare case where a whole ecclesiastical precinct is visible, allowing the excavators to develop a model of the organisation and sub-divisions of the enclosed space and the positions and uses of buildings.[37] The two main divisions correspond to an upper and lower terrace. Close to the river, on the lower terrace, is the zone of the inner ecclesiastical core with a rectangular burial ground and, on the highest point of this lower terrace, a church built with re-used Roman stone. On the upper terrace, the outer zone is the working area with the kilns and related structures, the processing centre for an agricultural estate: the sacred and the productive economy are both contained within the outer precinct boundary, each in its own zone.

Although the most intensive period of building and processing dates from the middle of the eighth century onwards, as it did at Whithorn, there is little sense of anything like a trading surplus being produced here. Unless it is to be found elsewhere on the site, the evidence for secondary products and crafts – smithing and weaving, bone and antler working, a scriptorium or even pottery use – is negligible. The exception is the carving of stone sculpture, without which Hoddom's possible ecclesiastical status as a mother church for Annandale – which it enjoyed in later centuries – would be difficult to argue.

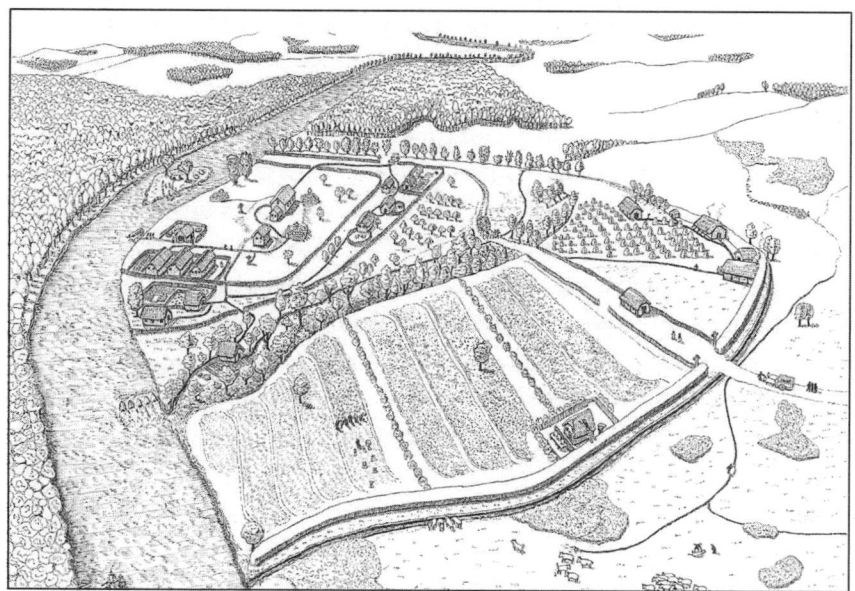

Artist's impression of the monastic complex at Hoddom

If the sculpture from Hoddom exhibits strong 'Anglian' affiliations, the architecture, like that at Whithorn, also reflects a much more local vernacular tradition. Pairs of opposed uprights, within which wattle or panel infills covered with clay daub provided insulation but no additional structural value, are a distinctive feature of the timber buildings. These uprights are recognised as supporting so-called 'Celtic' couples: pairs of crucks split from trees with natural curves caused by regrowth from cut stumps, forming a characteristic and very strong continuously curving roof and wall line, linked with horizontal sets of purlins acting as both wall plates and rafter supports.

The excavator Chris Lowe, in seeking a historical and political context for the evident 'Anglian' affinities of the architecture, highlights the reigns of Oswiu, Ecgfrið and Aldfrið as candidates for Northumbrian royal patronage at Hoddom. The case for Oswiu is threefold: his second, perhaps first legal marriage to Rhieinmelth, the great-granddaughter of Urien, offers the thought that the lands over which Hoddom may have exercised proprietorial control might have formed her dowry.* Oswiu's twenty-nine-year reign had

---

* The distinction between dowry and dower property is often overlooked. Dowry was property brought into the marriage from the bride's family,

seen an intense period of monastic foundation and the royal patronage of ecclesiastical entrepreneurs including Wilfrid, under whose acquisitive eye so many British churches were appropriated.

Hoddom also belongs to a landscape in which the name of Kentigern, a semi-legendary British saint and founder of Glasgow cathedral, has strong associations, even if the twelfth-century *Vita* by Jocelyn, in which he is said to have been based at Hoddom, is not independently supported by other evidence. Lowe might also have adduced the role of Alhfrið, very likely Oswiu's son by Rhieinmelth, who was probably bilingual and whose role in extending Anglian influence might have played better in communities with strong British cultural affiliations. His association with Elmet, with Wilfrid and with Ripon has already been highlighted.

* * *

Northumbrian kings enjoyed relatively easy access across the Pennines through the Tyne-Solway Gap, with the Roman Stanegate as a fast-paced road with convenient defensible campsites (the various forts) along the way. King Oswald had bivouacked with his small army at Heavenfield on his return from exile in Dál Riata; Kings Edwin and Ecgfrið were able to launch maritime assaults from somewhere along the west coast – perhaps the Roman harbour at Ravenglass; and Oswiu's dominant political alliance with the dynasty of Rheged through Rhieinmelth brought at least tributary control over what is now Cumbria.

The enigmatic insertion into the *Historia Brittonum* of a tradition that Edwin had first been baptised by Rhun, son of Urien, is, if nothing else, a hint that the nationalist antipathy towards Britons so pronounced in Bede's account did not get in the way of political or spiritual pragmatism. Charles Phythian-Adams, reviewing the evidence for Early Medieval Cumbria, believes that Anglian influence there was a gradual process from Edwin onwards,[38] involving the soft power of ecclesiastical and secular patronage and alliance; but it must always have been backed with the threat of military intervention. If Northumbrian kings were a potential menace to these

---

which became the possession of the groom. Dower lands were those gifted to the bride, more or less as insurance against widowhood. Hence dower lands like the Hexham estate might be gifted – if controversially – by a queen. Retiring queens were able to gift their dower lands to religious institutions as they entered them – as a sort of reverse dowry brought to the church in their role as brides of Christ.

communities and their élites, they also offered a measure of protection from potential enemies in the south and north and across the Irish Sea.

The very shadowy picture of lordship west of the Pennines and the fraught issue of where, when and what Rheged meant as a political entity are brought into focus by the constitutional crisis of 685. If Ecgfrið or his brother Ælfwine had produced the son named as Oslac in the *Historia Brittonum*, that child was too young to succeed in 685[39] – hence the need for high-level political consultation between Ælfflæd and Cuthbert. The case has been made that Oslac and his minor dynasty became *subreguli* in the west.[40] Were they among the dignitaries represented at the Ripon dedication? Queen Iurminburh was, during this most dangerous period, staying in Carlisle 'awaiting the issue of events'.[41] The same account in the *Anonymous Life* names Waga as the reeve, or *praepositus*, of the city, an indication that Anglian secular control was already established here. If the Annandale estates can be seen as lands gained through a queen's dowry – brought to Oswiu's possession by his British marriage – then Carlisle might be seen as her dower, or widow gift: insurance against her husband's early death. If that is the case, then Ecgfrið's second wife, Iurminburh, was the ultimate beneficiary.

In any case, Carlisle remained within the diocese of Lindisfarne, and fifteen church dedications to Cuthbert in Cumbria show how extensive the reach of the see became. The western boundary of the Hexham diocese, created after 678, is marked by the confluence of the Eden and Irthing valleys and the southerly course of the Eden. Phythian-Adams argues that Cuthbert's reluctant elevation to the bishopric in the year of Ecgfrið's death may have smoothed troubled ecclesiastical waters in the west – his unreformed sensibilities and probable bilingualism playing better, perhaps, than those of Trumbert, his orthodox predecessor, and of any of Hexham's decidedly orthodox bishops.

The material and place-name evidence used to map Anglian influence in Galloway and Lothian is paralleled in Cumbria, in pattern if not quantity. Names with *-ham* are few; the distribution of minsters and crosses is either coastal or confined to the Eden Valley and the plain of *Luel* around Carlisle. Unlike Whithorn, Carlisle did not see continual maritime trade throughout the post-Roman period, judging by the paucity of imported pottery from excavations here. A sense that the economy was dominated by transhumant pastoralism is reinforced by the distribution of *Caer-* names: peripheral to the corelands but dominating the heads of river valleys and routeways through the hills. A striking distribution of names containing the Old

English element *-bothl*, along the west coast and close to the Roman road between Carlisle and Maryport, suggests an idea of centralised military authority – these may be North-west equivalents of the Mercian and Deiran *burh-tuns*.* Angus Winchester notes that these sites, and a service obligation surviving in garbled form into the seventeenth century as 'seawake' – owed by coastal landholders to guard the maritime approaches,[42] bear a more than coincidental relationship to early estate territories and church sites.†

Cumbria has no Whithorn, but Bede records a miracle associated with the relics of St Cuthbert that occurred at a monastery on the River *Dacore*. Modern Dacre lies south-west of Penrith, close to the point at which three major routeways met at *Brocavum*, or Brougham as it later became: a regional centre of secular power, one of five identified by Phythian-Adams.[43] This may be the territory of *Lyvennet* associated with Urien in the Welsh poetic collections. Like Hoddom, the church site at Dacre‡ has yielded high-quality Early Medieval sculpture§ with Anglian-style iconography. Small-scale excavations took place here in the 1920s and then during the 1980s. In the latter campaign an extensive cemetery containing more than 200 graves was uncovered in advance of a housing development north of the Medieval graveyard. Soil conditions did not favour the preservation of bone but many of the graves contained iron fittings from chest-style wooden coffins – a feature recognised at a number of Northumbrian burial sites of the seventh to ninth centuries.[44] The cemetery was bounded on the west side by a ditch; beyond it lay two post-built timber structures – one of recognisable rectangular form; the other with a rounded eastern end. The latter contained two hearthstones, a reused millstone and Early Medieval metalwork including pins, buckles, strap-ends, spindle whorls, loomweights and glass from both drinking vessels and windows. Some Roman *spolia* was found – parts of a bridge or mill – reused as a covering for a substantial stone drain.

The site lacks the detailed chronology and layout seen at Hoddom; but it is suggestive of a community dominated, if not exclusively, by the church. Access to, or the production of, high-quality metalwork and glass, alongside

---

* See below in this chapter.
† As had Phythian-Adams 1996, 88–9.
‡ On the north bank of the Dacre Beck, 2 miles upstream from its confluence with the River Eamont south-west of Penrith.
§ Its four celebrated bear figures, which stand in the churchyard, are as yet undated.

evidence for weaving, shows a far from exclusively ecclesiastical settlement, prompting more questions than it answers. But given Dacre's location close to lordship sites and its proximity to major routeways, the temptation to see it as a key component in a well-established estate is strong.

The soft power of a still-expanding Northumbrian 'empire of the cross' cuts against the narrative of military and political decline. Northumbrian institutions, if they did not amount to what we would understand as a 'state', functioned to reinforce customary law, regional and territorial control and administrative logic. Political instability is not the same as anarchy. Bede alone is proof of a vibrant intellectual élite. Sculpture, metalwork, architecture and some of the finest manuscripts in Early Medieval Europe speak, and speak loudly, of a common creative output.

* * *

With such fragmentary material and annalistic evidence, it is difficult to paint a more nuanced portrait of early eighth-century Northumbria. But the reciprocal rise of Mercian royal power is solid enough. The first historically attested ruling warlord of the Icling dynasty in Mercia was Penda,* who rose to prominence in the Midlands as late as 630, when Northumbrian kings were already dominant over much of England. But his dynasty conventionally traced its roots back to Woden and, seven generations later, to Icil, the true dynastic progenitor. Two sons and two grandsons succeeded Penda in turn, able to coalesce the fragmented kingdoms and peoples of the Midlands under a single royal banner. The Iclings, like the Idings, became enthusiastic sponsors of religious communities beginning, it seems, with *Medeshamstede* (Peterborough) on the River Nene some time in the 650s or 660s and promoting the establishment of episcopal sees in its wake. After the Battle on the River Trent in 679 Mercian independence south of the Humber was permanently asserted – no subsequent Northumbrian king was able to claim *imperium* over Lindsey or, indeed, any of the other southern kingdoms.

The year 716 saw the deaths of both the Northumbrian King Osred at the hands of his kinsmen, perhaps somewhere in Mercia, and of the Mercian King Ceolred, Penda's childless grandson. The Mercians chose as their new king, willingly or otherwise, a grandson of Penda's brother Eowa, named

---

* His only known predecessor was the shadowy Cearl, whose daughter Edwin married. Penda's death in the Battle of the River *Winwaed* in 655 was King Oswiu's great military triumph.

Æðelbald. Something of his early career is known from his appearance in the *Vita* of a celebrated hermit, St Guðlac, whose wisdom and protection he sought while in exile in the kingdom of East Anglia and whose shrine at Crowland on the edge of the Fens he later endowed with magnificent gifts. Æðelbald rapidly established authority over the disparate peoples of the Midlands and ruled for forty-one years, longer than any English king before Edward III.

King Æðelbald came with an already-veteran *comitatus* of loyal, able and experienced fighting men, the support of a brother and the legitimacy of a celebrated holy man and his own Icling blood. His political strategies emerge across the first two decades of his rule: patronage, coercion and suppression where possible; war when necessary. He sponsored, or oversaw, a period of unprecedented economic expansion and settlement development, and his reign witnessed the creation of a novel system of royal administration, based on a keen strategic understanding of England's geographical realities and its Roman legacy.[45] He might almost be said to have engendered a revolution in English political history. By 736 he had styled himself *Rex Britanniae*.[46]

At the beginning of Æðelbald's reign Greater Mercia was served by five bishops, whose sees were broadly coterminous with once-independent tribal entities: Middle Anglia (at Leicester), *Hwicce* (at Worcester), *Magonsæte* (at Hereford), Lindsey (at Lincoln) and the 'original lands of the Mercians' along the Upper Trent (at Lichfield). In addition, sees at Dorchester on Thames and London came under Mercian control before or during his reign. He was able to impose successive Mercian nominees as archbishops of Canterbury.*

The wealth of charters relating to areas of peripheral Mercian control allow historians to see how the king's patronage of his senior ecclesiasts reinforced regional administrative control while encouraging them to engage in private commerce. Bishops of Worcester enjoyed rights to the valuable brine springs at Droitwich on the River Salwarpe;[47] their counterparts on the Thames were granted remission on tolls at the port of *Lundenwic*.[48] Direct patronage of minsters as far apart as Much Wenlock in Shropshire and Minster-in-Thanet on the Kent coast, with a string of monastic pearls along the Rivers Thames, Trent, Ouse and Nene, bound Æðelbald's élite into a tight network of control and exploitation, fostering new investment in

---

* Tatwine (731–734); Nothelm (735–739) and Cuthbert (740–760).

agriculture, technology and economic growth. Minsters and their 'home farms' began to specialise in secondary products – wool, metalwork, textiles – as well as winnable minerals like iron, lead and salt.[49]

A flood of Continental, mostly Frisian coinage, brought into England along the arteries of Mercian-controlled rivers and roads, shows how the Midlands and Thames corridor opened up to regional and international traders. Watling Street and the Fosse Way, key trunk roads of Roman administration and economic prosperity, formed a neat X-shape connecting navigable rivers that emptied into the North Sea and English Channel, Irish Sea and Bristol Channel. Under the king's unassailed *mund*, traders, ecclesiastical entrepreneurs and regional lords moved themselves, their ideas, their baggage trains and tradeable goods across Mercia and beyond.

Between about 710 and 740 England experienced an unprecedented economic boom and, increasingly, archaeologists are uncovering the hard evidence. The Mercian royal monastery at Cookham on the Thames, which became the subject of a bitter and long-running dispute between the archbishops of Canterbury and the widow of King Offa, has recently yielded evidence of a riverside industrial and agricultural processing site with loading facilities and a wealth of craft products and equipment.[50] Other important sites showing evidence of both spiritual and economic enterprise include Flixborough on the Lower Trent and Brandon on the Little Ouse in Suffolk, while so-called 'productive' sites are found across Mercia: in Lindsey, on the Warwickshire Avon, along the Thames and on the headwaters of the Fen-draining rivers of Middle Anglia.[51]

The charters likewise show how regional dynasts were suppressed without the need for overt military intervention. The sons of former kings of the *Hwicce* – the old tribal lands of the Severn Valley and its hinterland – were co-opted as signatories to the king's charters as mere ealdormen[52] – a sure sign of a new, if honourable, subordinate status: their rewards were a secure place in the king's wider itinerant household and rights to their own regional patronage networks. By controlling key economic and political assets Æðelbald and his canny counsellors were able to impose an administrative framework onto a superbly connected landscape. Royal functionaries – the *wicgerefa*, or wic-reeve, and *thelonarius*, or tax collector – were installed at key trading sites like *Lundenwic*.

The administrative web penetrated much deeper across Greater Mercia. Scholars have become increasingly sensitive to clusters of place-names originating in the eighth century that reference resources available from local settlements: Wittons and Rushtons,* for example.⁵³ John Blair has shown how a particular set of names can also be used to identify the systematic hand of the royal administrator on the ground. These clusters include *-tuns* with functional or stakeholder prefixes: Burtons, Charltons, Eatons, Knightons, Strattons and their variants and possibly cardinal names like Norton, Sutton, Weston and Easton.† Examples of these clusters indicate key nodes of administrative control and exploitation in the Mercian state, focused on defended or defensible enclosed sites – the *burhs* themselves: on the Upper Trent around Tutbury (a lookout and *burh* name); on the Fosse Way near Bourton-on-the-Water in the Cotswolds; south-east of Leicester at Great Glen and on the River Nene downstream from Northampton with a focus on Irthlingborough.

* * *

In 737 'a great drought made the land unfruitful'; King Ceolwulf gave up the Northumbrian throne after a turbulent eight years and entered the monastery at Lindisfarne, bequeathing the kingdom to his cousin Eadberht, brother of Archbishop Ecgberht.⁵⁴ And for the same year the *Anglo-Saxon Chronicle* records that King Æðelbald of Mercia harried Northumbria – a first recorded act of aggression against his northern neighbour. Three years later he brought a Mercian warband into Northumbria again while King Eadberht was campaigning further north in Pictland and laid waste the kingdom 'through wicked deceit'.⁵⁵ The following year, 741, saw a second drought⁵⁶ and a third raid by Æðelbald across the Humber: York was sacked; the minster burned.⁵⁷

In spite of the inauspicious reigns of his immediate predecessors, and despite such conflicts with both northern and southern neighbours, King Eadberht held the throne in Northumbria for more than twenty years. His brother Ecgberht, archbishop in York, might be thought of as something like

---

* Witton (*wudu-tūn*), or Rushton (*rysc-tūn) for settlements producing timber or rushes, or with a river crossing.

† Burton: the *tūn* servicing a fortress or stronghold; Charlton, the estate of a ceorl rendering services to the royal *vill*; Eaton: a *tūn* fulfilling a function at a river crossing, such as a ferry; Knighton: the *tūn* of a thegn owing a service – perhaps military protection or as a courier – to a royal *vill*; Stratton: a *tūn* on a Roman road – perhaps a place where stabling and fodder might be found. Directional names often come in pairs and seem to have well-understood (to their administrators) functions in the overall scheme. Blair 2018, 193.

a Deiran *subregulus*, holding the archdiocese until 766 – an astonishing tenure of more than thirty years in the mould of Theodore at Canterbury. He founded an important school and library at York, which nurtured scholarship and intellect in no way insulting to the memory of Bede. He wrote a detailed clerical legal text, the *Dialogus*, which survives. The two brothers promulgated a coinage bearing both their names.[58] Among his students, Alcuin – the diplomat, essayist and friend of Charlemagne – is the outstanding name.

The wealth and creativity of Early Medieval Northumbria was predicated on two fundamentals: a productive landscape whose roots lay in ancient corelands and in Roman exploitation of its resources and natural routeways; and a diverse, hybrid culture that drew on Irish, British, Pictish and Continental inspiration – forged, in the crucible of seventh-century lordship, into exuberant and prolific scholarship, sculpture, decorative arts and architecture under the jealous eyes of its martial but God-fearing kings. These are Northumbria's museum and library showpieces. The solid, customary institutions of territorial lordship and tribal patronage enabled kings, scholars and craftspeople to specialise, devoting their labours to more than mere subsistence on cattle ranching and sheep rearing. Circumstantial but compelling evidence for a broad geography of this hybrid Anglian culture hints at evidence for diversity and of the means of exploitation of the land's resources. But it is only with the all-too-rare excavation of the settlement base underlying an impressive pyramid of halls, churches, monastic estates and economic wealth, that the nine-tenths of the Northumbrian iceberg is revealed.

John Blair, in his great survey *Building Anglo-Saxon England*, made explicit what archaeologists know from long experience: Early Medieval settlement is missing most of the buildings and most of the burials of most of the population.[59] There do not seem to be enough people to create that conspicuous wealth. If the halls and farmsteads of the Anglo-Saxon squirearchy are under-represented – in Bernicia, only Thirlings has produced such a site so far – then their dependents, the *ceorls* and the unfree, are even harder to detect. Excavations at West Heslerton, Shotton and elsewhere show that substantial, otherwise unknown, Early Medieval settlements may be revealed in the right circumstances. Assiduous reporting of metal-detecting finds and excavation in advance of development are increasingly identifying signs of previously undetected settlements.

Many other settlements are hiding in plain sight. Not enough modern excavation has taken place at the so-called 'native' sites of the Roman period and Iron Age to rule out broad continuities. Many rural sites with upstanding features – familiar lumps and bumps in grassy fields – are assigned later 'Medieval' dates without excavation. Immediately east of the line of the Roman Devil's Causeway, near the hamlet of Bolam in south central Northumberland, a prehistoric hilltop enclosure called Huckhoe was excavated by George Jobey in the mid 1950s.[60] The earthworks are typical of the region: an enclosing bank revetted with drystone work; the outlines of roundhouse platforms in cell-like compounds: a classic, neatly self-contained Iron Age farmstead. Originally the farmstead had been enclosed by a wooden stockade; then by a wall up to 10ft thick at the base, furnished with a similarly impressive gateway complete with pivot stone for the massive wooden gate that it must once have held.

Finds allowed Jobey to date the first enclosure to the late centuries BC; the second to the Roman centuries. Dwellings and huts or workshops were represented by both wooden stake and post holes and by stone footings and floors – a substantial investment in labour over a long period of continued habitation. Ovens, a forge and many quern fragments are the remains of an active, self-sustained agricultural community, living beyond the imperial enceinte of Hadrian's Wall but probably well-integrated into the Romanised economy, with access to sources of iron and lead and even to fine tableware. Evidence that the site continued to be occupied into the post-Roman centuries comes in the form of possible fifth- to sixth-century 'wheel-thrown or wheel-finished' pottery fragments, with affinities to Early Medieval wares from Dunadd and Dalkey Island identified by Charles Thomas – he believed them to be imported wares.*[61] In addition, two sub-rectangular buildings with apsidal ends replaced one of the circular huts in or after the fourth century AD. Jobey pointed out the similarity of this sequence to an enclosure on Ingram Hill in the Breamish Valley excavated by Hogg; and we have elsewhere argued the case for Early Medieval continuity in the Breamish Valley.[62] Out of hundreds of such settlements identified as earthworks with 'Native Iron Age' affinities, how many more will eventually yield evidence for Early Medieval occupation?

* Maria Duggan, who has made an intensive study of the imported wares from across Britain and the western Atlantic seaboard, cannot find convincing imported or late material in the existing Huckoe archive. It is likely that either Thomas misidentified the sherds or that he took them into his private collection. Maria Duggan pers. comm.

'Permanent' settlement aside, we know that itinerant lords and their followers spent much of their lives in transit, even if their tents are very rarely found.* A hundred years ago excavators were just beginning to learn to identify the materially ephemeral remains of sunken-featured buildings, complementing the more easily recognised earth-fast timber halls. But John Blair highlights even more undetectable traditions in rubble and earth or turf-walled structures. Most such buildings leave no traces after their materials have been recycled, their walls levelled. If the body- and rubbish-depositing practices of small rural farmsteads were so discrete, the base of the settlement pyramid will always be invisible to us.[63]

Excavations on the north-facing slopes of Simy Folds, Upper Teesdale, in the late 1970s and early 1980s by Dennis Coggins revealed that upstanding remains of field enclosures and rectangular buildings in such landscapes might belong to Early Medieval settlement. Three small farmsteads, each consisting of a long, narrow house in the order of 8m by 4m internally with massive low stone walls and a second, smaller structure at right angles, were set in enclosed yards and integrated into the overall co-axial field pattern. Each structure had a hearth. Evidence of iron-smelting and of textile production suggests a mixed economy reliant on summer pasturing, local ore deposits and perhaps the small-scale cultivation of arable and garden foods. Radiocarbon dating shows occupation in the eighth century – but the building tradition, with internal posts supporting a ridged, hipped roof of light timber covered with turf or peat, was long-lasting in these areas and can be found from Cornwall to Scotland.[64]

Further south in the Pennines a cluster of upstanding earthwork and stone wall sites has been investigated over the last decades. At Crummack Dale, in the shadow of Ingleborough's imposing Iron Age hillfort, the remains of cellular field systems surround similar small farmsteads of long, narrow, rectangular buildings with low doorways and partially paved floors, attached to walled garths. No pottery was recovered – these communities may have been aceramic – but metal artefacts such as a draw-knives for woodworking, a copper alloy-plated iron bell and smithing tongs were retrieved. The farmsteads were occupied over at least two, perhaps three centuries from about

---

* The two tent frames found in the Oseberg ship excavations and a reference in the will of the Anglo-Saxon noblewoman Wynflæd are exceptions. Sjøvold 1957; Charter S1539: Will of Wynflæd concerning land at Ebbesborne, Wiltshire: https://esawyer.lib.cam.ac.uk/charter/1539.html

700. Sheep and/or goat, cattle and wild deer bones were recovered, along with a fragment of a wool comb.⁶⁵ This was a dispersed but coherent community of herders and craftspeople. To the immediate north of Ingleborough Hill, at the head of Chapel-le-Dale, further excavations under the direction of David Johnson and the Ingleborough Archaeology Group uncovered two comparable farmstead complexes. Poor in artefacts, they nevertheless produced radiocarbon dates ranging from the late seventh to the late ninth century.⁶⁶

There is no reason why such apparently self-contained farmsteads should not have been much more numerous and widespread; and no reason for them to have been an uncommon feature of the lowland landscapes of *vill* and shire, either. Like the roundhouses of later prehistory, they were constructed from materials available locally, with little thought of ostentation or communal ceremony. Just how their lives and economies were integrated into those of the *gesiðas* and *comites* of the élite is not yet clear; but it seems unavoidable that these are the dependent farmers who rendered cattle and sheep on the hoof, perhaps iron ingots and cloth to their lords in distant *vills*; probably also services in the form of military attendance and haulage, or cutting timber. The conservative structural traditions that they represent are also hinted at in the otherwise seemingly anomalous forms seen at Whithorn, Hoddom, Lockerbie and elsewhere and which Brian Hope-Taylor was convinced was an Anglo-British hybrid tradition. Their tribal affinities are ultimately unknowable, unless they represent the often-invoked miscellaneous 'Anglian settlers' of uncritical narratives, or those native Brittonic speakers persecuted by the ecclesiasts of Wilfrid's day. In some ways it does not matter: they were the foundations that held up the pyramid of the Northumbrian empire.

At the very end of the *Historia Ecclesiastica*, Bede brings his history up to date with a summary of important events between 725 and the present time – that is, 731.⁶⁷ Accounting for the names of the bishops currently presiding over the English sees, he tells us that 'All these kingdoms . . . right up to the Humber . . . are subject to Æðelbald, king of Mercia.' He describes how the Picts have a peace treaty with the English and are content to share in the joys of the universal, orthodox church; how the Irish in Britain (i.e. Dál Riata) are content within their own territories. The Britons, he says, who still oppose the English through their inbred hatred and their evil customs and 'incorrect' Easter, are partly their own masters but are partly under the rule of the English. Then, portentously, he addresses the present and future of his own people:

> In these favourable times of peace and prosperity, many of the Northumbrian race, both noble and simple, have laid aside their weapons and taken the tonsure, preferring that they and their children should take monastic vows rather than train themselves in the art of war. What the result will be, a later generation will discover.*

On that subject Bede had not quite had his last say; but in some sense, and literally for students of the period, this is the end of history, looking uncertainly into the future without his reassuringly continuous, if partisan, narrative.

---

* There follows a brief chronological summary from the incarnation to the present; an invaluable autobiographical note and a list of his works. Bede *HE* V.23; Colgrave and Mynors 1969, 290.

PART III: 738–867

CHRONOLOGY III: 738–867

740 – A Mercian warband under Æðelbald invades Northumbria while Eadberht is campaigning against the Picts (Bede *Continuatio*).

741 – A Mercian army burns and sacks York; minster burned (*Hist Reg*; *ASC*).

749 – Synod of Gumley (Leicestershire). Mercian King Æðelbald agrees to allow 'booking' of church estates to exempt them from taxes except bridge and fort building (*burhbot*) and military dues. Development of the Mercian 'common burdens' (John 1964; Charter S92).

750 – King Eadberht imprisons Bishop Cynewulf at Bamburgh; besieges the church at Lindisfarne; Offa, son of Aldfrið, is dragged from the church (*Hist Reg*); King Eadberht conquers parts of Ayrshire. He 'added the plain of Kyle and other places to his dominions' (Bede *Continuatio*).

The Strathclyde Britons defeat the Picts.

756 – King Eadberht of Northumbria and King Óengus mac Fergusso of Pictland unite to attack the British capital fortress at Dumbarton (*Hist Reg*). The Britons accept terms. Multiple coup attempts occur in Northumbria while Eadberht is away campaigning. The army of Eadberht is destroyed on its way from *Ovania* ([?] Govan) to *Niwanbrig* (*Hist Reg*) – possibly Newburgh (on Tyne; or in Fife; or Staffordshire).

757 – King Æðelbald of Mercia is murdered by his bodyguard; he is succeeded by King Offa, to 796.

758 – King Eadberht abdicates in favour of his son Oswulf (*Hist Reg*); joins the church at York.

759 – King Oswulf is killed by kinsmen/bodyguards, at *Meðel Wongtun* ([?] Market Weighton). Northumbria is claimed by a thegn, Æðelwald Moll, 'elected by his people' (Bede *Continuatio*), but unconnected to the royal family (*Hist Reg*).

'A pestilence occurred, which lasted almost two years, diverse grievous sickness causing havoc, more especially the disease of dysentery' (Bede *Continuatio*).

760 – An outbreak of plague (but see 759). Æðelwald Moll puts down a Bernician uprising.

761 – Battle of *Eldunum* (Eildon) near Melrose (759, in *Hist Reg*). King Æðelwald Moll kills Oswine, Oswulf's brother ([?] Bede *Continuatio*) at *Ædwinesclif* on 6 August (*ASC*).

762 – Æðelwald Moll marries Æðelðryð at *Catræth* (*Hist Reg*).

764 – *The great winter* (763–4). Former King Ceolwulf dies (*Hist Reg*; *ASC*) in retirement on Lindisfarne.

765 – Æðelwald Moll is deprived of the Northumbrian kingdom at *Pincanheale* on 30 October (*Hist Reg*); possibly by tonsure (*Libellus*; *AT*; *CA*). Alhred (supposedly an Iding) succeeds (*ASC*).

766 – Ecgberht, archbishop of York, dies after thirty-four years of office.

768 – Former King Eadberht dies in monastic seclusion at York (*Hist Reg*).

King Alhred of Northumbria marries Osgifu (*Hist Reg*), possibly a daughter of Oswulf.

769 – Catterick is burned by 'the tyrant' Eanred; he is burned to death the same year (*Hist Reg*).

774 – King Alhred is expelled, first to Bamburgh, then to the protection of Ciniod, son of Uuredach, in Pictland. He is succeeded in Northumbria by Æðelred (*Hist Reg*) (a child, son of Alhred or of Moll) (*ASC*).

778 – King Æðelred has Ealdormen Ealdwulf, Cynewulf and Ecga killed (*Hist Reg*).

[?] Æðelbald and Heardberht slay three high reeves on 22 March: Ealdwulf at Coniscliffe; Cynewulf and Ecga at *Heladurne* (*Hist Reg*).

779 – King Æðelred driven out of Northumbria; succeeded by Ælfwald, son of Oswulf (*Hist Reg*; *ASC*; *ASC* E s.a. 778), to 788.

780 – Ealdormen Osbald and Æðelheard 'collect an army' and burn Ealdorman Bearn in *Seletun* (*Hist Reg*; *ASC* 782).

Archbishop Æðelberht of York dies; succeeded by Eanbald, who receives the pallium from Rome (*Hist Reg*).

782 – Alcuin of York leaves Northumbria to join the court of Charlemagne. He becomes master of the palace school (Allott 1974).

786 – Pope Hadrian I sends legates to Britain possibly at Offa's invitation in alliance with King Ælfwald of Northumbria (*Hist Reg*).

787 – Synod at *Pincanheale* in Northumbria (*Hist Reg*; *ASC* F).

788 – King Ælfwald of Northumbria is assassinated by Ealdorman Sicga on Hadrian's Wall; afterwards, a church is dedicated to Oswald on the site at *Scythlescester* ([?] Halton Chesters). Ælfwald is buried in Hexham Abbey. Osred II (a youth, son of Alhred) succeeds, to 789 (*Hist Reg*).

789 – First recorded attack by three ships of Norwegian (from Horðaland) raiders on the south coast kills royal official (*ASC* A) Beauduherd, the king's man in Dorchester (*Æthelweard*).

790 – King Osred of Northumbria is expelled and forcibly tonsured at York; Æðelred is freed from exile and resumes his reign (*Hist Reg*).

Alcuin returns to York from Charlemagne's court (Allott 1974, 14 for letters).

791 – Ealdorman Eardwulf is captured and brought to Ripon; King Æðelred orders him to be killed outside the gates of the monastery; the monks place his body in a tent; in the morning he is found alive in the church (*Hist Reg* 789; and see year 796).

The sons of King Ælfwald are taken by force from York and killed by King Æðelred in *Wonwaldremere*; 'their names were Oelf and Oelwine' (*Hist Reg*).

792 – Osred returns from exile on Man; is captured and killed at *Aynburg* by King Æðelred. He is buried at Tynemouth (*Hist Reg*) (*ASC* E s.a. 794).

793 – Lindisfarne is attacked and plundered by Vikings; monks are abducted (*Hist Reg*; *ASC*). Preceded by a famine and evil portents.

Ealdorman Sicga, killer of King Ælfwald (and signatory to the papal legation reforms of 786 (cf. Story 2003, 92)), commits suicide and is later buried at Lindisfarne (*Hist Reg*).

794 – Pagans ravage *Portus Ecgfridi* and plunder the monastery at *Donemuða*; their chief is killed by the English and their fleet scattered by a storm (*ASC*; *Hist Reg*) but see Woolf 2007, 44 for 796 date.

796 – King Æðelred of Northumbria is assassinated near *Cover* (possibly Corbridge); succeeded by Osbald, for twenty-seven days; Osbald is exiled to Lindisfarne, then to Pictland (*Hist Reg*).

Ealdorman Eardwulf succeeds to the throne in Northumbria and is consecrated at York minster (*Hist Reg*) (see year 791).

King Offa of Mercia dies. Succeeded by his son Ecgfrið; he too dies, succeeded by the unrelated Coenwulf, to 821 (*Hist Reg*).

798 – A great battle in Northumbria at Whalley (*ASC* E) near Billington Moor between Ealdorman Wada and his fellow conspirators, against King Æðelred. They attack King Eardwulf, who wins a victory (*Hist Reg*); Alric, the son of Heardberht, is slain.

799 – First recorded Viking raid on Francia: islands off the coast of Aquitaine (Noirmoutier?) (Alcuin *Epp*; 65).

Ealdorman Moll killed by orders of King Eardwulf of Northumbria (*Hist Reg*).

Ealdorman Ealdred, murderer of King Æðelred, killed by Ealdorman Torhtmund in vengeance (*Hist Reg*).

800 – Probable destruction by Vikings of monasteries at Hartness and Tynemouth (*Flores Historiarum*).

801 – King Eardwulf of Northumbria attacks King Cœnwulf of Mercia inconclusively after a long campaign. Peace brokered by church and 'nobles' (*Hist Reg*).

Alcuin sends letters admonishing Archbishop Eanbald for supporting the king's enemies, taking property, keeping too large a retinue of soldiers and harming the monastics who support him (Alcuin *Epp* 20, 21; Allott 1974: 29–30).

802 – Death of King Beorhtric of Wessex (according to Asser, accidentally poisoned by his Mercian wife); *ASC* says he was buried at Wareham; Ecgberht (grandfather of Ælfred) succeeds to throne of Wessex, to 839 (see year 789).

End of Northumbrian Chronicle embedded in the *Historia Regum*; Norwegian raid on Iona (*AU*).

804 – Alcuin of York dies as abbot at Tours.

806 – King Eardwulf deposed in Northumbria (*ASC*), goes into exile at Charlemagne's court and visits pope (*RFA*; Story 2003, 146ff) – cf. year 808. Ælfwald II succeeds.

Second Norwegian raid on Iona; sixty-eight monks slaughtered in Martyr's Bay (*AU*).

808 – Ælfwald II dies; exiled Northumbrian King Eardwulf travels to Nijmegen seeking support from Charlemagne (*RFA*), who supports his return with an envoy called Aldulf. Pope Leo III sends delegation to Northumbria (Levison 1946, 16) to restore Eardwulf.

814 – Death of Charlemagne, aged seventy; succeeded by Louis the Pious (*RFA*).

821 – Tidfrið, last bishop of Hexham dies.

825 – Vikings sack monasteries at Movilla and Downpatrick; another attack on Iona: Abbot Blathmac and companions killed for refusing to reveal the location of Columban relics (*AU*).

829 – Conquest of Mercia by King Ecgberht of Wessex. *ASC* records meeting between Ecgberht of Wessex and unnamed Northumbrian king (Eanred) at Dore, South Yorkshire; probably the boundary of Northumbria and Mercia in ninth century. Northumbria submits: Ecgberht overlord of English kingdoms.

830 – Under Bishop Ecgred the church on Holy Island is moved to Norham (possibly as late as 845, according to *HSC* 9). Bishop Ecgred takes relics of Ceolwulf, including his body, to Norham (*Libellus* and *Annales Lindisfarenses*).

835 – Heathens 'devastate Sheppey' (*ASC*) the first great raid on an Anglo-Saxon kingdom.

c.839 – Cináed mac Ailpín becomes king of Dál Riata.

840 – King Eanred dies (*RWE*) but probably actually in 850s after coin evidence. Succeeded by Æðelred II (his son).

Louis the Pious dies, aged sixty-four (*NHF*); the Frankish empire splits and factionalises among three sons.

841 – Dublin becomes the principal *longphort* of the Vikings in Ireland: evidence of co-ordinated establishment of raiding bases in Ireland.

842 – Slaughter at London, Rochester, *Quentovic*; *Hamwic* and *Norðunnwig* (?Norwich) plundered (*ASC*; *NHF*) – and see year 840. Nantes attacked; raiders overwinter on Noirmoutier at the mouth of the Loire (*ASB*).

844 – [?] Æðelred II of Northumbria expelled from Mercia. Succeeded by Rædwulf, who is killed by Vikings (*RWE*). But see Kirby 1987; Woolf 2007, 69; Æðelred II restored.

845 – Paris plundered by Viking raiders (*ASB*).

846 – Dorestad plundered (*ASB*).

847 – [?] Cináed mac Ailpín becomes king of Scotia.

848 – King Æðelred II of Northumbria killed. Succeeded by Osberht (*RWE*).

851 – Fragmentary evidence in Irish Annals of Anglo-Saxon victory over Vikings in [?] Northumbria.

Some 350 heathen ships arrive at the mouth of the Thames; attack Canterbury and London, put King Beorhtwulf of Mercia to flight (*ASC*; *ASB*).

853 – Possible death of Æðelred II in Northumbria; accession of Osberht, to 866 (Kirby 1987, 17).

c.858 – Death of Cináed mac Ailpín.

861 – The Danes burn Paris (*ASB*).

862 – Causantín mac Cináeda becomes king of Alba.

Vikings penetrate defences along the River Marne, burning the bridge at *Traiectum*; Charles rebuilds bridge, trapping them upstream; they come to terms (*ASB*).

Construction begins of a fortified bridge at Pont de l'Arche, near Pîtres.

863 – Dorestad sacked by Vikings (*ASB*).

864 – Edict of Pîtres: (June) Charles the Bald reforms army, forms cavalry; reforms coinage; orders construction of fortified bridges to block Viking incursions (*ASB*).

865 – A great army comes to England ([?] from Dublin – the *Scaldingi*) and winters in East Anglia under Ívarr (Æðelweard). East Anglians submit; give them horses (*ASC*).

866 – The Viking army crosses the Humber; dissension among Northumbrian leaders. The Host take the city of York in November (*ASC*).

867 – King Osberht expelled. Succeeded by Ælle (possibly his brother).

Battle of York (21 March): city stormed by Northumbrian force. But Osberht and Ælle are killed along with eight leading noblemen; Wulfhere flees to Addingham. Danes seize York under Halfdan, impose a tributary King Ecgberht on Bernicia and Archbishop Wulfhere on Deira.

Minting of coins ceases in Northumbria (*ASC*).

9

SKY-FLAME: 738–803

Bede's parting shot – *De Abbatibus* – The fortunes of St Cuthbert – The common burdens – Uncivil wars – The raid on Lindisfarne – Alcuin

Bede's generalised forebodings at the end of his *Ecclesiastical History* would play out across the following century or so. But even in his last years he remained an active member of Northumbria's élite. The *Historia* was dedicated to King Ceolwulf, and Bede was a close friend and mentor to the king's cousin, Bishop Ecgberht of York. A year before his death in 735, the monk of Jarrow wrote a letter to Ecgberht, in which his urgent concerns for the spiritual welfare of the Northumbrian people were addressed in unapologetic detail. That letter survives.

The written word has necessarily been substituted, Bede tells him, for a private conversation prevented by his declining health; he cannot undertake the arduous journey from Jarrow to York, a hundred miles to the south – a week's uncomfortable journey by road; perhaps less by boat. Nevertheless, his intellectual energy seems undiminished. An opening salvo is directed at the bishop himself: Bede alludes to frivolous chatter and gossip as unbecoming to the sacred dignity of a bishop. He has heard it said of some bishops that they indulge too freely in laughter, storytelling, drinking and 'other temptations of an idle life'; his friend should be setting an example.[1] That example was vital since the bishop's diocese was too large for him alone to minister to all the people.

At that time three sees oversaw the spiritual welfare of the Northumbrians, at Hexham, Lindisfarne and York, with Whithorn either recently established or about to be established under Bishop Pecthelm as a Bernician offshoot. Abercorn had been lost after King Ecgfrið's disastrous Pictish campaign in 685. York covered the largest area; the bishop must, of necessity, ordain more priests to help him in his work; and if they and the lay people under their ministry were so vulgar as to not know Latin, they must at least learn the Apostles' Creed and the Lord's Prayer by rote in their own tongue.

Steeped in a culture of reciprocity, Bede is also concerned that overstretched bishops may be committing a grave social and moral error:

> There are many country houses and hamlets of our nation situated on inaccessible mountains and thick forests where, for many years, no bishop comes to perform any of the duties of holy ministry or Divine grace, yet none of these is free from paying tribute to the bishop...[2] [and] when a bishop, for the love of money, has nominally taken under his guardianship a larger portion of the people than he can by any means visit and preach to the whole year round, it is plain that he is only gathering danger and destruction for himself, as well as those whose false guardian he is.[3]

This is the earliest written confirmation that the services and renders – what would later be called tithes – due from dependent *vills*, were being claimed by ecclesiasts in their roles as territorial lords – in some cases fraudulently, for in return their dependants should receive proper pastoral care. Bede saw this as a social contract, to be honoured by all sides. The solution was to create more, and therefore more manageable, dioceses, following the original scheme conceived by Pope Gregory in his letters to Augustine; and Bede believed that the bishop's cousin, King Ceolwulf, would be amenable to the plan. An archdiocese for Northumbria ought to be created at York, as Gregory had envisaged, and Ecgberht himself should receive the pallium.

The church council convened by Archbishop Theodore at Hertford in 672 had been tasked with addressing provisions for more dioceses; but in the face of fierce resistance from existing bishops – Wilfrid included – the council had 'passed over that matter for the present';[4] that bird had now come home to roost.

Bede acknowledged that Ceolwulf's predecessors, from Ecgfrið onwards, had 'by negligence and foolish donations', given away so many estates for the founding of monasteries that it would now be difficult to find a vacant place – and he meant an existing monastery with sufficient wealth to support a bishop – where a suitable diocesan seat might be established. A general council should be held at which kings and bishops would consider suitable candidates, so that a place may be provided among the monasteries, where an episcopal see may be created. [Then] licence should be given them to choose some one from among themselves to be ordained bishop, and to rule with episcopal authority, over the adjoining country belonging to the same diocese, as well as the monastery itself.[5]

Now, warming to his theme, Bede set out to promote his scheme for providing sufficient estates to support a new diocese, while addressing the lax practices of many existing monastic establishments – harking back to the theme of his prophetic ending to the *Ecclesiastical History*:

> If it appear necessary that any addition of land or property should be made to such a monastery, that it may be the better able to undertake the episcopal duties, there are, as we know well, many places calling themselves monasteries, but exhibiting no sign whatever of a monastic system; some of which I should much like to see transferred by synodical authority, that their present luxury, vanity, and intemperance in meat and drink might be exchanged for chastity, temperance and piety, and that they may so help to sustain the episcopal see, which is to be created ... There are many such large establishments, which, as is commonly said, are of use to neither God nor man, because they neither observe regular monastic life, nor yet supply soldiers or attendants of the secular authorities to defend our shores from barbarians.[6]

No pre-Conquest Northumbrian charter survives in anything like its original form. The social and legal processes, to which Bede alludes, by which so much land had been transferred from the royal portfolio, must be reconstructed by analogy from well-attested Mercian examples, including the so-called Ismere charter of 736 which records that King Æðelbald donated ten *cassati* (the equivalent of *familiae*) to his *comes* Cyneberht for the construction of a minster.*[7]

As John Blair points out in his analysis of the letter, if some of these grants of estates to thegns were new transactions, many others must have involved

---

* Notable, amongst other things, for a very early use of the *Anno Domini* dating system popularised by Bede; for the Mercian overlord styling himself *Rex Britanniae*; and for preserving the name of an ancient territorial grouping, the *Husmerae*.

the formal written 'booking' of existing family property, establishing a novel and secure tenurial status for the family and its descendants.[8] In earlier centuries, to be noble meant to be weapon-worthy; in the first half of the eighth century it became fashionable to be considered charter-worthy and, increasingly, to be worthy of holding the office of abbot.

Searching for concrete examples in Northumbria, and drawn to episodes in Book Five of the *Ecclesiastical History*, one is struck by the career of Bishop John of Hexham (687–705), who rode between minsters with a large company of predominantly lay companions – that is to say, a *comitatus* – and who is to be found dedicating churches founded by *gesiðas*.[9] One of his visits, the subject of a miracle, took place at the Deiran minster of Watton, south of Driffield on a minor tributary of the River Hull. Abbess Hereburh's daughter (the abbess must, we infer, have been a married woman *before* she took holy orders) was sick and the abbess sought a cure for her 'whom she loved greatly and had planned to make abbess in her place' – a sure sign of the trend towards heritable monastic property.[10] Bede gives such 'imposters' short shrift. They

> have no experience of the regular monastic life, nor any love for the same, [and] commit a still greater scandal: – for they give money to the kings, and under pretence of erecting monasteries they acquire possessions, wherein the more freely to indulge their licentiousness; and procuring these by a royal edict to be assigned over to them in inheritance, they get the deed by which these privileges are confirmed . . . At one time they are occupied with their wives and the care of raising children, and at another time they rise from their beds to occupy themselves with the internal concerns of the monastery.[11]

'Well suited to them,' Bede wrote to Ecgberht, 'is the proverb that wasps, though they make combs, yet fill them with poison instead of honey.'

The foundation of a new see at Whithorn was one response to such concerns, although its administrative arrangements are invisible. Were productive monasteries like Hoddom brought under its control as part of a reforming process? One wonders how Bede envisaged the division of one or more of the other existing Northumbrian sees. The resulting potential for political conflict might have been one reason why Ecgberht did not implement such reforms. He was, however, elevated to the status of archbishop by the gift of a pallium from Pope Gregory III in 735, the year of Bede's death; Gregory I's intention for York was finally achieved.

If Bede saw a church in spiritual crisis, we are entitled, by contrast, to read into its eighth-century fortunes a flowering of the process by which Northumbrian culture had been partially reintegrated into a wider European milieu. During the eighth century, and continuing into the ninth, a distinctive school of monumental sculptural carving emerged in the Deiran cultural zone. It emulated the classical, Mediterranean style of carving in the half-round, in contrast to the low relief that was more typical of practice in England; figures, portrayed naturalistically, are clothed in Roman-style drapery; figures and scenes illustrated within arcaded panels draw on the iconography of Early Christendom. This style and its iconography emerged in Deira through two Continental routes. One was via the Carolingian world, mediated through the York-educated churchman and scholar Alcuin (c.735–804), whom Charlemagne appointed master of the palace schools in Aachen in 782.* The other was via Rome itself, which the church of York, now the seat of an archbishop, drew into closer contact, and where Late Antique sculptural models were prominent in city churches.

With metropolitan status at last achieved, the opportunity came to consolidate the church of York as the central authority for a Northumbrian church integrated into the mainstream of Western Christendom. As a model it looked to the Carolingian kingdom in Francia where Charlemagne, crowned emperor in Rome by Pope Leo III on Christmas Day 800, claimed the pedigree of empire and the universal church for the Frankish world. His people assembled an antique and Early Christian inheritance both by acquiring monuments from the Roman world and by imitating its subject matter and style in their own carving.

The most telling evidence surviving to us now of these connections is the ecclesiastical sculpture in which we see how, through the visual arts, the now-metropolitan church developed its position and its identity. The prominent use of figures of the apostles in the iconography, as seen at Collingham, Dewsbury and Otley[12] in the West Riding of Yorkshire, Easby and Masham in the North Riding, and Halton[13] in Lancashire, emphasises the teaching authority of the church through its historic roots via the church of Rome back to the New Testament. The deep source and inspiration of the Deiran sculpture was thus not Carolingian – they were the agents of transmission – but the Roman and Early Christian past which both sought to embrace.[14]

* See below in this chapter.

The early ninth-century poem *De Abbatibus* provides a further salutary lesson to historians reading Bede's black-and-white portrait of a church in crisis. Its author, a monk named Æðelwulf, spent most of his life in an unnamed dependent house of Lindisfarne and in his old age wrote a poem celebrating the virtues of its community. The poem is dedicated to Bishop Ecgberht of Lindisfarne (803–821). Equally valuable as a dating tool is the poet's explicit statement that his house had been founded a century before, during the reign of King Osred (704/5–716), son of King Aldfrið. The poet is no more charitable towards that king's reign than Boniface had been. An 'indocile' youth, he 'persecuted many';[15] and 'he did not honour his nobles, or even fittingly worship Christ, but alas he devoted his whole life to empty acts . . . he destroyed many by a pitiable death, but forced others to . . . live in monastic enclosures after receiving tonsure.'[16]

Despite several scholarly attempts, Æðelwulf's monastery has not been identified.* But it was certainly real rather than imagined – of the six abbots mentioned in the poem, five are attested in the Durham *Liber Vitae*.[17] In outline, the story of its fortunes can be traced by internal evidence from the poem. Its founder was a man named Eanmund. Like Wilfrid, Cuthbert and Benedict Biscop, he was a member of the Northumbrian nobility, a *gesið* who gave up a 'fruitless' military career. This may be a reference to a lack of martial opportunity under Osred; it is equally possible that he submitted to the tonsure to escape the king's vindictive persecutions. In any case he seems to have petitioned the king to book his family estates to him by charter.† He subsequently donated them to Lindisfarne, received instruction in the monastic way of life from its abbot/bishop,‡ acquired a teacher and entered the monastic life with his companions – his *comites*, now committed to a career as *milites Christi*.

That Lindisfarne still retained Irish affinities in the early eighth century is evident from the fact that Eanmund, now the proprietary abbot of a new monastic foundation, received visionary advice from an Ionan authority on

---

* Crayke, some 12 miles north of York, suits a visionary description of the site on a prominent hill; Bywell, sited in a bend on the north bank of the River Tyne downstream of Corbridge, has also been suggested (Campbell 1967; Howlett 1975).

† This is Campbell's reading of a slightly allusive passage. Campbell 1967, 8: lines 74–5 of the poem.

‡ Bishop Eadfrið (698–721).

where to build his new church – on a hill with a winding path, covered with thorny scrub which the brothers must clear to provide smooth foundations for their church, to be dedicated to St Peter. Eanmund's church and the lives of his community and successors are described in the sort of circumstantial detail that prompted Harold Taylor, the distinguished architectural historian, to attempt a reconstruction of its layout, complete with porticos, glazed windows, a roof clad with lead sheets and lavish adornments.[18] A second church, dedicated to the Holy Mary, was constructed by Abbot Sigbald, the third in succession to its founder.* This church, also roofed in lead and provided with bells,† was lavishly provided with glazed windows. The eucharist was celebrated with a golden chalice adorned with gems; the altar decorated with lovely pictures.[19] One of the brothers was a gifted smith named Cwicwine; another was something of an astronomer;[20] and a famous Irish scribe named Ultán, who spent his last years in the community, seems to have been a master of ornamental writing – no 'modern' scribe could equal him.[21]

Eanmund's distinctly secular upbringing, his blatant booking of heritable estates free of renders and services, and the lavish furnishing of the church, tend on the face of it to support Bede's portrayal of the worst sorts of foundation described in his letter to Bishop Ecgberht. Two of the six named abbots inherited the office from a brother. The story of a monk named Merðeof who, on his deathbed, suffered guilt-ridden visions of his children, dead from disease in infancy, and of the repudiation of his first wife for another, also seems to confirm Bede's scepticism regarding such establishments. But Æðelwulf also paints a picture of devotion and asceticism; of generosity to the poor; of fasting and extreme deprivation; of a love of psalm-singing.

Eanmund, the founder, was buried in a tomb inside the church, as was the Irish scribe Ultán – evidently something of a celebrity. Abbot Sigwine erected a high cross and was buried close to it after his death. A hundred years after its founding, having survived and thrived and not, at that time, having 'endured persecution' – Viking raids, we infer – Eanmund's monastery claimed an exemplary record of piety and devotion. Although we cannot know how far its priests and brothers ministered to their pastoral dependents, any archaeologist excavating the remains of this monastery

---

* So perhaps during the middle of the eighth century.
† One wonders whence the lead and, presumably, bronze for the bells, were acquired. For recent research on a lead source, see Chapter 10.

would find it indistinguishable from any of the great monastic complexes celebrated by Bede.

* * *

There is some evidence that King Ceolwulf, Bishop Ecgberht's cousin, may have taken Bede's admonitions on episcopal administration seriously. The king had enjoyed or endured a reign 'filled with serious commotions and setbacks',* being temporarily deposed in 731. On his eventual abdication in 737 Ceolwulf submitted himself to the tonsure and joined the community at Lindisfarne. Such retirements presented dilemmas for communities living traditionally under austere rules. Anglo-Saxon élite culture was steeped in the conviviality of the mead hall; in the bling of jewellery and fine clothes, feasting and storytelling; in comradeship and bonhomie. If some of the newer minsters established by married thegns were the subject of censure by Bede for just such behaviour, how were the Irish-flavoured ascetics of Lindisfarne to accommodate a former king? No doubt moral conflicts were soothed by the acquisition of generous gifts of cash and land; and then, as James Campbell pointed out in a classic essay on the development of the cult of St Cuthbert, even the most pious monks were themselves drawn from the same society. The proto-saint Guðlac, a former warband leader, had made himself unpopular at Repton because he *refused* to drink intoxicating liquor. As Campbell memorably noted: 'Modern historians judging eighth-century monasteries are often the denizens of Barchester applying the standards of Monte Cassino to establishments which resembled the former more than they did the latter.'[22]

As it happens, two land grants supposedly made by King Ceolwulf to Lindisfarne, and recorded retrospectively in the *Historia de Sancto Cuthberto*, reveal the extent of the generosity expected of a king wishing to enter the secluded, contemplative world of island life in the company of the sainted Cuthbert's followers. They reveal, too, the sorts of territorial acquisitions that the community sought in order to augment its existing portfolio of estates. This was, after all, the monastery that had produced the stunning and extraordinarily expensive Lindisfarne Gospels. We have argued elsewhere that the resources required for such projects – including fine-quality vellum from calves bred specifically for the purpose – drove an expansion of the monastic resource base.[23]

Elsewhere in England minsters were also increasing their surplus output of secondary products – wool and woven textiles, grain, leather, metalwork and

---

* Bede's allusive account. See Chapter 8.

so on – to generate profits for the acquisition of exotic imports – books, church plate, silks and embroidered vestments, oil and wine, for example.[24] Brian Roberts has shown how the estates owing services and renders to the twin monasteries of Wearmouth and Jarrow, where such wonders as the *Codex Amiatinus* and Bede's *Ecclesiastical History* were produced, can also be reconstructed, as the territorial estate of *Werhale*.[25] The key phrase that denotes large-scale estate parcels of contiguous territories comes in the form *Vill* X *cum suis appendiciis* YY: the *vill* of Warkworth (or Wearmouth or wherever), and its dependencies – subsidiary *vills* owing renders and services to the centre – which we suppose to have been a *villa regia*, a royal estate centre.

At the time of King Ceolwulf's abdication the abbot-bishop of Lindisfarne was Æðelwold, who held office from about 721 to 740. Internal evidence from marginalia in the text of the Lindisfarne Gospels credits him with taking the manuscript created by Eadfrið and having it bound by one Billfrið.[26] If he had reservations about the effects that the king's retirement there would have on his community, he must have swallowed them: a pill sugared by the consolidation of Lindisfarne's now huge estates.

The *Historia de Sancto Cuthberto*, which its successor community compiled in Durham in the eleventh century,[27] made claims to landholdings from as far south as York to as far north as the Forth and from east coast to west. It is a problematic document, both because it relies on faulty memory when reaching back to the seventh and eighth centuries and because it strikes a defensive tone against what it sees as thefts of land perpetrated against the community during the ninth century. Nevertheless, Geoffrey Barrow showed some time ago that it has geographical reality, when he elucidated a difficult paragraph to reveal an estate in the Bowmont valley, straddling what later became the Anglo-Scottish border.[28]

Three land units once belonging to Lindisfarne – Islandshire and Norhamshire in north Northumberland, and Bedlingtonshire in south-east Northumberland – retained a geographical and administrative identity, known collectively as North Durham, until 1844.[29] It is probable that Islandshire preserves the estate with which King Oswald endowed the monastery at its foundation in 635; a church and shrine were established at Norham-on-Tweed between 830 and 845;[30] and Bedlingtonshire was a land purchase early in the tenth century.[31] Section 4 of the *Historia* refers to the boundaries of Lindisfarne's territory, though without any chronological reference. It claims an area south of the Tweed which seems to imply two estates: one between the River Till in the west and Waren Burn in the south is more extensive than Islandshire and takes in most, but not all, of Norhamshire. It is difficult to reconcile this both with the North Durham units and with shire territories of Yeavering and Bamburgh;[32] one suspects that the *Historia* is faulty on this point. The second, on both sides of the Breamish, is identifiable as *Bromic*, an upland estate in the Cheviot Hills.[33] 'Beyond Tweed' there is an estate bounded by the Rivers Leader and *Edre*; it is not clear whether this is the Blackadder or the Whiteadder.[34] The text also claims the monastery of St Balðere between the Firth of Forth, River Esk and the Lammermuir hills (as discussed in Chapter 6).

Other passages in the *Historia* give better historical context, and it appears from these that there were three stages in which Lindisfarne's landholdings expanded: under the patronage of King Ecgfrið (670–685), then King Ceolwulf (729–737) and finally when Ecgred was the bishop (830–845). After the fall of York to the Danish army, Lindisfarne then suffered expropriation of some of its holdings but also gained new grants south of the Tyne.

Ecgfrið emerges from the *Historia* as being as much a patron to Lindisfarne as he was to Wilfrid.[35] He provided the monastery with a base in York and a stopping-off point at Crayke.[36] In thanks for his victory over the Mercians, he granted lands at Carham. This is on the south side of the Tweed, and it links Islandshire and the Bowmont estate in an unbroken block of land. An archaeological project currently in progress has identified a monastic focus between the parish church and the river.* He also gave an estate at Carlisle, where Bishop Cuthbert was in attendance on Queen Iurminburh at the time of Ecgfrið's death in 685.[37] If the Medieval parish of Carlisle St Cuthbert marks the Lindisfarne holding, then Carlisle St Mary might be the land of Iurminburh's sister's monastery. Also on the west side of the country, and the west side of Morecambe Bay, opposite the lands which Wilfrid had gained, he gave the territory of Cartmel. The text seems to link Cartmel with *Suðgedling*, whose identity is uncertain.[38]

The next patron is King Ceolwulf, who eventually resigned the kingship and entered Lindisfarne as a monk. He initiated the creation of a consolidated block of land taking in the major terrain types in the middle zone of Bernicia, linking them to the fertile upland pastures of *Bromic*; Ecgred completed the project a hundred years later.[39] He made two grants.[40] First, four *vills*: *Wudacestre* (Woodhorn), *Hwitingham* (Whittingham), *Eadwulfincham*

---

* This is a collaboration between the authors and Dr David Petts of Durham University.

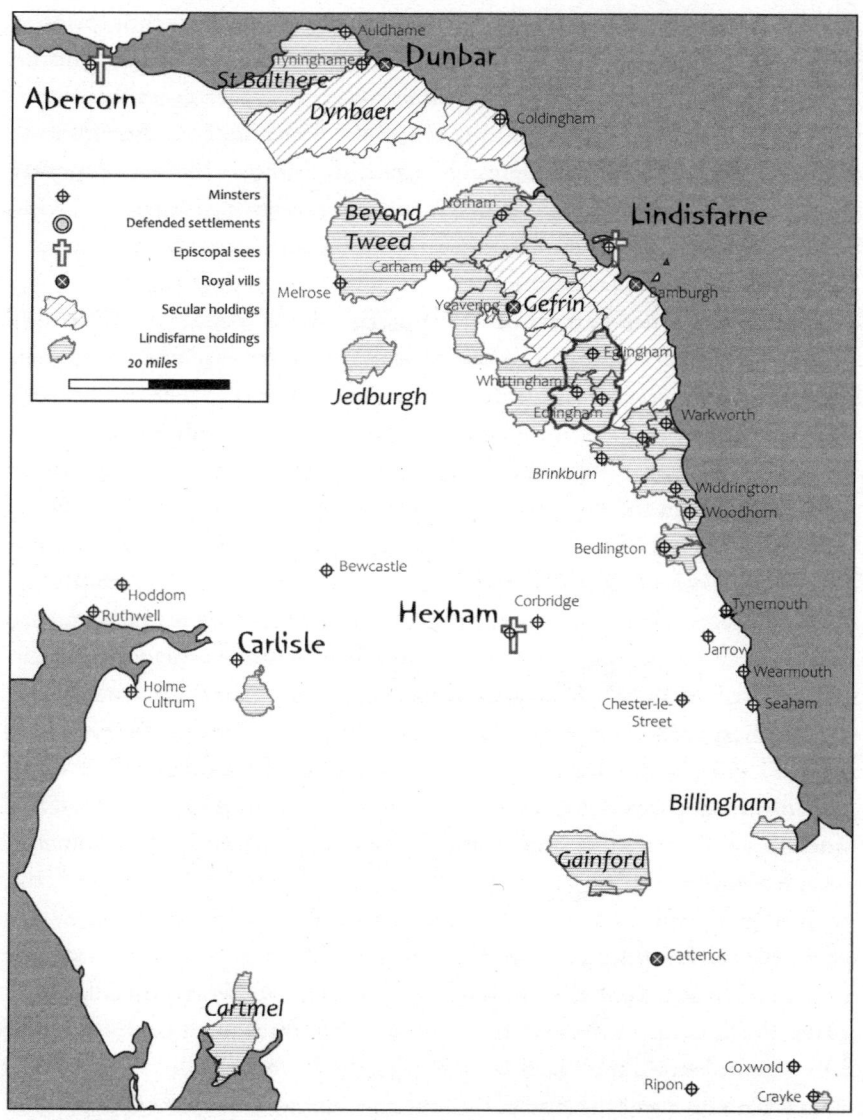

Map 18 The territorial interests of the monastic community on Lindisfarne. Note that a southern outlier, at York, is omitted

(Edlingham) and *Ecwulfincham* (Eglingham). The said bishop consecrated the churches of these *vills*. Woodhorn is coastal; the other three lie in the outer edges of the king's shire of Bamburgh.[41] And we might also see, in the detail of the grant, an attempt by Ceolwulf to bring a number of proprietary minsters – the sort described by the poet of *De Abbatibus*, of which Bede did not approve – under the diocesan control of Lindisfarne's exacting bishop-abbots. It is significant that in this scheme – which severely denuded the available land on which a king might settle his faithful warriors – the very large core shire of Bamburgh, which must have provided the Bernician royal household with its core supplies and revenue during long winter months, was never lost from the royal estate.

Ceolwulf's other grant was Warkworth, at the estuary of the River Coquet, with its dependencies. The *Historia* purports to define a boundary circuit from the River Lyne at the south, and then the Coquet and beyond. The geography here is confused but it can be read as four sub-units which in large measure carry forward into Medieval parishes and feudal landholdings and which adjoin the territory of the four-*vill* grant.[42]

Bishop Ecgred[43] had Aidan's church transported from Lindisfarne and rebuilt in Norham (further discussed in Chapter 10). In Teviotdale, he granted *Gedweade et altera Gedwearde* (Jedburgh and Old Jeddart) and the lands pertaining to them. South reads this to correspond to the northern half of the parish of Jedburgh, an area of some 7,000ha.[44] But the text refers to a boundary running along the River Teviot from Jedmouth to Wilton, near Hawick, indicating a much larger block of land than the valley of Jed Water and its surrounds, reaching from Teviot on the north-west side across to Dere Street on the north-east; this Roman road crosses Teviot by its confluence with Jed Water.

Bishop Ecgred also provided for Lindisfarne two estates on the north side of the River Tees. Billingham in Hartness is at the estuary. Roberts maps this as the ecclesiastical parish of Billingham, to include its Wolviston chapelry.[45] David Austin,[46] however, understands this as the larger topographical unit of Hartness, taking in the Hartlepool headland.* In the middle reaches of the Tees is Gainford and the land pertaining to it, along with Cliffe and Wycliffe

---

* On Map 18 on page 261 we take a cautiously conservative view on both Jedburgh and Billingham, following the smaller units of South and Roberts, and, *ultra Tweoda*, we map to the Blackadder and not the larger area to Whiteadder.

on the south side. This is a large land area reaching upriver north-west, to the River Wear in the north and bounded by Dere Street in the east.[47] Sir Edmund Craster, drawing on the evidence of ecclesiastical sculpture, observed that neither Billingham nor Gainford was a new foundation in the time of Bishop Ecgred.[48] The corpus of sculpture does not list any carved stones earlier than the ninth century at Gainford but, as Craster also noted, the *Historia Regum* records the burial in the church at Gainford in 801 of one Edwine, also called Eda,[49] thirty years before Ecgred became bishop. At Billingham there is a fragment of an inscribed name stone in which the treatment of the terminals of the cross carved into the stone bears comparison with examples from the monastery at Hartlepool.[50] This adds weight to Austin's suggestion that Billingham and its territory once belonged to Hild's monastery at Hartlepool. Ecgred was consolidating into Lindisfarne hands churches and lands which had been under other jurisdictions.

There is a tantalising footnote to the reconstruction of the Ceolwulf grants estates. The River Lyne is a minor landscape feature; but it was evidently an identifiable and important boundary in the eighth century. It rises as Heronsclose Burn, some 14km inland and due west from its outflow into the North Sea at Lynemouth. Medieval and later township boundaries follow it almost exclusively and at its source the townships of the Lyne–Warkworth estate butt against another pre-Conquest territorial unit, held from the early twelfth century by the House of Cospatric who descended from the Bamburgh-based earls of Northumbria, and through which the Roman road known as Devil's Causeway runs between Hadrian's Wall and Berwick.[51] The southern edges of the townships of this estate subsequently follow other natural features: the Fence Burn, whose source lies within 100m or so of the source of the Lyne; then the River Font; then the Mere Burn;* then the River Hart.

For more than 30km inland from the sea, almost all historic township boundaries respect this line. Its integrity, together with the Lyne boundary description, lead us to suggest that this is a major, primary landscape feature. In Hangingleaves Wood, just to the east of the modern A1 road, an upstanding ditch-and-bank earthwork substantially survives along the south side of the Lyne, and here it is possible to suggest a surviving fragment of what once must have been a monumental feature. A planned programme of testing for optically stimulated luminescence (OSL) dating may determine its date with

---

* The name is derived from the Old English word for 'boundary'.

some precision. If a boundary feature on this scale had been established by the eighth century – perhaps long before – it raises a number of questions about the nature of land division in the Early Medieval period. Were north and central Northumberland distinct entities with a recognised border; and, if so, why has it only survived as a faint territorial fossil in an early charter? Does the axis of this boundary – east-north-east to west-south-west, at right angles to a number of long-distance paths that seem to connect a crossing of the River Wansbeck with summer grazing lands in the Cheviots – reflect some underlying prehistoric topographic axiom?

* * *

The England-wide trend for the establishment of large numbers of proprietary minsters in the first quarter of the eighth century may have been driven by more than just fashion and the attractions of evading military service and the king's *feorm*. The devastating plague that swept through Britain in 664 and which recurred several times during the following decades, notably in 685/6, had two potentially significant consequences. Open warfare between kingdoms is a common feature of the annals in the middle third of the seventh century; much less so in the last quarter of that century and in the first third of the eighth, before becoming more common again thereafter. Depopulation may have played a part; so might the diplomatic skills of England's greatest archbishop, Theodore. Warfare was a principal source of wealth and prestige for kings and their *comites* through booty, tribute and the sale of slaves. Mercian kings, bishops and monastic entrepreneurs increasingly saw how to generate an alternative income, from trade and landed surplus; and depopulated – that is to say lordless – estates could be capitalised by fostering an injection of tax-free and military service-free monastic labour and the investment of technology, alongside security of tenure. Bede's kings – and one thinks of the Aldfrið coinage here as well as the proliferation of trading settlements – may not have been so short-sighted as he would have us believe.

Even so, Bede's fears about the alienation of land and the proliferation of spurious monastic communities were well-founded. If King Ceolwulf's successors in Northumbria are politically and biographically obscure, more tangible contemporary Mercian kings and bishops, even in the fuzzy silhouettes provided by charters, the records of church councils and annals, found themselves confronting the same issues – with momentous consequences. King Ceolwulf's abdication in 737 and subsequent Mercian aggression towards Northumbria (see Chapter 8) show how surface tensions in one kingdom were quickly exploited by its neighbours.[52] The outbreak of hostilities seems to coincide with a general economic decline in the Southern kingdoms; war, against a neighbour with insufficient armed men to defend itself, may have been the most expedient means of refilling the Mercian treasury.

The tension seems to have spread: the reign of King Cuðred of Wessex (740–756) is marked by the 'E' recension of the *Anglo-Saxon Chronicle* thus: '[He] resolutely made war against Æðelbald, king of Mercia.' Those military tensions are also reflected in a broader sense of insecurity. In 742 a council was held at the unidentified *Clofesho* (possibly a site near Hertford)* at which a newly enthroned Archbishop Cuthbert of Canterbury sought and secured from King Æðelbald, among other things, the following promise:

> in all things the honour and authority and security of the church of Christ on this side of the River Humber be denied by no person and also all of the monasteries established within Kent should remain both free from secular services and also secure from all burdens, major or minor.[53]

Five years after this seemingly harmonious agreement, Boniface, the former English missionary to Frisia and now archbishop of Mainz, along with seven other missionary bishops, wrote to the Mercian king with accusations that he had revoked the privileges of many churches, depriving them of property. He also cited the examples of Æðelbald's predecessor, King Ceolred, and of King Osred of Northumbria, both of whom had (he said) been notorious for violating nuns and destroying monasteries.[54] He wrote to Archbishop Ecgberht in York on the same theme, taking the opportunity to request that he send him some of the works of Bede.† In the same year, 747, Boniface wrote to the archbishop in Canterbury with this admonition: 'As to the forced labour of monks upon royal buildings and other works, a thing unheard of anywhere excepting only in England, let not the priests of God keep silence or consent thereto. It is an evil unknown in times gone by.'[55]

In what seems to have been a direct response, a second council was held at *Clofesho* in September of that year in which Boniface's admonitions were

---

* See Adams 2025, 339ff for a discussion of the debate around the name and its location.
† *EHD* 179; Letters LI. He made the same request of Abbot Hwætberht of Wearmouth (*EHD* 180; Letters LX), adding that he would like a warm cloak, sending in return a coverlet of goat's hair.

repeated almost word for word.[56] Bishops were now adjured to inspect the monasteries in their dioceses 'if they can be called monasteries', in particular those 'we know not how, possessed by secular men . . . by presumptuous human invention'.[57] But if King Æðelbald was prepared to restate the privileges of the Kentish church, protecting their liberty, security and authority and exempting them from *all* secular services, he now exacted a price in the form of an exemption: 'except [military] expedition and building of a bridge, or fortification'.[58] Monastic estates must provide labour and resources sufficient to fight in the king's army, repair his fortifications and construct his bridges.

This is the first formal statement to survive defining the three so-called 'common burdens'. The proliferation of new monasteries had driven kings in Mercia and Kent to confiscate monastic lands and to impose on monks 'forced . . . labour on royal buildings and other works'. The churches had resisted. The second *Clofesho* council was both a compromise and a hardening of royal – one might almost now call it 'state' – authority. The Ceolwulf grants show that favoured minsters might still benefit from endowments of land but, since the *Historia de Sancto Cuthberto* provides the only reliable record of such dealings in Northumbria, many others can only be a matter of speculation. Even so, there is no doubt that the tensions caused by competing political and territorial interests were played out across the rest of the century and into the next.

Very occasionally these tensions bubble to the surface and we catch glimpses of them. In about 757 or 758 a Northumbrian abbot named Forðred applied to Pope Paul in Rome for his intervention in a dispute with King Eadberht, who had forcibly deprived him of three monasteries given to him by a certain abbess, and instead given them to his brother, a certain *patricius* named Moll.[59] The dispute is known to us only because the pope's letter to King Eadberht and to Archbishop Ecgberht, requesting their restitution, survives – albeit in a badly scorched and barely legible manuscript.[60] The monasteries at stake were Stonegrave and Coxwold in Ryedale and *Donemuða* on the Tyne. At stake for the king and his brother was, in the pope's words, the 'ruin of your soul.' The *patricius* Moll would have his own consequential part to play in Northumbrian history. The outcome of the papal intervention is unrecorded.

A Mercian narrative, of a long-running legal dispute over the ownership of a valuable monastery and productive trading site at Cookham on the River Thames, shows how tenaciously the interested parties might defend their claims to such assets. Cookham had been given to Christ Church, Canterbury, but its deeds had been stolen and given to a West Saxon king. By the time that penitence prompted him to return the deeds, Cookham lay in lands claimed by King Offa of Mercia. Offa gave Cookham to his queen, Cyneðryð, who successfully defended her ownership at a synod held at *Clofesho* in 798 – but not without ceding to Canterbury 110 family farms in Kent and 110 more elsewhere.[61]

From across Mercia, evidence drawn from charters, excavation and place-names is revealing something of the reach and ambitions of kings in bending both secular and spiritual resources to a unified scheme of royal administration: the common burdens. A system of *burhs* – defensible enclosures at, or close to, probable royal estate centres – is coming into focus along key lines of communication – rivers and Roman roads. While only a single eighth-century Mercian bridge has been solidly identified, at Cromwell on the River Trent, others are suspected, and these can only have been conceived and constructed with all the resources available to royal administrators. King Æðelbald's martial record shows that he could muster sufficient armies to enforce his overlordship of the Southern kingdoms. *Burh* defences have been tentatively identified at a number of Mercian central places, including Irthlingborough (Northamptonshire), Hereford, Tamworth (Staffordshire) and Winchcombe (Gloucestershire).[62] Under Æðelbald's successor, King Offa (757–796), the physical existence, and provisions for guarding the great earthwork that bears his name, rather speak for themselves.

Eighth-century Mercian kings established a system of royal administration based on estate centres surrounded by clusters of the so-called functional *tūns*: settlements focused on strategic resources or locations and with a defined relationship to the *burh*.[63] In enclosing and formalising these centres of administration, they had to draw on labour from dependent *vills*. In the new Mercian state orthodoxy, those perfectly legitimate monasteries which had become wealthy through endowments and trade ought to contribute, just as monasteries booked by secular men under the guise of piety but in fact to protect their hereditary rights, must also contribute or face the confiscation of their estates.

That chance record of the dispute between Abbot Forðred and the king and archbishop in the 750s shows how inevitably sparse our knowledge really is of such arrangements in Northumbria. And beneath the surface of an apparently stable régime other forces were in play: ancient or recent rivalries threatening the king's peace. A notice in the *Historia Regum* for the year 750 describes how King Eadberht laid siege to the monastery on Lindisfarne and imprisoned Abbot-bishop Cynewulf of Lindisfarne in the nearby royal fortress of Bamburgh. The abbot had apparently been harbouring a fugitive pretender to the throne: an *ætheling* named Offa, son of the late King Aldfrið and brother of Osred. One wonders what part the retired but still very much alive King Ceolwulf played in these dangerous events. Offa, who had sought the sanctuary of the relics of St Cuthbert, was dragged from the church on Holy Island, 'almost dead with hunger'. No wonder the separation between secular and spiritual power had become blurred – both worlds were extensions of the politics of the mead hall and of the Old Testament.

The drivers for the secularising process lamented by Bede and seen across the Anglo-Saxon kingdoms are complex. Religious zeal and depopulation driven by recurrent episodes of plague in the late seventh century propelled a rash of almost certainly genuine monastic endowments – the activities of great spiritual entrepreneurs like Wilfrid and Benedict Biscop promoting religious communities to both kings and the ranks of nobility, male and female. An economic boom in the first third of the eighth century enabled, or was fostered by, the formation of extensive monastic landholdings, held in perpetuity, into which capital flowed in return for what prehistorians would call a 'secondary products revolution': surpluses of wool, salt, minerals, finished textiles and other craft items being exported regionally and to the Continent in return for an influx of silver and of active merchant venturers. English books – particularly the works of the Venerable Bede – were much in demand across the North Sea. The gifts sent by Abbot Cuthbert of Wearmouth and Jarrow to his friend Archbishop Lul of Mainz in about 759 included twenty knives, a robe made of otter skins, two palls of 'subtle workmanship', books and a bell.[64] Who could blame secular lords for wanting a share of England's wealth – especially during times of political instability but with few opportunities to enrich themselves by the sword? The king's thegns used their political capital to extract grants of booked land; kings began to resist and to demand labour on public works as the price of patronage; ecclesiastics reacted to defend their assets.

Where else might historians and archaeologists look in Northumbria for evidence of these tensions between an increasingly secularised church and the ambitions of its kings to construct and protect nascent state institutions? Monasteries exhibiting signs of conspicuous economic success are betrayed by expanded and formalised layouts; by the presence of coinage; by the archaeology of specialisation in agriculture and crafts. The long-established

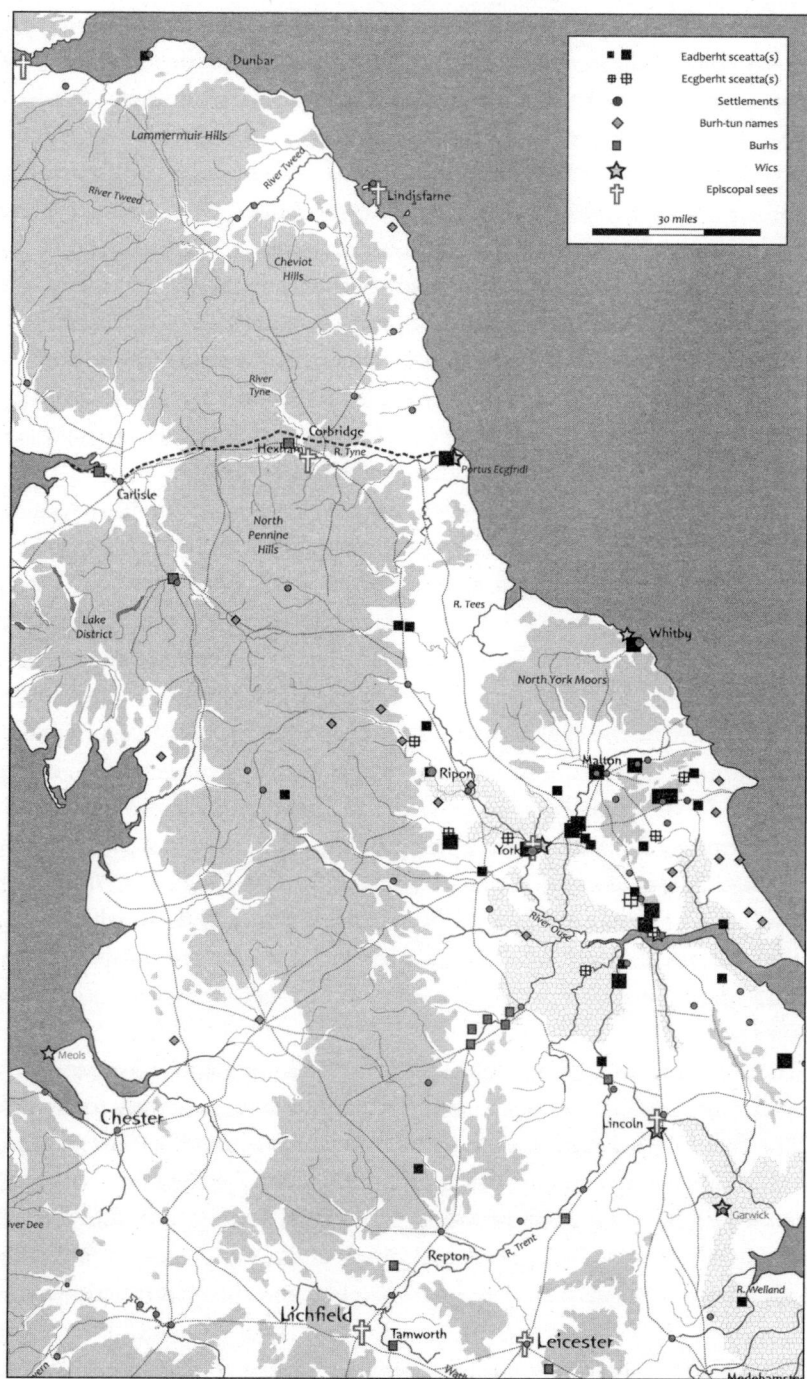

Map 19 Distribution of coins of King Eadberht and Archbishop Ecgberht

monastery and royal cult centre at Whitby, with its fine harbour, concentrations of coins and extensive layout, is a good candidate for the secularising trend, as are Whithorn, Hoddom, Carlisle, Wilfrid's grandiose minsters at Ripon and Hexham and Bede's own monastery.

The archbishop's minster at York is also a prime candidate. The trading settlement at Fishergate and its probable successors elsewhere in the city complemented the territorial and political power of its incumbent, the brother and cousin of kings. In Ecgberht's time a series of coins was jointly issued with King Eadberht.[65] Their distribution shows a concentration of economic activity and patronage that echoes and expands the evidence of King Aldfrið's coinage. The king had, it seems, been able to impose a controlled weight standard across Northumbrian coinage as a bulwark against economic decline; his brother endorsed and profited from it.

The long-lived and extensive settlement at West Heslerton has produced eighth-century *sceattas* from across the site.* From about 730 onwards it seems that livestock and grain production, crafts and industrial output here ensured its full integration into the wider economic world. Disciplined and planned zoning and demarcation of activities strongly suggests the hand of external authority, given the conspicuous lack of any outstanding dwelling here. At the time of excavation it was not by any means clear how unique this combination of functional and spatial zoning might be – no comparable sites had been identified, let alone investigated. In the last thirty years such features have increasingly come into focus, especially across the Midland counties, at sites like West Fen Road, Ely, Yarnton in Oxfordshire, Higham Ferrers in Northamptonshire and elsewhere. West Heslerton is still exceptional in many ways, but perhaps no longer such an outlier in an eighth-century milieu increasingly driven by economic optimisation.[66]

At Brandon in Suffolk, Cookham in Berkshire and Flixborough in Lincolnshire highly developed settlement complexes apparently focused on a church but with direct riverine access to regional economic routeways blur the line between the secular and spiritual, highlighting the potential role of monasteries in driving, or profiting from, this economic boom time. In Bernicia, Shotton provides the most conspicuous example so far; Whithorn seems also to have spanned the range of secular and spiritual functions.

---

* Dominic Powlesland has kindly allowed us access to the pre-publication coin report.

In the Cumbrian hinterland of Carlisle, with its important royal minster, a conspicuous pattern of *burh* and *botl/bothl* names suggests the hand of royal administrators in establishing control over key routes and resources. A similar pattern can be seen in the coastal coreland of East Lothian, with a focus of economic activity at Aberlady. In the eastern half of Deira, particularly along the River Hull and in Holderness, a number of *burh-tūn* names have been identified, seemingly a mirror of administrative initiatives in Mercia.[67] *Burh* and *burh-tūn* names also occur across what had once been the independent British kingdom of Elmet: at Aldborough, the former Brigantian *civitas* capital and further upstream along the River Ure. And a very dense concentration of possible *burh* sites along the River Don upstream of Doncaster seems to define a key frontier zone between Northumbria and Mercia.

Under King Eadberht and his brother, Northumbria entered two decades of apparent political stability, notwithstanding King Æðelbald's incursions across the Humber between 737 and 741, which marked a new phase of military conflict between the two kingdoms. Some 350 silver *sceattas* of Eadberht are known, and their consistency and sophistication is marked. Their quantity and distribution show an expanded penetration from King Aldfrið's coinage, across the south of Northumbria and beyond, contrasting with the contemporary debasement of coinage south of the Humber.[68] Even so, Eadberht seems to have been more interested in exploiting opportunities among his northern neighbours than in taking on the might of Mercia. In 750, according to an entry in the continuation of Bede's *Chronica*, King Eadberht took an army into Ayrshire and 'added the plain of Kyle to his dominions'. Perhaps he was protecting Bernician interests in Galloway – at any rate he found the time to put down a nascent coup at Lindisfarne. Six years later he is to be found in alliance with a Pictish force under Óengus mac Fergusso, attacking the British kingdom of Strathclyde at the great Clydeside fortress of *Alt Clud*: Dumbarton Rock. The British accepted terms. But the *Historia Regum* records that 'on the tenth day of the same month there perished almost the whole army which he led from *Ovania* to *Niwanbrig*'.

Neither *Ovania* (perhaps Govan on the Clyde) nor *Niwanbrig** has been positively identified, nor has the identity of the enemy. If Mercia was the antagonist, its political advantage lasted less than a year. In 757 King

---

* There are Newburghs or Newbroughs, the modern equivalents, in Fife and on the River North Tyne.

Æðelbald was murdered at Seckington, near Tamworth, by his bodyguard. A year later King Eadberht abdicated in favour of his son, Oswulf, and retired to his brother's monastery at York. Mercian stability was quickly restored under a new king, Offa, who held the throne for thirty-nine years. But in Northumbria King Oswulf Eadberhting was 'wickedly killed' by his household near *Meðel Wongtun** – as if, perhaps, treachery was infectious.

From this crisis in the succession a warlord unrelated to his predecessors emerged and was 'elected by his people' in 759.[69] This was Æðelwald, 'who was also called Moll' – very probably the *patricius* to whom the three disputed monasteries had been given two years previously. These are murky waters; but it seems very likely that Æðelwald's power base lay in Deira, where two of his proprietary minsters also lay – although he has no place in the Bernician or Deiran genealogies. He was married formally to a woman named Æðelðryð at the royal *vill* and former Roman town of Catterick in 762, according to the *Historia Regum*; and they had at least one son, named Æðelred. But the fates seem already to have set themselves against the usurper. In the year in which he took power, 'A pestilence occurred, which lasted almost two years, diverse grievous sickness causing havoc, more especially the disease of dysentery.'[70]

In 761† the new king faced rebellion in Bernicia from Oswine, son of King Eadberht and brother of the Oswulf who had been killed so wickedly. They seem to have fought a 'very severe' three-day battle at *Eldunum* – Eildon, where three distinct hills known by the Romans as *Trimontium*, near Melrose, were the focus of military roads and ancient fortresses. Oswine was killed – the *Chronicle* recorded that he died at an unidentified place called *Ædwinesclif*.

The former King Ceolwulf died in retirement on Lindisfarne during the winter of 764: a season of apparently unprecedented severity:

> An immense snowfall, hardened into ice, unparalleled in all former ages, oppressed the land from the beginning of winter almost until the middle of spring; through its severity the trees and plants for the most part withered, and many marine animals were found dead.[71]

---

* Perhaps Market Weighton in East Yorkshire.
† The date comes from the *Anglo-Saxon Chronicle*; but the battle is listed under 759 in the *Historia Regum*.

In Ireland the Ulster annalist remembered a great snowfall which lasted three months. It was lucky for Abbot Cuthbert of Wearmouth and Jarrow that his friend Archbishop Lul had sent him a 'multi-coloured coverlet' to protect him from the cold. In return he sent copies of Bede's two *Lives of St Cuthbert* but he wrote that 'the conditions of the past winter oppressed the island of our race very horribly with cold and ice and long and widespread storms of wind and rain, so that the hand of the scribe was hindered from producing a great number of books'.[72]

The fortunes of Early Medieval peoples were tied inextricably to those of their God-given kings, so it is perhaps no wonder that in the year after this dreadful winter King Æðelwald was 'deprived' of his kingdom at a place called *Pincanheale*.[73] This unidentified site was the location for two synods in the late eighth century, so it is perhaps apt that Æðelwald is said to have been forcibly tonsured.[74] He was probably lucky not to lose his head.

The former *patricius* was succeeded by Alhred, who appears in the Anglian genealogies as a sixth-generation descendant of Ida, although his genealogy, compiled at the beginning of the ninth century, may have been at least a partial fiction.[75] His intent to demonstrate legitimacy is evident from his marriage in 768 to Osgifu who, according to Symeon, was a daughter of the short-lived King Oswulf and therefore a more solidly Bernician Iding. A sense of restored continuity is apparent in the succession of a new archbishop in York after the death of the long-lived Ecgberht in the previous year. The new incumbent was a relative of his predecessor:[76] Archbishop Ælberht was a York insider and genuine career monk; a pilgrim, teacher and scholar, founder of a great library and teacher of Alcuin, whose glowing praise of him forms a set piece of his long poem on the *Bishops, Kings and Saints of York*, composed for the visit of the papal legates in 786.[77] In Ælberht's time the minster at York, which had been razed in 741, was rebuilt as a lofty basilica, supported by columns with curving arches, inlaid ceilings and windows and many chapels; embellished with a chandelier with twenty-seven tiers, an altar cross covered with precious metals and a cruet of pure gold.[78]

The new king and queen actively patronised the church and its missionary activities on the Continent. They were correspondents of Archbishop Lul, whose help they secured in sending embassies to the greatest power in Early Medieval Europe, the court of Charlemagne (768–814) at Aachen. With a letter of 773, begging for Lul's prayers in a time of 'disturbances' among Northumbrian churches and people, they sent him small treasures: twelve cloaks – an English speciality – and a gold ring, a 'substantial gift for an endowment'.[79]

Those disturbances to which the royal couple alluded are illuminated by passages in the *Vita* of St Liudger of Utrecht (742–809).[80] Liudger was sent to study at York under Alcuin and stayed there for three years, but his studies were interrupted when York's citizens became engaged in a conflict with unidentified 'enemies', during which a Deiran *comes* was killed by a Frisian merchant. The Frisian community, including Liudger, 'hastened to leave the land of the English, fearing the wrath of the kindred of the slain young man'.[81]

Such were the realities of the blood feud; such were also, probably, the inevitable tensions between regional landed interests and communities of 'foreign' merchants and traders. More internal instability is evidenced by notice of the burning of the royal *vill* at Catterick in 769[82] by 'the tyrant Eanred' even if his career as a usurper was short-lived – he was burned to death the same year.

Five years later, while residing in York during Easter ceremonies, King Alhred was expelled – first to Bamburgh, the ancient Iding heartland fortress; then into Pictland. According to Symeon's much later testimony, he was replaced by Æðelred, supposedly a son of Æðelwold Moll.[83] The new king was himself expelled after four years and replaced in 779 by Ælfwald, a grandson of King Eadberht. The new king's decade-long reign was marked, says Symeon, by outstanding piety and justice. He was able to mint a substantial series of coins, of which forty-one specimens are now known, compared to seventeen from his immediate predecessor and, by way of comparison, his grandfather's 350 or so. He was also a signatory – at least, with the mark of a cross – to the decrees of a Legatine Mission that visited Britain in 786. Accompanying the legation as a reader and likely diplomat was Alcuin, the Northumbrian-born scholar, poet, clergyman and man of letters who, since 782, had been master of Charlemagne's palace school at Aachen/Aix-la-Chapelle.

Alcuin is the first Northumbrian whose likeness has been preserved – at least, it was made within a decade or so of his death, as a grey-bearded, slightly stooped figure, presenting one of his works to the archbishop of Mainz.[84] His family were members of the Deiran élite, holding land near Spurn Point at the bleakly exposed mouth of the Humber estuary. Alcuin, born in about 732, was schooled under Archbishop Ecgberht at York – he may have been a witness to the burning of the minster by Mercian forces in 741. After Ecgberht's death and the succession of Ælberht as archbishop in 767, Alcuin had become the master of York's monastic school and its well-endowed library.*

---

* A list of its books is contained in Alcuin's long poem on the *Bishops, Kings and Saints of York*. Allott 1974; Godman 1982, 123ff.

Upon Eanberht's succession to the archdiocese in 780, Alcuin travelled to Rome to petition Pope Hadrian for a pallium for the new archbishop. On his return journey he met – apparently for the second time – the Emperor Charlemagne, who invited him to become master of the palace school at Aachen. It was an irresistible opportunity for Alcuin – the intellectual descendant of Bede, to whom he was linked by their mutual friendship with Ecgberht – to introduce serious scholarship, and the liberal arts, to the Carolingian court.[85]

It was natural that Alcuin should volunteer, or be invited, to join the papal legation of 786 – the first to visit these shores since the days of Theodore, a century before. Like that embassy, the mission was partly motivated by papal concerns for the state of the English church and partly by a Frankish desire to update its knowledge of the political state of the Anglo-Saxon kingdoms – particularly of the powerful Mercian state under King Offa. After visiting Canterbury and then Offa's court, the legation divided – one party went into Wales, the other to Northumbria, where the archbishop and the king, the four Northumbrian bishops, the bishop of the Anglian community in Mayo and a *patricius*, Sicga – who 'subscribed with a serene mind' – signed the decrees. These covered baptism, monastic elections, the observation of the Nicene creed, priestly ordination and papal privileges. They included chapters concerned with separating secular from ecclesiastical business, the legitimacy of royal heirs* and the suppression of pagan rites.

The decrees were read aloud by Alcuin and his assistant, in both English and Latin, and they preserve some intriguing social detail – ox-horn was condemned as a material for making chalices and patens; bare legs were not to be shown when celebrating mass; just and equal weights and measures were to be used in assessing tithes; pagan mores in tattooing, dress and feasting, including the eating of horse-flesh, were to be repudiated.[86]

We may read into this grand visitation the monumentalisation of a set of relations between church, state and people: a social contract for eighth-century England to be read alongside its literature, sculpture and coinage – in parallel with Northumbria's descent into dynastic warfare. Two years after the departure of the Legatine Mission, in the year 788, King Ælfwald was murdered at a place called *Scythlescester*,† and, for once, the name of the assassin is known: the *dux* Sicga, the previously 'serene' signatory to the papal decrees.

---

* King Offa had been determined to ensure recognition for his son, Ecgfrið.
† Probably Halton Chesters on Hadrian's Wall. *EHD* 3; *Hist Reg*.

How can the modern historian comprehend the dynamics of such power struggles at so great a remove? They cannot, except by vague analogy with the politics of tyranny, tribal rivalry and, perhaps, the thuggery of organised crime. Northumbria's kings were weak; or their dynastic rivals were too strong. Fifty years after the death of Bede, his prescient words must have been ringing with grim satisfaction in the ears of wise counsellors. But a year after Ælfwald's murder a louder alarm sounded. On the south coast a king's reeve, sent to conduct some Scandinavian seafarers from their three vessels drawn up on the beach at Portland Bill to the court of the West Saxon king, seems to have misread the foreigners' motives: they killed him.[87] The Viking Age had begun.

Alcuin must have been a prolific correspondent long before the first of his surviving letters – a friendly lecture delivered to Ecgfrið, King Offa's son and heir-apparent, in the year of the Legatine Mission.[88] In 790, the year after the portentous events on the south coast, Alcuin was in York writing to his Irish pupil, Joseph, back in Aachen. The reader is instantly immersed in an eighth-century milieu of royal politics, monastic conviviality and the business of maintaining Alcuin's wide network of correspondents. After the assassination of King Ælfwald, Osred – a son of the late King Alhred – had held the throne for a year before being tonsured and expelled. Now the exiled former King Æðelred, Moll's son, returned to seize power in Northumbria. Alcuin neatly précised the situation: the king 'has just come from misery to majesty, from prison to the throne! The new reign keeps me here against my inclination.'[89]

He asks for news from the court in Aachen: is Charlemagne there; is there peace or war ... Is everyone well? Then to business. He asks if Joseph will send him 10lbs of silver and some three-ply goat's hair garments; wool for the use of the boys in his care; linen for his own use; black and red goat's hair hoods; and fine sulphur paints and dyes for colouring. These are the sorts of detail that archaeologists and historians pounce on: evidence for precious but otherwise intangible materials traded and exchanged across the North Sea. And behind the commodities lie the income: money to be collected from his monastery and from 'Wormec's township'. But he urged his pupil to be generous with bread and wine and to make 'our brothers' welcome with wine and mutton; to help the widows with corn, wine and butter. Like a good territorial lord – like a model squire, in fact – he indulged his dependants while admonishing their faults.

Later that same year, 790, he confided in a letter to his friend, Abbot Adalhard, that the state of his native land troubled him: 'I found things in my country somewhat disturbed and the new king's attitude not as I hoped or wished [but] I have given some advice to him [and] we are working against injustice... with certain men of power.'⁹⁰

A sermonising letter to King Æðelred also survives. But it is Alcuin's reaction to the disaster of 793 that has most often drawn historians' attention. That year ominous portents were observed

> and miserably frightened the people: these were immense flashes of lightning, and fiery dragons were seen flying in the air. A great famine immediately followed these signs; and a little after that in the same year on 8 June the raiding of heathen men miserably devastated God's church in Lindisfarne island by looting and slaughter.⁹¹

The Northern annalist compared the raiders to stinging hornets, recording that they not only slaughtered cattle and sheep but also some of the brethren, enslaving others. Monasteries were wealthy, vulnerable communities. Lindisfarne was not the first to have been attacked – Wilfrid's foundation at Oundle had been razed by a warband after his death.⁹² But the Lindisfarne raid was seen then, as now, to herald a new age of uncertainty, of universal peril. Alcuin, back in Aachen at his emperor's request, expressed the Christian world's deep shock:

> Lo, it is nearly 350 years that we and our fathers have inhabited this most lovely land, and never before has such terror appeared in Britain as we have now suffered from a pagan race, nor was it thought that such an inroad from the sea could be made. Behold, the church of St. Cuthbert spattered with the blood of the priests of God, despoiled of all its ornaments; a place more venerable than all in Britain is given as a prey to pagan peoples.⁹³

Bede's fears had been realised. For Alcuin, the irresistible conclusion was that this catastrophe was a divine judgement on moral failure: luxury and licentiousness, fornication, adultery and incest had flooded the land; greed, robbery and judicial violence were rife. A plundered people was proof: when powerful men seized the property of the weak, they lost their own; kings would lose kingdoms; peoples their lands. The violence done to his native land was punishment by blood from the North.*

---

* Alex Woolf raises the possibility that the Pictish King Constantín may have had a hand in encouraging or sponsoring the first Norse raid. Woolf 2007, 57.

The blow struck against Lindisfarne was followed by others – coastal and riverine monasteries were easy pickings for intrepid Scandinavian farmer-seafarers who knew Britain's coastlines and navigable rivers from decades of trade: King Ecgfrið's port* and *Donemuða* in 794; Hartness and Tynemouth in 799; Iona, Northumbria's mother church, in 802 or 803. Who can say if the raid on Lindisfarne was premeditated, or a trade deal that went horribly wrong; whether the raiders were known to the community of St Cuthbert or if their arrival was opportunistic? Scandinavian skippers must already have been familiar with these waters; must have known of their undefended potential for theft and slavery. In Norse mythology, treasure was jealously guarded by dragons, fought over with lethal weaponry, potentially the inciting incident in a blood feud; in England's monasteries it was protected by prematurely balding men whose only weapons were prayers; their only protection the power of St Cuthbert's relics.

As though the moral calamity had corrupted the soul of Bede's *gens Anglorum*, Ealdorman Sicga – signatory to the canons of the Legatine Mission and murderer of King Ælfwald – committed suicide during the same year, 793; his body was taken to Lindisfarne for burial.[94] In 796, the year in which King Offa died in Mercia after a reign of thirty-nine years, the Northumbrian King Æðelred was assassinated at a place called *Cover* (probably Corbridge, the old Roman town on the River Tyne).[95] His successor, Osbald, reigned for twenty-seven days before being exiled to Lindisfarne; thence to Pictland. The implication is that Pictish kings were harbouring and backing rival candidates for the Northumbrian kingship. But since Æðelred had married Ælfflæd, a daughter of King Offa, one might also read into this latest royal murder the abrupt absence of Mercian protection for its northern ally. Northumbria lay under the twin catastrophes of coastal raiding, picking off the cream of its monasteries, and civil war, while in Mercia King Ecgfrið, Offa's son and chosen heir, died within a year of his father's death. Alcuin consoled King Æðelred's mother, Abbess Æðeltrude, with a letter; but he wrote to Archbishop Eanbald: 'Times are dangerous in Britain. The death of kings is a sign of misery, and divisions a cause of bondage.'[96]

---

* *Portus Ecgfridi*, which Symeon believed to be Jarrow. The story passed down to Symeon was that the raiders had themselves suffered the fate of such risky enterprises: their leader had been slain; their ships destroyed in a storm. *Libellus* II.5.

Nevertheless, Northumbria's institutions proved tenacious. In the same year a new archbishop, Eanbald II, consecrated a new king: Eardwulf, a *dux* seemingly unrelated to Northumbria's competing dynasties.* It was likely in relation to an earlier conflict between Eardwulf and King Æðelred in 790 that Alcuin had written his admonishing words. The annalist of the *Historia Regum* had recorded that

> Eardwulf was taken prisoner, and conveyed to Ripon, and there ordered by the aforesaid king [Æthelred] to be put to death without the gate of the monastery. The brethren carried his body into the church with Gregorian chanting, and placed it out of doors in a tent; after midnight he was found alive in the church.[97]

Eardwulf must previously have been known to Alcuin. The latter wrote to him in that tumultuous year of his accession, 796, reminding him of their former friendship and suggesting that his earlier salvation was providential: he had been 'saved for better times' to set his country right.[98]

Better times did not come – at least, not during Alcuin's lifetime. In 798 a battle was fought at Whalley in what is now Lancashire, where the River Calder meets the Ribble.[99] The king's antagonists, led by a *dux* named Wada, were said to have been the conspirators who had murdered Æðelred. The king's army was victorious and the following year two more of the conspirators were hunted down and killed. Alcuin, writing to his bemused master at Aachen, approved: the rules of the blood feud were immutable.[100]

But the king's troubles were not ended by any means. In the year 800 – the year in which Charlemagne was crowned Emperor of the Romans by Pope Leo III in Rome – another victim of Northumbria's blood feud was killed: Alhmund, probably the son of King Alhred (765–774). Then, at Christmas, a great wind 'by its indescribable violence destroyed and threw to the ground cities, many houses and numerous vills. Innumerable trees were torn up by the roots and thrown to the earth [and] . . . an inundation of the sea burst beyond its bounds.'[101]

Some of the politics behind Northumbria's ongoing conflicts are revealed by events in the following year, when King Eardwulf took an army into Mercia and attacked the forces of King Cœnwulf 'because he had given asylum to his enemies'.[102] After a long campaign without decisive victory on

---

* But see Yorke 2013, 90, for a genealogical chart.

either side, peace was brokered, as it had been in 679, by agreement between senior counsellors and churchmen. But if both Pictish and Mercian kings were harbouring Northumbrian exiles, it is no wonder that its kings struggled to maintain their rule.

Once again, Alcuin provides deeper insight. He had already written to Archbishop Eanbald that year in optimistic terms, sending him gifts: a little wine and 100lbs of tin and four lattices so that York's minster belfry might be roofed with distinction.[103] Then he received intelligence from Canterbury's archbishop concerning 'troubles' from which Eanbald was suffering. Writing to the archbishop again, he suggested allusively that Eanbald might be at least partly to blame for them; that he was playing dangerous politics. From the same year, a letter from Alcuin to two of his pupils, then in Northumbria, provides the devil in the detail. The archbishop had, it seems, been giving succour to the king's enemies and had been taking bribes of land from them in return. Why, the ageing scholar asked from his retirement in Tours, did Eanbald need such a large retinue of soldiers in his household – some of whom were criminals?[104] As for the king, Alcuin would not be surprised if he should lose his throne – he had repudiated his wife and was openly living with a mistress.[105] 'It looks,' he wrote to his Mercian correspondent, 'as if England's good fortune is nearly over . . .'

10

SHIELD-CLASH: 804–867

King Eardwulf abroad – The Eanred *stycas* –
Mercia, Wessex and the Vikings – Norham
– Green Shiel and the 'styca' sites – Civil
war – The fall of York – Epilogues

With Alcuin's death in Tours in 804 the last contemporary window onto the fortunes of Northumbria's kings is effectively shuttered.* In order to reconstruct the barest narrative for the ninth century north of the Humber, historians rely on off-stage noises from Francia, Mercia, Wessex and Ireland, and on dubious eleventh- and twelfth-century Northumbrian traditions.† There is no definitive regnal list or genealogy for kingship north of the Humber after 800. The age of Bede, the Lindisfarne Gospels and the great high crosses was long gone. But that should not be taken as corroboration of Alcuin's lament that England's fortune was indeed over.

If the frequent notices of raids on coastal monasteries in Ireland and the western seaboard reflect a wider trend, religious communities along the North Sea are likely to have suffered the same fate: from Portmahomack on the Moray Firth, where excavations have uncovered the physical evidence of destruction, to Hartness and Tynemouth in Northumbria, both recorded as having been raided by a late source with access to earlier, lost annals.[1] Of Northumbria's monastic communities, only that of St Cuthbert demonstrably survived the Viking Age, and that by relocating far from its spiritual

---

* The first, more or less reliable part of the Northern Annal ends in 802 – possibly not unconnected with Alcuin's own demise.
† David Dumville surveyed the standing ruins in a symposium dedicated to the ninth-century Northumbrian coinage in the late 1980s. Dumville in Metcalf 1987. David Kirby reconstructed what might be known of Northumbria in the ninth century in the same volume.

home. But historians over-read the doom-laden annals at their peril. There are few signs in the archaeological record of the widespread fortification of settlement or royal estate centres that would indicate endemic violence. Æðelwulf's monastic poem *De Abbatibus* celebrates a thriving religious foundation in the first quarter of the ninth century. York's archbishops maintained, if periodically, contact with their Frankish counterparts. Bishops at Whithorn, Hexham and Lindisfarne are recorded into the middle of the century. At least one Northumbrian king reigned for more than thirty years, and a still-thriving economy is evinced by settlement stability and by the widespread circulation of a numerous, if low value, coinage. In fact, the coinage may provide our most reliable chronological compass for much of that period and it speaks, literally in volumes, of a productive, thriving land. A decline-and-fall linear narrative leading up to the seizure of York in 867 by the Great Heathen Army does reality a disservice.

King Eardwulf, beset by enemies at home and in neighbouring kingdoms, was deposed in 806, according to an entry in the *Chronicle*. Roger of Wendover, writing in the thirteenth century but with access to now-lost Northumbrian material, recorded Eardwulf's fall two years later, in 808;[2] and that he was succeeded by Ælfwald II, very likely the son of the Ælfwald who had been assassinated some twenty years previously. To what extent Archbishop Eanbald II, or King Cœnwulf in Mercia, were complicit in the coup is unknown. Roger's testimony is independently corroborated by a modest number of Ælfwald's coins from a moneyer named Cuðheard, probably operating in York. But he was able to hold the kingdom for just two years – Roger has him dying in 810.[3]

The now twice-exiled King Eardwulf had fled to Francia, and there he was able to deploy otherwise unsuspected political capital – probably also a large quantity of cash – to gain the backing of an ailing Emperor Charlemagne, then at Nijmegen. From there he travelled to Rome to beg support from Pope Leo and also, perhaps, to make a pilgrimage to the tomb of St Peter. At any rate he seems to have been successful in his mission. The compiler of the contemporary Royal Frankish Annals took sufficient interest in Eardwulf's adventures that he recorded the outcome. After returning to the Frankish court, '[Eardwulf] was taken back to his own kingdom by the envoys of the Roman pontiff and the Lord Emperor... As his envoy, the Deacon Aldulf, a Saxon from Britain, was sent.'[4]

After that, the narrative trail goes cold. Ælfwald's fate is unknown; perhaps he ended his days in exile, either in Mercia or Pictland. The archbishop's career, once assumed to have ended in the year of Eardwulf's return from Francia, is now thought to have continued.* King Eardwulf's own resumption of power is also arguable, for a second reign appears in no insular notices. Before 1994 his reign was not even testified by the solid evidence of coins; the total is now something like seven.[5] Within two or three years of his Frankish adventure, King Eardwulf seems in any case to have been succeeded by a long-reigning son, Eanred – perhaps during 810, when a cattle pestilence is recorded by both the Welsh Annals and in Frankish sources; but no remotely contemporary Northumbrian chronicle survives to record the detail of death, abdication or succession.†

Roger of Wendover allows King Eanred thirty-two years from 810.[6] Such is the paucity of primary evidence for his reign that his biography might be told in a single page, were it not for the dispassionate testimony of the coins. Indeed, it is now generally accepted that numismatists do much of the heavy lifting in sorting out the complex and contradictory chronology of Northumbria's ninth-century kings. Some 740 coins are known from Eanred's reign – a third of them provenanced more or less accurately.[7] These are exclusively of a type known as *stycas*, each weighing a little over a gram. Almost all feature the king's name on the obverse, circling a central motif such as a crucifix; the reverse features the name of the moneyer. The earliest *stycas*, dating to the 790s, were made of a debased silver alloy, but from the fourth decade of the ninth century they are of a copper alloy or pure copper. So far as twentieth-century numismatists and art historians were concerned they are a retrograde coinage, by comparison with the Frankish denier or King Offa's stupendous silver portrait pennies. But numismatists are now reassessing both their value and their significance:

> It has been the convention to describe (and until quite recently, denigrate) Northumbria's unprepossessing, base coins as token *stycas*, but it is better to regard them as an attempt by Eanred to resurrect the silver penny or *sceat* following a three-decade long period of economic stagnation. The success in this renovation of minting through the,

---

* See below in this chapter.
† Alex Woolf interprets the Eardwulf coinage as evidence that his second reign may have lasted into the 820s. He provides a tabulated recalculation of Northumbria's coin-minting of ninth-century kings in his 2007 synthesis of Scottish history from 789 to 1070: Woolf 2007.

sometimes chaotic, mass production of base coins by Eanred and his successors and episcopal contemporaries, is due to the denomination being commensurate with the quotidian needs of the populace.[8]

The distribution of Eanred *stycas* both echoes that of the much earlier coins of Kings Aldfrið (685–705) and Eadberht (737–758) and extends evidence for the commercial reach of Northumbrian trade and patronage beyond its core. From Aberlady on the Forth to Whithorn in Galloway and Minster-in-Thanet in north-east Kent, they are found at coastal trading and religious sites, along navigable rivers and Roman roads and at so-called productive sites, often intersections on such routeways where trade was carried on. Overwhelmingly they are concentrated east of the Pennines and between the Humber and Tees. They are not (yet) found in inland Bernicia – perhaps partly because of the historically small numbers of excavations in this region.* The conclusion must be that this is a trading currency, its geographical reach echoing economic activity at settlements where surplus was either produced or traded, or both. The largest concentrations are found at York and across the East Riding. Whitby, Tynemouth, Bamburgh, Lindisfarne and Carlisle – all sites with both royal and monastic affiliations – have produced multiple finds. Unsurprisingly, the areas with the densest concentrations map satisfactorily onto Roberts's (and our putative) cultural corelands – with a notable gap in the Tees Valley.

Ninth-century Northumbria, especially Deira, was busy with some form of commerce. Wheat and meat surpluses account for much of the productivity, judging by environmental evidence from excavations. In recent decades the economic role of secondary products – particularly metalworking (iron production was a speciality of the Yorkshire Wolds), textiles and books, for which material and textual evidence is strong – has been much in evidence from archaeological research. Recently, another component has been added to the mix. Evidence from the study of chemical isotopes in lead from both insular and Scandinavian sites shows that Pennine lead mines, having been a cornerstone of the Roman lead mining industry, were once again productive from about 800 onwards.[9] Lead was both valuable in its own right – one thinks of the lead sheets that covered the Lindisfarne church in the late

---

* They are beginning to turn up in very small numbers on the Portable Antiquities Scheme website: https://finds.org.uk/database/search/map/q/styca.

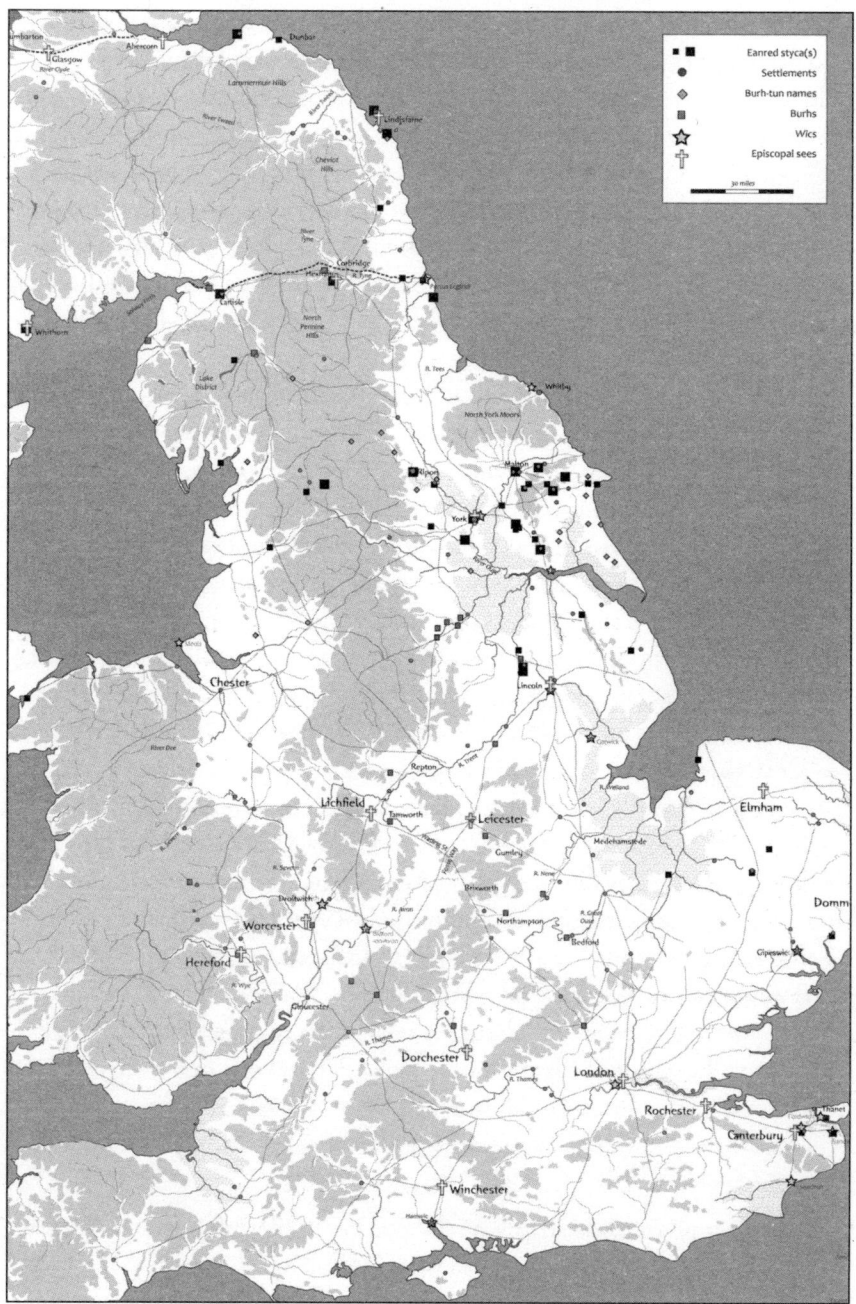

Map 20 Distribution of *stycas* of Kings Eanred and Æðelred II

seventh century – and as a by-product of the extraction of more valuable silver from the same deposits. Church window glass was held in place by lead cames; lead gaming pieces turn up at Norse military sites in some abundance.*

Given the riverine and coastal distribution of the Eanred *stycas*, and given their association with powerful and wealthy monasteries, it seems odd that little attention has been paid to the possibility that Scandinavian seafarers might also, and contemporaneously, have been trading with the communities on which they periodically fell with violence. *Stycas* turn up at or near their mainland camps in substantial numbers, including sites at Torksey on the River Trent and near Felton on the River Coquet/Great North Road.† Might one dare to suggest that the extraction of slaves, church plate and other ecclesiastical assets involved, at times, payment in cash? It seems overly simplistic to believe that seafarers were exclusively either raiders *or* traders: traders may loot; looters may trade. Just as speculatively, we might offer the idea that a base coinage lacking inherent value as scrap might be a pragmatic trading medium, obviating the propensity for Norse raiders to convert it into their favoured bullion bars or silver armbands. The corollary is that a currency based on alloy coins with a very low intrinsic value says much about trust – and the economic potency of royal authority. In any case, archaeologists may be underestimating the potential for these low-value coins to be used increasingly in place of the food and services which custom and law obliged them to render to their lords. Many of those lords were ecclesiastical; many *stycas* may have changed hands as tithe payments: renders commuted to cash.

North of the Humber only York (*Eoforwic*), which has yielded hundreds of *stycas*, would emerge in the Viking Age as a great centre of commerce and industry – its Coppergate excavations made world famous by the wealth of artefactual and environmental evidence it produced. York, Norse *Jorvik* – a royal estate centre and heart of a huge diocese, connected by Roman roads with all points of the compass, lying on a navigable river and with demonstrable links to Scandinavia, Francia and Frisia. Its archbishops were powerful territorial lords in their own right. They were on occasion collateral members of royal families, and their diplomatic reach must have helped oil the wheels

---

* At Torksey and at the recently discovered putative Viking camp in Central Northumberland near Felton. Kershaw and Merkel 2023; Hadley and Richards 2016.

† The Felton site has produced *stycas* of indeterminate date, which we have mapped for both Eanred and Æðelred II (see Map 20 on page 285).

of trade, as Alcuin's correspondence testifies. The seeds of York's Viking period dominance may have been sown before their conquest of the city in 867 – may, even, have prompted it.

If King Eanred could not command the imperial powers of some of his predecessors; could not, we must suppose, secure silver supplies from the Continent to mint his own silver coinage,* he was nevertheless able to control his mint and profit from the internal economic wealth of the kingdom: the coins of almost no other king penetrated north of the Humber during his reign. That reign is conventionally dated from c.810 to c.842, on the testimony of Roger of Wendover. But two coin finds have spectacularly overturned both his chronology and that of the archbishop who had plotted against his father. Eanbald II had been archbishop in York from 796 and was generally supposed to have been deposed on Eardwulf's return from Francia. But very recently a coin has been found, near Driffield, which proves that his career continued under Eanred. It belongs to a joint issue *styca* with obverse EANBALD (the letter 'L' is inverted) and reverse +EANRED R. Bradley Hopper and Tony Abramson, who have analysed the find, consider it to have been struck during the late 820s or early 830s, giving the archbishop, who also independently minted coins, including a silver *sceat*, a much longer career at the apex of the ecclesiastical hierarchy.[10] A further implication is that king and archbishop were in a long-lasting relationship of fiscal co-operation during a period when political instability is generally suspected – a distant echo, perhaps, of the relationship between King Eadberht and his brother Archbishop Ecgberht a century before. Might these men also have been brothers, or cousins?

A second, so far unique find, of a silver penny bearing a portrait and the inscription +EANRED REX, was discovered as long ago as 1774, in a hoard from Trewhiddle in Cornwall.[11] Stylistically the coin belongs to the mint at Canterbury and can be dated to the middle of the ninth century – specifically about 850. Historians and some numismatists have proposed an otherwise unknown Kentish king of that name; or that it was a memorial issue. Hugh Pagan has studied Eanred's coinage and believes that in all probability Eanred had a small silver *sceat* issue struck on commission by the Canterbury moneyer, there being insufficient silver in Northumbria at the time to service

---

* The implication of the new lead isotope data, and the single known silver coin of Eanred described below, may hint at a more local, regional supply of silver.

Silver penny of King Eanred

its evidently very active economy. Whatever the truth – and it is conceivable that others of this remarkable issue will one day come to light – numismatists are now adamant that Eanred's reign must be extended to about 850. This presents its own problems for Northumbrian chronology in the decades before the fall of York in 867.

Useful and dispassionate as these coin finds are, they barely hint at the political and military context of Eanred's reign, except to demonstrate his longevity. That context, thin as it is, must be sought on a broader canvas, to the north and south and in Francia. Charlemagne, the greatest ruler of the age, died in 814 and was succeeded by his only surviving son, Louis the Pious. That same year Abbot Cellach of Iona completed a programme to move Colm Cille's relics to a new mainland church complex at Kells in County Meath. Iona had been attacked in 802 or 803; and four years later sixty-eight of its *familia* were murdered by raiders.[12] Lindisfarne's mother church, the font of Northern Christianity, could not be defended by its former royal sponsors in Dál Riata.

The history of Pictland and of Dál Riata is deeply obscure during the first part of the ninth century, but Alex Woolf has teased out the very limited evidence to suggest a Pictish conquest of the Gaelic-speaking dynasty in the west by around 811 and the establishment of a pan-Alba hegemony, with cultural cores in Strathearn and in Fortriu around the

Moray Firth.¹³ A new ecclesiastical centre at Dunkeld, traditionally founded under the patronage of the long-reigning King Constantín (c.789–820) to house other relics of Colm Cille, was designed to appropriate him as a royal saint of Alba. Hints of Pictish involvement in Northumbrian politics are no more than shadows but since their mutual interests marched in the central belt, political, if not military, interaction is inevitable. There was certainly ecclesiastical contact.*

In his last years Charlemagne had been preoccupied by ongoing campaigns against a very aggressive heathen Danish king, Godfrið. In 810 Godfrið sent a fleet of 200 ships to harry the Frisian coast, exacting a tribute of 100lbs of silver.¹⁴ Godfrið's murder the same year paved the way for a peace treaty with Francia in 811, but in 813 Norse raiders again attacked the Frisian coast, with its concentration of wealthy trading settlements, and by 820 small fleets of raiders from the North were harrying further south along the coast of Flanders and then Aquitaine, carrying off 'an immense booty', according to the Royal Frankish Annals.¹⁵ Such predations were much harder to counter than land-based military campaigns. Periodic notices of raids on Irish monasteries and coastal settlements in these years show how widespread the raiding culture had become. In 825 raiders sacked Movilla, Downpatrick and Iona again, killing Abbot Blathmac when he refused to reveal the location of Colm Cille's remaining relics.¹⁶ By the late 830s Norse forces were sufficiently confident to take on, and beat, a Pictish army in battle.¹⁷

So far as Anglo-Saxon kings were concerned, such raids were as yet only peripherally significant; their preoccupations remained the subjection of neighbours and the suppression of dynastic rivals while they enriched their treasure chests with the fruits of the land. In Wessex King Ecgberht, like Eardwulf a former exile at the court of Charlemagne, had succeeded in 802 – his predecessor, Beorhtric, was said to have been accidentally poisoned by his Mercian wife.¹⁸ The *Chronicle* records a battle in that year between the men of Wiltshire and the *Hwicce* which seems to have resulted in Wessex throwing off Mercian overlordship. No further conflict between the two kingdoms is recorded until 821, when Ecgberht won a victory against a Mercian army. The Mercian King Cœnwulf died that year, perhaps as a result of wounds sustained in battle. His successor, King Ceolwulf, was

---

* Constantín, his brother Onuist and his son, Wen, are entered in the Durham *Liber Vitae*, as patrons of the Cuthbert community. Rollason 2004; Woolf 2007, 67.

deposed in 823 and two years later King Ecgberht's forces defeated the new Mercian king, Beornwulf, at Ellendun in Wiltshire. After the long eighth century of Mercian dominance in which two kings had between them reigned for eighty years, the fortunes of its great Icling dynasty had faltered, like those of the Northumbrian Idings. In 829 Wessex decisively conquered Mercia and King Ecgberht began to mint coins at *Lundenwic*. That same year, the *Chronicle* records a meeting been Ecgberht and King Eanred at Dore in what is now South Yorkshire, the ancient border between Mercia and Northumbria. Eanred recognised the Wessex king as overlord of all the English kingdoms and must, by custom, have surrendered a great tribute to him. But a king named Wiglaf reasserted Mercian independence the following year, and we may infer that Northumbria's tributary status was similarly shrugged off.

Within a few years West Saxon attention was distracted by a Norse attack on the Isle of Sheppey in the Thames estuary. In 836 King Ecgberht had to raise a fleet to fight a force of twenty-five Norse ships off Carhampton in Somerset; and two years after that the Britons of Cornwall, in alliance with a 'pirate host', fought against him in an attempt to assert British independence in the South-west peninsula. He saw them off; but told his Frankish counterpart Louis the Pious, in a letter, of an apocalyptic vison of darkness and of heathen fleets invading the land.[19] That same year, 839, he died (perhaps in exile in Francia) and was succeeded by his eldest son, Æðelwulf.* In Francia Louis's son attempted a coup against *his* father; and a very large Norse raid on Fortriu resulted in the deaths of the kings of Pictland and Dál Riata and the wiping out of the Pictish dynasty.† From that time, no English or Scottish king could pursue their domestic or regional policies in ignorance of the threat of seaborne attack. The first record of a raiding force overwintering on English soil, on Thanet in 850, marks the beginning of the Age of the Viking Wars in England.

* * *

Through these turbulent years Eanred ruled in Northumbria, minting coins with his archbishop and profiting from long-established trading networks sustained in the face of such turbulence. There is no record of a Norse raid on

---

* The father of King Ælfred.
† Two years later the year 841 marks the traditional accession of Cináed mac Ailpín, first as king of Dál Riata, then of all the nation that became known as Alba.

either the east or west coast of Northumbria during Eanred's reign; but that silence is probably illusory. So too, the failure of contemporary sources to record successive bishops of Whithorn and Hexham after the 830s is more likely to be illusory than real.[20] Against this backdrop almost the only internal notice of Northumbrian affairs comes from the dubious testimony of an entry in the *Historia de Sancto Cuthberto*, which says that Bishop Ecgred of Lindisfarne (830–845)*

> transported a certain church, originally built by St Aidan in the time of King Oswald, from the Isle of Lindisfarne to Norham† and there rebuilt it, and translated to that place the body of St Cuthbert and [that] of King Ceolwulf and gave the *vill* itself to the holy confessor with two other *vills*, Jedburgh and Old Jeddart and whatever pertains to them . . .[21]

Questions about the likelihood that Bishop Ecgred was in a position to donate such gifts have been raised on several occasions.[22] The distinct northern and southern components of the grants probably relate to separate acquisitions, and both may have been ascribed to the bishop through the mis-reading of disparate earlier sources. King Eanred might have been responsible for granting the *vill* at Norham if, indeed, it was not already part of the founding gift to Lindisfarne in the seventh century. More important, in the present context, is the record of a move of the church itself and the relics of St Cuthbert and King Ceolwulf away from Lindisfarne. Two independent sources confirm that Cuthbert's body, in its wooden coffin, was at some point taken to Norham; and the surviving stone sculpture there is regarded as suitably early.[23] How long it lay there and the date of its move, if any, to Chester-le-Street later in the ninth century, are matters of dispute.[24] But if we can accept that some time during the reign of Eanred and the episcopate of

---

* A letter survives written by Ecgred some time in the 830s to Archbishop Wulfsige of York in response to concerns about a book written by a priest named Pehtred which contained unorthodox views. The letter shows that Ecgred was literate and thoughtful, keen to assure the archbishop of his own orthodoxy; also that the archbishop's authority was still recognised in the northern diocese. *EHD* 214.

† Known originally, and named in other sources, as *Ubbanforda*. South 2002, 84.

Ecgred, St Cuthbert and, by implication, the bishop and episcopal seat, were relocated, a number of questions arise. Why did the community move from Lindisfarne; why to Norham – inland but lying on the navigable River Tweed and therefore hardly less vulnerable than Lindisfarne; is the orthodox interpretation of the move, as a reaction to the threat of Viking raids, credible; and what can be said about the contemporary fortunes of Holy Island and its church?

It is immediately striking that the Cuthbert community should so successfully have curated the original wooden church built by Aidan in 635. It had been superseded by a wooden church 'suitable for an episcopal see', constructed under his successor, Finán. That church was preserved until the end of the seventh century, as shown by Bede's recollection that it was then encased in lead sheets. Aidan's, presumably smaller, wooden original may have been preserved *within* that later building. The specific removal of Aidan's church, when many of his relics had already been taken to Ireland in the aftermath of the Synod of Whitby,[25] may be seen as part of a shadowy narrative in which the post-664 split between Irish and orthodox factions at Lindisfarne persisted into the ninth century; and that suspicion is corroborated by the story of the later travels of Cuthbert's relics recounted in Section 20 of the *Historia*: the unsuccessful attempt to take them to Ireland.* Aidan's church had itself, perhaps, become a holy relic – a life-size version of the sort of house shrine often constructed to receive and access a saint's relics. In that church Cuthbert and Aidan (perhaps Oswald and Oswiu too) had prayed; it embodied their sanctity. If the saint's and King Ceolwulf's relics were housed in that structure, it was natural to take them too; but it is hard to imagine that an orthodox rump of Lindisfarne monks did not try to stop them.

A cultural or spiritual split in the community is perhaps more credible than the idea that the whole community moved, with the saint and episcopal seat, to Norham when other Lindisfarne estate centres would have offered a much more secure location – especially when Northumbrian kings, or their proxies, lay just a few miles over the water from Holy Island at Bamburgh. Norham certainly provided economic security: a large shire-estate with access to ample resources – possibly even larger after the grants of land beyond the Tweed. It may already have supported a self-sufficient estate centre; but no more so than Lindisfarne. One possibility is that the

---

* See below in this chapter.

alliterative Beorning dynasty, who had been such prominent sub-kings during the late seventh and eighth centuries, maintained a power base along the Tweed – perhaps at Sprouston – and that they offered more active protection to the community than absentee kings at Bamburgh.

In any case, there is every reason to suppose that the church on Lindisfarne was not abandoned in the mid ninth century. An ongoing campaign of excavation immediately east of the Medieval priory in Sanctuary Close has exposed substantial areas of burial and industrial activity and, while detailed analysis is not yet forthcoming, the tell-tale of substantial quantities of *stycas* indicates very active occupation in the area of the monastery site across the ninth century and there are at least as many pieces of ecclesiastical sculpture from the ninth to eleventh centuries as from the earlier periods.[26] The cemetery was receiving burials from at least the eighth century until the twelfth, some commemorated by Lindisfarne's distinctive name-stones. Notably, however, the burial population included males, females and children – the cemetery of a township rather than an exclusively monastic settlement.[27]

Lindisfarne was never a merely ecclesiastical island. In the nineteenth century workmen constructing a waggonway from lime kilns in the sand dunes at the north end of the island came across ruined stone walls; they took some of the stone to build their track. Nearby, two coins were found and identified as *stycas* – distinctly Northumbrian and ninth-century. The site where the buildings were exposed is called Green Shiel. It was relocated in 1980 during fieldwork and a campaign of excavations was begun here in 1985 by Deidre O'Sullivan and Rob Young.[28] Their work showed that Green Shiel was a substantial farmstead, consisting of a complex of rectangular longhouses laid out co-axially, a series of fenced yards or compounds connecting them (see Map 21, page 294). The walls were of unmortared limestone, readily available on the beach nearby. Only the lower courses remained, but such structures of this tradition that survive in upland areas today are usually gable-ended, with walls to a full head height. Buildings A and B, aligned east to west end on end, were designed as bicameral compartments, with paved floors at the east end and a door on the south side. Typically, such buildings house humans at one end and livestock at the other. Building A had a hearth at one end and showed signs of periodic abandonment and refurbishment. A third house and its probable associated barn (Structures D and E) lay at right angles, facing onto a large yard area. A fourth stone structure (C) was internally divided into compartments, suggesting its use as a byre for milking, calving and winter feeding.

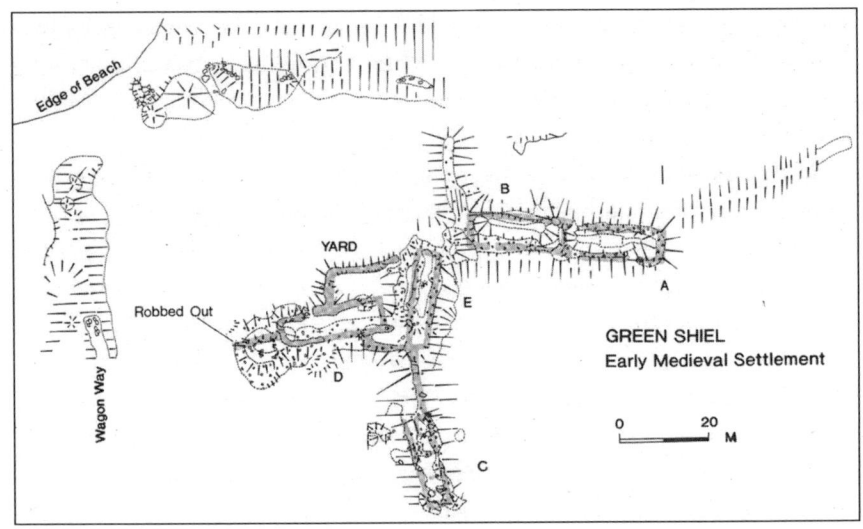

Map 21 Excavated structures of the Early Medieval settlement at Green Shiel on Holy Island

The farmers of Green Shiel apparently did not use pottery. Their diet was predictably varied, with animal and fish bone and shellfish common finds. A ninth-century spear head and iron key, a fragment of bone comb, a bronze strip, an amber bead and a small lead disc comprise the bulk of the small finds. Occupation of the site throughout the century is confirmed by the presence of nineteen coins, all but one *stycas*. The exception is a coin of King Æðelred of Wessex (866–871), the older brother and immediate predecessor of Ælfred.

The Green Shiel economy seems principally to have been based on dairying, judging by the age range of cattle bones. The farmers' diet was supplemented by fish and the occasional whale or hunted bird and deer. Before the post-Medieval accumulation of wind-blown sand on this part of the island, good arable soils were available in the area, and the excavators suggest that there may have been a ring of such settlements in these parts. How archaeologists integrate the Green Shiel evidence with that of the monastic relocation – or partial relocation – to Norham, and with the apparently thriving contemporary occupation in the vicinity of the monastery, is a question for future fieldwork and analysis. But despite its evident exposure to sea raiders, Lindisfarne was equally accessible to commercial trade and its mainland estates are likely to have remained productive. The apparently extreme jeopardy which the sparse historical sources imply in this period masks the simple fact that communities got by even in hard times: an odd raid every twenty years or so might have had less deleterious long-term effects on the island's communities than periodic visitations of the plague, a terrible storm or a drought. The relocation of Aidan's church to Norham seems to have been driven by other considerations.

If we take the presence of multiple *styca* finds as an indicator of ninth-century sites integrated into the Northumbrian economy, then a consideration of them as a whole offers a more nuanced insight into Northumbria's fortunes at the beginning of the Viking Age than the woeful, if sparse records of the chroniclers. At its most northerly extent, the *styca* distribution takes in the coastal sites of Aberlady and Dunbar. Aberlady has produced four *stycas* of Eanred and four of his son and successor, Æðelred II, turned up by metal detectorists and by a small community-led excavation in the Glebe Field. Here, in 2016, small-scale trenches revealed the presence of stone structures, following a geophysical survey that appeared to show two rectangular timber buildings. The artefacts, including two bone combs, are consistent with the coin dates and a radiocarbon date from one of the structures.[29] A cross fragment found locally in the nineteenth century suggests an ecclesiastical component to the settlement, which lies on the Forth estuary between Dunbar and the eighth-century Northumbrian episcopal see at Abercorn.

The archaeological history of the royal estate centre at Dunbar, which has produced just two *stycas* so far, has been described in Chapters 6 and 8. South along the North Sea coast from Dunbar lies the monastery of Coldingham, founded by King Oswald's sister Æbbe.[30] Recent small-scale excavations in the Glebe Field here have yielded suitable dating evidence and the possible location of the monastery's *vallum*; but no *stycas* have so far been found.[31]

Immediately south of Lindisfarne the royal township of Bamburgh, with its extensive township cemetery and ongoing excavations in the north interior of the castle, has produced twenty-eight *stycas*, many from metal-detected finds in the immediate surroundings, complementing a hoard of more than 300 *stycas* from an undisclosed site nearby.[32] Bamburgh fell off the historical radar in the ninth century, but evidently maintained its pre-eminence as a regional centre of lordship, if not kingship, and was well integrated into Northumbria's broader regional economy. Early results from excavations by the Bamburgh Research Project under Graeme Young have demonstrated that industrial activity was concentrated at the north end of the castle promontory. As at Lindisfarne, its township community – the inhabitants buried at the Bowl Hole – continued to inter their dead in the cemetery they had used since the seventh century.

Across the Tyne-Solway Gap, from Tynemouth and Jarrow in the east to Hexham and further west to Carlisle, *stycas* show up in more than trivial numbers, confirming the ancient routeway's continued use as a conduit for people and commerce. Whithorn, too, yielded significant numbers, and Hoddom a single *styca*, while finds of the coinage of Æðelred II occur not just in the corelands of Dumfries and Galloway but much further north and west: on Colonsay and North Uist. Here we detect the spoor of Norse trader-raiders operating in the former territorial waters of Dál Riata.

Like the late seventh-century coins of King Aldfrið, ninth-century *styca* finds are concentrated most densely in Deira: along the Rivers Ouse and Humber and across the Pennines in smaller numbers, with finds from all the major settlement sites in East Yorkshire, from the south side of the Vale of Pickering to the major routeways leading from York to the Humber along the edge of the Wolds. *Stycas* made their way along the Trent and have been found in abundance at the post-872 camp of the Great Army at Torksey. If nothing else, this shows how long some of these coins remained in circulation, a generation and more after their minting. Archaeologists are comfortable using coins to date the latest phases of settlements but in some cases, Whithorn being a prime example, they may need to extend their chronologies substantially beyond the emotively tempting end date of 867.

If that argument applies to the Anglian settlement at West Heslerton and to its even more substantial, but barely excavated neighbour at Sherburn, we can say that the southern edge of the Vale of Pickering between the coast at Bridlington and the Roman fort at Malton was fully integrated into the regional economy for the entire half-millennium covered in this book – and certainly extending back into prehistory. West Heslerton produced twenty-four Anglo-Saxon coins in all but it was, over the years, subject to high levels of illegal metal-detecting. If some, perhaps all, of the fifty-four unprovenanced coins known as Malton Productive Site 2 come from the Anglian settlement here, the numbers, and their value as artefacts, would be substantially greater.[33] As it is, their wide distribution across the site does not suggest that any one part of the settlement had been abandoned or was in decline – although none came from the concentration of houses in the north-east part of the site, where metal-detectors had been at their most predatory. A dearth of coins from the years between 790 and 830 may be a factor of a general decline in silver circulation in Northumbria; or of a reduction in economic activity at the site otherwise undetectable in the stratigraphic record. West Heslerton's economic heyday lay in the boom decades of the eighth century; but its persistence across the centuries is nevertheless a monument to the endurance and stability of Northumbrian communities.

* * *

The 840s saw a change in the intensity, perhaps in the aspirations, of Norse raiders. In 840 Louis the Pious died and the Frankish empire split and factionalised under his three sons. In the west, Charles the Bald succeeded and in his reign (d. 877) Viking forces began increasingly to penetrate Frankish heartlands along its navigable rivers and arterial roads, forcing Charles to innovate and refine a new form of counter-attacking warfare from which, belatedly, English kings would learn.

In 841 Dublin became the principal *longphort*, or pirate base, for Scandinavian raider-traders in Ireland, giving them control of the Irish Sea and its vulnerable coastal communities. The Channel port of Rouen was burnt by Vikings; and in the following year reports of destructive raids on London, Rochester, *Quentovic*, *Hamwic*, *Norðunnwig* (Norwich) and Nantes were recorded in the *Anglo-Saxon Chronicle*, Nithard's Frankish Chronicle and in the annals of the abbey of St Bertin. The latter recorded that they overwintered on the monastic island enclave of Noirmoutier at the mouth of the River Loire.[34]

In Roger of Wendover's chronology, probably based on a now-missing Northumbrian regnal list, King Eanred had died in 840 and his son Æðelred II had succeeded, the third generation of that dynasty to reign. Roger says that Æðelred was driven from his kingdom four years later by one Rædwulf.[35] His name appears in no other contemporary records and so he might be dismissed by historians, for whom he is a chronological inconvenience, but for the *stycas* that bear his name: more than 100 of them struck by a series of moneyers. Most of them are, unfortunately, unprovenanced; but the distribution of the few find spots to be recorded bears comparison with those of Eanred and of Æðelred. Rædwulf is particularly problematic because Roger implies that his reign lasted less than a year: 'he was no sooner invested with the diadem than he fought a battle with the pagans at *Aluthelia*,* in which he

---

* The place has not been identified.

himself and his general Ælfred fell, with the greatest part of their forces, on which Æðelred again obtained the kingdom'.[36]

For a single year's reign, Rædwulf's moneyers seem to have been awfully busy. Four years later, according to Roger, Æðelred II was himself slain and succeeded by Osberht, who reigned for eighteen years (to a putative 866). Symeon allows the same king just thirteen years.[37] Given the numismatists' insistence that Eanred must be allowed to have reigned until the late 840s, Roger's scheme must now be treated with grave suspicion. Many historians have wrestled with the problem. Two causes for the confusion seem probable: the lost annals or regnal list to which Roger had access contained serious errors or were cobbled together from contradictory sources which Roger confused; or more than one king was reigning in Northumbria at times during the ninth century and Roger has rationalised them into a single sequence. That is by no means improbable, given the historic semi-independence of Deira and Bernicia. The weak link would seem to be Osberht, for whose reign only marginally more coins are known than from the reign of Rædwulf. Roger knew that Osberht's reign ended within a year or so of 867 because of his well-attested role in the catastrophic events of that year and the next in York. Alex Woolf has attempted to reconcile all the evidence, squeezing Osberht's reign into the five years before 867, placing Rædwulf in 858 and Æðelred II's two reigns either side of him.[38] That still seems problematic given the Rædwulf coinage; but we must accept that the chronology of Northumbria's ninth-century kings will remain frustratingly unco-operative.

King Osberht warrants his own ignominious footnote, for the community of St Cuthbert remembered that he had 'stolen' from the saint two *vills*, Warkworth and Tillmouth: the former was part of the eighth-century Ceolwulf grant; the latter is recorded in the list of Cuthbert *mansiones* concentrated along and north of the River Tweed (see Chapter 8).* If nothing else, the royal appropriation of monastic *vills* in Bernicia suggests that Osberht's focus was northern and that he was unsympathetic to the Cuthbert community; but how we are to map that idea onto the removal, during the previous twenty years, of at least part of the community to Norham – 5 miles downstream from Tillmouth – is unclear. These are murky waters whose outfall can only be established in the broadest outline by retrospection from

---

* *HSC* 10; *Hist Reg* 854; *mansiones* may be understood as residences for a bishop or his officials on circuit.

subsequent events. At any rate, during Osberht's reign raiders in 350 ships were said to have arrived in the mouth of the Thames and proceeded to attack London and Canterbury. Coin production at those mints was interrupted; but in 851 King Æðelwulf of Wessex won a 'great victory' against a Scandinavian force at *Acleah* – probably in Surrey.[39]

During these troubled times the intercourse between English and Continental churches, and therefore also between intellectuals and traders in the higher arts, had been strained to the point of breakage. Two surviving letters confirm the discontinuity but show how keen ecclesiastics were to restore former bonds of friendship and gift exchange. Abbot Lupus of Ferrières, who had been taught by men who had known Alcuin, wrote to Archbishop Wigmund of York in about 852 when, he believed, 'the grace of peace is beginning'. It is no more than an acknowledgement of the 'great space of time' during which 'increased disorders' the ancient Anglo-Frankish alliance of churches had been disrupted.[40] But a second letter written by the abbot in the same year to Abbot Ealdsige of the minster community at York is more confident, asking him to send copies of works by Jerome and Bede, among others.[41]

The hope of better times was not, in the end, fulfilled. By the end of that decade Vikings were to be found attacking settlements on the Somme, Rhine and Seine. In 860 a force struck the West Saxon royal centre at Winchester and a year later they burned Paris. In 864 Charles the Bald issued a celebrated edict at Pîtres, in which he initiated reforms to Frankish military structures: forming cavalry units; ordering the construction of fortified bridges across key strategic rivers; reversing the decline in the quality of his coinage. The result was spectacular: as if Francia had suddenly become too hot, a great Viking force, the *Scaldingi*, now landed in eastern England, overwintering in East Anglia. The East Anglians submitted to them and gave them horses.* A Viking force remained in Kent and on Thanet while the bulk of the army, which became known to chroniclers as *micel here* or *hæðen here*, a great heathen host, moved inland.

The *Anglo-Saxon Chronicle*, whose pages are empty of Northumbrian entries during the preceding half-century, takes up the story:

866: This year the army went from the East-Angles over the mouth of the Humber to the Northumbrians, as far as York. And there was much

---

* Their king, Edmund, was murdered in 869 after a battle with the Great Heathen Army at Hoxne, and he subsequently became the focus of a cult.

dissension in that nation among themselves; they had deposed their King Osberht, and had admitted Ælle, who had no natural claim. Late in the year, however, they returned to their allegiance, and they were now fighting against the common enemy; having collected a vast force, with which they fought the army at York [March 867]; and breaking open the town, some of them entered in. Then was there an immense slaughter of the Northumbrians, some within and some without; and both the kings were slain on the spot. The survivors made peace with the army.[42]

The compiler of the *Chronicle* believed that Ælle and Osberht were brothers.[43] Symeon interpolates into this record the tradition that York fell to the Host on 1 November 866 and that it ravaged Northumbria as far north as the River Tyne; that the two kings were reconciled to each other out of desperation before their fatal attempt to recover York at the end of March 867. In the aftermath, he records the installation of a native, Ecgberht, as king in Bernicia under their overlordship. Danish forces ruled directly between Tyne and Humber in Deira.[44] The *Historia* adds that subsequently the Host returned to Mercia; but came back to York a year later and 'ravaged with its customary cruelty'. Inferentially, this is the period during which many monastic communities, such as Hexham, must have been despoiled.

In Wessex a year (870–1) of running battles against the Host across the breadth of Southern England below the Thames left King Æðelred dead. He was succeeded by the twenty-one-year-old Ælfred, fifth and last surviving son of King Æðelwulf.* In the Host's absence the Northumbrian élite expelled Ecgberht and Archbishop Wulfhere in about 872 and set up as their king a man named Ricsige. The Host suppressed the uprising, restored their proxy king and archbishop and then moved to Torksey on the east bank of the River Trent. A concerted campaign of metal-detecting and small-scale excavation of the site has allowed archaeologists to estimate the scale and range of the Host's activities. Their camp covered more than 40ha, defended on the west side by the river and by marshy ground to the east and controlling the confluence of the Trent with the Roman Fossdyke, which connected it to Lincoln. There is clear evidence here of trading, coin striking, smithing

---

* This narrative is more fully explored in *Ælfred's Britain*. Adams 2017.

and textile production, and recent estimates accept that the army and its camp followers must have numbered comfortably in the thousands. This was an army of occupation.

In 873 the bulk of the *Micel Hæðen Here* moved from Torksey to the Mercian royal minster at Repton, in the Mid Trent Valley, where they constructed a fortification which incorporated the royal Mercian mausoleum and church as a gatehouse.[45] The following year they returned to Northumbria, splitting into three groups. One of these, under Hálfdan, wintered on the River Tyne and, according to the *Chronicle*, embarked on a series of raiding forays against the Picts and the Britons of Strathclyde. A dramatic entry in the same *Chronicle* for 875 records that 'Hálfdan shared out the lands of Northumbria, and they were engaged in ploughing and in making a living for themselves'.[46]

In the *Historia*'s version Halfdan sailed with his fleet up the River Tyne as far as *Wircesforda*, 'devastating everything and sinning cruelly against St Cuthbert' (i.e. despoiling minsters belonging to the Lindisfarne *paruchia*).[47] *Wircesforda* has not yet been identified. The lowest fording point on the river was historically Newburn, the possible royal *vill* some 10km upstream from Newcastle. The highest navigable point is another 6km upstream at Wylam, close to the tidal reach, although there are hints that the river may have been navigable further up in the Medieval period. *Wircesforda* probably lay not far from Newburn and would evidently have been a strategically vital bridgehead for Hálfdan to take and hold. Subsequent events seem to reinforce the importance of the location.

Dramatic confirmation of the effects of the army's arrogation of territory in the North comes from the large number of Scandinavian place-names, either with Norse personal names or Norse suffixes *-by*, *-thorpe*, etc., and Norse names with English *-tūn* suffixes, the so-called Grimston hybrids that dominate Yorkshire. These are concentrated in the old East Riding* – they are almost entirely absent north of the River Tyne. At West Heslerton the latest, ninth-century occupation of the Anglian site is overlain wholesale by the marks of a heavy plough; its excavator, Dominic Powlesland, believes that this is the direct imprint of Hálfdan's sharing out of the land among his veterans.[48]

---

* Also in Lincolnshire, parts of East Anglia and the Midlands counties north-east of Watling Street.

Scandinavian place-names are a familiar feature of East and North Yorkshire

In executing the large-scale invasion of East Anglia, Eastern Mercia and Deira, Scandinavian forces at once secured precious agricultural land for their veterans and took control of the key trading centres and routes that gave access to the North Sea and Channel. That they were able to do so against competent military leaders and dynasts in long-established English kingdoms says much about the institutions through which those native dynasties had ruled. Their social, economic and military mindsets were based on a model of territorial lordship whose strong points were dispersed centres of consumption – royal estates and fortresses occupying often marginal landscapes. Against a battle-hardened, highly motivated and mobile enemy who knew England's rivers and Roman road network from long experience as traders, this static, centripetal model was inadequate.

In Francia, Charles the Bald had made the reforms which rendered such conquest much more challenging, fortifying his rivers with bridges at strategically key points and creating mobile cavalry units. In Wessex, at first surviving by the skin of his teeth, the last of King Ecgberht's grandsons, Ælfred, learned the same lessons the hard way, over a period of a decade and a half. Fortified bridges, the development of a defensible *burh* system and reform of his armies so that a force might be kept in the field at all times, allowed Ælfred to stem the tide and his son and daughter, eventually, to dominate all England south of the Humber.

Ælfred makes his own, superficially ludicrous cameo appearance in the story of the community of St Cuthbert.[49] The saint, appearing in a vision that the young king is said to have experienced while in hiding in the Somerset marshes in the late winter of 877–8, adjured him to have faith; to believe that the saint would succour him in his distress and bring him future victory – just as Colm Cille had appeared to the exiled *ætheling* Oswald at Heavenfield in 634. The Ælfred episode was almost certainly written retrospectively into the Durham tradition at a time when King Æðelstan, Ælfred's grandson, was making diplomatic overtures to the Cuthbert community at Chester-le-Street* in the 930s.[50]

In later centuries the Lindisfarne community, re-established at Durham, remembered various disjointed traditions concerning the saint and his see in the aftermath of the fall of York and Deira: how they had fled Bernicia, had wandered for seven years and then settled for the best part of a century at Chester-le-Street, a former Roman fortress on the banks of the River Wear in County Durham. In the aftermath of Hálfdan's territorial conquest in 875

> Bishop Eardulf and Abbot Eadred† bore the body of St Cuthbert from the Isle of Lindisfarne and wandered with it through the land, carrying it from place to place for seven years, and finally they arrived at the mouth of the river that is called Derwent‡ and there they placed it in a boat so that they might thus transport it across the adjoining sea to Ireland.[51]

---

* Or Norham, if Neil McGuigan's thesis casting doubt on the Chester-le-Street location is accepted. McGuigan 2015, 178–90.
† The *Historia* identifies him as abbot of the Cuthbert community at Carlisle.
‡ That is, Derwentmouth in Cumbria.

Whose initiative drove this extraordinary attempt is left unstated; the *Historia* makes it clear that Cuthbert's faithful followers, weeping and wailing on the beach at the prospective loss of their saint and patron, were distraught. Fortunately for them, God intervened: a great storm arose, huge waves forced the ship back and the water was turned to blood. Suitably admonished, the bearers returned to shore, carried the saint's body and relics to his *mansio* at Crayke, near York, and from there, a few months later, translated the body to Chester-le-Street. Symeon records variants on the story, as do other twelfth-century histories.[52] Significant doubt has now been cast on the timing of the move, if any, to Chester-le-Street, by Neil McGuigan.[53] Eric Cambridge, who has studied the Durham traditions, offered a key insight into the so-called 'seven years' of wandering: that the community, or part of it, displaced from Lindisfarne (or Norham), embarked on a period during which the bishop, like other itinerant territorial lords, visited his estates in turn along a long-established route between Lindisfarne and York where sites with Anglian sculpture and grants recorded in the *Historia* indicate that Cuthbert possessed *mansiones*.[54] In visiting these estates the community was able to subsist from their surplus by turns and at the same time reassert their proprietorial rights.

Many elements of the narrative are unconvincing, particularly the seemingly symbolic journey of seven years' length, which led to a traditional arrival date at Chester-le-Street of 883. If insecurity from Viking predation was the underlying motivation, passage across the Irish Sea followed by relocation to Crayke and then to Chester-le-Street, both well within zones of Scandinavian control, are at best illogical. We might, alternatively, see the continuation of a factional split, with a pro-Irish party led by Bishop Eardulf being thwarted in their attempt to take the saint's relics to Ireland (and thence where: to the 'Anglian' establishment at Mayo? To Kells?). We might also see, in the 'theft' of Lindisfarne estates under Osberht and Ælle and in subsequent gains for the community south of the River Tyne, a sense that Bernician kings had failed Cuthbert in their duties as patrons.

That the community might make accommodation with the new régime at York is shown by one of the most remarkable episodes in English history, recorded by the *Historia*, apparently out of sequence, as a sequel to Hálfdan's penetration of the Tyne Valley in 875.[55] In this episode, Abbot Eadred of Carlisle appears once again as the protagonist. The saint came to him in a vision and told him to cross the River Tyne and approach the army of the Danes. They would show him a certain young man named Guthred (properly the Norse Guðrøðr), who was the son of Harðaknútr but was enslaved to a certain widow. Eadred and the Danes should offer her his *wergild*, his head price, and then take him before the 'whole multitude' so that they may elect him king. He should then be led with the army to the hill that is called *Oswigesdune*; there a golden armlet – the symbolic token of Scandinavian royal power – was to be placed on his right arm and he should be constituted king. These things Eadred did, bringing the body of St Cuthbert to the hill of inauguration. The boy and the army swore fidelity to him (that is, to Cuthbert).

If the story sounds wildly improbable, King Guðroðr was real enough – his death in 895 is recorded in the tenth-century *Chronicle of Æðelweard*; he was buried in York minster. He is also the first Scandinavian ruler of York to have issued coins that survive: just one, so far, carrying the inscription *Godet*.[56] The realpolitik of this episode is more prosaic than it sounds. After Hálfdan's death in unknown circumstances, there appears to have been an interregnum. It was in the interests of the Danish army that a king should be elevated from Norse royal stock, and we may infer that Guðroðr's father had been such a man. His enslavement could have been the result of a number of misfortunes – as a prisoner of war, or captured by a Northumbrian warlord during the battle for York. We may also infer that Guðroðr had been baptised, perhaps by the widow in whose possession he was found. At any rate he was deemed to be a candidate suitable to both conquering and native élites – the Northumbrian élite, in this case, being represented by the imprimatur of Northumbria's greatest saint. The site of the inauguration, *Oswigesdune*, has not been positively identified, although elsewhere Adams has suggested that a prominent mound close to the church of the Holy Cross at Ryton on the south bank of the Tyne opposite Newburn, might be a suitable site for a royal inauguration mound.*

The support of the Cuthbert community and its bishop came at a suitable price: for the *Historia* adds to the narrative of the Guðroðr story the detail that the new king was to grant him (Cuthbert) all the land between the Rivers Tyne and Wear and sanctuary therein for all who might flee to the saint's protection. If Lindisfarne had lost faith in its Bernician patrons, it had

---

* Adams 2017, 169. A number of royal inauguration sites are known to have associations with the tidal reaches of navigable rivers: at Scone on the River Tay; at Kingston upon Thames, at Govan on the River Clyde and perhaps at Norham-on-Tweed. Alex Woolf pers. comm.

Ryton church overlooking the Tyne at its lowest historical fording point. Was the mound in its churchyard *Oswigesdune*?

found new lines of patronage among York's Norse rulers. After this date, with one exception, all subsequent land grants to Cuthbert involved land south of the Tyne. If there had, indeed, been a factional split among the Lindisfarne community, only the narrative of those who finally settled at Durham with the saint's relics survives.

* * *

The earliest Northumbrian ecclesiastical foundations at York and Lindisfarne long outlasted their original patrons, Northumbria's seventh-century royal dynasties. Subsequent to the political catastrophe of the late ninth century, Norse kings and their successors in turn became active supporters of the church, as did the descendants of the Viking veterans in their roles as minor territorial lords. St Cuthbert remained a potent force of regional power and identity after the Norman Conquest – his banner was taken into battle against the Scots as late as 1513. Bishops of Durham successfully retained their new landed assets, and their quasi-regal power south of the River Tyne, recording them in the *Boldon Book* survey of 1183, Durham's equivalent of *Domesday Book*. Into the nineteenth century those possessions still included estates in Islandshire and Norhamshire.

In exploring the narrative history of Northumbria across the half-millennium before the symbolic fall of York in 867, we have used models of territorial lordship to show how power was exercised in the land. Deeply ancient customary obligations between minor lords and their kings were exercised through a two-way system of patronage that extracted food renders and services, particularly military service in the king's warband, from known parcels of land in return for a life interest in that land. Small-scale lordships were grouped into shires administered under a system of extensive lordship which, despite periodic fragmentation, acquisition, theft and the vagaries of the fates, reinforced those structural relationships between territorial lords and their dependants across centuries.

After the introduction, during the middle and later decades of the seventh century, of new tenurial relationships driven by grants for genuine and spurious ecclesiastical foundations, investment in agricultural and intellectual surplus brought infrastructural cohesion, economic wealth and a cultural flowering. It led to a period of Northumbrian military overlordship and intellectual-spiritual leadership whose legacy survives in the works of Bede and Alcuin and the output of the monastic artisans behind illuminated gospels, stone sculpture and other material expressions of creativity. Bernicia and Deira were probably never comfortably unified – the one-nation

'Northumbrian project' was wish-fulfilment on the part of the Venerable Bede. Under pressure they split into their constituent parts and, in the end, could not compete with the more cohesive geographies and more fertile and interconnected lands of Mercia and Wessex. But the robustness of hierarchical territorial lordship, which substantially survives from parish level upwards into the present day, still seems extraordinary. It is a monumental legacy, written into boundary and place-name and in hundreds of parish churches across the lands north of the Humber.

The Northumbrian intellectual and artistic tradition was forged in the ancient three-way relationship between lords, their secular dependents and their holy men and women. In Northumbria, from the third decade of the seventh century, it was increasingly eclectic. Intermarriage, exile, fostering and the active, intellectual curiosity of a literate, Latinate clergy drew Irish, Pictish, Roman, Scandinavian and Frankish influences together. The innate wealth of the land, investment in productivity under the secure freehold of the church and the release of huge quantities of recycled Roman booty drove an exuberant literary outpouring, with Bede and Alcuin as outstanding Northumbrian scholars towering over the European scene. That exuberance extended to sculpture, warrior-bling, manuscript illumination and a rich aesthetic in textiles, architecture, memorial and poetry of which the merest, if suggestive, fragments survive.

Because of Bede's rich literary legacy and his brilliance as a historian and in spite of his prejudices, which have helped to foster an enduring sense of English exceptionalism, we also know that his world was one of great cultural, linguistic and intellectual diversity. His belief in a universal, united *Angelcynn* was an ironic myth. Northumbria was just that – a description of the lands north of the Humber and south of the Forth–Clyde isthmus. Even so, its distinct sense of identity and legacy seem to have long outlasted its existence as an independent kingdom.

NORTHUMBRIAN REGNAL LIST

This list of Northumbrian monarchs begins after the death of Aldfrið in 705. Before this date the genealogies of the Northumbrian kins are sufficiently secure to portray them as 'family trees' – see the genealogies on pages xvii–xix. Significantly long reigns are in **bold**. In addition:

* Claiming descent from Ida in Anglian genealogies; Latin (Roman) lower case numerals are regnal years from Anglian list Manuscript CCCC 183 (Dumville 1976).
** Only known from Anglian regnal list.
*** From Roger of Wendover, *Flores Historiarum*.

Eadwulf	less than 1 year (705)
Osred	11 years
Eadwulf	months
Cœnred**	ii years – son of Cuðwine, son of Ceolwald
Osric	11 years (718–729)
Ceolwulf *Cuðwining**	viii years – brother of Cœnred, according to Bede
Eadberht Eating	21 years (737–758) – **abdicated in favour of son**
Oswulf	1 year
Æðelwald Moll	6 years
Alhred *Eanwining**	ix years (765–774) – expelled
Æðelred I	iv years (774–779) – a child, son of Moll; driven out
Ælfwald I	**x years (779–788) – son of Oswulf; 41 coins**
Osred II	i year – a youth, nephew of Ælfwald, son of Alhred; tonsured and expelled
Æðelred I	vii years – returned from exile; assassinated
Osbald	27 days – exiled to Lindisfarne, then Pictland
Eardwulf	**10 years (from 796) – exiled in Francia**
Ælfwald II	3 years – uncertain and not chronicled

Eardwulf	[?] 1 year, second reign likely from coin evidence
Eanred*	**[?] 30 years (810–840/843 but see coinage) – son of Eardwulf**
Æðelred II***	3–4 years, first reign – son of Eanred
Rædwulf***	[?] months
Æðelred II***	3–4 years, second reign
Osberht	**[?] 19 years (to 867)**
Ælle	[?] months (867)
Ecgberht	5 years
Ricsige	[?] months
Ecgberht	2 years
Interregnum	3 years
Ecgberht II	6 years
Guðrøðr	12 years (to 895)

NOTES ON THE WRITTEN SOURCES

It would be hardly possible to write a Northumbrian history without *Bede's Ecclesiastical History of the English People* of AD 731, which traces the origins of the English, their dealings with other peoples of the island and the actions of kings and great prelates. But Bede is to be read with care: he wrote to give moral instruction, and, in his mind, history was the working out of God's plan for the English people. He derived his model of the ethnic cleansing of the British inhabitants at the hand of the English from Gildas, a Latin-educated British Christian cleric of the sixth century, whose text *On the Ruin of the Britons* was largely a moral diatribe against the actions of the kings of his day, within which is a historical narrative of how the Britons came to their ruin. From an earlier date, during the fifth century, the *Confessions* of St Patrick, gives insight into conditions in the early post-Roman years.

Life stories of some prominent individuals active within the seventh–eighth centuries, written within a period of some twenty years from late in the seventh century, have survived and, like the *Ecclesiastical History*, these can be quarried for historical detail of people, their actions, places and events. But these *Lives* are not quite biographies in the modern sense; rather, they were written within the genre of hagiography whose main purpose was to show the holiness of the individual concerned. Thus, the *Life of Cuthbert*, written by an anonymous monk of Lindisfarne, and Bede's own reworking of the *Life*, are to a great extent structured around miracle stories. *The Life of Wilfrid* by Stephen of Ripon, while conceived within this genre, is nevertheless more overtly a politically engaged narrative, a defence of Wilfrid and a response to criticism of his actions. The monastic institution of Wearmouth-Jarrow, Bede's lifelong home, is documented in the *Anonymous Life of Ceolfrith*, his teacher and abbot and in Bede's own *History of the Abbots of Wearmouth-Jarrow*. An anonymous *Life of St Gregory*, written within the monastery of Whitby, gives an account of the Deiran King Edwin. Also from Bede's pen, shortly before his death in 735, is the *Letter to Egbert*, his former pupil, then bishop in York, a sharp polemic against the shortcomings of the Northumbrian church at that time.

From the eighth century, after Bede's death, Alcuin, who became a prominent councillor to Charlemagne, king of the Franks, composed a long narrative poem, *The Bishops, Kings and Saints of York*, written around 780, reflecting on his early years and his education in York when Bede's former pupil Egbert was then archbishop; his *Letters* includes reactions to the raid on Lindisfarne of 783. From early in the ninth century, a poem, *De Abbatibus*, refers to an unknown monastery thought to have been a Lindisfarne daughter house and contains a hostile account of the Northumbrian king Osred I (704–716).

In addition to the narrative texts, historical information is derived from year-by-year brief listings of events contained in annals and chronicles. Bede had compiled a chronicle of world history in 703 and then a revised and extended version in his text *De Temporum Ratione* of 725. Then, at the end of the *Ecclesiastical History*, he included a chronicle which, in the oldest surviving texts of the *Ecclesiastical History*, runs to the year 734. This was kept up in a *Continuatio* (Continuation), now lost, to which Symeon of Durham had access early in the 12th century and which he used for dates up to 887 in the *Historia Regum*. Most widely known of these is the *Anglo-Saxon Chronicle*, with its origins in the Wessex of King Alfred (871–899). There are seven extant manuscripts deriving from a lost archetype which was itself a composite drawn from different sources which included material from Bede and from Annals, including a lost *Northumbrian Annals* down to the year 957. The closely related D (Worcester) and E (Laud, or Peterborough) manuscripts of the *Anglo-Saxon Chronicle* show strong interest in northern matters which D continued well into the eleventh century. A set of *Lindisfarne Annals* records accessions and burials of Kentish and Northumbrian kings between 616 and 704. These no longer survive as a complete text but are found in marginal notes with easter tables in one English and six Frankish manuscripts dating between about 740 and 830. From further afield, the compilation known as the Royal Frankish Annals, covering the period 741–829, makes occasional note of events in England.

A compiler known by the name Nennius brought together in Wales in the first half of the ninth century a disparate body of materials called the *British History and Welsh Annals* presented in the form of chronicles of historical events and genealogies. One section of this draws on British and English traditions concerning Northumbria, with Bernician and Deiran genealogies and historical events up to the death of king Ecgfrith in 685. A regnal list of Bernician kings working back from 737 known as the *Moore Memorandum* is attached to an early manuscript of Bede's *Ecclesiastical History* and a collection of records known as the *Anglian Collection of Royal Genealogies* and regnal lists gives lists of kings of Deira and Bernicia, as well as other English kingdoms. This collection is represented by four manuscripts written between the ninth and twelfth centuries, deriving ultimately from a Northumbrian source written between the years 765 and 774. Such king lists provide a basis for establishing chronologies, though, as our discussion of the *Moore Memorandum* and *Historia Brittonum* lists in Chapter 2 show, they are not without problems of interpretation.

Because of the Bernician kings' connections with the monastery of Iona and the kingdom of Dál Riata, Irish sources take an interest in events in Northumbria and Pictland. In a narrative text, the *Life of Columba*, founder of the monastery of Iona in the sixth century, written at the end of the seventh century by Adomnán, one of his successor abbots, gives an account that differs in some detail from Bede's of the arrival of Oswald to regain the kingship at Heavenfield. A lost chronicle compiled on the island of Iona noted events between the years 563 and 740, some of which concerned Northumbria, as well as Dál Riata and Pictland. These found their way into another now lost *Chronicle of Ireland* thence into the fifteenth-century manuscript of the *Annals of Ulster* and the incomplete fragments the *Annals of Tigernach* in medieval manuscripts and the seventeenth-century compilation the *Annals of the Four Masters*.

Historians active in Northumbria during the twelfth century provide another layer of historiography as they looked back to earlier Northumbrian history. Symeon of Durham traced the history of the church of Durham back to its seventh-century origins on Lindisfarne in his *Libellus on the Origins and progress of the Church of Durham*, drawing heavily in its first section on Bede's *Life of Cuthbert*, while his younger contemporary Reginald of Durham wrote a *Life of King Oswald* which contains some material not in Bede. A little earlier, in the eleventh century, a writer in Durham compiled a document known as the *Historia de Sancto Cuthberto*. This too traces the life of St Cuthbert from the early sources, but it is in great part a set of claims made retrospectively on landholdings belonging to Lindisfarne. Hexham too had its historians in the twelfth century. Richard, prior of Hexham, wrote a *Brevis Annotatio*, a short history of that church from its foundation to 1138, drawing on Bede, Stephen and Symeon. Ælred, a son of Eilaf, priest of Hexham, and who became abbot at Rievaulx, wrote a memoir on the *Saints of Hexham*. Somewhat later, in the thirteenth century, Roger of Wendover, working from St Albans, had access to now-lost Northumbrian material for his chronicle *The Flowers of History*.

NOTES

Chapter 1

1. *Res Gestae* Book 14, Chapter 5
2. Zosimus *Historia Nova* III.5
3. Sulpicius Severus *Chronicorum XLI*
4. *Res Gestae* Book 20, Chapter 1. Translation by Hamilton 1986, 185
5. *Res Gestae* Book 27, Chapter 8
6. *Res Gestae* Book 28, Chapter 3
7. Zosimus *Historia Nova* VI.5
8. Adams 2021a, 76ff
9. Van Der Noort 2004, 109; Dark 2000, 27
10. Higham 1993; Boek, undated master's thesis
11. Wood 2018; Collins 2012, 18
12. Wilmott 2010, 13
13. Wilmott and Wilson 2000, 12
14. Wilmott 2010, 13
15. Birley *et al.* 1999; Wilmott 2010, 14
16. Jackson 1982
17. Birley and Alberti 2021
18. Wilmott 2010, 14
19. Petts 2013, 319–21
20. Bidwell and Speak 1994, 103
21. Wilmott 2010, 14
22. Collins 2012
23. Roberts 2010, 127
24. McCarthy 2018
25. McCarthy 2018, 301
26. Hall 2011, 72–3
27. Petts 2013, 324
28. Petts 2013, 325
29. Wilson *et al.* 1996
30. *Hist Reg*; *EHD*, Whitelock 1979, 267; 272

31. Bede *HE* II.14
32. Koch 1997
33. Higham 1993
34. For example, Roberts and Wrathmell 2002; Roberts 2010; Wood 2011; Gelling and Cole 2014; Oosthuizen 2017
35. Roberts 2010, 121
36. Now available online at the National Library of Scotland's outstanding mapping site: https://maps.nls.uk/geo/find/#zoom=6.0&lat=53.39954&lon=-3.03050&layers=65&b=1&z=0&point=0,0
37. Roberts 2010, 121
38. Sources for these maps: Brooke 1991; Phythian-Adams 1996; the Canmore portal of Historic Scotland: https://canmore.org.uk/. Thomas 1992; McNeil and Nicholson 1975; National Library of Scotland Land Utilisation Map 1931–1938: https://maps.nls.uk/series/land-utilisation-survey/info.html; Aliaga-Kelly 1986
39. Bassett 1997
40. Dark 2000, 100ff
41. Dark 2000, 108
42. Tipping 2010, 182
43. Powlesland 1999, 58
44. Haughton and Powlesland 1999, 78ff
45. Penelope Walton Rogers: report in Haughton and Powlesland 1999, 142ff
46. Budd *et al.* 2004; Montgomery *et al.* 2005. Budd's report has to be read with caution: some of the oxygen data may have been mis-read, according to Dominic Powlesland (pers. comm.)
47. Gretzinger *et al.* 2022
48. Barrow 1973; South 2002, 125–9
49. Patrick *Confessio* I.
50. Thomas 1981, 312; Hassall 1976, 113–14
51. Forsyth 2005.
52. Gildas *De Excidio*; Winterbottom 1978
53. Gildas *De Excidio* 13–18
54. Gildas *De Excidio* 19
55. Gildas *De Excidio* 24
56. *HB* 56; Morris 1980, 36
57. Alcock 1971

Chapter 2

1. Bede *HE* II.5
2. Bede *HE* III.2
3. Bede *HE* III.1; III.23
4. Bede *HE* II.14
5. Bede *HE* III.4; Hunter Blair 1949, 53
6. Hunter Blair 1948, 99
7. Bede *HE* II.5
8. Hunter Blair 1948
9. Hunter Blair 1949
10. Hunter Blair 1949, 50–1; *Richard*, 1–2; *Reginald*, 339
11. Hunter Blair 1949, 54–6
12. Bede *HE* III.14
13. *Richard*, 20
14. Cramp 1988
15. Sherlock and Welch 1992; Cramp 1988, 74
16. Brooks 1989, 160–2
17. Rollason 2003, 20–43; 27; 28
18. Higham 2006, 400
19. Higham 2006, 405–6
20. Higham 2006, 408–11
21. Higham 2006, 412–16
22. Roberts 2010, 120–121, figs. 13.1, 13.3
23. Roberts 2010, 121
24. Wood 2007, 108–110
25. Neal 2007
26. Lucy 1998, 98–9; fig. 7.40
27. Lucy 1998, Gazetteer, 127–32; Buckberry 2004, 441–2; Pickles 2018, 24–5
28. Leahy 2007, 123–8
29. Lucy 1998, 87–9; 98–9; figs. 7.40, 7.41, 7.45; Pickles 2018, Appendix 1.
30. Stoertz 1997
31. Fenton-Thomas 2003, 28
32. Mortimer 1905, frontispiece
33. Stoertz 1997, 65; Fenton-Thomas 2003, 32–41, figs. 33–68
34. Mortimer 1905, 50–2; Barrow No. 127
35. Fenton-Thomas 2003, 146–7; figs. 35–8
36. Mortimer 1905, 264–70, fig. 731; Grantham, C. and E. 1965; Fenton-Thomas 2003, 149–50

37. Mortimer 1905, 247–57, fig. 621; Fenton-Thomas 2003, fig. 132; Lucy 1988, 26
38. Lucy 1998
39. Mortimer 1905, 294–5; Lucy 1998, 11
40. Mortimer 1905, 290–4; Barrow C44; Lucy 1998, 19
41. Mortimer 1905, 271–83; Lucy 1998, 42
42. Mortimer 1905, 245–6; Lucy 1998, 43
43. Mortimer 1905, 245–6; Barrow No. 112; Lucy 1998, 44
44. Mortimer 1905, 235; Lucy 1998, 45
45. Mortimer 1905, 358–64
46. Stoertz 1997, 34–9
47. Stead 1991
48. Wilson 2006; Oakey 2015
49. Evans 1989; Bidwell 1996; Whyman 2001, Chapter 8.
50. Loveluck 1996, 28
51. Stoertz 1997, 67
52. Stoertz 1997, 55–9, fig. 30
53. Abramson 1996
54. Hayfield 1987, 201
55. Fenton-Thomas 2003, 93–8
56. Gelling 2004
57. Fenton-Thomas 2003, 98
58. *HB* 56, 57, 61
59. Dumville 1989, 216–17
60. Charles-Edwards 1989
61. Bede *HE* II.14
62. Hope-Taylor 1977
63. *VW* 39
64. *EHD*, 406
65. *VW* 17; Bede *HE* III.26
66. Charles-Edwards 1989, 29
67. Bede *HE* III.21, 22
68. Charles-Edwards 1989, 29–31
69. Charles-Edwards 1989, 30
70. Kinsella 1969
71. Fern, Dickinson and Webster 2019
72. Bede *HE* III.14
73. Bede *HE* II.5; III.24
74. *VW* 20
75. Bede *HE* IV.26

76. Dumville 1977
77. Wood 1997
78. Bede *HE* II.1
79. Bede *DTR* 226
80. Bede *HE* I.34
81. *HB* 57
82. Hunter Blair 1950
83. *HB* 57
84. *HB* 63
85. *HB* 63
86. Bede *HE* I.34
87. Bede *HE* I.34
88. Koch 1997, xxiv
89. In the Battle of Gweith Gwen Ystrat. Lewis and Williams 2019, 6–7
90. Taliesin 6 in Lewis and Williams 2019
91. Fleming 1994
92. *HB* 63; Bede *HE* III.6; III.16
93. Breeze 2009
94. Bede *HE* II.2
95. Tolley 2016; Mason 2001

Chapter 3

1. Bede *HE* II.14
2. Adams 2013, 78–9
3. Bede *HE* II.12
4. Bede *HE* III.1
5. Moisl 1983
6. Bede *HE* II.5, 9
7. Bannerman 2016, 148–54. The manuscript of the *Senchus* is late fourteenth-century; but it appears to describe the world of sixth- and seventh-century Dál Riata
8. *Beowulf*, line 2195
9. O'Daly 1952; Bhreathnach 2005, 98–9; Bhreathnach 2014, 67; Charles-Edwards 2005
10. Kelly 2000
11. *HB* 63
12. Bede *HE* III.23
13. Bede *HE* II.16
14. Hind 1980; the meaning is contested; see Coates and Breeze 2000, 345 and Watts 2004

15. Jones 1975
16. Wood 1996
17. Roberts 2001, 280–5
18. Holbrey and Burgess 2001, 101–4
19. The survey is not fully published, but is referenced in Blair 2018, 240–1
20. James 2009, 125
21. James 2009, 132–3; Barrow 1973, 19–21.
22. Smith 1962; Faull 1977; Faull and Moorhouse 1981, I, Map 10
23. Smith 1962, end pocket maps
24. Bede *HE* II.14
25. Bede *HE* II.14
26. Jones 1975
27. Colgrave and Mynors 1969, 189, note
28. Faull and Moorhouse 1981, 157–63
29. Faull and Moorhouse 1981, 184
30. Clarke 2021, 173
31. Clarke 2021
32. Rivet and Smith 1979, 292–3
33. Clarke 2021, 175–81
34. Faull and Moorhouse 1981, 157–63
35. Wilmott 1993, 65–72
36. Wheelhouse and Burgess 2001, 123–48
37. Faull and Moorhouse 1981, 157–63
38. Wilmott 1993, 73–4
39. Alcock 1954
40. Higham 1993, 85–6; Jones 1975, 23
41. Kapelle 1979, 80
42. Wallace-Hadrill 1988, 75
43. Clarke 2021, 184 n. 74
44. Kapelle 1979, 80ff
45. Bede *HE* II.9–16
46. Bede *HE* II.9
47. Bede *HE* II.9
48. Bede *HE* II.10, 11, 18
49. Bede *HE* I.29
50. Bede *HE* II.17
51. *HB* 63
52. Rollason 2003, 88 is doubtful; Stancliffe 2007, 11–16 thinks it possible
53. Adams 2013, 76–8

54. O'Brien 2017, 229–30
55. Gittos 2024
56. Filmer-Sankey 1996
57. Bede *HE* II.16
58. Charles-Edwards 2013, 390
59. Parker 1992, 45–6
60. *Vit Greg Anon* 18; Parker 1992
61. Adams 2013, 124
62. Bede *HE* II.20
63. Bede *HE* II.14
64. O'Brien 2002, 66
65. Hope-Taylor 1977
66. Cramp 1957
67. Caroline Ware 2005 analyses the movement patterns implicit in the layout of these structures
68. Hope-Taylor 1977, 161
69. Barnwell 2005.
70. Hope-Taylor 1977, figs. 25 and 26 for this alignment
71. Hope-Taylor 1977, 200–3
72. Hope-Taylor 1977, fig. 29; 78–83
73. Hope-Taylor 1977, 181
74. Hope-Taylor 1977, 267, 280
75. O'Brien 2011 reviews these points in detail. Roger Miket and Sarah Semple now have radiocarbon dates showing that the massive palisade phase of the Great Enclosure is in fact Iron Age, though Hope-Taylor's seventh-century dating for the buildings sequence is confirmed. We are most grateful to them for sharing with us their findings from a programme of site investigations still in progress
76. Bradley 1987
77. Driscoll 2005, 169
78. Wood 2011, 64
79. Lucy 2005
80. Alcock 1988
81. Bede *HE* II.14
82. Waddington 2005
83. Fig. 1 in Gates and O'Brien 1988
84. Smith 1991
85. Smith 1991, Illus. 4
86. O'Brien proposed a mapping of this shire (2002, fig. 5). Its extent shown on Map 10 is slightly smaller than the 2002 version in view of

information kindly given by Dr Richard Lomas (pers. comm.) that the chapelry of Lowick was originally part of the Lindisfarne holdings
87. O'Brien and Miket 1991
88. O'Brien 2002, 66
89. Johnson and Waddington 2008
90. Stafford 2007; Waddington 2009
91. Gates and O'Brien 1988
92. Gates and O'Brien 1988
93. Gates and Deegan 2009
94. Bede *HE* II.9
95. Thwing, East Yorkshire: https://intarch.ac.uk/journal/issue25/2/4.4.57.html retrieved 04.09.24; https://www.heritagegateway.org.uk/Gateway/Results_Single.aspx?uid=79885&resourceID=19191 retrieved 04.09.24
96. Watts 1994, 320

Chapter 4

1. Bannerman 1974
2. Lane and Campbell 2000
3. Campbell 2007; Duggan 2018
4. Lacey 2013
5. Sharpe 1995
6. Bede *HE* II.10
7. But see Adams 2021b
8. Enright 1996
9. Charles-Edwards 1989
10. Dunn 2003
11. Thomas 1981; Adams 2021a
12. Sharpe 1995, 19
13. *Vit Col* I.9
14. Lacey 2013, 119ff
15. Judging by a story told in *Vit Col* II.3
16. *Vit Col* I.1
17. Adams 2013, 145; *Hergest* 15: Skene 1868
18. Bede *HE* II.20
19. Bede *HE* III.1
20. Adams 2013, 132
21. Bede *HE* II.1
22. *Vit Col* I.1; Sharpe 1995, 111
23. Bede *HE* III.2

24. Bede *HE* III.2
25. Bede *DTR* 66
26. *VW* 57
27. Wood 2006
28. Corfe 1997
29. Bede *HE* III.3–6
30. *Donegal*, 231
31. Bede *HE* III.3
32. Breeze 2005
33. Barrow 1973; Jones 1972; O'Brien 2002; O'Brien and Adams 2016
34. O'Brien and Adams 2016
35. *Vit Col* II.3
36. McErlean and Crothers 2007
37. South 2002, 47
38. Petts 2017
39. Petts 2017; Bede *HE* III.17
40. Bede *HE* III.25
41. Blair 1991, 47
42. Bede *Vit Cuth* 20; *Vit Col* II.16
43. Groves 2010; Groves *et al.* 2013
44. Castling and Young 2011; Kirton and Young 2017
45. Bede *HE* III.3
46. Gretzinger *et al.* 2022
47. Collins and Turner 2018
48. Collins and Turner 2018, 42
49. Bede *HE* II.14
50. Muncaster *et al.* 2014, 138
51. *HSC* 21; South 2002, 59–60
52. Kershaw *et al.* 2023; Muncaster 2019
53. Muncaster 2019, 136
54. Bede *HE* III.6
55. *AFM* 3303–3330. https://celt.ucc.ie/published/T100005A.html
56. Hermann Moisl pers. comm.
57. Bede *HE* III.6
58. Bede *HE* III.7, 9
59. Bede *HE* II.20; III.11
60. Bede *HE* III.7
61. Bede *HE* III.7–9
62. Adams 2013, 232–3
63. Tudor 1995, 190

64. Bede *HE* III.12
65. See Thacker 1995 especially
66. Bede *HE* III.9
67. Bede *HE* III.12
68. Thacker 1995, 98
69. Stancliffe 1995a, 33–46
70. Bede *HE* IV.14
71. Stancliffe 1995a, 43
72. Bede *HE* preface
73. O'Brien, Conor 2017
74. Foot 2018, 33; McClure 1983; DeGregorio 2010
75. Kendall 2008, 8–14
76. Holder 1994; Connolly and O'Reilly 1995; DeGregorio and Love 2019; Brown 2009, 14–15 for dates of composition
77. McClure 1983; DeGregorio 2010, 136
78. Collingwood 1946, 49–52
79. Bede *HE* I.15
80. Bede *HE* V.24
81. Bede *HE* I.34; II.2
82. McClure 1983, 90–2
83. Bede *HE* II.2
84. Bede *HE* II.9
85. Bede *HE* II.9–17; O'Brien 2017
86. Bede *HE* III.9
87. Bede *HE* II.20
88. Bede *HE* III.1
89. Bede *HE* III.2
90. Bede *HE* III.6
91. Bede *HE* III.9
92. Bede *HE* III.9–13

Chapter 5

1. Bede *HE* II.5
2. *Vit Cuth Anon* I.7; *AT* 643 retrieved 01.04.24 from https://celt.ucc.ie/published/T100002A/
3. Byrne 1973, 104
4. Adams 2013, 263
5. Bede *HE* III.15, 21
6. Bede *HE* III.15

7. Bede *HE* III.14
8. Bede *HE* III.14
9. Bede *HE* III.5; III.3
10. Bede *HE* IV.23
11. Bede *HE* IV.24; IV.23
12. Daniels 2007
13. Bede *HE* IV.25
14. Bede *HE* II.20; III.21
15. Bede *HE* III.7
16. Bede *HE* III.24
17. Bede *HE* III.7
18. Bede *HE* III.22
19. Bede *HE* III.21
20. Bede *HE* III.21, 22
21. Bede *HE* III.9, 10
22. Bede *HE* III.11
23. Bede *HE* III.24
24. Bede *HE* III.20; *Vit Greg Anon* 15–19. His head had been placed in St Peter's York after the battle
25. *Vit Greg Anon* 15–19
26. Lang 1991, 135–41; Higgitt 1995, 231; Karkov 1999, 133; Wood 2008b, 23
27. Bede *HE* II.9, 13
28. Pickles 2018, 128–35
29. Bede *HE* III.14
30. *Vit Ceol* 2
31. Bede *HE* IV.12, 28
32. *VW* 2
33. Bede *HE* IV.16
34. *Vit Ceol* 5, 16; Bede *Hist Abb* 7, 13
35. Bede *HE* V.24
36. Bede *HE* III.16
37. Bede *HE* III.17
38. *HB* 65; *ASC* A; Bede *HE* III.18
39. Bede *HE* III.24
40. *HB* 3, 4
41. Adams 2013, 283–5
42. Bede *HE* III.24; *HB* 64
43. Bede *HE* III.24
44. *AC* s.a. 658

45. Bede *HE* III.24
46. *Vit Cuth Anon* 3.6; *Bede Vit Cuth* 24; *VW* 60. See below in Chapters 6 and 7
47. Bede *HE* III.24
48. Bede *HE* III.14
49. Morris 2004, 2015; Wood 2008b; Pickles 2009a
50. Bede *HE* III.23
51. Morris 2015
52. Wood 2008b, 18
53. Roberts 2010, 124
54. Blair 2005, 143–60
55. Pickles 2009b, 18–20
56. Pickles 2009b, 5
57. Pacitto and Watts 2007
58. Lang 1991, 144–8; Hawkes 1993, 254; Morris 2015, 142–3. Lang, in the *Corpus of Anglo-Saxon Stone Sculpture* (1991, 136–8), has a different reading of panels 5–7
59. Morris 2015, 138–143
60. Pickles 2009b, 26–8; Map 6
61. Lang 1991, 133
62. Pickles 2009b, 21–2; Map 3
63. Lang 1991, 133, 215–20
64. Morris 2004, 22–3; *Vit Ceol* 29
65. Rahtz and Watts 2021, 284–6
66. Lang 1991, 161–3; Morris 2015, 144
67. Rahtz and Watts 2021, 290–2
68. Fletcher 1997, 524; Rahtz and Watts 2021, 306, 311–12
69. Bede *HE* III.23
70. Morris 2015, 126–35
71. Morris 2015, 132–3
72. Lang 1991, 152–4; Morris 2015, 146
73. Pickles 2009b, 24–6; Map 5
74. Lang 1991, 187; Morris 2015, 146–7
75. Pickles 2009b, 22–4; Map 4
76. *HSC* 5
77. Lang 2001, 88–9; Alcuin *BKSY* 1388–93
78. Adams 1990, 49 and figs. 6 and 8
79. Morris 2015, 145–6
80. Bede *Vit Cuth* 7
81. *VW* 8; Bede *Vit Cuth* 8

82. Jones 1979, 29–32
83. *Bede HE* V.19
84. Hall and Whyman 1996, 142
85. Hall and Whyman 1996, 137–40
86. Bede *Vit Cuth* 7, 8
87. Hall and Whyman 1996, 142
88. *Richard*, 14–15
89. Bede *HE* III.21, 22
90. Cramp and Miket 1982, 8 and fig. 6
91. Nolan, Harbottle and Vaughan 2010
92. Snape and Bidwell 2002, 111–27
93. Wood 2008b
94. Nolan 2007, 114
95. Wood 2008b, 17
96. Jobey 1967, 42–9
97. Turner, Semple and Turner 2013, 146
98. Wallis 1999, xxxiv–lxiii
99. Bede *HE* III.26
100. Bede *HE* III.28; *VW* 11–12, 14
101. Bede *HE* III.14
102. Bede *HE* III.27
103. Bede *HE* III.28
104. Bede *HE* III.27, 29; IV. 1
105. Lapidge 1995

Chapter 6

1. Higham 2015, 26
2. Bede *HE* III.24
3. *VW* 19
4. Fraser 2009, 200–1
5. Higham 2015, 148–9
6. *VW* 20; Bede *HE* IV. 12
7. *VW* 20; *HSC* 7
8. *VW* 17
9. Jones 1995, 29–30
10. Jones 1995, 30 fn
11. Wood 1996
12. Smith 1961, 155
13. Jones 1995, 30–6

14. Wood 1987, 24
15. Clarke 2010
16. Roper 1974, 72
17. Bede *HE* I.34; II.16
18. Clark 2011
19. *VW* 22
20. Watts 1994
21. Corfe 2005, 6–9
22. *VW* 22
23. Cambridge 1995, fig. 16; Bidwell 2010, fig. 41
24. Cambridge 1995, 79–80
25. *Richard*, 14–15, 183
26. *VW* 57
27. *Richard*, 183–4
28. Cambridge 1995, 73–6
29. Lowe and Brooke 2006
30. Corfe 2005, 21
31. Hall 1993; Bailey 1993
32. Bailey 1991, 21
33. Crook 2000, 92
34. Bailey 2013, 117–23
35. Wood, 1995, 15
36. *VW* 22
37. Duval 1991, 197–202; Reynaud 1998
38. Hamar 1970, 27–8
39. *Vit Cuth Anon* IV. 8
40. Bede *HE* II.16
41. Filmer-Sankey 1996
42. Bidwell 2010, 116–20
43. Hall 1993, 51
44. Roper 1974, 73
45. Bede *HE* IV.19
46. *VW* 24
47. Colgrave and Mynors 1969, 350 fn. 1 re: Bede *HE* IV.5
48. Bede *HE* IV.12
49. Bede *HE* IV.23
50. Bede *HE* III.26
51. *VW* 13
52. Roper 1974, 73–4
53. Fraser 2009, 211–12

54. *VW* 51
55. *VW* 36; 38–9
56. Barrow 1973, 66–7
57. Alcock and Alcock 1990
58. Kaufmann-Heinimann 2013; Blackwell *et al.* 2017, 45–67
59. Blackwell *et al.* 2017, 141; Blackwell 2018, 298–300
60. Youngs 2013, 411; Blackwell 2018, 300
61. Kaufmann-Heinimann 2013, 259
62. Maldonado 2013
63. Orsini 2017
64. Maldonado 2013, 7
65. Orsini 2017, 88
66. Perry 2000
67. Cramp 2005, 93–5, 101
68. *VW* 38
69. Crone and Hindmarsh 2016
70. Woolf 2007, 82, 235
71. Canmore https://canmore.org.uk/site/57717/tyninghame accessed 04.09.2024
72. *HSC* 4
73. Woolf 2016
74. Alcock, Alcock and Foster 1986
75. As Alan James suggests, 2019, 31
76. Woolf 2016, 169
77. Morrison, Oram and Oliver 2008
78. Nicolaisen 1976, 77
79. James 2010
80. Cowie 1977–78
81. Rutherford and Ritchie 1974
82. Forsyth 2005, 118
83. Smith 1995
84. Smith 1995, 117–18
85. Higham 2015, 140–1
86. Bede *Hist Abb* 6
87. Cramp 2005, 73–114
88. Turner, Semple and Turner 2013, 113–15; figs. 3.21 a and b
89. Cramp 2005, fig. 24.3
90. Bailey 1991, 14
91. Cramp 2005, 147–241
92. Turner, Semple and Turner 2013, 133, fig. 3.32

93. Bede *Hist Abb* 5
94. *VW* 14
95. Cramp 2005, 93–5; Hüglin 2011
96. Cramp 2006, fig. 27.1.11
97. Cramp 2006, 56–80; 126–55
98. Cramp 2006, 49–53
99. *VW* 16; Bede *HE* III.25
100. Cramp 2006, 37–49
101. Cramp 2006, 18–19
102. Turner, Semple and Turner 2013, 140–52
103. Bede *Hist Abb* 6; 15
104. *VW* 14; 47
105. Bede *Hist Abb* 6
106. Bede *Hist Abb* 5; 15
107. *VW* 16
108. Bede *Hist Abb* 9
109. Bede *Hist Abb* 6; 9
110. Bede *Hist Abb* 4; 15
111. Bede *Hist Abb* 15
112. Ó Carragáin 1994, 26
113. Nordhagen 1977
114. Brown 2013, 359
115. Bidwell 2010, 132
116. Bede *Hist Abb* 4, 7; *Vit Ceol Anon* 33
117. Roberts 2008a
118. Roberts 2008a, 127, 134
119. Dunsford and Harris 2003
120. Roberts 2008a, fig. 4
121. Roberts 2008a, 147
122. Roberts 2008a, 136–47; Tables 1 and 2 and 136–47 for this analysis, with variation in the units of measurement and other caveats on numbers carefully noted
123. O'Brien and Adams 2016, 15–17
124. *Boldon* 12–13
125. Bede *DTR* 15
126. Hope Dodds 1935, 301–6
127. Bede *HE* IV.12
128. Bede *HE* IV.21
129. Bede *HE* IV.12
130. Bede *HE* V.24

131. Wood 2008a
132. Wood 2008a, 6
133. *Vit Ceol Anon* 18
134. Bede *Vit Cuth* 3
135. Wood 2008a 27–8; 2008b, 20
136. *Vit Cuth Anon* 3.6; Bede *Vit Cuth* 24
137. Bede *HE* IV.26
138. Higham 2015, 202–7
139. Fraser 2009, 212–15
140. Bede *Vit Cuth* 27
141. Bede *HE* IV.26; *VW* 20; *HSC* 7.

Chapter 7

1. Bede *HE* IV.26
2. Bede *Vit Cuth* 24
3. Lacey 2006, 208
4. Ireland 1991
5. Yorke 2009, 9
6. Moisl 1983, 120
7. Yorke 2010, 40
8. Lapidge and Herren 2009, 12
9. Bede *HE* V.18
10. It is recorded in *Vit Ceol Anon* 13
11. *AU* 687.5; *AT* 687.5
12. Sharpe 1995, 43ff; see also Fraser 2009, 219ff
13. *Adomnán*; Bede *HE* V.15
14. Bede *HE* V.16
15. *Vit Col* II.46. Sharpe 1995, 203–4
16. Bede *Hist Abb* 9
17. Yorke 2009, 6
18. O'Brien, Conor 2015, xviii–xx for the chronology of Bede's writings.
19. Colgrave, Introduction, 48–49 in *Vit Greg Anon*, in the context of the tomb cult nurtured by Abbess Ælfflæd. Stephen of Ripon's Life of Wilfrid was completed between 712 and 714. Stancliffe 2013, 24
20. Carver 2008
21. Bailey 1978, 3–4. Its library catalogue number is B II 30
22. Bede *Hist Abb* 15; Bruce-Mitford 1967, 8–9; Gameson 2017
23. *Vit Ceol Anon* 37, 39
24. O'Brien and Adams 2016

25. Adams and O'Brien 2021
26. McErlean and Crothers 2007
27. Adams, M. and O'Brien, C. 2016, the Bernician Studies Group on Inishowen 2016: unpublished Interim report
28. Thomas 1971
29. Adams and O'Brien 2021, 162
30. Bede *HE* III.25
31. Roberts 2008a, 151
32. *VW* 63
33. Gelling and Cole 2014
34. Maddicott 2005; Kelly 1992
35. Muncaster *et al.* 2014
36. Blair 2018
37. Alcock 2003, 107–8
38. Bede *HE* III.21
39. Wood 2008a
40. *Vit Ceol Anon* 33
41. Bede *Hist Abb* 8
42. https://emc.fitzmuseum.cam.ac.uk/search retrieved 19.01.24
43. Metcalf 2006, 153
44. Metcalf 2006, 152–3
45. Adams 2025
46. Crabtree 2018, 118–21
47. Godman 1982, 5
48. Richards 2003, 158–9
49. Richards 2003, 165
50. Richards 2003, 158
51. Smith 2006, 85
52. Smith 2006, 148
53. *ASC* D and E
54. Loveluck 1996
55. Loveluck 1996, 44–5
56. Maritime Archaeological Research Agenda for England. https://researchframeworks.org/maritime/early-medieval-ad-400-to-1000/#:~:text=A%20second%20wooden%20revetment%20for,%3B%20Dent%20et%20al%202000 retrieved 12.03.25
57. Loveluck 1996, 29
58. Colgrave 1985; Adams 2025
59. Bede *HE* III.11
60. Bede *HE* IV.12

61. Bede *HE* III.11
62. *Vit Greg Anon* 18–19
63. Bede *HE* IV.19
64. Bede *HE* III.25
65. Bede *Vit Cuth* 42
66. Adams and O'Brien 2021, 161
67. *VW* 19
68. Bede *HE* IV.26
69. ASC 710; Bede *HE* V.24
70. *VW* 60
71. Fraser 2009, 200–1
72. Smith 1991
73. *VW* 36
74. *VW* 44
75. *VW* 44
76. Bede *Vit Cuth* 40
77. *VW* 46
78. *VW* 46
79. *VW* 43
80. *VW* 58
81. *VW* 59
82. *VW* 60
83. *VW* 60

Chapter 8

1. Bede *HE* V.21
2. *Boniface* Letter LVII to King Æðelbald of Mercia, 746–7, Emerton 2000, 107
3. Dumville 1976, 30
4. Wallis 1999
5. Bede *HE* V.23
6. *Hist Reg* I.47; 52; 201
7. Dumville 1976
8. *HB* 61
9. *VW* 17
10. Adams 2025
11. *HSC* 4
12. *HSC* 3; Barrow 1973, 32–5; South 2002, 43; 72–9; O'Brien 2002
13. *HSC* 3

14. *HSC* 4
15. Woolf 2018, 235
16. *Vit Cuth Anon* I.5
17. *Vit Cuth Anon* II.8; Bede *Vit Cuth* XV
18. *Vit Cuth Anon* IV.3; *Bede Vit Cuth* XXIX
19. *Vit Cuth Anon* I.7
20. Aliaga-Kelly 1986, 58–64; 70
21. Phythian-Adams 1996, 84ff
22. Barrow 1973
23. Quinton 2009; Elsworth 2011
24. Bede *HE* III.4
25. Bede *HE* V.23
26. Hill 1997, 12
27. *VW* 17
28. Phythian-Adams 1996, 61
29. Thomas 1971
30. Toolis and Bowles 2017
31. Hill 1997, 614
32. Campbell 2007; Duggan 2018; Adams 2021a
33. James 2009, 36–7
34. Phythian-Adams 1996, 53
35. Kirby 2011
36. Lowe and Brooke 2006, 8
37. Lowe and Brooke 2006, 186–90
38. Phythian-Adams 1996, 103
39. Phythian-Adams 1996, 60
40. Phythian-Adams 1996, 60
41. *Vit Cuth Anon* IV.8; Bede *Vit Cuth* XXVII
42. Winchester 2008, 18
43. Phythian-Adams 1996, 101
44. Newman *et al.* 2022
45. Adams 2025
46. Charter S89: AD 736. Æthelbald, king of the Mercians and of the South Angli, to Cyneberht, *comes*; grant of ten hides (*cassati*) at Ismere by the River Stour and land at Brochyl in Morfe forest, Worcs., for the construction of a minster. https://esawyer.lib.cam.ac.uk/charter/89.html retrieved 17.06.24
47. Charter S102: AD 716 x 717. Æthelbald, king of Mercia, to the church of Worcester; grant of land south of the River Salwarpe, Worcs., at Lootwic and Coolbeorg, for the construction of salt works, in exchange

for salt works north of the same river. https://esawyer.lib.cam.ac.uk/charter/102.html retrieved 17.06.24
48. Charter S103b: AD 716 x 745. Æthelbald, king of Mercia, to Ingwald, bishop of London; grant of the toll on one ship. https://esawyer.lib.cam.ac.uk/charter/103b.html retrieved 17.06.24
49. Wright 2015; Adams 2025
50. Thomas *et al.* 2022
51. Adams 2025
52. For example Æðelric, son of a Hwiccian king, now *comes*. Charter S94: AD 716 x 737. Æthelbald, king of Mercia and of the South Angles, to Æthelric, *comes*; grant of twenty hides (*cassati*) *in regione* . . . Stopping as at Wootton, Warwicks. https://esawyer.lib.cam.ac.uk/charter/94.html retrieved 17.06.24
53. Gelling 1984; Gelling and Cole 2014; Cole 2013
54. *Hist Reg*; *ASC* E
55. Bede *Continuatio*
56. Bede *Continuatio*
57. *Hist Reg*; *ASC* E
58. Wood 2008a; Sawyer 2013, 76; Bude 2016; Corpus of Early Medieval Coins: https://emc.fitzmuseum.cam.ac.uk/ retrieved 01.08.24
59. Blair 2018
60. Jobey 1959
61. Jobey 1959, 245–6; 258–9
62. O'Brien and Adams 2016
63. Blair 2018, 51ff
64. Coggins *et al.* 1983
65. Johnson 2015
66. Johnson 2017
67. Bede *HE* V.23

Chapter 9

1. Colgrave and Mynors 1969, 344; *EHD* 170; Bede *Eps Egbert*, 140
2. Bede's Letter to Ecgberht Section 6. Bede *Eps Egbert*, 142
3. Bede's Letter to Ecgberht Section 8. Bede *Eps Egbert*, 144
4. *EHD* 151: Whitelock 1979, 708
5. Bede's Letter to Ecgberht Sections 9–10. Bede *Eps Egbert*, 144–5
6. Bede's Letter to Ecgberht Sections 10 and 11. Bede *Eps Egbert*, 146
7. Charter S89: AD 736. Æthelbald, king of the Mercians and of the

South Angli, to Cyneberht, *comes*; grant of ten hides (*cassati*) at Ismere by the River Stour and land at Brochyl in Morfe forest, Worcs., for the construction of a minster. https://esawyer.lib.cam.ac.uk/charter/89.html retrieved 24.08.24

8. Blair 2005, 104
9. Bede *HE* V.4, 5, 6
10. Bede *HE* V.3; Blair 2005, 105
11. Bede *Eps Egbert*, 12, 147–8
12. Collingham: Coatsworth 2008, 117–19; Lang 1999, 276–9; Dewsbury: Coatsworth 2008, 129–33; Lang 1999, 273–5; Otley: Coatsworth 2008, 215–19; Lang 2000, 113–14
13. Easby: Lang 1999, 273–4; 2001, 98–102; Masham: Lang 1999, 273–7; 2001, 168–71; Halton: Bailey 2010, 185–7
14. Lang 1990, 2; 1999; 2000, 111; 2001, 9
15. *De Abbatibus* 11: Campbell 1967
16. *De Abbatibus* 2: Campbell 1967
17. Campbell 1967, xxix
18. Taylor 1974
19. *De Abbatibus* 10
20. *De Abbatibus* Section 21
21. *De Abbatibus* Section 8
22. Campbell 1989, 11–12
23. O'Brien and Adams 2016 and see above, Chapter 4
24. Adams 2025
25. Adams 2025 and see above, Chapter 6
26. *Libellus* II.13
27. South 2002, 25–32
28. Barrow 1973, 2–35 re *HSC* 3
29. Raine 1852
30. *HSC* 9
31. *HSC* 21
32. O'Brien 2002
33. O'Brien 2002, 66–7
34. South 2002, 80 reads this as the Blackadder
35. *HSC* 5–7
36. *HSC* 5. See above Chapter 6 re Crayke
37. Bede *Vit Cuth* 27
38. Discussed by South 2002, 81–2
39. O'Brien, Adams and Whaley 2018, 99
40. *HSC* 8, 11

41. O'Brien 2002, 56–61; O'Brien 2023, 196–7
42. O'Brien, Adams and Whaley 2018, 79–99
43. *HSC* 9
44. South 2002, 84
45. Roberts 2008b, 155, fig. 6.2
46. Austin 1976, 73–4
47. Roberts 2008b, 155, fig. 6.2
48. Craster 1954, 187
49. *Hist Reg* 2, 65
50. Cramp 1984, 51–2
51. O'Brien 2023
52. *Hist Reg*; *ASC*
53. Charter S90: AD 742 (*Clofesho*). Æthelbald, king of Mercia, to the Kentish churches; confirmation of privileges. https://esawyer.lib.cam.ac.uk/charter/90.html retrieved 24.08.24
54. *Boniface* Letters LVII; *EHD* 177
55. *Boniface* Letters LXII
56. Keynes 1993, 6
57. Johnson 1850, Volume 1, 238
58. Johnson 1850, Volume 1, 238
59. Levison 1946, 18
60. *EHD* 184; *Cart Sax* 184: Birch 1885
61. Thomas *et al.* 2022; Adams 2025, pp. 229–30
62. Blair 2018
63. Blair 2018
64. *EHD* 185
65. Bude 2016
66. Hamerow 2012
67. Blair 2018
68. Pagan 2018, 21ff
69. Bede *Continuatio. EHD* 5
70. Bede *Continuatio. EHD* 5
71. *Hist Reg. EHD* 3
72. *EHD* 185
73. *Hist Reg. EHD* 3
74. *AT* 764
75. Kirby 2000, 127
76. Alcuin *BKSY*, line 1429
77. Alcuin *BKSY*, lines 1393 onwards; Ward 2012
78. Alcuin *BKSY*, lines 1495–1515; 1

79. *EHD* 187
80. *EHD* 159
81. *EHD* 159; Whitelock 1979, 788–9
82. *Hist Reg. EHD* 3
83. *Libellus* II.4
84. Fulda – Manuscript: Wien, Österreichische Nationalbibliothek, cod. 652, fol. 2v
85. Story 2003, 150ff
86. *EHD* 191, Wormald 1991
87. *ASC* 789
88. Alcuin *Epp.* Allott 1974, 35
89. Alcuin *Epp* 9. Allott 1974, 14–15
90. Alcuin *Epp* 10. Allott 1974, 16–17
91. *ASC* 793: Garmonsway 1972, 54–6
92. *VW* 67
93. *EHD* 193: Whitelock 1979, 842–4
94. *Hist Reg. EHD* 3
95. *Hist Reg. EHD* 3
96. Alcuin *Epp* 7. Allott 1974, 10
97. Stevenson 1855, 455
98. Alcuin *Epp* 16. Allott 1974, 24–5
99. *Hist Reg. EHD* 3
100. *EHD* 206
101. *Hist Reg.* Stevenson 1855, 462
102. *Hist Reg.* Stevenson 1855, 463
103. Alcuin *Epp* 19. Allott 1974, 27–8
104. Alcuin *Epp* 21. Allott 1974, 30–1
105. Alcuin *Epp* 46. Allott 1974, 57–8

Chapter 10

1. *RWE*, 169
2. *RWE*, 172
3. *RWE*, 172
4. *RFA*, 808
5. Pagan 2018, 29
6. *RWE*, 172
7. According to the online Early Medieval Coin corpus maintained by the Fitzwilliam Museum in Cambridge. https://emc.fitzmuseum.cam. ac.uk/advanced-results?rulername%5B%5D=Eanred&Find-spot=&e

mcnumb=&Preservation=&startdate=&enddate=&emc-scbi= retrieved 20.08.24
8. Bradley Hopper and Tony Adamson. British Numismatic Journal blog, November 2021. https://britnumsoc.blog/2021/11/12/a-unique-joint-issue-of-king-eanred-of-northumbrian-and-archbishop-eanbald-ii-bradley-hopper-tony-abramson/ retrieved 20.08.24
9. Kershaw and Merkel 2023
10. British Numismatic Journal blog, November 2021. https://britnumsoc.blog/2021/11/12/a-unique-joint-issue-of-king-eanred-of-northumbrian-and-archbishop-eanbald-ii-bradley-hopper-tony-abramson/ retrieved 20.08.24
11. Pagan 2018, 30ff
12. *AU*
13. Woolf 2007, 63–5
14. *RFA* 810. Scholz 1972, 91–2
15. *RFA*. Scholz 1972, 107
16. *AU* 825
17. *AU* 839.9. Woolf 2007, 66
18. *ASC*
19. *ASB*. Nelson 1991, 43. Nelson interprets the letter as having been sent by his son and immediate successor, Æðelwulf.
20. McGuigan 2015, 58ff
21. *HSC* 9. South 2002, 50
22. South 2002, 84–5; O'Brien *et al.* 2018
23. South 2002, 84; Cambridge 1989, 375
24. McGuigan 2019
25. Bede *HE* III.26
26. Petts and Wilkins 2022, 480; Cramp 1984 194–251
27. Petts and Wilkins 2022, 478–9
28. O'Sullivan and Young 1995
29. Discovery and Excavation in Scotland 17, 2016: 58. https://www.archaeologyscotland.org.uk/wp-content/uploads/2022/05/2016.pdf retrieved 23.08.24
30. Bede *HE* IV.25
31. https://digventures.com/wp-content/uploads/2022/06/Col18_EvaluationReport_V2–0.pdf retrieved 23.08.24
32. Pirie 2004
33. Unpublished coin report, kindly provided by Dominic Powlesland
34. *ASC*; Scholz 1972, 167–8; Nelson 1991, 52–3; 56n
35. *RWE*. Giles 1849, 180

36. *RWE*. Giles 1849, 180
37. Stevenson 1855, 761
38. Woolf 2007, 69
39. *ASC*
40. *EHD* 217
41. *EHD* 218
42. *ASC* E under 865, correctly 866. Giles 1914
43. *HSC* 10
44. *Libellus* II.6
45. Biddle and Kjølbye-Biddle 1992
46. *ASC* E
47. *HSC* 13
48. Powlesland pers. comm.
49. *HSC* 14–19a
50. Adams 2017, 366
51. *HSC* 20
52. South 2002, 95ff
53. McGuigan 2015; 2019
54. Cambridge 1989
55. *HSC* 13
56. Gooch 2012, 46

BIBLIOGRAPHY

Abbreviations and primary sources

AC *Annales Cambriae*, The Welsh Annals. Morris, J. (ed. and trans.) 1980 *Nennius: British History and the Welsh Annals*. London and Chichester: Phillimore.

Adomnán Meehan, D. (ed. and trans.) 1983 *Adamnan's De Locis Sanctis*. Dublin: Dublin Institute for Advanced Studies

Æthelweard Campbell, A. (ed. and trans) 1962 *The Chronicle of Æthelweard*. London: Nelson's Medieval texts.

AFM *Annals of the Four Masters*. CELT: The Corpus of Electronic Texts. https://celt.ucc.ie/published/T100005A/ retrieved 15.11.24.

Alcuin *BKSY* Godman, P. 1982 *The Bishops, Kings, and Saints of York*. Oxford: Clarendon Press.

Alcuin *Epp* Allott, S. 1974 *Alcuin of York, c.* AD *732 to 804: His Life and Letters*. York: William Sessions.

Annales Lindisfarnenses Levison, W. 1961 Die Annales 'Lindisfarnenses et Dunemenses' kritisch untersucht und neu herausgegeben. https://www.digizeitschriften.de/id/345858735_0017%7Clog41?tify=%7B%22pages%22%3A%5B465%5D%2C%22view%22%3A%22info%22%7D retrieved 29.09.24.

ASB Nelson, J.L. (trans.) 1991 *The Annals of St Bertin: Ninth Century Histories, Volume 1*. Manchester: Manchester University Press (Manchester Medieval Sources).

ASC Garmonsway, G.N. (ed.) 1972 *The Anglo-Saxon Chronicle*. London: J.M. Dent.

AT *The Annals of Tigernach*. CELT: The Corpus of Electronic Texts. https://celt.ucc.ie/published/T100002A/ retrieved 16.09.24.

AU *The Annals of Ulster* https://celt.ucc.ie/published/T100001A/index.html retrieved 16.09.24.

Bede *Continuatio* Continuations from the Moore Manuscript. Colgrave, B. and Mynors, R.A.B. (eds and trans.) 1969 *Bede's Ecclesiastical History*. Oxford: Clarendon Press, 572–577.

Bede *DTR* *De Temporum Ratione*. Wallis, F. (trans.) 1999 *Bede: The*

Reckoning of Time. Liverpool: Liverpool University Press (Translated Texts for Historians, Volume 29).

Bede *Eps Egbert*   Bede's Letter to Egbert. Giles, J.A. 1843 *The Historical Works of Venerable Bede*. London: James Bohn, 138–55. https://archive.org/details/historicalworks002bede/page/n21/mode/2up   retrieved 23.05.24.

Bede *HE*   Historia Ecclesiastica. Colgrave, B. and Mynors, R.A.B. (eds and trans.) 1969 *Bede's Ecclesiastical History*. Oxford: Clarendon Press.

Bede *Hist Abb*   Historia Abbatum. Grocock, C. and Wood, I.N. (eds and trans.) 2013 *Abbots of Wearmouth and Jarrow*. Oxford: Clarendon Press (Oxford Medieval Texts), 22–75.

Bede *Vit Cuth*   Vita Sancti Cuthberti, The Life of Cuthbert by Bede. Colgrave, B. (ed. and trans.) 1940 *Two Lives of Saint Cuthbert*. Cambridge: Cambridge University Press.

Beowulf   Alexander, M. (ed. and trans.) 1973 *Beowulf*. London: Penguin.

Boldon   Austin, D. (ed. and trans.) 1982 *Boldon Book: Northumberland and Durham*. London: Phillimore.

Boniface   Emerton, E. (trans.) and Noble, T.F.X. (ed.) 2000 *The Letters of Saint Boniface*. Chichester: Columbia University Press.

CA   Campbell, A. 1962 (ed. and trans.) *The Chronicle of Æthelweard*. London: Nelson's Medieval texts.

Cart Sax   Birch, W. de G. (ed.) 1885 *Cartularium Saxonicum: A Collection of Charters Relating to Anglo-Saxon History. Volume 1, AD 430–839*. Cambridge: Cambridge University Press edition 2012.

Chronica Gallica   Burgess, R. 2001 The Gallic Chronicle of 452: A New Critical Edition with a Brief Introduction. In Mathisen, R.W. and Shanzer, D. (eds), *Society and Culture in Late Antique Gaul: Revisiting the Sources*. Aldershot: Ashgate.

De Abbatibus   Campbell, A. 1967 *Æthelwulf: De Abbatibus*. Oxford: Clarendon Press.

Donegal   Todd, J.H. and Reeves, W. 1864 *The Martyrology of Donegal: A Calendar of the Saints of Ireland*. Dublin: Irish Archaeological and Celtic Society.

EHD   Whitelock, D. (ed.) 1979 *English Historical Documents*, Volume 1, 2nd edition. London: Eyre Methuen.

Flores Historiarum   Giles, J.A. 1849 *Roger of Wendover's Flowers of History*. London: Henry G. Bohn.

Gildas *De Excidio*   De Excidio Britonum. Winterbottom, M. (ed. and trans.) 1978 *Gildas: The Ruin of Britain and Other Works*. London and Chichester: Phillimore.

HB *Historia Brittonum*. Morris, J. (ed. and trans.) 1980 *Nennius: British History and the Welsh Annals*. London and Chichester: Phillimore.

Hergest The Red Book of Hergest. Skene, W.F. 1868 *The Four Ancient Books of Wales*. Edinburgh: Edmonston and Douglas.

Hist Reg *Historia Regum*. Arnold. T. (ed.) 1883–5. *Symeonis Monachi Opera Omnia*, Volumes 1 and 2. London (Rolls Series 75).

HSC South, T.J. (ed. and trans.) 2002 *Historia de Sancto Cuthberto: A History of Saint Cuthbert and a Record of His Patrimony*. Cambridge: D.S. Brewer (Anglo-Saxon Texts 3).

Libellus Rollason, D. 2000 *Symeon of Durham*: Libellus de exordio atque procursu istius hoc est Dunhelmensis ecclesiae. *Tract on the Origins and progress of this the Church of Durham*. Oxford: Clarendon Press.

NHF Scholtz, B.W. (trans.) 1972 *Carolingian Chronicles: Royal Frankish Annals and Nithard's Histories*. Ann Arbor, MI: University of Michigan Press.

Patrick Confessio Hood, A.B.E. (ed. and trans.) 1978 *St Patrick: His Writings and Muirchu's Life*. London and Chichester: Phillimore.

Reginald (of Durham) Arnold, T. (ed.) 1882 *Symeonis monachi opera omnia. Volume 1 Historiae Ecclesiae Dunelmensis*. Cambridge: Cambridge University Press 2012 edition.

Res Gestae (of Ammianus Marcellinus) Hamilton, W. 1996 *Ammianus Marcellinus: the Later Roman Empire (AD 354–378)*. Harmondsworth: Penguin (Penguin Classics).

RFA Scholtz, B.W. (trans.) 1972 *Carolingian Chronicles: Royal Frankish Annals and Nithard's Histories*. University of Michigan Press.

Richard (of Hexham) Raine, J. (ed.) 1864 *The Priory of Hexham, its Chronicles, Endowments and Annals, Volume 1*. Durham: Surtees Society of Durham, Volume 44.

RWE Roger of Wendover. Giles, J.A. 1849 *Roger of Wendover's Flowers of History*. London: Henry G. Bohn.

Sulpicius Severus *Chronicorum* Schaff, P. and Wace, H. (eds) 1894 *The Nicene and Post-Nicene Fathers Second Series, Volume 11: Sulpicius Severus, Vincent of lerins, John Cassian*. Christian Literature Company.

Vit Ceol Anon *Vita Ceolfridi*: The Anonymous Life of Ceolfrith. Grocock, C. and Wood, I.N. (trans. and eds) 2013 *Abbots of Wearmouth and Jarrow*. Oxford: Clarendon Press (Oxford Medieval Texts), 78–121.

Vit Col Anderson, A.O. and Anderson, M.O. (eds and trans.) 1961 *Adomnan's Life of Columba*. London and Edinburgh: Thomas Nelson and Son.

Vit Cuth Anon The Anonymous Life of Cuthbert. Colgrave, B. (ed. and trans.) 1940 *Two Lives of Saint Cuthbert*. Cambridge: Cambridge University Press.

Vit Germ Constantius *Vita Germani*. Hoare, F.R. 1954 *The Western Fathers*. London: Sheen and Ward (The Makers of Christendom).

Vit Greg Anon Colgrave, B. (ed. and trans.) 1985 *The Earliest Life of St Gregory the Great, by an Anonymous Monk of Whitby*. Cambridge: Cambridge University Press.

Vit Guth Colgrave, B. (ed. and trans.) 1985 *Felix's Life of Saint Guthlac*. Cambridge: Cambridge University Press.

VW Vita Wilfridi. Colgrave, B. (ed. and trans.) 1927 *The Life of Bishop Wilfrid by Eddius Stephanus*. Cambridge: Cambridge University Press.

Zosimus *Historia Nova* Vossius, G.J. 1814 *The History of Count Zosimus*. London: Green and Chaplin.

Secondary sources

Abramson, P. 1996 Excavations along the Caythorpe Gas Pipeline, North Humberside. *Yorkshire Archaeological Journal* 68, 1–88.

Abramson, T. and Pirie, E.J.E. 2018 *Coinage in the Northumbrian Landscape and Economy, c.575–c.867*. Oxford: British Archaeological Reports, British Series 641.

Adams, K.A. 1990 Monastery and Village of Crayke, North Yorkshire. *Yorkshire Archaeological Journal* 62, 29–50.

Adams, M. 2013 *The King in the North: The Life and Times of Oswald of Northumbria*. London: Head of Zeus.

Adams, M. 2017 *Ælfred's Britain: War and Peace in the Viking Age*. London: Head of Zeus.

Adams, M. 2021a *The First Kingdom: Britain in the Age of Arthur*. London: Head of Zeus.

Adams, M. 2021b St Columba as a Territorial Lord. *Donegal Annual* 73, 85–92.

Adams, M. 2025 *The Mercian Chronicles*. London: Head of Zeus.

Adams, M. and O'Brien, C. 2021 A Sparrow in the Temple? The Ephemeral and the Eternal in Bede's Northumbria. In Hüglin, S., Gramsch, A. and Seppänen, L. (eds) *Petrification Processes in Matter and Society*. European Association of Archaeologists. Cham: Springer, 155–66.

Alcock, L. 1954 Aberford Dykes: the First Defence of the Brigantes? *Antiquity* 28, 147–54.

Alcock, L. 1971 *Arthur's Britain: History and Archaeology, AD 367–634*. Harmondsworth: Allen Lane.

Alcock, L. 1988 *Bede, Eddius and the Forts of the North Britons*. Jarrow: Jarrow Lecture.

Alcock, L. 2003 *Kings and Warriors, Craftsmen and Priests in Northern Britain* AD *550–850*. Edinburgh: Society of Antiquaries of Scotland.

Alcock, L., Alcock, E. and Foster, S. 1986 Reconnaissance Excavations on Early Historic Fortifications and Other Royal Sites in Scotland, 1974–84: 1, Excavations near St Abbe's Head, Berwickshire, 1980. *Proceedings of the Society of Antiquaries of Scotland*, 116, 255–79.

Alcock, L. and Alcock, E. 1990 Reconnaissance Excavations on Early Historic Fortifications and other Royal Sites in Scotland, 1974–84: 4, Excavations at Alt Clut, Clyde Rock, Strathclyde, 1974–75. *Proceedings of the Society of Antiquaries of Scotland* 120, 95–149.

Aliaga-Kelly, C. 1986 The Anglo-Saxon Occupation of South-East Scotland. Unpublished PhD thesis, University of Glasgow. https://theses.gla.ac.uk/1007/1/1986aliaga-kellyphd.pdf retrieved 26.02.24.

Allott, S. 1974 *Alcuin of York, c.* AD *732 to 804: His Life and Letters*. York: William Sessions, 1974.

Austin, D. 1976 Fieldwork and Excavation at Hart, Co. Durham, 1965–1975. *Archaeologia Aeliana* Series 5, 4, 69–132.

Bailey, R.N. 1978 *The Durham Cassiodorus*. Jarrow: Jarrow Lecture.

Bailey, R.N. 1991 St Wilfrid's Crypts at Hexham and Ripon. In Karkov, C. and Farrell, R.T. (eds) *Studies in Insular Art and Archaeology*, American Early Medieval Studies I, 4–25.

Bailey, R.N. 1993 *Saint Wilfrid's Crypts at Ripon and Hexham: A Visitor's Guide*. Newcastle upon Tyne: Society of Antiquaries of Newcastle upon Tyne.

Bailey, R.N. 2010 *Corpus of Anglo-Saxon Stone Sculpture: Volume 9, Cheshire and Lancashire*. Oxford: British Academy.

Bailey, R.N. 2013 St Wilfrid – A European Anglo-Saxon. In Higham, N.J. (ed.) *Wilfrid: Abbot, Bishop, Saint*. Shaun Tyas, 112–23.

Bannerman, J. 1974 *Studies in the History of Dalriada*. Edinburgh: Scottish Academic Press.

Bannerman, J. 2016 *Kinship, Church and Culture: Collected Essays and Studies*. Edinburgh: John Donald.

Barnwell, P. 2005 Anglian Yeavering: A Continental Perspective. In Frodsham, P. and O'Brien, C. (eds) *Yeavering: People, Power and Place*. Stroud: Tempus, 174–84.

Barnwell, P., Butler, L.A.S. and Dunn, C.J. 2003 The Confusion of Conversion: Streanæshalch, Strensall and Whitby and the Northumbrian Church. In Carver, M. (ed.) *The Cross Goes North: Processes of conversion in Northern Europe,* AD *300–1300*. York: York Medieval Press, 311–26.

Barrow, G.W.S. 1973 *The Kingdom of the Scots: Government, Church and Society from the Eleventh to the Fourteenth Century*. London: Edward Arnold.

Bassett, S. (ed.) 1989 *The Origins of Anglo-Saxon Kingdoms*. London: Leicester University Press.

Bassett, S. 1997 Continuity and Fission in the Anglo-Saxon Landscape: The Origins of the Rodings (Essex). *Landscape History* 19:1, 25–42.

Bhreathnach, E. 2005 The Airgíalla Charter Poem: the Political Context. In Bhreathnach, E. (ed.) *The Kingship and Landscape of Tara*. Dublin: Four Courts Press, 95–9.

Bhreathnach, E. 2014 *Ireland in the Medieval World* AD *400–1000*. Dublin: Four Courts Press.

Biddle, M. and Kjølbye-Biddle, B. 1992 Repton and the Vikings. *Antiquity* 66, 36–51.

Bidwell, P. 1996 The Dating of Crambeck Parchment Ware. *Journal of Roman Pottery Studies* 12, 15–21.

Bidwell, P. 2010 A Survey of the Anglo-Saxon Crypt at Hexham and its Reused Roman Stonework. *Archaeologia Aeliana* Series 5, 39, 53–144.

Bidwell, P. and Speak, S. 1994 *Excavations at South Shields Roman Fort, Volume 1*. Newcastle: Society of Antiquaries of Newcastle upon Tyne.

Birley, A. and Alberti, M. 2021 *Vindolanda Excavation Research report: Focusing on Post-Roman Vindolanda*. Hexham: Vindolanda Trust.

Birley, R., Birley, A. and Blake, J. 1999 *The 1998 Excavations at Vindolanda: The Praetorium Site Interim Report*. Greenhead: Roman Army Museum Publications.

Blackwell, A. 2018 A Reassessment of the Anglo-Saxon Artefacts from Scotland: Material Interactions and Identities in Early Medieval Northern Britain. Unpublished PhD thesis, University of Glasgow. https://theses.gla.ac.uk/30708/ retrieved 06.08.24.

Blackwell, A., Goldberg, M. and Hunter, F. 2017 *Scotland's Early Silver: Transforming Rome's Pay-offs to Pictish Treasures*. Edinburgh: National Museums Scotland.

Blair, J. 1991 The Early Churches at Lindisfarne. *Archaeologia Aeliana* Series 5, 19, 47–53.

Blair, J. 2005 *The Church in Anglo-Saxon Society*. Oxford: Oxford University Press.

Blair, J. 2018 *Building Anglo-Saxon England*. Princeton, NJ: Princeton University Press.

Boek, J.A. (undated) Taxation in the Later Roman Empire: A Study on the Character of the Late Antique Economy. Unpublished MPhil thesis, University of Leiden.

Bonner, G., Stancliffe, C. and Rollason, D. (eds) 1989 *St Cuthbert, his Cult and his Community to* AD *1200*. Woodbridge: Boydell Press.

Bradley, R. 1987 Time Regained: The Creation of Continuity. *Journal of the British Archaeological Association* 140, 1–17.
Breeze, A. 1999 Was Durham the *Broninis* of Eddius's Life of St Wilfred? *Durham Archaeological Journal* 14–15, 91–2.
Breeze, A. 2005 *Medcaut*: the Brittonic Name of Lindisfarne. *Northern History*, 42:1, 188–9.
Breeze, A. 2009 *Din Guoaroy*, the Old Welsh Name of Bamburgh. *Archaeologia Aeliana* Series 5, 38, 123–7.
Brooke, D. 1991 The Northumbrian Settlements in Galloway and Carrick: An Historical Assessment, *Proceedings of the Society of Antiquaries of Scotland* 121, 295–327.
Brooks, N. 1989 The Formation of the Mercian Kingdom. In Bassett S. (ed.) *The Origins of Anglo-Saxon Kingdoms*. Leicester: Leicester University Press, 159–70.
Brown, G.H. 2009 *A Companion to Bede*. Woodbridge: Boydell.
Brown, M.P. 2023 *Bede and the Theory of Everything*. London: Reaktion Books.
Brown, P. 2013 *The Rise of Western Christendom: triumph and diversity* AD *200–1000*. Hoboken, NJ: Wiley.
Bruce-Mitford, R. 1967 *The Art of the Codex Amiatinus*. Jarrow: Jarrow Lecture.
Buckberry, J.L. 2004 A Social and Anthropological Analysis of Conversion-Period and Later Anglo-Saxon Cemeteries in Lincolnshire and Yorkshire. Unpublished PhD thesis, University of Sheffield. https://etheses.whiterose.ac.uk/12793/ retrieved 17.02.14.
Budd, P., Millard, A., Chenery, C., Lucy, S. and Roberts, C. 2004 Investigating Population Movement by Stable Isotope Analysis: A Report from Britain. *Antiquity* 78, 127–41.
Bude, R. 2016 The Joint Coinage of Ecgberht and Eadberht of Northumbria. *British Numismatic Journal* 86, 118–39.
Byrne, F.J. 1973 *Irish Kings and High Kings*. London: Batsford.
Cambridge, E. 1989 Why Did the Community of St Cuthbert Settle at Chester le Street? In Bonner, G., Stancliffe, C. and Rollason, D. (eds) *St Cuthbert, his Cult and his Community to AD 1200*. Woodbridge: Boydell Press, 367–86.
Cambridge, E. 1995 Discussion pages 72–94 in Cambridge, E. and Williams, A. Hexham Abbey: A Review of Recent Work and its Implications. *Archaeologia Aeliana* Series 5, 23, 51–138.
Campbell, A. 1967 *Æthelwulf: De Abbatibus*. Oxford: Clarendon Press.
Campbell, E. 2007 *Continental and Mediterranean Imports to Atlantic*

Britain and Ireland, AD 400–800. York: Council for British Archaeology. Research Report 157.

Campbell, J. 1989 Elements in the Background to the Life of St Cuthbert and his Early Cult. In Bonner, G., Rollason, D. and Stancliffe, C. (eds) *St Cuthbert, his Cult and his Community to AD 1200.* Woodbridge: Boydell.

Canmore: National Record of the Historic Environment. Edinburgh: Historic Environment Scotland. https://canmore.org.uk/ retrieved 22.08.24

Carver, M. 2008 *Portmahomack: Monastery of the Picts.* Edinburgh: Edinburgh University Press.

Castling, J. and Young, G.L. 2011 Medieval Britain and Ireland, Northumberland, 2010: a 9th Century Industrial Area at Bamburgh Castle. *Medieval Archaeology* 55, 311–17.

Charles-Edwards, T.M. 1989 Early Medieval Kingship in the British Isles. In Bassett, S. (ed.) *The Origins of Anglo-Saxon Kingdoms.* London: Leicester University Press, 28–39.

Charles-Edwards, T.M. 2005 The Airgíalla Charter Poem: the Legal Content. In Breathnach, E. (ed.) *The Kingship and Landscape of Tara.* Dublin: Four Courts Press, 100–24.

Charles-Edwards, T. 2013 *Wales and the Britons 350–1064.* Oxford: Oxford University Press.

Clark, F.H. 2010 Wilfrid's Lands? The Lune Valley in its Anglian Context. In Sever, L. (ed.) *Lancashire's Sacred Landscape.* Stroud: History Press, 130–46.

Clark, F.H. 2011 Thinking about Western Northumbria. In Petts, D. and Turner, S. (eds) *Early Medieval Northumbria: Kingdoms and Communities, AD 450–1100.* Turnhout: Brepols, 113–28.

Clarke, D. 2021 *Loidam Civitatem*: Leeds from Tribal Capital to Viking Backwater. *Northern History* 58:2, 169–96.

Coates, R. and Breeze, A. 2000 *Celtic Voices, English Places: Studies of the Celtic Impact on Place-names in England.* Stamford: Shaun Tyas.

Coatsworth, E. 2008 *Corpus of Anglo-Saxon Stone Sculpture: Volume 8 Western Yorkshire.* Oxford: British Academy.

Coggins, D., Fairless, K.J. and Batey, C.E. 1983 Simy Folds: An Early Medieval Settlement Site in Upper Teesdale, Co Durham. *Medieval Archaeology* 27, 1–26.

Cole, A. 2013 *The Place-name Evidence for a Routeway Network in Early Medieval England.* Oxford: Archaeopress, BAR British Series 589.

Colgrave, B. (ed. and trans.) 1985 *Felix's Life of Saint Guthlac.* Cambridge: Cambridge University Press.

Colgrave, B. and Mynors, R.A.B. (trans. and ed.) 1969 *Bede's Ecclesiastical History.* Oxford: Clarendon Press.

Collingwood, R.G. 1946 *The Idea of History*. Oxford: Clarendon Press.

Collins, R. 2012 *Hadrian's Wall and the End of Empire: The Roman Frontier in the 4th and 5th Centuries*. London: Routledge.

Collins, R. and Allason-Jones, L. (eds) 2010 *Finds from the Frontier: Material Culture in the 4th–5th Centuries*. York: Council for British Archaeology. Research Report 162.

Collins, R. and Turner, S. 2018 The Eslington Sword and the Kingdom of Northumbria. *Medieval Archaeology* 62:1, 28–52.

Connolly, S. and O'Reilly, J. 1995 *Bede on the Temple*. Liverpool: Liverpool University Press.

Corfe, T. 1997 The Battle of Heavenfield. *Hexham Historian* 7, 65–86.

Corfe, T. 2005 The Hagustaldian Church: Some Notes on Early Hexham. *Hexham Historian* 15, 1–25.

Cowie, T.G. 1977–78. Excavations at the Catstane, Midlothian 1977. *Proceedings of the Society of Antiquaries of Scotland* 109, 166–201.

Crabtree, P.J. 2018 *Early Medieval Britain: The Rebirth of Towns in the Post-Roman West*. Cambridge: Cambridge University Press.

Cramp, R. 1957 Beowulf and Archaeology. *Medieval Archaeology* 1, 55–77.

Cramp, R. 1984 *Corpus of Anglo-Saxon Stone Sculpture I: County Durham and Northumberland*. London: British Academy.

Cramp, R. 1988 Northumbria: The Archaeological Evidence. In Driscoll, S.T. and Nieke, M.R. (eds) *Power and Politics in Early Medieval Britain and Ireland*. Edinburgh: Edinburgh University Press, 69–78.

Cramp, R. 2005 *Wearmouth and Jarrow Monastic Sites*, Volume 1. Swindon: English Heritage.

Cramp, R. 2006 *Wearmouth and Jarrow Monastic Sites*, Volume 2. Swindon: English Heritage.

Cramp, R. and Miket, R. 1982 *Catalogue of Anglo-Saxon and Viking Antiquities in the Museum of Antiquities*. Newcastle upon Tyne: Museum of Antiquities.

Craster, H.H.E. 1954 The Patrimony of Saint Cuthbert. *English Historical Review* 69, 177–99.

Crone, A. and Hindmarsh, E. 2016 *Living and Dying at Auldhame*. Edinburgh: Society of Antiquaries of Scotland.

Crook, J. 2000 *The Architectural Setting of the Cult of Saints in the Early Christian West c. 300–1200*. Oxford: Clarendon Press.

Crow, J. 2004 Survey and Excavation at Bremenium Roman fort, High Rochester, 1992–98. In Frodsham, P. (ed.) *Archaeology in Northumberland National Park*. York: Council for British Archaeology. Research Report 136, 213–23.

Daniels, R. 2007 *Anglo-Saxon Hartlepool and the Foundations of English Christianity: An Archaeology of the Anglo-Saxon Monastery*. Hartlepool: Tees Archaeology.

Dark, K. 2000 *Britain and the End of the Roman Empire*. Stroud: Tempus.

DeGregorio, S. 2010 Bede and the Old Testament. In DeGregorio, S. (ed.) *The Cambridge Companion to Bede*. Cambridge: Cambridge University Press, 127–41.

DeGregorio, S. and Love, R. 2019 *Bede on First Samuel*. Liverpool: Liverpool University Press.

Driscoll S.T. 2005 *Ad Gefrin* and Scotland: The Implications of the Yeavering Excavation for the North. In Frodsham, P. and O'Brien, C. (eds) 2005 *Yeavering: People, Power and Place*. Stroud: Tempus, 161–73.

Driscoll, S.T. and Nieke, M.R. (eds) 1988 *Power and Politics in Early Medieval Britain and Ireland*. Edinburgh: Edinburgh University Press.

Duggan, M. 2018 *Links to Late Antiquity: Ceramic Exchange and Contacts on the Atlantic Seaboard in the 5th to 7th centuries* AD. Oxford: Archaeopress. BAR British Series 639.

Dumville, D.N. 1976 The Anglian Collection of Royal Genealogies. *Anglo-Saxon England* 5, 23–50.

Dumville, D.N. 1977 Kingship, Genealogy and Regnal Lists. In Sawyer, P.H. and Wood, I.N. (eds) *Early Medieval Kingship*. Leeds: University of Leeds, 72–104.

Dumville, D.N. 1989 The Origins of Northumbria: Some Aspects of the British Background. In Bassett, S. (ed.) *The Origins of Anglo-Saxon Kingdoms*. London: Leicester University Press, 213–22.

Dumville, D.N. (ed.) 1993 *Saint Patrick* AD *493–1993*. Studies in Celtic History 13. Woodbridge: Boydell Press

Dunn, M. 2003 *The Emergence of Monasticism: From the Desert Fathers to the Early Middle Ages*. Oxford: Blackwell.

Dunsford, H.M. and Harris, S.J. 2003 Colonisation of Wasteland in County Durham, 1100–1400. *Economic History Review* 56:1, 34–56.

Duval, N. 1991 L'Architecture Culturelle. In Duval, N. (ed.) *Naissance des Arts Chretiéns: Atlas des Monuments Paléochrétiens de France*. Paris: Imprimerie Nationale, 186–219.

Elsworth, D.W. 2011 Eccles Place-names in Cumbria. *Transactions of the Cumbria and Westmoreland Antiquary and Archaeological Society* 11, 234–8.

Enright, M.J. 1996 *Lady with a Mead Cup: Ritual, Prophecy and Lordship in the European Warband from La Tène to the Viking Age*. Dublin: Four Courts Press.

Evans, J. 1989 Crambeck: The Development of a Major Pottery Industry. In Wilson, P.R. (ed.) *Crambeck Roman Pottery Industry*. Leeds: Yorkshire Archaeological Society, 43–90.

Fafinski, M. 2014 The Moving Centre: Trade and Travel in York from Roman to Anglo-Saxon Times. In Owen-Crocker, G.R. and Schneider, B.W. (eds) *The Anglo-Saxons: The World through their Eyes*. Oxford: British Archaeological Reports, British Series, 71–7.

Faull, M. 1977 British Survival in Anglo-Saxon Northumbria. In Laing, L. (ed.) *Studies in Celtic Survival*. Oxford: British Archaeological Reports, 1–55.

Faull, M. and Moorhouse, S. 1981 *West Yorkshire: An Archaeological Survey to AD 1500*, Volumes 1–4. Wakefield: West Yorkshire Metropolitan County Council.

Fenton-Thomas, C. 2003 *Late Prehistoric and Early Historic Landscapes of the Yorkshire Chalk*. Oxford: Archaeopress. BAR British Series 350.

Fern, C., Dickinson, T. and Webster, L. (eds) 2019. *The Staffordshire Hoard: An Anglo-Saxon Treasure*. Report of the Research Committee of the Society of Antiquaries of London, LXXX.

Filmer-Sankey, W. 1996 The 'Roman Emperor' in the Sutton Hoo Ship Burial. *Journal of the British Archaeological Association* 149, 1–9.

Fletcher, R. 1997 *The Conversion of Europe from Paganism to Christianity 371–1386 AD*. London: HarperCollins.

Fleming, A. 1994. Swadal, Swar (and Erechwydd?): Early Medieval Polities in Upper Swaledale. *Landscape History* 16, 17–30.

Foot, S. 2018 Bede's Kings. In Naismith, R. and Woodman, D.A. (eds) *Writing Kingship and Power in Anglo-Saxon England*. Cambridge: Cambridge University Press, 25–51.

Forsyth, K. 2005 *Hic Memoria Perpetua*: The Early Inscribed Stones of Southern Scotland in Context. In Foster, S.M. and Cross, M. (eds) *Able Minds and Practiced Hands*. Leeds: Society for Medieval Archaeology, 113–34.

Fraser, J.E. 2009 *Caledonia to Pictland: Scotland to 795*. New Edinburgh History of Scotland. Edinburgh: Edinburgh University Press.

Frodsham, P. and O'Brien, C. (eds) 2005 *Yeavering: People, Power and Place*. Stroud: Tempus.

Gameson, R. 2017 *Codex Amiatinus: Making and Meaning*. Jarrow: Jarrow Lecture.

Gates, T. and O'Brien, C. 1988 Cropmarks at Milfield and New Bewick and the Recognition of *Grubenhäuser* in Northumberland. *Archaeologia Aelliana* Series 5, 16, 1–9.

Gates, T. and Deegan, A. 2009 Monuments in the Landscape: The Aerial

Photographic Resource. In Passmore, D. and Waddington, C. *Managing Archaeological Landscapes in Northumberland*, Till–Tweed Studies Volume 1. Oxford: Oxbow, 125–71.

Gelling, M. 1984 *Place-names in the Landscape*. London: John Dent.

Gelling, M. 2004 Appendix I: A Regional Review of Place-names. In Rahtz, P.A. and Watts L. (eds) *Wharram, A Study of Settlement in the Yorkshire Wolds, IX: The North Manor Area and North-west Eenclosure*. York: York University, 347–51.

Gelling, M. and Cole, A. 2014 *The Landscape of Place-names*, 2nd edition. Donington: Shaun Tyas.

Gittos, H. 2024 Sutton Hoo and Syria: The Anglo-Saxons who Served in the Byzantine Army. *English Historical Review* 139:601, 1323–58. Hyyps://doi.org110.11093/her/ceae213 retrieved 07.10.24.

Godman, P. 1982 *The Bishops, Kings, and Saints of York*. Oxford: Clarendon Press.

Gooch, M.L. 2012 Money and Power in the Viking Kingdom of York, c.895–954. Unpublished PhD thesis, Durham University. https://etheses.dur.ac.uk/3495/ retrieved 28.09.24.

Grantham, C. and E. 1965 An Earthwork and Anglian Cemetery at Garton-on-the-Wolds, East Yorkshire. *Yorkshire Archaeological Journal* 62, 51–63.

Green, C. 2012 *Britons and Anglo-Saxons: Lincolnshire AD 400–650*. Studies in the History of Lincolnshire 3. Lincoln: History of Lincolnshire Committee.

Gretzinger, J., Sayer, D., Justeaue, P. *et al.* 2022 The Anglo-Saxon Migration and the Formation of the Early English Gene Pool. *Nature* 610, 112–19.

Groves, S.E. 2010 The Bowl Hole Burial Ground: A Late Anglian Cemetery in Northumberland. In Buckberry, J. and Cherryson, A. (eds) *Burial in Later Anglo-Saxon England, c.650 to 1100 AD*. Oxford: Oxbow Books, 114–25.

Groves, S.E., Roberts, C.A., Lucy, S., Pearson, G., Nowell, G., Macpherson, C.G., Gröcke, D. and Young, G. 2013 Mobility histories of 7th–9th century AD people buried at Early Medieval Bamburgh, Northumberland, England. *American Journal of Physical Anthropology* 151:3, 462–76.

Hadley, D.M. and Richards, J.D. 2016 The winter camp of the Viking Great Army, AD 872–3, Torksey, Lincolnshire. *Antiquaries Journal* 96, 23–67.

Hall, R.A. 1993 Observations in Ripon Cathedral Crypt 1989. *Yorkshire Archaeological Journal* 65, 39–53.

Hall, R.A. 2011 Recent Research into York and its hinterland. In Petts, D. and Turner, S. (eds) *Early Medieval Northumbria: kingdoms and communities, AD 450–1100*. Turnhout: Brepols, 71–84.

Hall, R.A. and Whyman, M. 1996 Settlement and Monasticism at Ripon from the 7th to 11th Centuries AD. *Medieval Archaeology* 40, 62–150.

Hamar, R. 1970 *A Choice of Anglo-Saxon Verse*. London: Faber.
Hamerow, H. 2012 *Rural Settlement in Anglo-Saxon England*. Oxford: Oxford University Press.
Hassall, M.W.C. 1976 Britain in the Notitia. In Goodburn, R. and Batholomew, P. (eds) *Aspects of the Notitia Dignitatum*, papers presented to the conference in Oxford, 13–15 December 1974. Oxford: British Archaeological Reports, 103–18.
Haughton, C. and Powlesland, D. 1999 *West Heslerton: The Anglian cemetery. Volume 1: The Excavation and Discussion of the Evidence*. Yedingham: Landscape Research Centre.
Hawkes, J. 1993 Mary and the Cycle of Resurrection: then iconography of the Hovingham panel. In Spearman, J. and Higgitt, J. (eds) *The Age of Migrating Ideas: Early Medieval Insular Art in Northern Britain and Ireland*. Edinburgh: National Museums of Scotland, 245–60.
Hawkes, J. and Mills, S. (eds) 1999 *Northumbria's Golden Age*. Stroud: Sutton.
Hayfield, C. 1987 *An Archaeological Survey of the Parish of Wharram Percy, East Yorkshire I: The Evolution of the Roman Landscape*. Oxford: British Archaeological Reports. BAR British Series 172.
Higgitt, J. 1995 Monasteries and Inscriptions in Early Northumbria – The Evidence in Whitby. In Bourke, C. (ed.) *From the Isles of the North: Early Medieval Art in Ireland and Britain*. Belfast: HMSO, 229–36.
Higham, N. 1993 *The Kingdom of Northumbria AD 350–1100*. Stroud: Alan Sutton.
Higham, N. 1995 *An English Empire: Bede and the Early Anglo-Saxon kings*. Manchester: Manchester University Press.
Higham, N. 2006 Northumbria's Southern Frontier: A Review. *Early Medieval Europe* 14:4, 391–417.
Higham, N.J. 2015 *Ecgfrið King of the Northumbrians, High-King of Britain*. Donington: Shaun Tyas.
Hill, P. 1997 *Whithorn and St Ninian: the Excavation of a Monastic Town 1984–91*. Stroud: Sutton.
Hind, J.G. 1980 *Elmet* and *Deira* – Forest Names in Yorkshire? *Bulletin of the Board of Celtic Studies* 28, 541–52.
Holbrey, R. and Burgess, A. 2001 Parlington Hollins. In Roberts, I., Burgess, A., Berg, D. (eds) 2001 *A New Link to the Past: The Archaeological Landscape of the M1–A1 Link Road*. Leeds: West Yorkshire Archaeological Service, 83–105.
Holder, A.G. 1994 *Bede and the Tabernacle*. Liverpool: Liverpool University Press.
Hope Dodds, M. 1935 *Northumberland County History*, Volume 14. Newcastle upon Tyne: Northumberland County History Committee.

Hope-Taylor, B. 1977 *Yeavering: An Anglo-British Centre of Early Northumbria*. London: HMSO.

Howlett, D.R. 1975 The Provenance, Date and Structure of *De Abbatibus*. *Archaeologia Aeliana* Series 5, 3, 121–50.

Hüglin, S. 2011 Medieval Mortar Mixers Revisited, Basel and Beyond. *Zeitschrift für Archäologie des Mittelalters* 39, 189–212.

Hunter, F. and Painter, K. (eds) 2013. *Late Roman Silver*. Edinburgh: Society of Antiquaries of Scotland.

Hunter Blair, P. 1948 The Northumbrians and their Southern Frontier. *Archaeologia Aeliana* Series 4, 26, 98–126.

Hunter Blair, P. 1949 The Boundary between Bernicia and Deira. *Archaeologia Aeliana* Series 4, 27, 46–59.

Hunter Blair, P. 1950 The Moore Memoranda on Northumbrian History. In Fox, C. and Dickens, B. (eds) *The Early Cultures of North-West Europe*. Cambridge: Cambridge University Press, 245–57.

Ireland, C. 1991 Aldfrith of Northumbria and the Irish Genealogies. *Celtica* 22, 64–78.

Jackson K.J. 1953 *Language and History in Early Britian: A Chronological Survey of the Brittonic Languages, from First to Twelfth Centuries* AD. Edinburgh: Edinburgh University Press.

Jackson, K.J. 1982 Brigomaglos and St Briog. *Archaeologia Aeliana* Series 5, 10, 61–5.

James, A.G. 2009 **Eglēs / Eclēs* and the Formation of Northumbria. In Quinton, E. (ed.) *The Church in English Place-Names*. Nottingham: English Place-Name Society, 125–50.

James, A.G. 2010 Scotland's *-Ham* and *-Ingham* Names: a Reconsideration. *Journal of Scottish Name Studies* 4, 103–30.

James, A.G. 2019 New Thoughts on Old Place-Names: Tyninghame and Whittinghame. *Transactions of the East Lothian Antiquarian and Field Naturalists' Society* 32, 28–35.

Jobey, G. 1959 Excavations at the Native Settlement at Huckhoe, Northumberland, 1955–7. *Archaeologia Aeliana* Series 4, 37, 217–78.

Jobey, G. 1967 Excavation at Tynemouth Priory and Castle. *Archaeologia Aeliana* Series 4, 45, 5–48.

John, E. 1964 Land Tenure in Early England. Studies in Early English History, Volume 1. Leicester: Leicester University Press.

Johnson, B. and Waddington, C. 2008 Prehistoric and Dark Age Settlement Remains from Cheviot Quarry, Milfield Basin, Northumberland. *Archaeological Journal* 165, 107–264.

Johnson, D. 2015 *The Crummack Dale Project: Excavation of three Early*

Medieval Steadings and a Lime Kiln, Austwick, North Yorkshire. Ingleton: Ingleborough Archaeology Group.

Johnson, D. 2017 *Excavation of Two Anglo-Saxon Period Farmsteads in Brows Pasture, Chapel-le-Dale, North Yorkshire*. Ingleton: Ingleborough Archaeology Group.

Johnson, J. 1850 *A Collection of the Laws and Canons of the Church of England*. Oxford: John Henry Parker.

Jones, G.R.J. 1972 Historical Geography and our Landed Heritage. *University of Leeds Review* 19, 53–78.

Jones, G.R.J. 1975 Early Territorial Organisation in Gwynedd and Elmet. *Northern History* 10, 3–27.

Jones, G.R.J. 1979 Multiple Estates and Early Settlements. In Sawyer, P.H. (ed.) *English Medieval Settlement*. London: E.J. Arnold, 9–34.

Jones, G.R.J. 1995 Some Donations to Bishop Wilfrid in Northern England. *Northern History* 31, 22–38.

Kapelle, W.E. 1979 *The Norman Conquest of the North: The Region and its Transformation, 1100–1135*. London: Croom Helm.

Karkov, C.E. 1999 Whitby, Jarrow and the Commemoration of Death in Northumbria. In Hawkes, J. and Mills, S. (eds) *Northumbria's Golden Age*. Stroud: Sutton, 126–35.

Kaufmann-Heinimann, A. 2013 The Traprain Treasure: Survey and Perspectives. In Hunter, F. and Painter, K. (eds) 2013. *Late Roman Silver*. Edinburgh: Society of Antiquaries of Scotland, 243–61.

Kelly, F. 2000 Early Irish Farming. Early Irish Law Series Volume 4. Dublin Institute for Advanced Studies.

Kelly, S.E. 1992 Eighth-Century Trading Privileges from Anglo-Saxon England. *Early Medieval Europe* 1, 3–28.

Kendall, C. 2008 *On Genesis: Bede*. Liverpool: Liverpool University Press.

Kershaw, J., Jarman, C., Weber, H. and Horton M. 2023. The Viking Great Army North of the Tyne: A Viking Camp in Northumberland? In Hedenstierna-Jonson, C. and García Losquiño, I. (eds) *Routledge Archaeologies of the Viking World*. Abingdon: Routledge, 96–116.

Kershaw, J. and Merkel, S. 2023 International Trade in Outland Resources: the Mining and Export of Lead in Early Medieval England in Light of New Isotope Data From York. *Medieval Archaeology* 67:2, 249–82.

Keynes, S. 1993. The Councils of *Clofesho*. 11th Brixworth Lecture.

Kinsella, T. 1969 *The Tain*. Dublin: The Dolman Press.

Kirby, D.P. 2000 *The Earliest English Kings*. London: Routledge.

Kirby, M. 2011 Lockerbie Academy: Neolithic and Early Historic timber halls, a Bronze Age Cemetery, an Undated Enclosure and a Post-medieval

Corn-drying Kiln in South-west Scotland. *Scottish Archaeological Internet Report* 46. www.sair.org.uk retrieved 21.02.24.

Kirton, J. and Young, G.L. 2017 An Anglo-Saxon Mortar-mixer at Bamburgh Castle. *Archaelogia Aeliana* Series 5, 41, 251–8.

Koch, J.T. (ed.) 1997 *The Gododdin of Aneirin: Text and Context from Dark Age North Britain.* Cardiff: University of Wales Press.

Lacey, B. 2006 *Cenél Conaill and the Donegal Kingdoms AD 500–800.* Dublin: Four Courts Press.

Lacey, B. 2013 *Saint Columba: his Life and Legacy.* Dublin: Columba Press.

Lane, A. and Campbell, E. 2000 *Dunadd: an Early Dalriadic Capital.* Oxford: Oxbow.

Lang, J. 1990 *The Anglian Sculpture of Deira: The Classical Tradition.* Jarrow: Jarrow Lecture.

Lang, J. 1991 *Corpus of Anglo-Saxon Stone Sculpture III: York and Eastern Yorkshire.* London: British Academy.

Lang, J. 1999 The Apostles in Anglo-Saxon Sculpture inn the Age of Alcuin. *Early Medieval Europe* 8:2, 271–82.

Lang, J. 2000 Monuments from Yorkshire in the Age of Alcuin. In Geake, H. and Kenny, J. (eds) *Early Deira: Archaeological Studies of the East Riding from the fourth to the ninth centuries AD.* Oxford: Oxbow.

Lang, J. 2001 *Corpus of Anglo-Saxon Stone Sculpture VI: North Yorkshire.* London: British Academy.

Lapidge, M. 1995 The Career of Archbishop Theodore. In Lapidge, M. (ed.) *Archbishop Theodore.* Cambridge: Cambridge University Press, 1–29.

Lapidge, M. and Herren, M. 2009 *Aldhelm: The Prose Works.* Woodbridge: D.S. Brewer.

Leahy, K. 2007 'Interrupting the Pots': *The Excavation of Cleatham Anglo-Saxon Cemetery.* York: Council for British Archaeology.

Levison, W. 1946 *England and the Continent in the Eighth Century: the Ford Lectures Delivered in the University of Oxford in the Hilary Term, 1943.* Oxford: Oxford University Press.

Lewis, G. and Williams, R. 2019 *The Book of Taliesin: Poems of Warfare and Praise in an Enchanted Britain.* London: Penguin Classics.

Loveluck, C.P. 1996 The Development of the Anglo-Saxon Landscape, Economy and Society, 'On Driffield', East Yorkshire, 400–750 AD. *Anglo-Saxon Studies in Archaeology and History* 9, 25–48.

Lowe, C. and Brooke, D. 2006. *Excavations at Hoddom, Dumfriesshire: An Early Ecclesiastical Site in South-West Scotland.* Edinburgh: Society of Antiquaries of Scotland.

Lucy, S. 1998 *The Early Anglo-Saxon Cemeteries of East Yorkshire: An*

Analysis and Reinterpretation. Oxford: Archaeopress. BAR British Series 272.

Lucy, S. 2005 Early Medieval Burial at Yeavering: A Retrospective. In Frodsham, P. and O'Brien, C. (eds) 2005 *Yeavering: People, Power and Place.* Stroud: Tempus, 127–44.

Maddicott, J.R. 2002 Prosperity and Power in the Age of Bede and Beowulf. *Proceedings of the British Academy* 117, 49–71.

Maddicott, J.R. 2005 London and Droitwich, c. 650–750: Trade, Industry and the Rise of Mercia. *Anglo Saxon England* 34, 7–58.

Maldonado, A. 2013 Burial in Early Medieval Scotland: New Questions. *Medieval Archaeology* 57, 1–34.

Mason, D.J.P. 2001 Battle Victims Found at Heronbridge. *Past Uncovered.* Chester Archaeology, 1–2. https://archaeologydataservice.ac.uk/library/browse/details.xhtml?recordId=3100325&recordType=Journal retrieved 28.08.24.

Mawer, A. 1920 *The Place-Names of Northumberland and Durham.* Cambridge: Cambridge University Press.

Mayr-Harting, H. 1972 *The Coming of Christianity to Anglo-Saxon England.* London: Batsford.

McCarthy, M. 2018 Carlisle: Function and Change between the First and Seventh Centuries AD. *Archaeological Journal*, 175:2, 292–314.

McClure, J. 1983 Bede's Old Testament Kings. In Wormald, P. (ed.) *Ideal and Reality in Anglo-Saxon Society: Studies presented to M. Wallace-Hadrill.* Oxford: Blackwell, 76–98.

McErlean, T. and Crothers, N. 2007 *Harnessing the Tides: The Early Medieval Tide Mills at Nendrum Monastery, Strangford Lough.* Northern Ireland Archaeological Monographs 7. Belfast: The Stationery Office.

McGuigan, N. 2015 Neither Scotland nor England: Middle Britain, c.850–1150. Unpublished PhD thesis, University of St Andrews.

McGuigan N. 2019 Cuthbert's Relics and the Origins of the Diocese of Durham. *Anglo-Saxon England* 48, 121–62.

McNeil, P. and Nicholson, R. 1975 *An Historical Atlas of Scotland, c.400–c.1600.* St Andrews: Atlas Committee of the Conference of Scottish Medievalists.

Metcalf, D.M. 1987 *Coinage in Ninth-century Northumbria: The Tenth Oxford Symposium on Coinage and Monetary History.* Oxford: Archaeopress. BAR British Series 180.

Metcalf, D.M. 2006 The Coinage of King Aldfrið of Northumbria (685–704) and some Contemporary Imitations. *British Numismatic Journal* 76, 147–58.

Moisl, H.L. 1983 The Bernician Royal Dynasty and the Irish in the Seventh Century. *Peritia* 2, 103–26.

Montgomery, J., Evans, J.A., Powlesland, D. and Roberts, C.A. 2005 Continuity or Colonisation in Anglo-Saxon England? Isotope Evidence for Mobility, Subsistence Practice, and Status at West Heslerton. *American Journal of Physical Anthropology* 126, 123–38.

Moore, K.B. 2018 Adomnán's On the Holy Places: Pilgrimage Manuscripts and Architectural Translation from Jerusalem to Europe. *Art in Translation* 10:1, 11–29.

Morris, J. (ed.) 1980 Nennius. British History and the Welsh Annals. *Arthurian Period Sources* Volume 8. London: Phillimore.

Morris, R. 2004 *Journeys from Jarrow*. Jarrow: Jarrow Lecture.

Morris, R. 2015 Landscapes of Conversion among the Deirans: Lastingham and its Neighbours in the Seventh and Eighth Centuries. In Barnwell, P.S. (ed.) *Places of Worship in Britain and Ireland, 300–950*. Donnington: Shaun Tyas, 119–51.

Morrison, J., Oram, R. and Oliver F. 2008. Ancient Eldbottle Unearthed: Archaeological and Historical Evidence for a long-Lost Early Medieval East Lothian Village. *Transactions of the East Lothian Antiquarian and Field Naturalists' Society* 27, 21–45.

Mortimer, J.R. 1905 *Forty Years' Researches in the British and Anglo-Saxon Burial Mounds of East Yorkshire*. London: A. Brown & Sons.

Muncaster, W. 2019 Excavation of an Early Medieval Settlement at Felton, Northumberland. *Archaeologia Aeliana* Series 5, 48, 57–92.

Muncaster, W., McKelvey, J. and Bidwell, P. 2014 Excavation of an Anglo-Saxon settlement and of prehistoric features at Shotton, Northumberland. *Archaeologia Aeliana* Series 5, 43, 77–140.

Naismith, R. 2012 *Money and Power in Anglo-Saxon England: the southern English kingdoms 757–865*. Cambridge: Cambridge University Press.

Naylor, J. 2006 Mercian Hegemony and the Origins of Series J Sceattas: The Case for Lindsey. *British Numismatic Journal* 76, 159–70.

Neal, C. 2007 The Dynamics of Human Activity in Landscape Process on the Yorkshire Wolds: An assessment of the Dry Valley Deposits at Cowlam Well Dale. *Yorkshire Archaeological Journal* 79, 1–15.

Nelson, J.L. 1991 *The Annals of St Bertin*. Ninth Century Histories, Volume 1. Manchester: Manchester University Press, Manchester Medieval Sources.

Newman, R., Howard Davis, C. and Leech, R. 2022 *The Early Medieval Site at Dacre, Cumbria*. Lancaster: Oxford Archaeology.

Nicolaisen, W.F.H. 1976. *Scottish Place-Names: Their Study and Significance*. London: Batsford.

Nolan, J. 2007 Gateshead: An Archaeological and Historical Overview. *Archaeologia Aeliana* Series 5, 36, 111–23.

Nolan, J., Harbottle, B. and Vaughan, J. 2010 The Early Medieval Cemetery at the Castle, Newcastle upon Tyne. *Archaeologia Aeliana* Series 5, 39, 147–287.

Nordhagen, P.J. 1977. *The Codex Amiatinus and the Byzantine Element in the Northumbrian Renaissance*. Jarrow: Jarrow Lecture.

Oakey, M. 2015 New Evidence for the *Vicus* at Malton Roman Fort. *Yorkshire Archaeological Journal* 87, 193–7.

O'Brien, C. 2002 The Early Medieval Shires of Yeavering, Breamish and Bamburgh. *Archaeologia Aeliana* Series 5, 30, 53–73.

O'Brien, C. 2011 Yeavering and Bernician Kingship: A Review of Debate on the Hybrid Culture Thesis. In Petts, D. and Turner, S. (eds) 2011 *Early Medieval Northumbria: Kingdoms and Communities, AD 450–1100*. Turnhout: Brepols, 207–20.

O'Brien, C. 2017 The Hero's Journey in Bede's *Ecclesiastical History*: The Case of King Edwin. In Cambridge, E. and Hawkes, J. (eds) *Crossing Boundaries: Interdisciplinary Approaches to the Art, Material Culture, Language & Literature of the Early Medieval World*. Oxford: Oxbow, 225–231.

O'Brien, C. 2023 The Northumbrian Landholdings of the House of Cospatric. *Archaeologia Aeliana* Series 6, 2, 181–208.

O'Brien, C. and Adams, M. 2016 The Identification of Early Medieval Monastic Estates in Northumbria. *Medieval Settlement Research* 31, 15–27.

O'Brien, C. and Miket, R.F. 1991. The Early Medieval Settlement of Thirlings, Northumberland. *Durham Archaeological Journal* 7, 57–91.

O'Brien, C., Adams, M. and Whaley, D. 2018. King Ceolwulf's Land Grants to St Cuthbert and their Loss in the Ninth Century. *Archaeologia Æliana* Series 5, 47, 79–116.

O'Brien, Conor 2015 *Bede's Temple: An Image and its Interpretation*. Oxford: Oxford University Press.

O'Brien, Conor 2017 Kings and Kingship in the Writings of Bede. *English Historical Review* 132:559, 1473–98.

Ó Carragáin, É. 1994 *The City of Rome and the World of Bede*. Jarrow: Jarrow Lecture.

O'Daly, M. 1952 A Poem on the Airgialla: Contributions in Memory of Osborn Bergin. *Ériu* 16, 179–88.

Oosthuizen, S. 2017 *The Anglo-Saxon Fenland*. Oxford: Oxbow.

Orsini, C. 2017 Negotiating Identity in North-East England and South-East Scotland. In Semple, S., Orsini, C. and Mui, S. (eds) *Life on the Edge:*

Social, Political and Social frontiers in Early Medieval Europe. Braunschweig: Braunschweigisches Landesmuseum, 83–8.

O'Sullivan, D. and Young, R. 1995 *Lindisfarne: Holy Island.* English Heritage series. London: Batsford.

Ottaway, P. 2013 *Roman Yorkshire: People, Culture and Landscape.* Pickering: Blackthorn Press.

Pacitto, A. and Watts, L. 2007 Excavations at the Church of All Saints, Hovingham, Yorkshire. *Church Archaeology* 11, 51–60.

Pagan, H. 2018 SCBI 68 and the Coinage of Northumbria c.685–867. *British Numismatic Journal* 88, 17–39.

Palliser, D.M. 2014 *Medieval York: 600–1540.* Oxford: Oxford University Press.

Parker, M.S. 1985 An Anglo-Saxon Monastery in the Lower Don Valley. *Northern History* 21, 19–32.

Parker, M.S. 1992 The Province of Hatfield. *Northern History* 28, 42–69.

Perry, D.R. 2000 *Castle Park Dunbar: Two Thousand Years on a Fortified Headland.* Edinburgh: Society of Antiquaries of Scotland.

Petts, D. 2013 Military and Civilian: Reconfiguring the End of Roman Britain in the North. *European Journal of Archaeology* 16:2, 314–35.

Petts, D. 2017. 'A Place more venerable than all in Britain': The Archaeology of Anglo-Saxon Lindisfarne. In Gameson, R. (ed.) *The Lindisfarne Gospels: New Perspectives.* Library of the Written Word 57. Leiden: Brill, 1–18.

Petts, D. and Turner, S. (eds) 2011 *Early Medieval Northumbria: Kingdoms and Communities,* AD *450–1100.* Turnhout: Brepols.

Petts, D. and Wilkins, B. 2022 Early Medieval and Medieval Burials and Industries on Lindisfarne. *Medieval Archaeology* 66:2, 476–81.

Phythian-Adams, C. 1996 *Land of the Cumbrians: A Study in British Provincial Origins,* AD *400–1120.* Aldershot: Scolar Press.

Pickles, T. 2009a Locating Ingeltingum and Suthgelting: Gilling West and Gilling East. *Northern History* 46:2, 313–25.

Pickles, T. 2009b *Power, Religious Patronage and Pastoral Care: Religious Communities, Mother Parishes and Local Churches in Ryedale, c.650–c.1250.* Kirkdale: Trustees of the Friends of St Gregory's Minster Kirkdale. Kirkdale Lecture.

Pickles, T. 2018 *Kingship, Society and the Church in Anglo-Saxon Yorkshire.* Oxford: Oxford University Press.

Pirie, E.J.E. 2004 The Bamburgh hoard of Ninth-Century Northumbrian Coins. *Archaeologia Aeliana* Series 5, 33, 65–75.

Powlesland, D. 1999 The Anglo-Saxon Settlement at West Heslerton, North Yorkshire. In Hawkes, J. and Mills, S. (eds) *Northumbria's Golden Age.* Stroud: Sutton, 55–65.

Pythian-Adams, C. 1996 *Land of the Cumbrians: a study in British provincial origins, AD 400–1120*. Aldershot: Scolar Press.

Quinton, E.J.P. and English Place-Name Society 2009 *The Church in English Place-names*. Nottingham: English Place-Name Society.

Rahtz, P. and Watts, L. 2021 *St Gregory's Minster, Kirkdale, North Yorkshire: Archaeological investigations and historical context*. Oxford: Archaeopress.

Raine, J. 1852 *The History and Antiquities of North Durham*. London and Durham.

Reynaud, J.-F. 1998 *Lugdunum Christianum: Lyon du IVe au VIIIs.: topographie, nécropoles et édifices religieux*. Paris: Edition de le Maison des Sciences de l'Homme.

Richards, J.D. 2003 The Anglian and Anglo-Scandinavian sites at Cottam, East Yorkshire. In Pestell, T. and Ulmschneider, K. (eds) *Markets in Early Medieval Europe: Trading and Productive Sites, 650–850*. Macclesfield: Windgather, 155–67.

Rivet, A.L.F. and Smith, C. 1979 *The Place Names of Roman Britain*. Cambridge: Cambridge University Press.

Roberts, B.K. 2007 Between the Brine and the High Ground: The Roots of Northumbria. In Colls, R. (ed.) *Northumbria: History and Identity 547–2000*. Chichester: History Press, 12–32.

Roberts, B.K. 2008a The Lands of Werhale – Landscapes of Bede. *Archaeologia Aeliana* Series 5, 37, 127–59.

Roberts, B.K. 2008b *Landscape, Documents and Maps: Villages in Northern England and Beyond AD 900–1250*. Oxford: Oxbow Books.

Roberts, B.K. 2010 Northumbrian Origins and Post-Roman Continuity: an Exploration. In Collins, R. and Allason-Jones, L. (eds) *Finds from the Frontier: Material Culture in the 4th–5th Centuries*. York: Council for British Archaeology Research Report 162, 119–32.

Roberts, B.K., Wrathmell, S. and English Heritage 2002 *Region and Place: A Study of English Rural Settlement*. London: English Heritage.

Roberts, I. 2001 The Post-Roman Evidence c. AD 450–700. In Roberts, I., Burgess, A. and Berg, D. (eds) *A New Link to the Past: The Archaeological Landscape of the M1–A1 Link Road*. Leeds: West Yorkshire Archaeological Service, 280–5.

Roberts, I., Burgess, A. and Berg, D. (eds) 2001 *A New Link to the Past: The Archaeological Landscape of the M1–A1 Link Road*. Leeds: West Yorkshire Archaeological Service.

Rollason, D. 2003 *Northumbria 500–1100: Creation and Destruction of a Kingdom*. Cambridge: Cambridge University Press.

Rollason, D.W. 2004 *The Durham* Liber Vitae *and its Context*. Suffolk: Boydell Press.

Roper, M. 1974 Wilfrid's Landholdings in Northumbria. In Kirby, D.P. (ed.) *Saint Wilfrid at Hexham*. Newcastle upon Tyne: Oriel Press, 61–79.

Rutherford, A. and Ritchie, J.N.G. 1974 The Catstane. *Proceedings of the Society of Antiquaries of Scotland* 105, 183–8.

Sawyer, P.H. 2013 *The Wealth of Anglo-Saxon England*. Oxford: Oxford University Press.

Sharpe, R. 1995 *Life of St. Columba*. Harmondsworth: Penguin.

Sherlock, S.J 2012 *A Royal Anglo-Saxon Cemetery at Street House, Loftus, North-East Yorkshire*. Hartlepool: Tees Archaeology.

Sherlock, S.J. and Welch, M. 1992 *An Anglo-Saxon Cemetery at Norton, Cleveland*. London: Council for British Archaeology.

Sjøvold, T. 1957 *The Oseberg Find and the Other Viking Ship Finds*. Oslo: Universitetets Oldsaksamling.

Smith, A.H. 1961 *The Place-Names of the West Riding of Yorkshire, Part VI*. Cambridge: Cambridge University Press.

Smith A.H. 1962 *The Place-Names of the West Riding of Yorkshire, Part VII*. Cambridge: Cambridge University Press.

Smith, A.N. 1995 The Excavation of Neolithic, Bronze Age and Early Historic Features near Ratho, Edinburgh. *Proceedings of the Society of Antiquaries of Scotland* 125, 69–138.

Smith, C.N.J. 2006 The Economic History of Anglian Deira, 700–870. Unpublished PhD thesis, University of York. https://etheses.whiterose.ac.uk/11017/ retrieved 13.07.24.

Smith, I.M. 1991 Sprouston, Roxburghshire: An Early Anglian Centre of the Eastern Tweed Basin. *Proceedings of the Society of Antiquaries of Scotland* 121, 261–94.

Snape, M. and Bidwell, P. 2002 The Roman Fort at Newcastle upon Tyne. *Archaeologia Aeliana* Series 5, 21, 1–295.

South, T. Johnson 2002 *Historia de Sancto Cuthberto*. Anglo-Saxon Texts 3. Cambridge: D.S. Brewer.

Spall, C.A. and Toop, N.J. 2008 Before *Eoforwic*: New Light on York in the 6th–7th Centuries. *Medieval Archaeology* 52:1, 1–25.

Stancliffe, C. 1995a Oswald: Most Holy and Most Victorious King of the Northumbrians. In Stancliffe, C. and Cambridge, E. (eds) 1995, 33–83.

Stancliffe, C. 1995b Where was Oswald killed? In Stancliffe, C. and Cambridge, E. (eds) *Oswald: Northumbrian King to European Saint*. Stamford: Paul Watkins, 84–96.

Stancliffe, C. 2007 *Bede and the Britons*. Whithorn: Whithorn Lecture.

Stancliffe, C. 2010 British and Irish Contexts. In DeGregorio, S. (ed.) *The Cambridge Companion to Bede*. Cambridge: Cambridge University Press.

Stancliffe, C. 2013 Disputed Episcopies: Bede, Acca and the Relationship between Stephen's Life of Wilfrid and the Early Prose Life of Cuthbert. *Anglo-Saxon England* 41, 7–39.

Stancliffe, C. and Cambridge, E. (eds) 1995 *Oswald: Northumbrian King to European Saint*. Stamford: Paul Watkins.

Stafford, L. 2007 *Excavation at Lanton Quarry, Northumberland*. Archaeological Research Services Ltd. https://www.archaeologicalresearch-services.com/lantonwebsite/downloads/phase1.pdf retrieved 26.10.23.

Stead, I. 1991 *Iron Age Cemeteries in East Yorkshire*. London: English Heritage.

Stevenson, J. 1855 (ed. and trans.) *The Historical Works of Simeon of Durham*, Volume 3, Part II. London: Seeleys.

Stoertz, C. 1997 *Ancient Landscapes of the Yorkshire Wolds: Aerial Photographic Transcription and Analysis*. Swindon: Royal Commission on the Historical Monuments of England.

Story, J. 2003 *Carolingian Connections: Anglo-Saxon England and Carolingian Francia, c.750–870*. Ashgate Studies in Early Medieval Britain 2. Aldershot: Ashgate.

Taylor, H.M. 1974 The Architectural Interest of Æthelwulf's *De Abbatibus*. *Anglo-Saxon England* 3, 163–73.

Thacker, A. 1995 *Membra Disjecta*: The Division of the Body and the Diffusion of the Cult. In Stancliffe, C. and Cambridge, E. (eds) *Oswald Northumbrian King to European Saint*. Stamford: Paul Watkins, 97–127.

Thacker, A. 2020 St Wæburh: the Multiple Identities of a Regional Saint. In Langlands, A.J. and Lavelle, R. 2020 *The Land of the English Kin: Essays in Honour of Professor Barbara Yorke*, 26. Brepols: Brill, 443–66.

Thomas, C. 1971 *The Early Christian Archaeology of North Britain*. Oxford: Oxford University Press.

Thomas, C. 1981 *Christianity in Roman Britain to AD 500*. London: Batsford.

Thomas, C. 1992 The Early Christian Inscriptions of Southern Scotland. *Glasgow Archaeological Journal* 17, 1–10.

Thomas, G., Mudd, D., Clarke, A., Eaton, J., Garland, C. and Pankhurst, N. 2022 In Search of the Early Medieval Monastic Archaeology of the Middle Thames. *Interim Report No. 2 on University of Reading Excavations at Cookham, East Berkshire*.

Tipping, R. 2010 *Bowmont: An Environmental History of the Bowmont Valley and the Northern Cheviot Hills, 10 000 BC–AD 2000*. Edinburgh: Society of Antiquaries of Scotland.

Tolley, C. 2016 Æthelfrith and the Battle of Chester. *Journal of the Chester Archaeological Society*, New Series, 86, 51–95.

Toolis, R. and Bowles, C.R. 2016 *The Lost Dark Age Kingdom of Rheged: The Discovery of a Royal Stronghold at Trusty's Hill, Galloway*. Oxford: Oxbow.

Toop, N.J. 2011 Northumbria in the West: Considering Interaction Through Monumentality. In Petts, D. and Turner, S. (eds) 2011 *Early Medieval Northumbria: Kingdoms and Communities, AD 450–1100*. Turnhout: Brepols, 85–112.

Tudor, V. 1995 Reginald's Life of St Oswald. In Stancliffe, C. and Cambridge, E. (eds) *Oswald: Northumbrian King to European Saint*. Stamford: Paul Watkins, 178–94.

Turner, S., Semple, S. and Turner, A. 2013 *Wearmouth and Jarrow: Northumbrian monasteries in an historic landscape*. Hatfield: University of Hertfordshire Press.

Van Der Noort, R. 2004 *The Humber Wetlands: The Archaeology of a Dynamic Landscape*. Oxford: Windgather Press.

Van Der Veen, M. 2022 All Change on the Land? Wheat and the Roman to Early Medieval Transition in England. *Medieval Archaeology* 66:2, 304–42.

Waddington, C. 2005 Yeavering in its Stone Age Landscape. In Frodsham, P. and O'Brien, C. (eds) *Yeavering: People, Power and Place*. Stroud: Tempus, 84–97.

Waddington, C. 2009 A Note on Neolithic, Bronze Age, Iron Age and Anglo-Saxon Remains at Lanton Quarry near Milfield, Northumberland. *Archaeologia Aelina* Series 5, 38, 23–29.

Wallace-Hadrill, J.M. 1988 *Bede's Ecclesiastical History of the English People: A Historical Commentary*. Oxford: Clarendon Press

Wallis, F. 1999 *Bede: The Reckoning of Time*. Liverpool: Liverpool University Press.

Ward, S. 2012 Church and State in Eighth-century Northumbria: Alcuin's York Poem. *Archaeologia Aeliana* Series 5, 41, 217–36

Ware, C. 2005 The Social Use of Space at *Gefrin*. In Frodsham, P. and O'Brien, C. (eds) 2005 *Yeavering: People, Power and Place*. Stroud: Tempus, 153–60.

Watson, W.G. 2015 Change in Northumbria: Was Aldfrith of Northumbria's reign a period of innovation or did it merely reflect the development of processes already underway in the late seventh century? Unpublished PhD thesis. University of St Andrews. http://hdl.handle.net/10023/7607 retrieved 10.04.24.

Watts, V. 1994 The Place-Name Hexham: A Mainly Philological Approach. *Nomina* 17, 119–36.

Watts, V. 2004 *The Cambridge Dictionary of English Place-Names*. Cambridge: Cambridge University Press.

Wheelhouse, P. and Burgess, A. 2001 The Linear Earthworks. In Roberts, I., Burgess, A. and Berg, D. (eds) *A New Link to the Past: The Archaeological Landscape of the M1–A1 Link Road*. Leeds: West Yorkshire Archaeological Service.

Whitelock, D. (ed.) 1979 *English Historical Documents*, Volume I, 2nd edition. London: Eyre Methuen.

Whyman, M. 2001 Late Roman Britain in Transition, AD 300–500: A Ceramic Perspective. PhD thesis, University of York. https://etheses.whiterose.ac.uk/2515/ retrieved 02.08.24.

Wilmott, T. 1993 Excavation and Survey on the Line of Grim's Ditch, West Yorkshire 1977–83. *Yorkshire Archaeological Journal* 65, 55–74.

Wilmott, T. 1997 *Birdoswald: Excavations of a Roman Fort on Hadrian's Wall and its Successor Settlements, 1987–92*. London: English Heritage.

Wilmott, T. 2010 The Late Roman Frontier: The Structural Background. In Collins, R. and Allason-Jones, L. (eds) *Finds from the Frontier: Material Culture in the 4th–5th Centuries*. York: Council for British Archaeology Research Report 162, 10–19.

Wilmott, T. and Wilson, P. 2000 *The Late Roman Transition in the North: Papers from the Roman Archaeology Conference, Durham 1999*. Oxford: Archaeopress. British Archaeological Reports 229.

Wilson, D.M. (ed.) 1976 *Archaeology in Anglo-Saxon England*. Cambridge: Cambridge University Press.

Wilson, P. 2006 A Yorkshire Fort and 'Small Town': Roman Malton and North Revisited. *Yorkshire Archaeological Journal* 78, 35–60.

Wilson, P., Cardwell, P., Cramp, R.J., Evans, J., Taylor-Wilson, R.H., Thompson, A. and Wacher, J.S. 1996 Early Anglian Catterick and Catraeth. *Medieval Archaeology* 40, 1–61.

Winchester, A.J.L. 2008. Early Estate Structure in Cumbria and Lancashire. *Medieval Settlement Research* 23, 14–21.

Wood, I.N. 1987 Anglo-Saxon Otley: An Archepiscopal Estate and its Crosses in a Northumbrian Context. *Northern History* 23, 20–38.

Wood, I.N. 1995 *The Most Holy Abbot Ceolfrid*. Jarrow: Jarrow Lecture.

Wood, I.N. 1997 Before and After the Migration to Britain. In Hines, J. (ed.) *The Anglo-Saxons from the Migration Period to the Eighth Century: An Ethnographic Perspective*. Woodbridge: Boydell, 41–54.

Wood, I.N. 2006 Constantinian Crosses in Northumbria. In Karkov, C.E., Keefer, S.R. and Jolly, K.L. (eds) *The Place of the Cross in Anglo-Saxon England*. Woodbridge: Boydell, 3–13.

Wood, I.N. 2007 Bernicii and Deirii. In Orton, F., Wood, I.N. and Lees, C.A. (eds) *Fragments of History: Rethinking the Ruthwell and Bewcastle Monuments*. Manchester: Manchester University Press, 108–10.

Wood, I.N. 2008a *The Origins of Jarrow: The Monastery, the Slake and Ecgfrith's Minster.* Jarrow: Bede's World.

Wood, I.N. 2008b Monasteries and the Geography of Power in the Age of Bede. *Northern History* 45:1, 11–25.

Wood, I.N. 2018 The Roman Origins of the Northumbrian Kingdom. In Balzaretti, R., Barrow, J. and Skinner, P. (eds) *Italy and Early Medieval Europe: Papers for Chris Wickham.* Oxford: Oxford University Press, 39–49.

Wood, M. 2011 Bernician Transitions: Place-Names and Archaeology. In Petts, D. and Turner, S. (eds) *Early Medieval Northumbria: Kingdoms and Communities,* AD *450–1100.* Turnhout: Brepols, 33–70.

Wood, P.N. 1996 The Little British Kingdom of Craven. *Northern History* 32, 1–20.

Woolf, A. 2004 Cadualla Rex Brettonum and the Passing of the Old North. *Northern History,* 41, 5–24.

Woolf, A. 2007 *From Pictland to Alba 787–1070.* Edinburgh: Edinburgh University Press.

Woolf, A. 2016 A Historian's View of the Evidence from Auldhame. In Crone, A. and Hindmarsh, E. 2016 *Living and Dying at Auldhame.* Edinburgh: Society of Antiquaries of Scotland, 166–70.

Woolf, A. 2018 The Diocese of Lindisfarne: Organisation and Pastoral Care. In McGuigan, N. and Woolf, A. (eds) *The Battle of Carham: A Thousand Years On.* Edinburgh: John Donald.

Wormald, P. 1991 In Search of Offa's Law Code. In Wood, I. and Lund, N. (eds) *People and Places in Northern Europe 500–1600: Essays in Honour of Peter Hayes Sawyer.* Woodbridge: Boydell Press, 25–46.

Wright, D. 2015 Early Medieval Settlement and Social Power: The Middle Anglo-Saxon 'Home Farm'. *Medieval Archaeology* 59, 24–46.

Yorke, B. 2009 Rex Doctissimus: *Bede and King Aldfrið of Northumbria.* Jarrow: Jarrow Lecture.

Yorke, B. 2010 Adomnán at the Court of King Aldfrith. In Aist, R., Owen Clancy, T., O'Loughlin, T. and Wooding, J.M. (eds) *Adomnán of Iona: Theologian, Lawmaker, Peacemaker.* Dublin: Four Courts Press, 36–50.

Yorke, B. 2013 *Kings and Kingdoms of Early Anglo-Saxon England.* Abingdon: Routledge.

Youngs, S. 2013 From Chains to Brooches: the Uses and Hoarding of Silver in North Britain in the Early Historic Period. In Hunter, F. and Painter, K. (eds) 2013. *Late Roman Silver.* Edinburgh: Society of Antiquaries of Scotland, 403–25.

IMAGE CREDITS

In-text images

All in-text maps and plans copyright Max Adams except:
Page 46: Mortimer 1905, Fig. 731
Page 80: Colm O'Brien after Hope-Taylor 1977, Figs 12, 76–79
Page 84: Smith 1991, Fig. 4
Page 87: O'Brien and Miket 1991, Fig. 2
Page 106: Helena Hamerow in Sherlock 2012, Fig. 2.1
Page 108: Muncaster, McKelvey and Bidwell 2014, Fig. 12
Page 147: Colm O'Brien after Hall and Whyman 1996, Fig. 36
Page 159, Hexham: Colm O'Brien
Page 227: Lowe 2006, Fig. 9.1
Page 261: Colm O'Brien
Page 294: P. Dunn / English Heritage in O'Sullivan and Young 1995, Fig. 56

All in-text photographs copyright Max Adams except:
Page 141: Colm O'Brien
Page 191: Keith Chapman
Pages 221, 288: Flora Carr

Plate section

All plates copyright Max Adams except:
Plate 15: Christopher Lowe, by permission of Rev. David Glover
Plate 16: Wien, Österreichische Nationalbibliothek, cod.652, fol. 2v
Plate 17: Historic England
Plate 18: British Museum, photograph by Mike Peel (www.mikepeel.net). Licence CC-BY-SA-4.0
Plate 19: from De Locis Sanctis (public domain)

Plate 20: © Alicia Canter / Guardian / eyevine
Plate 21: British Library Add Ms 89000. Creative Commons, public domain CC0.10 Universal

SUBJECT INDEX

Page numbers in italic are references to photographs or maps.

ætheling 65, 95, 211, 268, 303
agriculture (*see also* material culture) 10, 12, 49, 216, 233, 268
    arable 12, 25, 29, 69, 89, 176, 218, 237, 294
    corn driers 145, 203
    crops 7, 16–17, 24, 29, 89, 101, 108, 187, 195, 226, 203–4, 226, 258, 270, 284
    grazing, pasture, meadows 16, 25, 28–9, 89, 106–8, 176, 177, 229, 264, 280
    livestock (see also cattle; geese; hens; sheep/wethers/goats) 22, 49, 53, 89, 108, 187, 195, 203, 208, 217, 270, 293
    horses 52, 109, 112–13, 250, 275, 299
    produce (*see also* salt; wool) 30, 52, 108, 109, 177, 193, 195, 276, 284
    technology 204
    wood pasture 25, 29, 108, 176
Anglian cultural influence 24, 28, 165, 170–1, 217–19, 223, 227–9, 235, 239
Anglian Tower, York 201, *202*
archaeological sites and excavations: *see individual site names*
archbishops: *see name index*
architecture: *see* structures

armies 8, 96
    size and composition 136, 165, 249
    Great Viking Host / *micel here* 250, 282, 296, 299–300, 301, 302, 304
    military service 127, 218, 266
    weaponry 52, 254

battles
    Arfderydd (573) 61
    Argoed Llwyfain (sixth century) 60
    Cantscaul: see Denisesburn
    Catræth (?590) 60–1
    Chester/*Legacæstir* (616) 5, 62, 114
    Degsastan (604) 5, 58–9, 62, 114
    Denisesburn (634) 6, 98, 159; see also Heavenfield
    Hæthfelth, Hatfield Chase (633) 76, 134, 207
    Maserfelth (642) 6, 111, 116, 127
    River Trent (679) 122, 177, 183, 188, 231
    River Idle (617) 5, 63
    Nechtansmere (685) 181, 211
    unlocated 131
    Winwæd (655) 120, 136, 231
    York (866) 250, 299–300
books and manuscripts 193
    Anglian Collection of Royal Genealogies 216, 313

Anglo-Saxon Chronicle 50, 55, 56, 57, 58, 59, 151, 179, 183, 184, 207, 213, 214, 234, 265, 282, 289 297, 299, 312
Annales Cambriae 36
Anonymous Life of Cuthbert 207
Bede's works: see under Bede *in name index*
Bishops, Kings and Saints of York 273
Boldon Book 177, 307
Codex Amiatinus 124–5, 175, 187–8, 214
De Abbatibus 256–8, 262, 282, 312
Durham *Liber Vitae* 128, 208–9, 256, 289
Historia Brittonum 36, 50, 55, 57, 76, 216, 228, 312
Historia de Sancto Cuthberto 258, 259–64, 266, 313
Historia Regum 214, 263, 267, 271, 279
Irish Annals 65, 125, 127, 214, 273, 313
Life of St Columba 65, 185, 313
Life of Pope Gregory the Great 186
Lindisfarne Gospels: see under Lindisfarne *in name index*
Northern Annals 213, 281
scriptoria 95, 100, 187–8, 226
Tribal Hidage 40, 66, 68, 132
boundaries and frontiers
  of Lindisfarne estates 101, 215, 217
  linear earthworks and dykes 39, 40, 44, 45, 72–3, 213
burial 21, 24, 69, 92, 105, 133, 143, 147, 148, 161, 179, 220, 222, 235, 312
  Bernician 50, 81–2, 103–5, 293
  cemeteries 29–31, 45, 88, 149, 167–8, 226, 230, 295–6
  cist/long-cist 103, 166, 170
  cremation 42–3, 81, 170
  Deiran 12, 42–47, *46*, 88, 105, 144, 205
  grave goods 43, 49, 105, 149
  grave memorials 19, 143, 178, 263; see also memorials
  inhumations/earth-cut graves 42, 81, 103, 168
  isotope analysis 103, 284, 287
  pathology 103–4

Carolingian kingdom 255
cattle (*see also* raiding) 11, 16, 21, 54, 66, 82, 93, 109, 168, 177, 194, 203–4, 226, 235, 238, 277, 283, 294
Christianity
  Augustinian mission 57, 59
  baptism 5, 6, 74, 76, 82, 97, 111, 120, 132, 134, 228, 305
  British 69, 89, 131, 146 170, 219
  conversion 61, 74, 76, 89, 95, 115, 134, 188
  miracles 92–3, 112–13, 128, 135, 206, 230, 254, 311
  pilgrimage 97, 113, 125, 144, 187, 223, 230, 282
chronology 35, 44, 89, 114, 148, 189, 287, 297
  annals 92
  coins: see coins and coinage
  genealogies xvii–xix, 36, 49ff, 54–5, 57, 213–14, 216, 272–3, 279, 281, 313
  general problems with dating 28, 48, 288, 298
  radiocarbon dates 10, 49, 69, 89, 103, 141, 145, 168, 169, 237, 238, 295, 321n
  regnal lists 56ff, 283, 298, 309
churches and monasteries
  Beverley, East Yorkshire 88, 205
  Brandon, Suffolk 233, 270

churches and monasteries *continued*
  Bywell, Northumberland 256
  Carlisle 22, 123, 181, 220, 229, 260, 303
  Chester-le-Street, County Durham, 119, 290–1, 303–4
  Coldingham, Northumberland 119, 131, 138, 169, 295
  Cookham, Berkshire, 233, 266, 270
  Coxwold, North Yorkshire 138, 142, 266
  Crayke, North Yorkshire 138, 145, 256, 304
  Dacre, Cumbria 230–1
  Donemuða, Tyne and Wear 246, 266, 278
  Downpatrick, Co. Down 248, 289
  Escomb, County Durham 173–4
  Flixborough, Lincolnshire 233, 270
  Gateshead, Tyne and Wear 128–9, 138, 149, 196
  Gilling West, North Yorkshire 119, 138, 142
  Hartlepool, County Durham 119, 129, 131, 137, 262–3
  Hartness 247, 278, 281
  Heavenfield, Northumberland 97
  Hexham, Northumberland: *see main entry in name index*
  Hoddom, Dumfries and Galloway 219, 223–4, 226–7, *227*, 228
  Hovingham, North Yorkshire 88, 138, 140–1, *141*, 142
  Iona, Inner Hebrides 4, 92, 95, 98, *102*, 185, 247, 248, 288–9
  Jarrow, Tyne and Wear 123–4, 138, 151, 171, *172*, 173, 178–9, 186, 188, 191, 196, 251, 259, 278
  Kirkdale, North Yorkshire 142–3, 144
  Lastingham, North Yorkshire 120, 138, 140, 143–4
  Lindisfarne, Northumberland: *see main entry in name index*
  Mailros (*see* Old Melrose)
  Medeshamstede (Peterborough), Cambridgeshire 137, 231
  Minster-in-Thanet, Kent 232, 284
  Monkwearmouth, Tyne and Wear: *see* Wearmouth *in name index*
  Movilla, Co. Down 248, 289
  Norham, Northumberland 102, 248, 262, 29–2, 295, 298
  Old Melrose, Roxburghshire 119–20, 121, 145, 148, 153, 154, 165, 217
  Oundle, Northamptonshire 125, 210, 211, 277
  Portmahomack, Easter Ross 187, 281
  Repton, Derbyshire 258, 301
  Ripon, North Yorkshire: *see main entry in name index*
  Stonegrave, North Yorkshire 138, 142, 266
  Tynemouth, Tyne and Wear 151, 196, 246, 247, 278, 281
  Watton, East Yorkshire, 254
  Wearmouth, Tyne and Wear: *see main entry in name index*
  Whitby: *see main entry in name index*
  Whithorn (*Candida Casa*), Wigtownshire 33, 38, 169, 170, 219–20, *221*, 222–3, 251, 270, 284, 296
  York Minster, North Yorkshire x, 5, *75*, 121, 175, 201, 246, 273, 280, 305
church buildings 5, 81, 102, 122, 141, 142, 143, 160–1, 168, 171, 173, 188, 190, 191, 223, 292

church foundations and endowments 122, 133, 135, 138–40, 168, 176, 191
church landholdings 138, 176ff, 259
    Bardney, Lincolnshire 111, 122, 206–7, 210
church organisation 35, 122, 164, 178, 252, 266; *see also under* Whitby; Theodore of Canterbury
church topography 143–4, 145, 146, *147*, 148, *159*, 161, 171
civitas/civitates 14, 16, 22, 33, 35, 96, 146, 271
coins and coinage 189, 196ff, 200, 213, 222
    as dating evidence 10, 48, 310
    end of Northumbrian coinage (867) 250
    Frankish coinage 249, 282
    Frisian coinage 233
    mints 206
    royal issues 196, *197*, 197–200, 201, 203, 264, 270–1, 274, 282–4, *285*, 286–8, *288*, 290, 296, 297, 298, 299
    sceattas 197, 198, 201, 203, 222, 270, 271, 283, 287
    stycas 283, 284, 285, 286, 294–6
    York coinage of Archbishop Ecgberht and King Eadberht 235, 270
comes /comites/comitatus 8, 82, 85, 86, 87, 93, 94, 105, 107, 109, 184, 217, 218, 232, 238, 239, 253, 254, 256, 264, 276
common burdens 243, 266, 267
crosses and cross-shafts 25, *26*, *27*, 190, 219
    high crosses 98, 189, *192*, 219, 224, *225*, 257

cults 61, 93, 110, 112–13, 133–4, 137, 144, 186, 193, 206–7, 219, 222, 258, 270, 299
    shrines 30, 31, 89, 141, 143, 144, 206, 222–3, 232, 259, 292
cultural corelands: *see under* territorial lordship
crypts *53*, 122, 148, 160, 161, *162*, 163, 164, 191, 222

dark earth 10, 21, 22
dating: *see* chronology
depopulation 264, 268
DNA studies 30
dower and dowry 159, 160, 165, 179, 187, 195, 227n, 229
drought 126, 234

Easter controversy 151ff, 169, 184, 191, 213, 214, 238,
economy 10, 18, 28, 108–9, 193ff, 196, 203, 229, 233, 237, 268, 270, 282, 288, 294–6
    secularisation of monasteries 268, 270
    see also coins and coinage; markets and trade
estates, estate centre: *see under* territorial lordship
excavations: *see under individual site names*

familiae 176, 253
food render: *see under* territorial lordship
frontier zones 7, 11, 17, 21, 22, 28, 40, 160, 271
gaming pieces 151, 286
geese 52, 100
genealogies: *see under* chronology

gens Anglorum 61, 189, 278
gesiðas 100, 194, 205, 218, 238, 254, 256
gift-giving 12, 22, 76, 93, 109, 110, 112, 185, 186, 187, 198, 201, 206, 208, 227n, 232, 268, 273, 280, 291
   see also kingship (endowments)
glass: *see under* material culture
Great Viking Host: *see under* armies
Grubenhaus/*Grubenhäuser*: *see under* structures

hens 52
hides, unit of assessment 176, 253
hoards 54, 73, 166, 287, 295

identity xiii–xv, 11, 20, 25, 28, 30, 38, 43, 44, 61–2, 69, 165, 167, 217, 307, 308
   DNA studies 30
   isotope analysis 30, 103, 284
imperium: *see under* kingship
Irish Annals 214, 273, 313
iron production: *see under* minerals
isotope analysis 30, 103, 284

kingship (*see also* territorial lordship; Yeavering) 42, 50, 51–2, 55, 56, 113
   abdication/retirement 121, 210, 243, 258, 259, 260, 264, 272, 283, 309
   Bede on kingship 54, 91, 111, 114–16
   Christian kingship 61, 89, 92, 113, 114–16
   diplomacy 52, 77, 111, 128–9, 132, 146, 148, 149, 164, 183, 185, 210, 220, 274
   eligibility 62, 77, 92, 110, 128, 182, 214, 216, 273, 275

endowments 78, 94, 99, 129, 137, 138, 146, 169, 176, 177, 215, 217, 253, 260ff, 289
genealogies: *see under* chronology
king lists, regnal lists: *see under* chronology
marriage alliances 62, 111, 128, 132, 156, 165, 184, 220
imperium/overlordship 54, 57, 59, 65–7, 89, 96, 110, 127, 131, 136, 156, 177, 181, 216, 231, 248, 253, 267, 290, 300, 307
patronage 22, 54, 65, 93, 98, 132, 134, 138, 146, 165, 182, 194, 206, 218, 227–8, 232, 233, 235, 268, 270, 307
praefecti/reeves 200, 203, 209, 216, 218, 233, 245, 276; *see also under* ealdormen *in name index*
sub-reguli 156, 157, 183, 208, 216, 217, 229, 235
tonsure, forced 126, 215, 244, 245, 256, 273, 276, 309

language/languages 10, 71, 110, 128
Legatine Mission (786) 274–6, 278
libraries 175, 186, 187, 188, 235, 273, 274
linear earthworks: *see under* boundaries and frontiers
lordship: *see* territorial lordship

markets and trade 10, 48, 82, 53–4, 55, 109, 193, 299
   beach markets 88, 196, 200, 218
   coinage: *see* coins and coinage
   harbours and ports 101, 166, 178, 193, 196, 200, 203, 218, 220, 228, 270
   Mediterranean trade and exchange 91, 222

markets and trade *continued*
  monastic 'trading' sites: *see main entry*
  navigable rivers 14, 65, 88, 149, 213, 233, 278, 284, 286, 292, 297, 301, 305
  productive sites 233, 266, 284, 296
  routes for trade 65, 206, 255, 270, 284, 302,
  Scandinavian traders and raiders 276, 278, 286, 297
  traded goods 89, 193–4, 200–1; *see also under* material culture
  traders and merchants 193, 200–22, 203, 232–3, 268, 274, 286
  trading settlements 193–4, 200ff, 233, 249, 264, 290, 297
  see also economy; gift-giving; kingship (diplomacy); slavery
marriage alliances: *see under* kingship
material culture
  animal bone 20, 21, 24, 49, 88, 168, 195, 204, 221
  antler 167, 194, 203, 226
  dress and ornament 18, 149, 167, 191, 193, 200
  dyes 188, 193, 276
  gaming pieces 151, 286
  glass 89, 106–7, 149, 173, 191, 194, 203, 222, 223, 230, 286
  lamps 203
  leather work 186, 194, 258
  metalwork 21, 43, 49, 88, 107, 108, 109, 110, 151, 166, 194, 195, 196, 202, 203, 204, 205, 219, 221, 222, 230, 237, 258, 283, 284, 294
  mortar mixers: *see under* structures
  paintings 164, 175, 193
  pottery/ceramics 10, 24, 43, 47, 48, 49, 86, 88, 91, 107, 195, 203, 204, 219, 221, 222, 226, 229, 236

quernstones 88, 89, 194, 203, 204, 236
sculpture: *see main entry*
spinning and weaving 107, 167, 170, 230
textiles 30, 86, 157, 187, 195, 203, 233, 258, 268, 284, 308
timber 21, 28, 94, 194, 234, 238
vellum 100, 177, 187, 188, 258; *see also* books (*scriptoria*)
weaponry 30, 43, 47, 54, 74, 105, 294
whetstones 203
memorials 33, 133, 134, 170, *180*, 181
  inscribed stones 19–20, *26*, *27*, 170, 178, 189, 219, 221, 263
  see also crosses and cross-shafts
metreth 177
micel here (*hæðen here*) / Great Viking Host: *see under* armies
mills 89, 95, 101, 187, 189, 195, 204, 217, 226, 231
military service 17, 65, 67, 76, 85, 86, 93, 127, 193, 264, 307; *see also* common burdens
minerals and mining 16, 193, 233, 268
  iron 193, 205, 237, 238, 284
  lead 173, 193, 233, 257, 284–6
  salt 62, 194, 195, 232
monasteries: *see* churches and monasteries
monastic 'trading' sites 232–3
  see also Whitby *in name index*; churches and monasteries (Brandon, Cookham, Flixborough, Whithorn)

OSL (Optically Stimulated Luminescence) dating 263–4

palisade: *see under* structures
parishes / parochial structure 28, 29, 71,

140–142, 144–5, 157, 170, 260, 262, 308
parish church 141, 160, 171, 178, 260, 308
paruchia 92, 94, 301
petrification 188ff, 191, 206; *see also* skeuomorphism
pilgrimage: *see under* Christianity
place-names
　general discussion 71, 176
　-bot(h)l names 169, 229–30, 271
　brettas names 69
　burh-names 234, 267, 271
　burh-tuns 230, 234, 271
　-by names 301
　caer names 218, 229
　cumbra names 69
　eccles names 69, 70, 71, 146, 218–19, 223
　as evidence for Northumbrian hegemony 71, 217, 219
　as evidence for trade and travel 194
　functional *-tuns* 233–4, 267
　Grimston hybrids 301
　-ham names 49, 169, 217, 229
　-ingaham names 217
　-ingas names 140
　and language 82
　Scandinavian 25, 49, 152, 301, *302*
　Tarbet names 65
　-thorpe names 301
　walas names 69
plague/pestilence and disease 34, 54, 121, 124, 134, 154, 178, 184, 185, 244, 264, 268, 272, 283, 295
pottery/ceramics: *see under* material culture

raiding 32–5, 53–4, 60, 62, 75, 93, 109, 119, 135, 137, 179, 185, 234, 245, 247, 248, 249, 257, 277–8, 281, 286, 288–90, 294, 297, 299
regio/regiones: *see under* territorial lordship
render of food or service: *see under* territorial lordship
rivers
　Blackadder 217, 260, 262
　Breamish 78, 100, 101, 236, 260
　Coquet 262, 286
　Glen 82, 83
　Gypsy Race 42,
　Humber 12, 38, 42, 265,
　Jed Water 262
　Leader 217, 218
　Ouse 23, 88, 203, 232
　Swale 5, 24, 41, 61, 146
　Tees 14, 39, 262
　Tweed 83, 101, 145–6, 217, 259, 292; 'beyond Tweed' 217, 260
　Tyne (East Lothian) 166, 168, 169
　Tyne (Northumberland) 14, 28, 39, 41, 52, 149, 159, 195, 300, 301, 304, 307
　Wear 20, 191, 263, 303
　see also markets and trade (navigable rivers)
roads (*see also* Roman Roads)
　　Great North Road 286
Roman forts 19, 20, 48, 86, 146, 149, 151, 157, 164, 173, 296, 303
Roman roads 14, *15*, 16, 19, 20, 22, 23, 33, 77–8, 96, 97, 129, 130, 218, 228, 233, 236, 262, 263, 302
royal *vills*: *see under* territorial lordship

salt: *see under* minerals and mining
sceatta: *see under* coins and coinage
scriptoria: *see under* books

sculpture 88, 95, *141*, 142, 144, 158,
    224, 226–7, 230, 244, 255, 263
settlement 16, 21, 24, 28, 30, 42, 48, 49,
    61, 69, 194–5, 204, 235–6, 238,
    291, 293
  burhs 234, 267, 271, 303
  'Butterwick'-type settlements 203–4
  defended settlements 218, 234, 267
  excavations: *see under individual site
    names*
sheep/wethers/goats 52, 204, 277
shires 74, 91, 204, 307
shrines: *see under* cults
skeuomorphism 143, 189, *190*
slavery 32, 33, 53–4, 55, 181, 193, 264,
    305
structures 237
  auditorium 79, 81, 82
  churches and monasteries: *see main
    entry*
  defences 8, 19, 167, 168, *202*, 267
    fences 194
  Grubenhaus/Grubenhäuser 24, 48,
    69, 83, 86, 89, 167–8, 170, 203,
    237
  halls / timber halls 19, 24, 79, 86, 88,
    108, 131, 151, 194, 223, 226, 237;
    see also Yeavering *in name index*
  mausolea 104, *105*, 143, 160, 191, 301
  mortar mixers 104, 167, 173, 191
  palisades 81–2, 83, 84, 167, 170, 224
  Roman survivals 49, 163
  spolia 191, 224, 230
  steadings 22, 28, 49, 135, 235–6,
    237–8, 293ff
  sunken-floored building: see
    Grubenhaus/Grubenhäuser
  tents 237
  wooden structures 18, 20, 167, 228,
    230, 237, 295

styca: *see under* coins and coinage
synods and church councils 41, 121, 122,
    125, 151ff, 164, 185, 196, 208, 211,
    243, 245, 252, 265, 267, 273; *see
    also* Whitby *in name index*

technology 195–7, 204–5; *see also*
    mills; agriculture
territorial lordship xiv, 7, 19, 21, 22, 28, 29,
    31, 33, 35, 36, 89, 140, 217, 224, 235,
    259, 302, 307, 308
  bookland xiv, 140, 189
  cultural corelands 25, *26*, *27*, 41–2,
    91, 101, 149, 191, 194, 216, 218,
    219, 221, 235, 284, 288–9
  dependent settlements 21, 23, 73–4,
    77, 88, 100, 140, 141, 143, 169,
    204, 238, 252, 267
  endowments: *see under* kingship
  estates and holdings 137–8, 203,
    217; see also *familiae*
  estate centre /*caput* 22, 33, 51, 73–4,
    83–4, 86, 88, 100, 101, 107, 108,
    138, 140, 141–2, 143, 145, 146,
    157, 158, 165–6, 169–70, 201,
    204, 217, 218–19, 220, 224, 230,
    267, 282, 286, 292, 295
  extensive lordship/territory 31, 77,
    78, 89, 94, 144, 307
  feasting 51, 52, 76, 109, 158, 168,
    189, 258, 276,
  imperium/overlordship: *see under*
    kingship
  mansiones 217, 298, 304
  parochial structure and 140
  regio/regiones 140, 157, 158, 218,
    335n
  render, of food or service 21–2, 35,
    36, 51–2, 67, 71, 77, 83, 85–7,
    100, 107, 108, 109, 136, 145, 169,

177, 188, 189, 193, 194, 234, 238, 252, 257, 259, 264, 286, 307
royal *vills / villae regiae* xiv, 51, 77, 82, 88, 105, 140, 204, 234, 259, 272, 274, 301
tribute 40, 52, 53, 56, 66, 109, 158, 208, 252, 289, 290
vill/township 22, 31, 218, 295
textiles: *see under* material culture
tithe payments 252, 286
trade: *see under* markets and trade
travel 51, 122, 148, 172, 193, 206, 223
  on horseback 112
  navigable rivers: *see under* markets and trade

ports: *see under* markets and trade
Roman roads: *see main entry*
sea voyages 129, 303
Tribal Hidage 40, 66, 68, 75, 132
tribute: *see under* territorial lordship

Vikings / Viking Age 179, 246–50, 276, 286–7, 290, 297, 299

warfare (*see also* armies; battles; raiding) 11, 61, 264, 275, 297
warbands: *see comites/comitates*
wool 28, 76, 108, 194, 195, 201, 233, 258, 268, 276

NAME INDEX

Page numbers in italic are references to photographs or maps.

Aachen/Aix-la-Chapelle 255, 273, 274, 275, 276, 277, 279
Abercorn, East Lothian 123, 170, 178, 181, 220, 251, 295
Aberford, West Yorkshire 73
Aberlady, East Lothian 168, 271, 284, 295
Aberlemno II *180*
Acca, bishop of Hexham 97–8, 215, 220
Acca's Cross, Hexham 142, 158
Acha, wife of King Æðelfrið 62–3, 64–5, 91, 134
Acleah (location uncertain, prob. Surrey) 299
Adalhard, abbot 276
Ad Caput Caprae: see Gateshead
Adda, king of Bernicia (572–580) 4, 56–8
Adda, priest 133
Adomnán, abbot of Iona (628–704)
    author of *De Locis Sanctis* 124, 185–6
    author of *Life of Columba* 65, 92–8, 313
    friendship with king Aldfrith and visits to Northumbria 124, 184, 185
Ad Gefrin: see Yeavering
Ad Murum, royal *vill* 52, 120, 132, 149

Æbbe, sister of King Oswald (died 683) 123, 138, 164, 165, 169, 295
Ædwinesclif (location uncertain) 272
Ælfflæd, abbess, daughter of King Oswiu and Eanflæd 120, 121, 122, 123, 125, 152, 183, 186, 205
    Cuthbert, meeting with 179, 229
    Whitby, abbess of 134, 137
    Wilfrid's champion at the Synod of Nidd 208, 210, 211
Ælfflæd, daughter of King Offa 278
Ælfred, Bernician ætheling 65
Ælfred, king of Wessex (886–899) 247, 290, 294, 300, 303
Ælfwald, king of Northumbria (779–788) 244, 245, 246, 274, 275, 276, 278, 309
Ælfwald II, son of Ælfwald 247, 282, 309
Ælfwine, brother of King Ecgfrið (died 679) 38, 63, 122, 157, 177, 183, 216, 229
Ælle, king of Deira (560–588) 4, 5, 50, 54–5, 57, 59, 62, 63, 64, 96
Æðelbald, king of Mercia (716–757) 126, 212, 213, 232, 233, 243, 245, 265, 266, 272
Æðelberht, king of Kent (died 616) 74

Æðelburh, daughter of King Æðelberht 5, 74, 75, 77, 110, 128, 134
Æðelðryð, wife of King Ecgfrið 122, 156, 159–60, 164, 195, 207
Æðelðryð, wife of Æðelwald Moll 244, 272
Æðelðryð, wife of King Ecgfrið
Æðelfrið, king of Bernicia (604–616) and Deira (592–604) 4, 5, 6, 38, 52, 55–63, 64–5, 68, 77, 83, 111, 114–15, 128, 131, 158, 216
Æðeltrude, mother of King Æðelred 278
Æðelred, king of Mercia (675–704) 210, 278
Æðelred, king of Northumbria (774–779) 244, 245, 247, 274, 276, 277, 278, 279, 309
Æðelred II, king of Northumbria 248, 249, 297–8, 310
Æðelric, king of Bernicia (580–584) 4, 55–9, 61, 62
Æðelsige, son of Aldhun 216
Æðelwald Moll, *patricius* and king of Northumbria (759–765) 244, 266, 272, 273, 274, 276, 309
Æðelwold, bishop of Lindisfarne (721–740) 259
Æðelwold, king of the East Saxons (died 664) 154
Æðelwulf, monk and author of *De Abbatibus* 256, 257, 282
Æðelwulf, king of Wessex (839–858) 290, 299, 300
Ælle, imposed as king in Northumbria (867) 250, 300, 310
Acca, bishop of Hexham (died 740/2) 97, 98, 142, 158, 215, 220
Áed mac Ainmirech, king of the Northern Úi Néill (died 598) 94

Áedán mac Gabrain, king of Dál Riata (574–609) 5, 59, 59, 94
Agilbert, bishop of the West Saxons (c.650–660) 121, 146, 153
Aidan, abbot/bishop of Lindisfarne (635–651) 6, 98, 99, 119, 127, 130, 131, 135, 153, 165, 191, 219, 291, 292, 295
  arrival at Lindisfarne 100–2
  with King Oswald 99, 109–12
  with kings Oswiu and Oswine 128–9
Airgíalla, Irish tribal group 67
Alba, kingdom of 249, 288–9, 290
Alcuin, scholar 145, 155, 203, 203, 235, 245, 247
  accompanied the 786 Legatine Mission 274
  appointed in 782 master of the palace schools in Aachen 245, 255
  correspondence 247, 276–7, 278, 279, 280, 287
  retirement and death at Tours 247, 280, 281
  summary of his life 274–5
Aldborough, North Yorkshire 41, 96, 146, 164, 271
Aldfrið, king of Northumbria (685–704) 41, 92, 124, 137, 175, 179, 181, 182–5, 188, 194, 201, 205, 208, 209, 214, 215, 218, 227, 243, 256, 268, 309
  coinage 196, *197*, 198, *199*, 200, 203, 264, 270, 271, 284, 296
  core territory at Driffield 88, 204–5
  death at Driffield 125, 204, 210, 213
  economics 194ff, 198–200, 201, 203, 206, 208
  Irish background and name of *Flann Fína* 127, 131, 182–3

Aldhelm, abbot of Malmesbury 184, 185, 213, 220
Aldhun, son of Oslac 216
Aldulf, deacon, envoy of Charlemagne 248, 282
Alhflæd, wife of Peada of Mercia 120, 132, 137
Alhmund, probable son of King Alhred 279
Alhred, king of Northumbria (765–774) 216, 244, 245, 273, 274, 276, 279, 309
Aliortus 69
Alric, son of Heardberht 246
Alt Clud 60, 181, 271
Aluthelia (location uncertain) 297
Ana Cross 144
Aneirin, British poet 60
Anglesey 5, 60, 65, 66, 76
Anglo-Scottish Border 25, 97, 145, 259
Anna, king of East Anglia (died 654) 135, 156
Annandale 28, 219, 226, 229
Anthony, saint 92
Antonine Wall 16, 34, 130
Aquitaine 247, 289
Ardwall Island 20, 221
Arbeia (South Shields), Tyne and Wear 20, 151, 173, 196
archbishops
    Æðelberht of York (died 780) 245
    Ælberht of York (766–780) 273
    Augustine of Canterbury (601–604) 54, 55, 94, 115, 252
    Berhtwald of Canterbury (693–731) 124–5, 210, 211
    Cuthbert of Canterbury (731–734) 232, 265
    Eanbald I of York (780–793) 245, 247, 278
    Eanbald II of York (793) 247, 279, 280, 282, 287; minting coins 289
    Ecgberht of York (735–766): see main entry
    Lul of Mainz (754–786) 268, 273
    Theodore of Canterbury: *see* main entry
    Wigmund of York (837–854) 299
    Wulfhere of York (854–?892) 250, 300
    Wulfsige of York (c.808–838) 291
Arculf, Frankish bishop 185
Arfderydd (battle, 573) 61
Argoed Llwyfain (sixth-century battle) 60
Argyll 58, 91
Arosæte 28
Atlantic province 29
Atswinapathe: see Austerfield
Augustine of Canterbury (c.601–4): *see under* archbishops
Ad Caput Caprae (Gateshead), Tyne and Wear 128, 196
Auldhame, East Lothian 168–9
Austerfield, synod of 41, 125, 210, 211
Avon Valley 132
Aynburg (location uncertain) 246
Ayrshire 60, 243, 271

Bannavem Taburniae (location uncertain) 32
Balðere, St 168, *169*, *260*
Bangor Iscoed (*Bancornaburg*) 62
Bamburgh, Northumberland 4, 77, 82, 100, 104, 105, 110, 113, 119, 125, 133, 135, 146, 166, 169, 181, 211, 243, 244, 263, 268, 274, 284, 292, 293, 295
    King Oswald's uncorrupted arm at 112, 119

known as *Bebbanburg* 62
known as *Din Guaire* 41, 50, 82
Bamburghshire 77, 103, 260, 262
Bangor, Gwynedd 62
Barwick-in-Elmet, South Yorkshire 23, 69
Bath, Somerset 163, 223
Bawtry, South Yorkshire 5, 68, 210
Bebba, wife of King Æðelfrið 4, 62, 83, 96
Bebbanburg: see Bamburgh
Bede 259, 264, 270, 271, 278, 292, 307
   age of Bede 281
   attitude to the Britons 220, 228, 238
   cited as a source of information 22, 24, 38–9, 50–1, 54–9, 61–2, 65–8, 71–4, 76–7, 80, 83, 85–6, 92, 96–7, 99, 102–4, 106–7, 109–12, 129–9, 131–2, 134–7, 140, 142–3, 143, 145, 148–9, 151–5, 164, 168, 175–9, 181–4, 193, 196, 201, 206–7, 209–10, 212–13, 215, 219, 230–1, 238–9
   Continuatio 213, 271
   criticisms of the church in the *letter to Ecgberht* 251–5, 256, 257, 258, 262, 277
   De Temporum Ratione, On the Measurement of Time 126, 214, 312,
   Ecclesiastical History 114–15, 126, 151, 251, 254, 259, 311–12
   elements of his life and works 85, 92, 123, 135, 185–7, 214–15, 268, 265, 273, 299
   literary legacy 308
   on petrification 188–91
   Prose Life of St Cuthbert 210, 273
   providential history 113–16
   Verse Life of St Cuthbert 273

Bedlingtonshire 107, 259
Benedict Biscop, abbot of Wearmouth–Jarrow (died 690) 124, 135, 155, 171, 188, 194, 256, 268
   founding Wearmouth and Jarrow 122, 123
   travels to Rome 120, 156, 178, 186, 191, 193
Berctred, son of Beornæð 179, 181
Bernicia/*Berneich*, kingdom 4, 5, 6, 24, 28, 33, 68, 74, 75, 77, 98, 100, 103, 105, 119, 159–60, 164, 165, 166, 170, 178, 194, 196, 201, 204, 205, 209, 214, 215, 217, 218, 220, 224, 235, 250, 262, 270, 271, 272, 273, 284, 298, 300, 303, 304, 305, 307–8
Bernician people 38
   frontiers of 38, 39, 41–2
   kingship of 36, 50, 55, 57–9, 60–3, 64–5, 96, 216, 256, 273
   Oswiu's hegemony and monasteries 120, 128, 133, 136–8
   sites of kingship and other archaeological sites 77–8, 82–6, 100, 107
Berhtfrið, Bernician warlord 125, 211
Bertha, wife of King Æðelberht 74
Beornings, a northern dynasty 156, 213, 216, 293
Beorwine, abbot 135
Berwick-upon-Tweed, Northumberland 16, 263
Betti, priest 133
Billingham, Teesside
Birinus, bishop of Dorchester-on-Thames (c.634–649) 111
Birrens, Dumfries and Galloway 224
Blathmac, abbot of Iona 248, 289
Blotmonað (the month of November) 177

Name index

Boisil, abbot of Melrose (died 664) 121, 154, 217
Bolam, Northumberland 236
Boniface, missionary and archbishop of Mainz 201, 214, 256, 265
Bosa, bishop of York (678) 165
Boroughbridge, North Yorkshire 146, 203
Bothlem, monk 116
Bowmont Valley, Northumberland/Borders 217, 259–60
Bowl Hole 103–4, 135
Branxton, Northumberland 78
Breamish Valley, Northumberland 78, 100–1, 236, 260
Bridei, king of Pictland 156, 181, 183
Brigid of Kildare 93, 99
Bristol Channel 233
Britannia (Roman Britain) 175
Brittany 33
Brocmail, British warlord 62
Bromic, Northumberland 78, 100, 260
  see also rivers (Breamish) *in subject index*
Broninis (location uncertain) 123, 165, 209
Brougham (*Brocavum*), Cumbria 230
Bryneich: see Bernicia
Buckton, Northumberland 100
Burnswark, Dumfries and Galloway 218, 223

Cadwallon, king of Gwynedd (c. 625–634) 5, 6, 53, 62, 63, 76, 96, 97, 98, 110, 115, 182
Cælin, priest 133
Cær Colud: see Coldingham
Caere (Stirling) 125
Caerlegion: see Chester
Calcaria: see Tadcaster

Campodunum 71–3
Candida Casa: see Whithorn
Canterbury 57, 75, 92, 184, 201, 208, 232, 233, 235, 245, 265, 267, 275
  archbishops of: see under archbishops
Cantiumv: see Canterbury
Cantscaul: see Deniseburn
Cardrona, Dumfries and Galloway 218
Carfrae, Dumfries and Galloway 218
Carham, Northumberland 84, 260
Carhampton, Somerset 290
Carlisle, Cumbria 14, 22, 23, 33, 41, 97, 123, 163, 181, 220, 223, 229, 230, 260, 270, 271, 284, 296, 303, 304
Cartmel, Cumbria 260
Castleford, West Yorkshire 39, 68
Catlow, Lancashire 157, 158
Catstane 170
Catterick 22, 23, 24, 33, 41, 50. 60, 61, 72, 77, 129, 146, 244, 272, 274
Causantín mac Cináeda, king of Alba (862–877) 249
Cearl, king of Mercia (fl. 620) 5, 64, 131, 231
Cedd, bishop (died 664) 120, 133, 137, 138, 141, 143, 144, 154
Cellach, abbot of Iona 288
Cenwealh, king of Wessex 131
Ceolfrið, abbot of Jarrow (685–716) 122, 125, 134–5, 142, 174–7, 178, 179, 186, 187, 188, 196, 213, 214
Ceolred, king of Mercia (709–16) 214, 231, 265
Ceolwulf, king of Northumbria (729–737) 55, 126, 214, 215, 216, 244, 248, 251, 252, 258, 259, 260–2, 263, 264, 266, 268, 272, 289, 291, 292, 298

Ceretic, king of Elmet (died c.617) 5, 67–8
Chad, bishop of Lichfield (669–672) 133, 137, 153, 154
Chapel-le-Dale, Yorkshire, excavation at 238
Charibert, Merovingian king (561–567) 74
Charlemagne, king and emperor of Francia (768–814) 235, 245, 247–8, 273, 276, 282, 289
 crowned emperor (800) 288
 died (814) 288
Charles the Bald, Carolingian Emperor (843–877) 249, 297, 299, 303
Chatton, Northumberland 77
Chelles, Seine-et-Marne 130, 131, 172
Chester 5, 22, 62–3, 115, 245
 Legacæstir, battle of (615/16) and cemetery at Heronsbridge 5, 62–3, 64, 114, 131
Chester-Le-Street, Co. Durham 119, 291, 303–4
Cheswick, Northumberland 100
Cheviot Hills 14, 29, 77, 78, 100, 108, 188, 217, 260, 264
Cheviot Quarry, Northumberland, excavations 86
Chillingham, Northumberland 77, 177
Cináed mac Alpín, king of Dál Riata and Alba (841–858) 248, 249, 290
Cliffe, Co. Durham 262
Coel Hen, legendary British king 60, 61
Coenburh, wife of King Edwin 5, 64
Cœnwulf, King of Mercia (796–821) 247, 279, 282, 289
Coifi, chief priest of King Edwin 109
Coldingham, Northumberland 82, 119, 123, 131, 138, 164, 166, 169, 295

Colmán, bishop of Lindisfarne (661–664) 121, 153
Colmán Rimid, father of Fín 127
Colm Cille: see Columba
Columba (*Colm Cille*), first abbot of Iona (565–593) 92, 95, *102*, 103, 153, 219, 288, 289, 302
 Life of St Columba 65, 185, 313
 in Oswald's vision 96
 as territorial lord 93–95
Compiègne, Oise 153
Conall mac Comgaill, king of Dál Riata (c.558–574) 94
Condercum (Benwell), Tyne and Wear 148
Conisborough, South Yorkshire 73
Constantín, king of Picts (c.789–820) 277, 289
Constantine, emperor of Rome (306–337) 71, 97, 98
Contrebis 158
Corbridge/*Coria*/*Corstopitum*, Northumberland 14, 96, 97, 98, *162*, 164, 195,
Corcu Réti 91
Cospatric, House of 263
Cottam, East Yorkshire 203–4
Cover (possibly Corbridge, Northumberland) 246, 278
Coxwold church, North Yorkshire 138, 142, 266
Craven, kingdom of 68, 146, 157
Crayke church, North Yorkshire 138, 145, 256, 304
Croesoswallt 111
Cromwell, Nottinghamshire, bridge at 267
Crowland, Guðlac's refuge 206, 213, 232
Cruggleton, Dumfries and Galloway 218

Name index

Crummack Dale, excavations at 237–8
Cumbria 17, 61, 71, 160, 187, 218, 228, 229, 230, 271, 303
Curghie, Dumfries and Galloway 219
Cuthbert, abbot of Wearmouth–Jarrow 273
Cuðburh, wife of King Aldfrið 183, 184
Cuðheard, bishop of Lindisfarne (c.900–915) 107
Cuðheard, moneyer in York 282
Cuðred, king of Wessex (740–756) 265
Cuthbert of Lindisfarne (634–687) 102, 103, 113, 120, 121, 123, 124, 127, 155, 163, 169, 179, 181, 183, 186, 191, 209, 218, 229, 230, 256, 258, 260, 268, 277–8, 279, 301, 307, 313
    as bishop 181, 220
    Community of 176, 208, 215, 216, 281, 289, 292, 298, 303, 304, 305
    exhumation of his body 186, 207
    relics and sanctuary 268, 278
    translation of his remains to Norham 291, 291
Cwichelm, king of Wessex 5, 74–5
Cynebil, priest 133
Cynefrið, brother of Ceolfrið 134
Cyneburh, wife of Alhfrið 120, 132
Cynegils, king of Wessex (c.611–642) 6, 111, 131, 132
Cyneðryð, Offa's queen 267
Cynewise, wife of King Penda 120, 131, 136, 155
Cynewulf, abbot and bishop of Lindisfarne 243, 268
Cyniburh, wife of King Oswald 111
Cynon of Aeron, British warlord 60

Dál Riata, Early Medieval kingdom 5, 6, 65, 91, 92, 94–7, 98, 100, 110, 125, 129, 136, 156, 182, 185, 228, 238, 248, 288, 290, 296, 313
Degsastan: see under battles
Deira, kingdom of 4, 5, 24, 28, 36, 60, 62, 77, 83, 86, 96, 100, 105, 119, 120, 122, 130, 133–4, 136, 146, 151, 153, 156, 158, 164, 165, 196, 207, 215, 230, 235, 250, 254, 255, 271, 272, 274, 300, 302, 303, 307, 311, 313
    Æðelfrið and Deiran kingship 62–3
    Æðelwold Moll's power base 272
    beginnings of Deiran kingship 49–50, 52, 54, 55, 57, 58–9
    boundaries of 36–41
    coinage and commerce of 284, 296–7, 298
    cremation and inhumation cemeteries 43–7
    as a cultural coreland 41–2
    Edwin's kingship in 64, 67, 68, 69, 73, 74
    King Aldfrith in 201, 204–6
    King Owiu's Deiran marriage 128–9
    King Oswiu's monasteries in 137–42
Denisesburn, battle site 6, 98, 159
Dent, Cumbria 158
Dere Street 14, 16, 20, 23, 96, 97, 129, 130, 218n, 262–3
Derventio: see Malton
Derwentmouth, Cumbria 303
Din Eidyn / Edinburgh 24, 60
Dinguoaroy / *Din Guaire*: see Bamburgh
Diuma, bishop of Middle Anglia 133, 136,
Domnall Brecc, king of Dál Riata (629–642) 95, 156
Donafelda 71–3
Doncaster, South Yorkshire 39, 68, 73, 136, 271

Donemuða, Tyne and Wear 246, 266, 278
Dorchester on Thames, Oxon. 232
Dore, Yorkshire 248, 290
Dorestad 193, 249
Drest, Pictish king (663–672) 156
Driffield, East Yorkshire 42, 44, 45, 48, 49, 88, 125, 201, 204–5, 254, 287
Droitwich, Worcestershire 232
Druim Ceatt, Convention of (575)
Dublin, Viking *longphort* 248, 250, 297
Dumbarton: *see Alt Clud*
Dunadd, Argyll and Bute 58, 91 146, 236
Dunbar, East Lothian 16, 28, 82, 123, 125, 165–6, 167, 168–70, 191, 194, 209, 217, 295
Dunkeld, Perthshire 289
Dunollie, Argyll and Bute 58, 91
Dunragit, Dumfries and Galloway 218
Dynbær: *see* Dunbar

Eadberht, king of Northumbria (737–758) 126, 142, 173, 215, 243, 244, 266, 268, 272, 309
Eadberht, bishop of Lindisfarne (668–698) 207
Eadfrið, son of King Edwin 6, 64, 77, 96
Eadhæd, bishop of Lindsey 156, 177
Eadred, abbot of Carlisle 303–5
Eadric, son of Ida 216
Eardwulf, king of Northumbria (705) 211, 213–14, 246, 247, 309
Eaglesfield, Dumfries and Galloway 223
ealdormen/reeves/*praefecti*
    Beauduherd, king's reeve in Dorchester 245
    Osfrið, Bernician praefectus 123, 165, 209

Tydlin, praefectus of Dunbar 123, 165, 168, 209
Ealdsige, abbot in York 299
Eanflæd, wife of King Oswiu and abbess of Whitby 52, 74, 119, 120, 121, 122, 123, 128, 133–5, 137, 152, 165, 179, 186
Eanfrið, king of Bernicia (634) 6, 62, 96
Eanred 'tyrant' 244, 274
Eanred, king of Northumbria, son of King Eardwulf 248, 283, 290, 310
Eardwulf, king in Northumbria 246, 247, 279, 282, 309
East Anglia, kingdom of 63, 131, 163, 200, 250, 299
East Lothian 170
Eata, abbot and bishop 121, 145, 146, 153, 165, 209
Ecca, son of Æðelsige 216
Ecclefechan, Dumfries and Galloway 223, 224
Ecgberht of York (735–766) 126, 213, 244, 265–6, 274–5
    appointed archbishop in 735 254
    brother of King Eadberht 215, 234–5
    coinage *269*, 270
    death of 244, 273
    influence over Iona 213
    letter from Bede 213, 251–4, 257
Ecgberht, king of Wessex (802–839) 247, 248 289, 290
Ecgberht, imposed as king in Bernicia 250, 310
Ecgberht II, king in Northumbria 310
Ecgfrið, king of Northumbria (671–685) 38, 51, 54, 59, 120–5, 127, 136, 137, 138, 145, 149, 151, 167, 169, 196, 201, 205, 206, 207, 208, 209, 216, 218, 220, 227, 228, 229
    final years 179, 181, 183, 185

marriages 156, 164
and Mercia 155, 176
patron of Lindisfarne 260
Pictish rebellion 156
relations with Wearmouth–Jarrow 171, 178–9
relations with Wilfrid 156–7, 160, 164–5
Ecgfrið, son of Offa 46, 276, 278
Ecgred, bishop of Lindisfarne (830–845) 102, 248, 260–63
Edlingham (*Eadwulfincham*), Northumberland 262
Edwin, king of Northumbria (617–633) 5, 6, 23, 49, 51, 52, 53, 54, 55, 57, 59, 62, 63, 67, 68, 86, 87, 89, 91, 92, 96, 109, 110, 114–16, 119, 123, 128, 129, 130, 131, 134, 136, 158, 163, 186, 188, 201, 202, 207, 228, 231, 311
  death at *Hæthfelth* and post-mortem cult at Whitby 76–77, 207
  early life and succession to the kingship 64, 65
  expansion of power into Elmet and Lindsey 68, 69, 71–4
  marriage and conversion 74–6
  and Yeavering 76–8, 82, 83, 85
Edwine (Eda), buried 263
Eglingham (*Ecwulfincham*), Northumberland 262
Eildon (hills), Borders 146, 244, 272
Eldbottle, East Lothian 169
Elmet, kingdom of 5, 41, 51, 60, 67–71, 73, 74, 76, 83, 128, 146, 158, 201, 228, 271
Elwick, Northumberland 100
Eobba 36, 37
Eochaid Buide, king of Dál Riata (c.608–629) 91
Eoforwic: *see* York

Eomer, agent of King Cwichelm, assassin 74
Eorcenberht, King of Kent (640–664) 128, 156
Eosterwine, abbot of Jarrow (died 686) 124, 184, 196
Eslington, Northumberland 105

Felton, Northumberland, 16, 108
Fenton, Northumberland 77
Fenwick, Northumberland 100, 101
Filey, North Yorkshire 3, 11, 12, 30
Fín, mother of King Aldfrið 127, 128, 131, 183
Finán, bishop/abbot of Lindisfarne (651–661) 102, 119, 120, 131–33, 137, 153, 183, 191, 207, 292
Firth of Clyde 218
Firth of Forth 120, 165, 178, 260
Fishergate, York 201–3, 270
Ford, Northumberland 77
Forðred, abbot 142, 266, 267
Fortriu, Pictish kingdom 288–9, 290
Francia 110, 121, 122, 153, 154, 247, 255, 281, 282, 283, 266, 287, 288, 289, 290, 299, 303, 309
Freodwald, king of Bernicia (591–597) 57
Frisia 43, 193, 200, 201, 203, 205, 233, 265, 274, 286, 289

Gainford, Co. Durham 262–3
Galloway, 16, 25, 28, 161, 187, 218, 229, 271, 284, 296
Garton, East Yorkshire 42, 45, 47
Gateshead, Tyne and Wear 14, 128, 129, 138, 149, 196
Gefrinshire 77–8
Gevr-vrinn: *see* Yeavering
Glappa, Bernician king (571–572) 56, 57, 58

Glendale, Northumberland 77
Gododdin 4, 16, 24, 50, 60, 166, 216
Govan, Strathclyde 243, 271, 305
Greenhead 14, 17, 32, 33
Green Shiel, Holy Island 293–5
Gressingham, Lancashire 158
Greta Bridge, Co. Durham 39
Guðlac, hermit 213, 258
Guðrøðr, king in Northumbria 310
Guthred (*Guðroðr*) 304–7

Hackness, monastery 123, 134
Hadrian, abbot 154
Hadrian's Wall 3, 14, 17, 22, 148, 236, 263
Hagustaldesham: see Hexham
Halfdan, leader of the Great Army 250, 301
Halton, Lancashire 158, 255
Hamwic (Southampton) 194, 198, 202, 248, 297
Hangingleaves Wood, Northumberland 263
Hartlepool, Co. Durham *(Heruteu)* 119, 129–31, 137, 151, 166, 262–3
Hawick, Borders 262
Heavenfield 6, 97–8, 115, 116, 133, 159, 228, 303, 313
Heiu, abbess of Hartlepool 119, 129
Hereric, nephew of King Edwin 68, 130
Heronbridge, Cheshire 63
Hexham, Northumberland 122, *159*, 160–3, 191, 245, 254
Heysham, Lancaster 158
Hild, abbess of Whitby (657–680) 119, 121, 123, 130
Hoddom, Dumfries and Galloway 161, 191, 219, 223–8, 230, 238, 254, 270, 296

Holderness, East Yorkshire 42, 44, 204, 271
Hornby, Lancashire 158
Hovingham 88, 138, 140–3
Huckhoe, Northumberland 236
Hussa, king of Bernicia (597–604) 5, 56, 57, 58–60
Hwætberht, abbot of Wearmouth 187, 265
Hwicce, kingdom of 232, 289

Ida, king of Bernicia (559–571) 114, 273
Idings, Bernician ruling dynasty 85, 96, 183, 210, 212, 231, 244, 273, 274, 290
Ingleborough, Yorkshire, Iron Age hillfort 237–8
Ingram Hill, Northumberland 236
Inner Farne 179
Inveresk, Dumfries and Galloway 216
Iurminburh, wife of King Ecgfrið 51, 122, 123, 128, 163–5, 177, 179, 181, 183, 229, 260
Ívarr, leader of the Great Army 250

James, deacon 77
Jarrow Slake, Tyne and Wear 172, 179, 196
Jedburgh (*Gedweade*), Borders 262, 291
Jedmouth, Borders 262
John, bishop of Hexham (687–705) 254
John, the cantor 171, 175

Kells, Co. Meath 288, 304
Kelso 83
Kentigern, founder of Glasgow church 228
Kilham, East Yorkshire 42

Kirkburn, East Yorkshire 4, 49
Kirby Misperton, North Yorkshire 144
Kirkbymoorside, North Yorkshire
    143–44
Kirkliston, West Lothian 33, 170
Kirkmadrine, Dumfries and Galloway,
    inscriptions 219

Lammermuir Hills 16, 165, 166, 168,
    169, 260
Lanton Quarry, Northumberland,
    excavations 86, 194
Lauder, Borders 218
Leeds (*Loidis*) 41, 69, 71–3, 157
Leicester 133, 232, 234
Leicestershire 43, 132, 243
Lichfield, Staffordshire 132, 133, 232
Liddesdale 33, 58, 59
Lilla, thegn of King Edwin 74
Lincoln 14, 33, 39, 41, 68, 73, 198, 232,
    300
Lincolnshire 42, 43, 51, 178, 200, 270,
    301
Lindisfarne (Holy Island),
    Northumberland 6, 110, 112, 119,
    124, 126, 129, 152–3, 165, 208,
    243, 246, 268, 271, 278, 292, 303,
    312
  after the Synod of Whitby 153
  churches on 120, 173, 191, 207, 284,
    291, 293
  Cuthbert's body and cult of 124, 186,
    208
  diocese of 39, 122, 165, 170, 178,
    229, 251, 262, 282
  Durham *Liber Vitae* 128, 208–9,
    256, 289
  endowments 215, 256
  etymology of 50–1
  excavations on 293

  founding of the monastery 98–100,
    104–5
  Gospels 100, 188, 258–9, 281
  and Iona 100, 102, 152, 186, 219
  King Oswald's head buried at 112,
    119
  landholdings of 77, 84, 100–1, 107,
    145, 168, 187–8, 216–17, 258–63,
    261, 292, 304
  Norham and: *see main entry*
  origins of name 50
  scriptorium at 186–8
  Viking raid (793) 246, 277–8, 294
Lindsey, kingdom of 41, 50, 51, 52, 65,
    66, 68, 76, 112, 122, 132, 134,
    156, 177, 200, 201, 205, 206, 222,
    231, 232, 233
Littleborough 52, 68
Lochmaben, Dumfries and Galloway 223
Loftus, Cleveland 105–6
London/*Londinium*/*Lundenwic* 193,
    213, 233, 248, 249, 290, 297
Lothian 25, 28, 60, 61, 166, 167, 209,
    216, 217, 220, 223, 229
  East Lothian coreland 16, 166, 167,
    167, 170, 171
  Midlothian 170
Louis the Pious, Carolingian Emperor
    (813–840) 248, 288, 290, 297
lower Tyne, valley and coreland of 28,
    41, 127, 149, 155
Lowick, Northumberland 77
Luce Bay, Dumfries and Galloway 218,
    220
Lugubalia: *see* Carlisle
Lune Valley 157, 258

Machars peninsula, Dumfries and
    Galloway 220, 222
Madawg of Elmet, British warlord 60

Mælmin: see Milfield
Mailros: see under churches and
    monasteries (Old Melrose) *in
    subject index*
Malton, East Yorkshire 30, 48, 52 77,
    86, 88, 140, 141, 296
Man, Isle of 5, 65, 66, 91, 246
Maserfelth: *see under* Oswald
Mayo, English community in 275,
    304
Medcaut: *see* Lindisfarne
Melrose, Borders 16, 28, 218, 244, 272
    see also under churches and
    monasteries (Old Melrose/
    Mailros) *in subject index*
Mercia, kingdom of 36, 51, 75, 124,
    154, 184, 205, 212–13, 214, 238,
    246, 265, 266, 271, 272, 278, 280,
    281, 282, 289, 290, 300–2, 308
  bishops in 133, 136–7, 156, 232
  coinage and economy of 109, 197,
    200, 233
  conflicts with Northumbria 6, 54, 62,
    73, 76–7, 111–12, 116, 119, 120,
    121, 122, 126, 131–2, 135–7, 153,
    155, 156, 165, 177, 201, 206, 207,
    231, 234, 243, 247, 249, 260, 264,
    274, 275, 279
  geography of and Northumbrian-
    Mercian frontier 39–41, 65, 131,
    210, 248, 271
  marriage alliances with Northumbria
    5, 61, 64, 120, 132, 133, 183,
  Mercian charters 193, 203, 216, 232,
    233, 253
  Mercian burhs 203, 230, 234, 267–8
  Tribal Hidage and 66, 68
  Wilfrid in 123, 124, 209, 210, 211
Middle Anglia, kingdom of 132, 133,
    135, 136, 232, 233

Middleton, North Yorkshire 42, 144–5
Milfield / Milfield Basin,
    Northumberland 82, 83, 85, 86,
    106, 168
  Maelmin (Milfield palace site) 82,
    83, 84, 85, 106
Moray Firth 281, 289
Morecambe Bay 260
Morcant 4, 59, 60
Mote of Mark, Galloway 218, 221, 222

Nechtan mac Derilei, king of Picts 213
New Bewick, Northumberland, 86
Newburn, Northumberland 301, 305
Newcastle upon Tyne, Tyne and Wear
    41, 149, 186, 301
  Pons Aelius (Roman fort at) 14, 16, 148
Nidd, Synod of 125, 208, 211
Ninian, bishop at Whithorn 219, 220
Nithsdale 28
Noirmoutier, Francia 247, 248, 297
Norham / Norham-on-Tweed,
    Northumberland 102, 248, 259,
    262, 291, 292, 294, 295, 298, 303,
    304, 305
Norhamshire 77, 78, 100, 259, 260,
    307
Nordanhymbrorum gentis 38
North Berwick, East Lothian 169
North Ferriby, Humberside 198, 200
North Sea 28, 41, 104, 193, 233, 263,
    268, 281, 295, 302
North Yorkshire Moors 12, 140, 196
Northallerton, North Yorkshire 158
Norton, Cleveland 40
Norton, East Yorkshire 48
Norwich, Norfolk 248, 297
Nothelm, archbishop of Canterbury
    (735–739) 232

Œðelwald, son of King Oswald
Offa, King of Mercia (757–796) 197, 212, 213, 245, 246, 278
Offa, Northumbrian *ætheling* 243, 268
Old Melrose: *see under* churches and monasteries *in subject index*
Old Jeddart (*altera Gedwearde*) 262, 291
Osbald, king of Northumbria 246, 287, 309
Osberht, king in Northumbria (to *circa* 867) 249, 250, 298, 299, 300, 304, 310
Osfrið, son of King Edwin 6, 64, 77
Osgifu, daughter of king Oswulf 244, 273
Osðryð, wife of King Æðelred of Mercia, daughter of King Oswiu 122, 133, 177, 183, 206, 207, 210
Osred, king of Northumbria (705–716) 125, 151, 184, 208, 210, 211, 213, 214, 245, 255, 256, 268, 276, 309, 312
Osred II, king of Northumbria (788–9) 245, 246 309
Osric, Bernician *ætheling* (died 633) 6, 65, 96, 129
Osric, son of Alfrið, king of Northumbria (718–729) 126, 184, 214, 215, 309
Oswald, king of Bernicia (634–642) 6, 52, 62, 64, 77, 78, 85, 86, 91–2, 99, 102, 109–10, 111, 123, 127, 131, 132, 136, 184, 201, 219, 313
death at Maserfelth, body parts, cult and miracles 110–12, 113, 116, 119, 127, 133, 206, 207
founding of Lindisfarne 100, 101, 259
overlordship 104, 110–11, 128
return to Northumbria and the Battle of Heavenfield 95–8, 159–60, 182, 228, 303

Oswestry, Shropshire 111, 119, 206
Oswiu, king of Bernicia (643–670) 6, 52, 64, 91, 92, 112–13, 119, 122, 127, 129, 131–2, 133, 146, 148–51, 156, 182
death at *Winwæd* and burial at Whitby 121, 134, 136, 231
marriages and children 127, 128, 129, 146, 149, 160, 165, 179, 214, 220, 228, 229
monasteries and land grants 120, 133, 137–8, 217, 227–8
overlordship 54, 120, 131 136, 137, 206
Peada and Penda in Mercia and Middle Anglia 120, 121, 132, 133, 135–7, 155
Whitby, synod of and its aftermath 121, 151–4
Oswine, son of Osric, Deiran *subregulus* 6, 39, 54, 119, 129, 133, 134, 138, 151, 217
Oswine, son of king Eadberht 244, 272
Oswulf Eadberthing, king of Northumbria 243, 244, 245, 272, 273, 309
Oundle, Northamptonshire 125, 210, 211, 277
Ovania (perhaps Govan) 243, 271

Paddock Hill, East Yorkshire 88
Parlington Hollins, West Yorkshire 69
Partney, Lincolnshire: *see under* churches and monasteries *in subject index*
Patrick, bishop 3, 32–4, 93–4, 131
Paulinus, bishop, missionary 68, 74, 76, 77, 82, 92, 133, 134, 188
Peada, son of King Penda 120, 132, 133, 136, 137

Pecthelm, bishop of Whithorn 219,
    220, 222, 223, 251
Pehtred, priest 291
Penda, king of Mercia (c.626–655)
    and Northumbrian kings 62, 76–7, 96,
        111–12, 116, 119, 120, 132, 135,
        136, 137, 153, 155
    sons and daughters of 111, 112, 116,
        131, 137, 156, 132, 206
Pennine hills 12, 14, 17, 23, 31, 39, 61,
        62, 71, 96, 108, 129, 140, 157, 158,
        176, 195, 201, 203, 237, 284, 299
    lands west of 39, 41, 60, 157, 157,
        222, 229, 296
Penrith, Cumbria 230
Pickering, North Yorkshire
    church territories around 138, 140–5
    as Deiran coreland 25, 28, 41, 42, 86
    parish and territory of *Pickeringas*
        140, 144, 145
    Vale of 12, 48, 88, 89, 203, 296
Picts/Pictland 7–8, 34, 60, 219, 238,
        244, 246, 247, 248, 282, 288, 290,
        301, 309, 313, 278
    conflicts with Northumbria 120, 123,
        124, 125, 136, 137, 155, 156, 181,
        183, 185 208, 213, 216, 234, 243
Piercebridge, County Durham 14, 23,
    39
Pincanheale (location uncertain) 244,
    245, 273
Plessey, Northumberland 107
Portus Ecgfridi (King Ecgfrið's Port)
    178, 246, 278
Powys, Early Medieval Welsh kingdom
    5, 111, 131

Quarry Hill, West Yorkshire 72–3
Quentovic 193, 248, 297

Rædwald, king of East Anglia (*c.*599–
    624) 5, 63, 64, 65, 74, 76
Rædwulf, king of Northumbria 249,
    297–8, 310
Ratho, City of Edinburgh 170
Rheged, British kingdom 4, 6, 41, 60,
    65, 124, 128, 146, 183, 220, 221,
    228, 229
    coreland, in the Eden Valley,
        Cumbria 160
    see also Rhieinmelth; Urien
Rhieinmelth (*Rægumeld*), second wife
    of King Oswiu 128, 228
Rhinns of Galloway 28, 218, 219
Rhionydd, Dumfries and Galloway 218
Rhun, son of Urien 76, 128, 228
Rhydderch Henn, British warlord 60
Ricsige, king set up by the Great Army
    300, 310
Ripon, North Yorkshire 52, 53, 121,
    122, 125, 134, 138, 145–6, *147*,
    147–8, 153, 157–8, 209–11, 216,
    246, 279
    crypt at 161, 163–4
    see also Wilfrid
Rome 7, 16, 55, 61, 74, 75, 76, 92, 97, 121,
    154, 163, 166, 175, 189, 207,
    219–20, 245, 255, 266, 275, 279, 282
Rouen, Francia 297
Royth, son of Rhun, son of Urien 128
Rudston, East Yorkshire 42, 48
Ruthwell, Dumfries and Galloway 98,
    189, 223, 224
Ryedale, North Yorkshire 28, 88, 203
    as a cultural coreland 25
    religious houses in 138–40, 149, 266

St Bertin, abbey of 297
Sancton, east Yorkshire, burials at 43
Saul, Old Testament king 114–15

Name index

Scilly Isles 91, 222
Scone, Perthshire 305
Scythlescæster (possibly Halton Chesters on Hadrian's Wall) 245, 275
Seckington, near Tamworth, Staffordshire 272
Sedbergh, Cumbria 157,
Segedunum (Wallsend, Tyne and Wear) 148, 173
Ségéne, abbot of Iona (623–652) 95
Seletun (loction uncertain) 245
Sergius, Pope (687–701) 97
Sheppey, Isle of, Kent 248, 290
Sherburn, East Yorkshire 49, 145, 296
Sherburn-in-Elmet, West Yorkshire 69, 74
Shotton, Northumberland 194, 235, 270
Sicgfrið, abbot of Wearmouth (died 688) 179
Sigbald, abbot of monastery described in *De Abbatibus* 257
Sigeberht, king of East Anglia (c.629–c.634) 132, 133
Sigwine, abbot of monastery described in *De Abbatibus* 257
Simy Folds, Co. Durham, excavated settlement 237
Skerne, East Yorkshire 205
Sledmere, East Yorkshire 42, 45, 49, 205
Solway Firth 218, 219
Spalda, Early Medieval territory 51, 132
Sprouston, Roxburghshire 83–4, 105, 194, 209, 224, 293
Spurn Point, Humberside 274
Stanegate 14, 19, 22, 33, 97, 228
Stanforda (location uncertain) 138, 146
Staple Howe, Yorkshire 29
Stonegrave, North Yorkshire 138, 142, 266

Strathclyde, Early Medieval kingdom 60, 63, 95, 136, 181, 243, 271, 301
Strathearn, Perthshire 288
Streanæshealh: see Whitby
Street House cemetery, Loftus 105–6
Suðgedling (location uncertain) 260
Sutton Hoo 64, 76, 133, 163
Symeon of Durham 50, 152, 176, 214, 273, 274, 278, 298, 300, 304, 312, 313, 314
Swaledale, North Yorkshire 23, 61
Sweodora, Early Medieval territory 132

Tadcaster, North Yorkshire 68, 72, 119
Taliesin, British poet 60
Talorcan king of Picts (653–7) 62, 96
Tees Valley 196
Teviotdale 262
Theodbald, brother of King Æðelfrið xviii
Theodore of Canterbury (668–690) 154, 235
  and Northumbrian politics 156, 177, 209
  Council/Synod of Hertford 122, 164, 252
Theodoric, king of Bernicia (584–591)
Thirlings, Northumberland 85–6, 87, 105, 106, 194
Three Howes 144
Thwing, East Yorkshire 88
Tidfrið, bishop of Hexham (died 821) 248
Tillmouth, Northumberland 298
Traprain Law, East Lothian 166, 216
Trimontium: see Eildon
Trumbert, bishop of Hexham 229
Trumhere, abbot of Gilling 134
Trumwine, bishop of Abercorn 178
Trusty's Hill 218

Tuda, bishop of Lindisfarne 153, 154
Tunberht, bishop of Hexham (681–?) 178
Tynemouth: *see under* churches and monasteries *in subject index*
Tyne–Solway gap 223, 228, 296
Tyne Valley 14, 61, 97, 159, 304
 as coreland 25, 149
Tyninghame, East Lothian 168–9
 associated with St Balðere 168–9, 260
 Lindisfarne landholding 169–70, 216

Ubbanforda: *see* Norham
Ulster 66–7, 179, 218, 273
Ultán, Irish scribe abbot in monastery described in *De Abbatibus* 257
ultra Tweoda 84, 262; *see also* Lindisfarne (landholdings of)
Urien, king of Rheged (fl. 580s) 4, 6, 50, 59–60, 76, 128, 183, 220, 227, 228, 230
Utta, priest and abbot of Gateshead 128–9, 133, 138, 149

Wales 33, 60, 62, 64, 69, 111, 275, 312
Wallsend, Tyne and Wear 148, 173
Waren Mill, Northumberland 101
Warkworth, Northumberland 166, 298
Wearmouth (monastery), Tyne and Wear 124, 163, 167, 171, 173, 175, 184, 191, 196, 311
 scriptorium 175, 187–8
Werhale, territorial estate of Wearmouth–Jarrow 176, 259
Wessex, kingdom of 281
West Bretton, West Yorkshire 69

Westerna, Early Medieval territorial people 132
West Fen Road, excavated settlement 270
West Heslerton, East Yorkshire 29–31, 44, 45, 49, 86, 89–90, 107, 143, 135, 201, 235, 270, 296–7, 301
Whalley, Lancashire 246, 279
Wharram Percy, East Yorkshire 49, 204
Whitby 121, 123, 131, 134, 179, 186, 196, 200, 270, 311
 Synod of (664) 121, 151ff, 196, 292
 scriptorium 76, 187, 207
Whithorn (*Candida Casa*), Wigtownshire 33, 38, 169, 170, 219–20, *221*, 222–3, 251, 270, 284, 296
Whithorn, Isle of 220
Whittingham (*Hwitingham*) 260
Wigheard, priest (died 664) 154
Wiglaf, king of Mercia (827–839) 290
Wilfaræsdun 129
Wilfrid, abbot and bishop 51, 52, 113, 155, 162–4, 167, 171, 172, 173–6, 182, 191–2, 194, 201, 207, 208, 209, 210–11, 220, 228, 238, 252, 256, 260, 268, 270, 311
 as bishop of York 121, 124, 153
 dealings with British churches 157–8
 his churches 98, 121–2, 125, 134, 146–8, 158, 159–61, 162–64, 173–6, 191, 210, 211, 213, 277
 his death 211, 213
 his lands 52, 122, 145, 220
 relations with kings and queens 39, 122–4, 164, 165, 209, 211

Rome, travels to 120, 122, 123, 125, 165, 191, 193, 209, 210, 211
Synod of Whitby and its aftermath 121, 152–4
Wilton, Borders 262
Winchester, Hampshire 299
Wine, bishop of the West Saxons and of London 154
Winwæd: *see under* battles
Wircesforda (location uncertain) on River Tyne 301
Woden 50, 54, 82, 114, 231
Wolds, Yorkshire 14, 25, 28, 29, 41, 42–9, 86, 88–9, 105, 200, 201, 203–5, 284, 296
Wolviston, Teesside 262
Wonwaldremere (location uncertain) 246
Woodhorn (*Wudacsetre*), Northumberland 262
Wooler, Northumberland 77
'Wormec's township' 276
Wrocensætna, Early Medieval territorial people 132

Wulfhere, king of Mercia (658–675) 121, 156
Wycliffe, Co. Durham 262

Y Gododdin 24, 50, 60
Yeavering 5, 51, 52, 77–83, 84, 86, 88, 106, 107, 119, 168, 194, 224
  excavated features 79–81
  shire territory 85, 260
Yeavering Bell, Northumberland 78, 81, 82
Yeadon, West Yorkshire 157
York 5, 23, 30, 44, 73, 86, 96, 126, 145, 146, 153, 163, 173, 200, 201–3, 234, 244, 245, 246, 247, 251, 259, 260, 274–6, 286–7, 291, 299, 304, 305, 307, 312
  ecclesiastical status 39, 76, 121, 122, 124, 164, 201, 209–10, 213, 215, 273, 287
  falls to Great Army 250, 260, 282, 288, 300, 303
  mints in 222, 270
  Vale of 12, 14, 29, 140

John Donald, an imprint of Birlinn Limited.

Head over to our website to find more Birlinn books across, fiction, non-fiction, sport, poetry, children's books, and academic history.

You can scan the QR Code below to sign up to our newsletter. Keep up to date with all our new publications, launch events, author interviews, special offers and much more!

Explore Scotland with our app, Scotland-by-the-Book, a new tool for readers at home and around the globe with an interest in Scotland.

Scan the QR Code below to find out more:

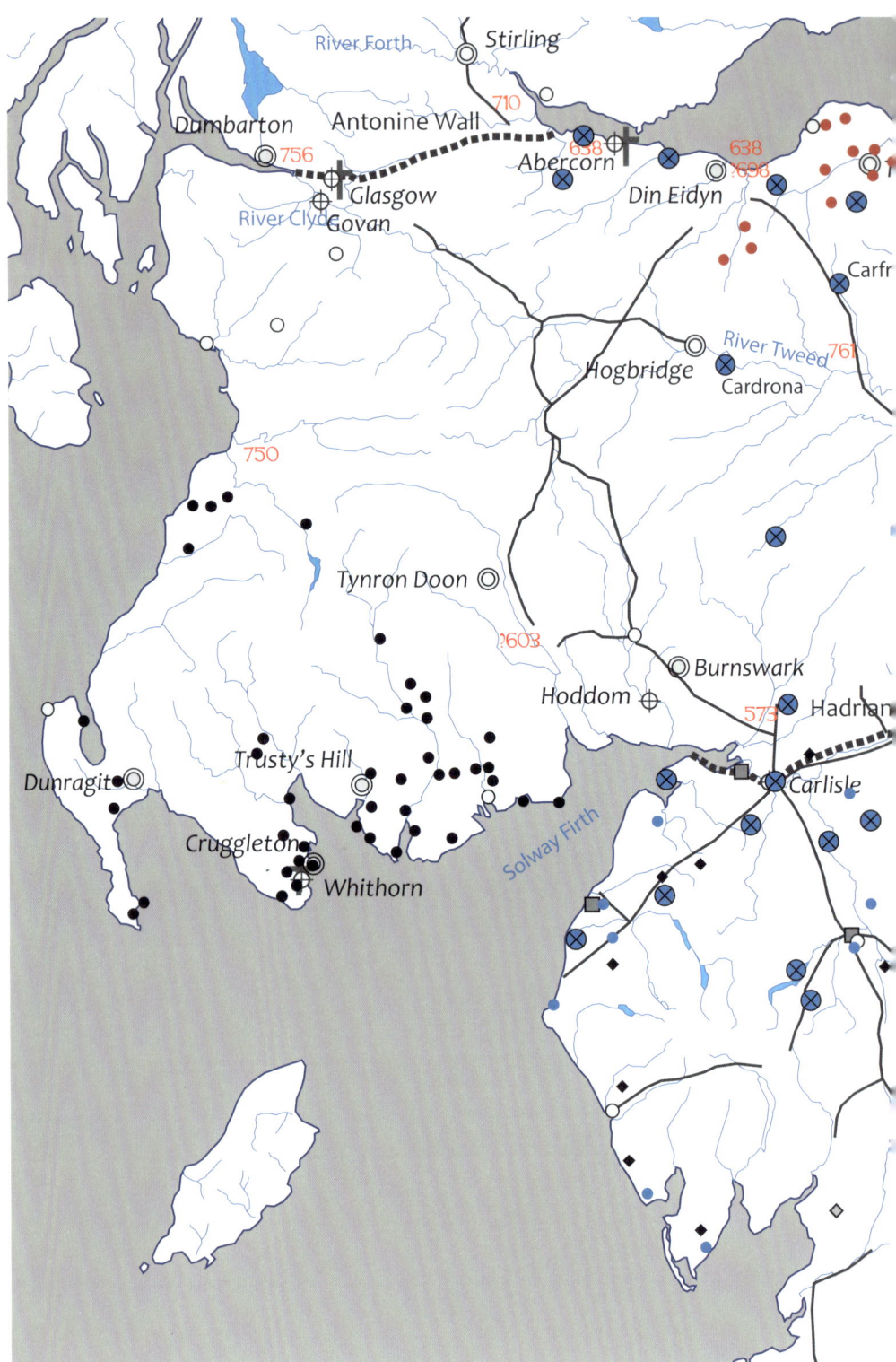